THE SCHOLAR
IN HIS STUDY

Ownership and Experience in Renaissance Italy

DORA THORNTON

YALE UNIVERSITY PRESS

New Haven & London

Designed by Gillian Malpass

Printed in Singapore

Library of Congress Cataloging-in-Publication Data

Thornton, Dora.
    The scholar in his study: ownership and experience in Renaissance
Italy/Dora Thornton.
        p.   cm.
    Includes index.
    ISBN 0-300-07389-5 (cloth)
    1. Studiolos – Italy.   2. Interior decoration – Italy – History –
15th century.   3. Interior decoration – Italy – History – 16th
century.   4. Decoration and ornament, Renaissance – Italy.
5. Decoration and ornament – Italy.   6. Renaissance – Italy.
I. Title.
NK2052.A1T48   1988
747.7′3 – dc21   97-30015
                                                             CIP

A catalogue record for this book is available from
The British Library

Page i: Hand-coloured woodcut showing an author in his study,
from the Malermi Bible, Venice 1490. London, British Library.

Frontispiece: Giovanbattista Moroni, *Giovanni Bressani in his Study*, 1562.
Oil on canvas, Edinburgh, National Gallery of Scotland.

For my parents

ANN THORNTON   PETER THORNTON

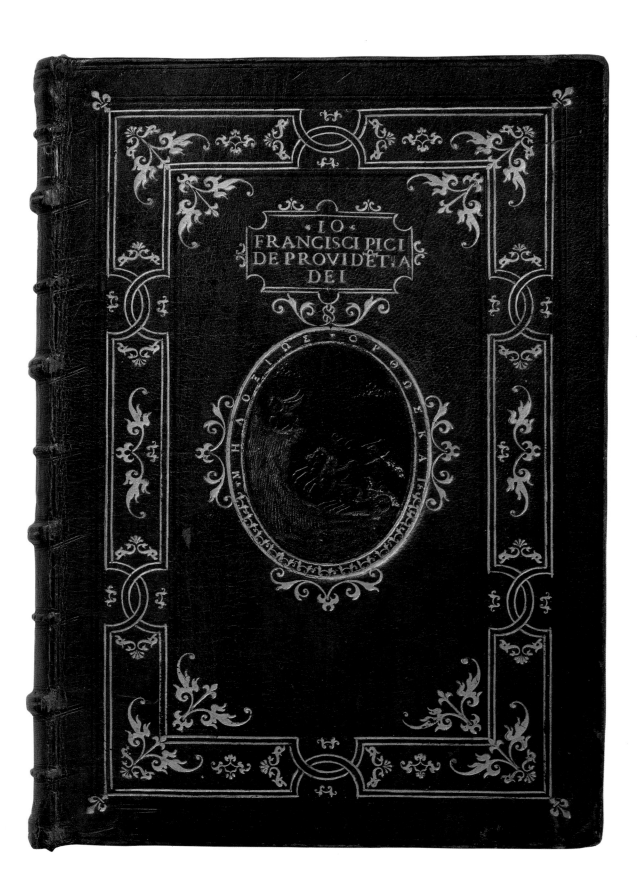

Contents

facing page   Binding on Pico
della Mirandola's *On the
Providence of God*. Copenhagen,
Kunstindustrimuseet. See
fig. 86.

Acknowledgements

THIS BOOK COULD NOT have been written without the assistance of a large number of people, and it is a pleasure to acknowledge them here. Starting with the thesis from which the book has grown, I would like to thank Michael Baxandall and David Chambers for their supervision and guidance, and my examiners, Brian Pullan and Bruce Boucher, for their comments. Giles Mandelbrote offered positive criticism, support and encouragement during the writing of the thesis, and was one of its first readers. I am also grateful to a number of friends who have since read drafts of the book and who have made invaluable suggestions: Marta Ajmar, Patricia Allerston, Peter Burke, Richard Goldthwaite, John Hale, Susan Haskins, Anthony Hobson, Deborah Howard and Zuzanna Shonfield. The work of Richard Goldthwaite, Peter Burke, John Hale and Marco Spallanzani has been crucial in shaping my own: I also owe Marco particular thanks for helping me obtain photographs from Florence. Kent Lydecker encouraged me from the beginning, and sent me a copy of his thesis before its reproduction by Ann Arbor, for which I am most grateful. A number of colleagues kindly showed me or granted access to their unpublished theses, some of which have since been published: Patricia Allerston, Amanda Lillie, Jacqueline Musacchio, Isabella Palumbo Fossati, Clare Robertson and Evelyn Welch.

Specific acknowledgements to those who alerted me to source material are made in the Notes. I would also like to list here those friends and colleagues who helped in a variety of ways: in giving me access to material in their care, in providing advice, information and photographs and in granting reproduction rights: Jörg Anders, Irina Arzhantseva, Giorgio Assirelli, Lorenzo Baldacchini, Sophie Baratte, Alan Bell, Cristina De Benedictis, Pierre Berès, Giovanna Gaeta Bertelà, Gian Carlo Bojani, Maria Bortolotti, Leonard Boyle, Clifford Brown, Paolo Caligula, Sauro Casadei, the late André Chastel, Polly Chiapetta, Julia Collieu, William Connell, Giancarlo Costa, Jill Dunkerton, Geoff Egan, Dagmar Eichberger, Pierre Ennès, Marzia Faietti, Irene Favaretto, Iain Fenlon, Anna Colombi Ferretti, Doris Fletcher, Ennio Gallo, Nubar Gianighian, Corinna Giudici, Philippa Glanville, Ernst Gombrich, Carmen Ravanelli Guidotti, Paul Gwynne, Arnold Hunt, Martin Israel, Pierette Jean-Richard, Simon Jervis, Bertrand Jestaz, Norbert Jopek, Frank Matthias Kammel, Daniel Katz, Pia Kehl, Michael Knuth, Thierry and Fabienne Crépin Leblond, Elizabeth Leedham-Green, Manfred Leithe-Jasper, Maria Lenzuni, Douglas Lewis, Ronald Lightbown, Kate Lowe, Richard Luckett, Martha Macrory, Bryan Maggs, Graziano Manni, Rodolfo Martini, Gabriele Mazzotta, Maria Serena Mazzi, Massimo Medica, Vitaly Michkine, Andrew Middleton, Shayne Mitchell, Daniela Moschini, Peta Motture, Hannelore Nussbaum, Nicholas Penny, John Perkins, Kirsten Aschengreen Piacenti, Mario Piana, Donato Pineider, Pierre-Yves Le Pogam, Julia Poole, Paul Quarrie, Anthony Radcliffe, Anthony Ray, Julian Roberts, Elise Roussel, Nicolai and Ruth Rubinstein, Sandra Saccone, Stanley Sadie, Mario Scaglia, Erich Schleier, Alison Shell, Pippa Shirley, Sally Spector, Simonetta Stagni, Wolfgang Steguweit, Anne Steinberg, Riccardo Steiner, Anthony Storr, Beatrice Paolozzi Strozzi, John Styles, Aase Sylow, Anne-Elizabeth and Christian Theuerkauff, Rosalia Manno Tolu, Elizabeth Turner, Hilary Wayment, Aidan Weston-Lewis, Lucy Whittaker, Johannes Willers, Timothy Wilson, Octavia Wiseman, Ole and Wibeke Woldbye, Martin Wyld and James Yorke.

Staff of the following libraries and archives have been unfailingly helpful: Biblioteca Apostolica Vaticana, Biblioteca Communale del Archiginnasio (Bologna), Bodleian Library (Oxford), British Library (London), Biblioteca Nazionale (Florence), Bibliothèque Nationale (Paris), Bibliothèque Cujas (Paris), Biblioteca Palatina (Parma), Biblioteca Medicea-Laurenziana (Florence), Biblioteca Malatestiana (Cesena), Pepys Library (Magdalene College, Cambridge), Warburg Library (London), National Art Library (Victoria and Albert Museum, London), London Library, Western Art Library (Ashmolean Museum, Oxford), Taylorian Library (Oxford), State Archives of Florence, Cesena, Venice, Padua, and the Archivio degli Innocenti (Florence).

My research was supported by the grant of an Andrew Mellon Fellowship at the Metropolitan Museum of Art in New York in 1989–90. I am grateful to Olga Raggio, and to James Draper, Clare Vincent and Antoine Wilmering for their part in making this so worthwhile. I would also like to thank the Gladys Krieble Delmas Foundation and the British School in Rome for grants towards the initial research in Italy.

The book, unlike the thesis, was written in my spare time. I am, however, grateful to the Keeper of the Department of Medieval and Later Antiquities in the British Museum, Neil Stratford, and the Deputy Keeper, John Cherry, for allowing me some days towards writing and proof reading. I doubt whether the book could have been written without the combined resources of the BM and BL to hand, and without the knowledge and contacts of current and former colleagues in both institutions. Those who assisted me include: Philip Attwood, Janet Backhouse, Don Bailey, Giulia Bartrum, Michael Borrie, Sheila Canby, Hugo Chapman, Stephen Coppel, Aileen Dawson, Anne Farrer, Mirjam Foot, David Gaimster, John Goldfinch, Ian Jenkins, Dafydd Kidd, Janet Larkin, Philippa Marks, Catherine Marsh, Chris Michaelides, Beverley Nenk, Anne Payne, Rita Phillips, Nigel Ramsay, John Reeve, Dennis Rhodes, Michael Rogers, Judy Rudoe, Tracy Ryan, Ruth Spires, Peter Stringer, Luke Syson, Susan Walker, Rachel Ward and Dyfri Williams.

That I have written the book I wanted to write, and that my part in its production could be completed before the arrival of my first child, is largely due to Gillian Malpass. Her role as editor, designer, adviser and friend has been crucial at every point, and she has given constant help and encouragement even in trying circumstances. My debt to her is considerable, as it is also to her assistant, Laura Church; to the copy editor, Ruth Thackeray; and to Pamela Turner, who compiled the index to my specifications.

I am grateful to my family, especially to my parents, Ann Thornton and Peter Thornton, to whom the book is jointly dedicated. They offered generous and tactful support during the writing of the thesis. My father's work on the role of inventories in the interpretation and reconstruction of historic interiors is well known, and this book makes frequent reference to his own, much wider study, *The Italian Renaissance Interior, 1400–1600* (London, Weidenfeld and Nicolson, 1991). Apart from drawing on his knowledge and experience, I have benefited from his example as a museum curator who has written a succession of scholarly books in his spare time. My mother's role and example has been no less important, and I have among other things consulted her as a critic, translator and master bookbinder.

I also recall my Danish great-uncle, the painter and writer Mogens-Kai Nørregaard. In a series of letters written in the 1970s from his eighteenth-century attic in Copenhagen, he encouraged my interest in Italy, where he himself had lived in the 1930s. His study-room, and the way in which he lived with his few, carefully selected things (a number of which I later inherited) was an inspiration in itself.

By far the greatest contribution has, however, been made by my husband, Jeremy Warren. Despite having a catalogue to write in his free time for the Ashmolean, he has never failed to give me support, advice and assistance whenever I needed it. I would like to thank him for his belief in the book, and in its author.

April 1997

Author's Note

As a GENERAL RULE, the English word 'study' has been used throughout this book, except for such well-known examples as Isabella d'Este's Studiolo and Grotta. The original term used by contemporaries to denote a given study is recorded in the Concordance.

In quoting from Italian sources, I have generally used standard translations, where these exist, specifying in the Notes if I have made any alterations. Translations of primary material are my own, except where I have acknowledged a particular individual in the Notes.

Author-date citations in both text and Notes, for example '(Barzizza 1444)', refer to inventories and other primary sources cited in the Concordance at the end of the book. Full bibliographical details of all secondary sources are given on their first occurrence in the Notes for each chapter, and are referred to by author and a short form of the title thereafter.

Esi gli
osi mar
tyris. a
atblet
xpi. bti
Georgii.
gesta. li

tteras. pugnam. palmaq; ttao
rum. m̃ morum nob scripta te
xuerint; quibs ochac gra nim as
actor honoris retiẽntur. mento
rum cumulus aucret. Hos tam
horum minimum; hec ozoem.
uel ipórum unum aliquod scp
ta isse. animo uiurabit. Quam

Introduction

To own a study was to lay claim to the civility, polite manners and educated tastes which came to define the ruling élite in the Italian Renaissance.[1] Through the medium of the study and its contents, this book is indirectly concerned with the expectations, behaviour and values of the urban élites and with the distinctive culture, both urban and urbane, which they created. The study as a room-type lies at the heart of that culture, for it represents not only the celebration of the individual, but also the prestige of education, learning and the arts, both of which have been taken to characterise the Italian Renaissance.[2] In itself, however humble the room, the study demonstrated the dignity of an individual, for it was (most unusually in the Renaissance household) a space set apart for the use of a single owner. More than any other room in the house – to a greater degree even than the principal bedchamber – the study was perceived by contemporaries as having an individual owner, and a secret identity of its own, which might persist long after that owner's death. Inventories and account books of the fifteenth century document the possessive and proprietorial spirit with which Renaissance Italians created and furnished their studies, and the kind of selfconsciousness which the rooms could represent.

It was not only the fact of owning a study, but also the nature of its decoration and contents which indicated an individual's credentials, and many of the characteristic things found in the room subtly suggest ways in which an individual related to the wider social world. Like the memoranda which they often contained, studies often represent their owners both as individuals and as responsible members of families, clans and neighbourhoods.[3]

Studies could represent a considerable investment in household fittings and furnishings, which (from the lists of their contents provided in inventories and account books) stimulated acquisitiveness and pride of possession. When Anton Francesco Doni complained about the expense involved in setting up house in the required bourgeois style in sixteenth-century Florence, he listed many of the kinds of object which were to be found in studies in the city:

> Then there are the household goods [. . .] a beaker, a carafe, a salt, a wine-cooler, a glass, a footed dish (these are of glass) and a wine flagon. Do you want anything else? [. . .] all the money ever minted would not serve to buy me half of the stuff.[4]

Doni's satirical observation points to the proliferation of household and domestic goods, as contemporaries perceived it. His comments about the proliferation of glass-forms, and the demand for them, is confirmed by an inventory of a Florentine glasshouse, which not only lists a remarkable variety of wares and types (including those which he mentions) but also covers both locally made and Venetian pieces, and two gold gem-set rings left with the workshop as payment in kind.[5] Above all, Doni's complaints point to the increasing costs of setting up house. An exaggerated sense of anxiety about the expanding material world is expressed by Leonardo in his drawing of a rain of artisan's tools and household necessities: lamps, plates, cooking vessels and the sardonic inscription 'O human misery – how many things you must serve for money' (fig. 2).[6]

Books stored in chests or displayed on shelves in the study could comprise the working

2 Leonardo da Vinci, ink drawing, *c.*1510, showing a rain of household objects and artisanal tools. Windsor, Royal Library. Royal Collection, © Her Majesty Queen Elizabeth II

library of an urban professional, or the corpus of corrected texts of a scholar, student or teacher.[7] Studies often contained an individual's reading library of vernacular texts (Colombe 1561) or the household books used for teaching children both in the vernacular schools and at home (Tura 1483; Fece 1450). Carefully bound and arranged, the works displayed in a gentleman scholar's library could be specifically set out to demonstrate the ways in which modern, Italian culture rivalled that of ancient Greece and Rome.

Beyond the presence of books, desks and writing equipment in the study, the activities of reading and writing which took place there conferred the prestige associated with literacy and learning in the eyes of the ruling élite. Reading, studying and thinking were considered by Renaissance writers to be free and pleasurable pursuits which gave shape and elegance to one's leisure, so that a study represented the ideal of making the pleasures of thinking and working continuous with the rest of one's existence. Sometimes inventories suggest this in a very practical way, in referring to 'the study where one writes' much as they refer to 'the room where one makes bread'.[8]

The study was also integral to the Renaissance cult of studious leisure, as praised by the mystic Isotta Nogarola in her description of St Jerome:

3 Antonio da Fabriano, *Saint Jerome in his Study*, 1451. The saint sits at a plain built-in desk unit. One end of his table is built into the wall, the other end being apparently supported by a single leg. His writing slope consists of a small portable desk. His texts lie, fore-edges outwards, in the book cupboard on the right. Paper labels have been tipped in to mark relevant pages for easy reference. The hands – those of an habitual writer – which hold his pen and eraser knife are closely observed, as is his strained, if focused, expression. Baltimore, Walters Art Gallery.

He understood that nothing is sweeter to a servant of God than studious leisure, than the study of letters through which we learn about the infinity of things and of nature, about the sky, earth, seas, and at last about God himself. He read so much that we can hardly imagine how he found time to write; he wrote so much that it is difficult to believe how he could have found time to read.[9]

The aim was not only to own selected classics in good editions, as we would call it, but to live with them in an easy and familiar way, in order to assume the best of both Christian and classical tradition. Proving the point that books do indeed furnish a room, one humanist scholar wrote to another:

I get up early [when at my villa] and walk about my garden in my little dressing gown [. . .] then I withdraw into my little study where I can scan the pages of some poet or other. [. . .] I do not have a library here like that of the Sassetti or Medici [families], but I do have a little shelf-ful of corrected texts, which I treasure more than any rich ornament.[10]

While the study certainly answered the new emphasis on self-improvement and perfection of the self, it was equally important in a practical and representative way as a repository of family history, and not just the private resource of an individual. Having not only a need, but also a dedicated space in which to keep family papers must surely have ensured their preservation; a fact which might help to explain their remarkable survival. Memoranda often resembled 'a salad of many herbs' (*un insalata di più erbe*, as one of the men who compiled them put it), for they contained a jumble of autobiography, familial and local history.[11] Those who wrote them were conscious of the sense of family identity and inheritance which should be preserved and passed on to future generations. If a family's history needed to be strengthened or even selfconsciously created, then this could be done most effectively through a book of memoranda. Giovanni Morelli opened his ledger with some telling statements about the role of genealogy in constructing a new sense of social class among the ruling élite in Florence:

Since this entry book hasn't been used yet, it occurred to me [. . .] to write about our ancient condition and ancestry, so far as I can remember, and also about our current and coming situation. I'll do this in order to pass the time and especially to let my sons and relatives know something about our origins and early condition. For everyone today pretends to a family background of great antiquity [*perche oggi ogni catuno si fonda in grande antichità*], and I want to establish the truth about ours.[12]

Similarly, the archives stored in the study – 'my papers [. . .] and those of my ancestors' in Alberti's words – constituted the memory not only of an individual, but also of the family and clan network to which he belonged. Such values were transmitted as much through art objects as through documents, for the treasures concentrated in the bedchamber and study were those core possessions (*masserizie*) which constituted a family's honour in the fifteenth century. These were the kinds of object which were thought important enough to be included among presents given by one Florentine patrician, Andrea Minerbetti, to his son Tommaso and his daughter-in-law in 1521, on the occasion of their setting up house together. A gift listed by Andrea in his account book was a birthdish (*desco da parto*), a painted or inlaid wooden tray presented to a woman at childbirth (Minerbetti memoranda; fig. 4).[13] Andrea himself had received a painted tondo on his marriage in 1494: perhaps this was the one he gave to his own son.[14] *Deschi* had proud familial associations, often being decorated with arms, and were treasured as commemorative objects, sometimes in the study.[15] The goldsmith Giovanni del Chiaro, for instance, kept two *tavolette di donna* in his study (Chiaro 1424). What may well have been a birth-

4 A ceremonial visit to a new mother, as painted on a poplar wood birth-tray (*desco da parto*). The men on the extreme right bear gifts, including a *desco*, which would have been presented on this kind of occasion and then kept as a family heirloom, often in the study of the head of a household. Attributed to Masaccio, Florentine, *c.*1427; the gilded frame, Florentine, *c.*1500. Berlin, Staatliche Museen zu Berlin, Preussischer Kulturbesitz, Gemäldegalerie.

5 The birth-tray of Lorenzo de' Medici, showing the Triumph of Fame. New York, Metropolitan Museum of Art. Purchase, in memory of Sir John Pope-Hennessy: Rogers Fund, The Annenberg Foundation, Drue Heinz Foundation, Annette de la Renta, Mr. and Mrs. Frank E. Richardson, and The Vincent Astor Foundation Gifts, Wrightsman and Gwynne Andrews Funds, special funds, and Gift of the children of Mrs. Harry Payne Whitney, Gift of Mr. and Mrs. Joshua Logan, and other gifts and bequests, by exchange, 1995.

tray, given the form of the description and the subject-matter of Romulus and Remus which was depicted on it, was kept in Marco d'Ugolino Bonzi's study.[16] Lorenzo de' Medici kept the *desco* commissioned from Scheggia at his birth in the room leading to his study with its gems and small-scale works of art (Medici 1492, p. 14; see fig. 5). The status of Lorenzo's *desco* exemplifies the process by which furnishings had attained a new status as a form of family capital: Alberti used the word 'masserizie' in his treatise on household management, echoed by wealthy Florentines in their household accounts.[17]

As accumulating and collecting elegant furnishings and antiquities came to be pursued by a much wider social group in the sixteenth century, the study, and the collection or collectables kept within it, conferred honour and dignity on its owner and his family. The word 'studio' even came to be used as shorthand for a collection, with its dignified associations. One of the earliest uses of the word in this way appears in a letter of 1552 concerning the fate of Valerio Belli's collection; the same meaning is intended by the reference made by Jacopo Contareno in his will of 1596 to his *studio*, 'by which I mean not only the place where the books are, but all those things contained in the four mezzanine rooms in which I ordinarily live'. He went on to add that the honour and esteem in which he was held had derived directly from his collection: that, in a very complex sense, his *studio* was intimately bound up not only with his sense of himself, but with the way in which others perceived him as an individual (Contareno 1596).

A further social value – or social virtue – expressed through the decoration, fitting and

6 The Florentine poet Bernardo Bellincioni (1452–92) reading in his study. This copper engraving, possibly based on a drawing by Leonardo da Vinci (a friend of Bellincioni's), is unique in its lively, informal pose and for its incisive portrait. Like Leonardo, with whom he collaborated in creating court spectacle, Bellincioni sought the patronage of Ludovico il Moro, ruler of Milan. This portrait was copied in woodcut form for the frontispiece of his book of poetry (*Rime* Milan in 1493). Paris, Louvre, Cabinet des Estampes, Collection Eduard Rothschild, H.589.53. Photo: © R.M.N.

7 Woodcut showing the Milanese court historian, Bernadino Corio, from his vernacular history of Milan from its origins to 1499 (published in 1503). Corio is presented as an individual of high social and intellectual status, as indicated by all the details of the study setting: his furred robe, dagger, X-frame chair, the lap-dog (named in Greek) at his feet, and by his arms, which appear on the intablature above his portrait and on the lower left. The architectonic frame with its classical pilasters and Latin inscription below add further dignity to the image. Corio, *Patria historia*, Milan 1503. London, British Library.

furnishings of the study was *gentilezza*: that cult of decorum, refinement and good manners, which distinguished the ruling élite. *Gentilezza* provided a sharp instrument for dividing the ruler from the ruled, as illustrated by an anecdote told of Cosimo 'Il Vecchio' de' Medici by the humanist Angelo Poliziano. When Cosimo proffered a visiting peasant muscatel pears – considered a great delicacy for their scent and taste despite their shrivelled and shrunken appearance – the peasant exclaimed 'Oh, we give those to the pigs'. Cosimo, motioning a servant to take the pears away, replied tartly: 'We don't'.[18] Beyond being a cruel joke (one of many circulating among worldly Florentines which supposedly proved the superiority of city culture over that of the countryside), the story points up the necessity of perceiving and recognising the aesthetic qualities inherent in things, as proof of being truly civilised; qualities which could not be recognised by the ignorant or uninitiated but demanded attuned and educated tastes. Discernment; enjoyment in one's things and in using one's skills in appraising them; a sense of elegance and civility – all these are intimately connected with the study as a distinctively Renaissance phenomenon, and as such are themes of this book.[19] The relationship between people and things in the context of the study is the focus of the last chapter.

The Italian Renaissance study has traditionally been seen as a predominantly courtly phenomenon.[20] Its emergence in fifteenth-century Italy has been traced to the convergence of two parallel traditions: the treasuries constructed in royal and papal palaces from the fourteenth century, and the monastic cell as a space for reflection and study.[21] The courtly studies of the mid- to late fifteenth century have received a great deal of attention in recent years. The earliest of these, the study-library of Paolo Guinigi of Lucca (Guinigi 1430), is less well known than the rest, even though it appears to have been a prototype in both its character as a treasury on the French royal model, and in its marquetry decoration, which was later adapted for use in the studies of Leonello, Borso and Ercole d'Este in Ferrara.

The courtly study culminated in the refined and elegant rooms created by Federico da Montefeltro at Urbino, and by his son Guidobaldo in Gubbio, in the 1470s.[22] Neither of these studies had direct successors[23] but, with the growing significance of collecting and antiquarianism as signs of social status, the collector's study as a focus for art treasures (including fine manuscripts) became ever more important in the North Italian courts. The studies of three generations of the Medici – Cosimo Il Vecchio, Piero di Cosimo and his son Lorenzo – were early examples of this phenomenon.[24] Isabella d'Este's Studiolo, and the Camerino d'Alabastro created by her brother, Alfonso d'Este, developed the theme.[25]

The study as collection was to become a much wider phenomenon in the sixteenth century, as individuals from the great collecting families, the Medici, Gonzaga and Farnese, were not the only ones who created study-collections of their own. Circles of collectors and antiquarians, and the agents and artists who worked to supply them, are now well documented for Rome, Mantua, Florence and the Veneto.[26]

Whether for the iconography of their painted or inlaid decoration, or the art treasures displayed in them, these courtly studies have been carefully analysed by scholars. Wolfgang Liebenwein's book on the study as a room-type, its role in architectural planning and its nature as an interior space in the Renaissance palace, has deservedly become a classic.[27] Yet the way in which these hybrid, courtly creations were tied into a wider urban culture has received very little attention, despite the richness and variety of the sources available. This book attempts to right the imbalance, in showing that the studies created by members of the urban élites had their own contribution to make to the history of the study as a distinctive feature of Italian Renaissance culture, one which was to be exported all over Europe.

Richard Goldthwaite has shown that the character of the ruling élites of Renaissance Italy was predominantly urban, to some degree – at least until the seventeenth century – independent of both the political control and culture of courts.[28] City élites not only developed institutions to maintain and consolidate their local position from the mid-fifteenth century, but also created a new sense of nobility and status, moving beyond feudal models.[29] Members of the Florentine ruling élite considered their *nobiltà civile* to be a match for feudal nobilities in other Italian cities, and the Medici's ability to turn them into courtiers, following Duke Cosimo's creation of an hereditary *principato*, was not a foregone conclusion. As the Medici supporter Ludovico Alamanni put it, writing four years after the restoration of the family's control over Florence in 1512, 'Florentines [. . .] only pay their respects to magistrates, and even then with great reluctance. They are therefore far removed from court manners'. They should, he argued, be bribed into subservience, and 'moulded into a more courtly mode of behaviour'.[30]

Alamanni was describing a highly evolved élite culture, one which was intimately linked to a distinctive pattern of consumption.[31] The magnificence of individual patrons, whether of the often short-lived dynasties of the fifteenth century or the princely families of the sixteenth, has distracted attention away from this much wider and more diffuse phenomenon. The history of the Italian Renaissance study throws light on this development, for studies were created by members of the administrative and professional classes who made up the ruling sector of society, by notaries, doctors of law and medicine, by clerics, by patricians, by merchants and bankers.[32] They were also created and owned by scholars, university teachers, graduates and students, and by artists and craftsmen; people who did much to create Renaissance culture as we now perceive it.[33]

It would, however, be both wilful and misleading to imply a strict dichotomy between the courtly study and that created by individuals lower down the social scale: emulation was always a spur in the impulse to create such a selfconscious space as a study. Moreover, some courtly studies – such as Leonello d'Este's – were originally intended to be visited by scholars and artists, who would best appreciate the intellectual refinement of their decoration. Some of the earliest examples of studies analysed in this book were based on courtly prototypes, like Petrarch's study at Arquà, which was to remain a model for later humanists. Petrarch has been recognised as the crucial linking figure between the two traditions which converged to create the Renaissance study: the courtly model and the monastic one. Petrarch had followed the papal court to Avignon, where John XXIII and Benedict XII both created private studies in the papal palace:[34] his own study was created on his return from Provence. Yet Petrarch's simple study, and his writings, also expressed the monastic yearnings of the contemporary layman; his book *On the Solitary Life* discusses solitude and meditation as necessary conditions for a Christian existence. The study offered its owner a space for reflection and seclusion from the pressures of ordinary, day-to-day life. Elements of Petrarch's philosophy are echoed in later writers' comments on the opportunities which their studies afforded them in maintaining a sense of balance and detachment. The 'humble study' of the notary Lapo Mazzei (1350–1412) in late fourteenth-century Prato is mentioned in his letters with particular affection, and it is clear that he used it both as an office and as a room for contemplation. Further to this need for psychological space was that prompted by an increased awareness of history – which has also been taken as characteristic of the Renaissance in Italy[35] – which heightened the importance of classical and Christian models of behaviour and the concern to integrate these into contemporary life. The study had a crucial role to play in the process of distilling moral virtue from classical and Christian tradition, in that it provided a physical framework for reading, meditation or prayer.[36] The room could become a layman's cell, in which he could follow a daily pattern of reflection; a kind of monastic rule which would confer balance and probity, qualities which had practical application in everyday life. As the great educator Vittorino da Feltre put it:

> Not everyone is obliged to excel in philosophy or law, nor are all equally favoured by nature; but all are destined to live in society and to practise virtue.[37]

It was in this very practical and worldly sense that another Florentine, Giovanni Pagolo Morelli, advised his son to spend part of each day reading in his study:

> Ensure that every day, for at least an hour, you study Virgil, Boethius, Seneca and other authors such as you read in school. From this you will gain great intellectual virtue: you will learn, thinking on the recommendations of the authors, what course you have to follow in this life, whether it be for the health of the soul or for the benefit and honour of the body. [. . .] Spend as much time as you please with Virgil in your study, for he will never deny you, but will answer whatever you put to him, and will counsel and teach you without demanding financial or any other rewards; and he will take away melancholy or brooding thoughts, and bring you pleasure and consolation.[38]

8 A doctor analysing a urine sample, seated at a built-in desk unit in his study. His medical texts are propped up against the wall on a narrow shelf, similar to the arrangement depicted in Ghirlandaio's *St Jerome* (fig. 25). This woodcut is from one of the finest Florentine illustrated books of the late fifteenth century, *The Book of the Game of Chess*, printed in 1493. Despite its title, the book is a didactic work written by a Dominican monk, presenting an allegory in which the different pieces in a chess set represent different ranks of society: this doctor represents one of the pawns. Photo: author.

'Pleasure and consolation', in the words of Ippolita Maria Sforza, were typical benefits associated with owning a study. In her case, however, it was more a matter of recognising familiar faces in the panel paintings around her than of colloquy with ancient authors, such as Morelli advocates.

Just as the wish to create a study was not an aristocratic preserve, neither was the custom of collecting and accumulating antiquities, art objects, curiosities and treasures. Circles of collectors were well established by the fourteenth century, particularly in the Veneto, as we know from the collecting activities of the notary Oliviero Forzetta of Treviso (1300–73), who produced a list of *desiderata* when planning a visit to Venice in 1335.[39] This book describes the combination of exactly those patterns and levels of collecting and the types of study created by Petrarch and Lapo Mazzei which provided the essential preconditions for the creation of studies by members of the urban élites from the fifteenth century. For these people, a study answered a range of needs. It could be used as an office or writing-room; as a storeroom or treasury for household valuables, or, like the principal bed-chamber in an apartment, as a focal point for collecting. Some studies were selfconscious creations, but the function of the room as an intimate, secret and secure room which was the particular property of an individual enabled accumulations of art objects and collec-tions to develop without forethought or design. While the studies of secular rulers and ecclesiastics served a representative function as an ideal retreat of an enlightened individual from public affairs, paintings and literary evidence point to the individual's demand for privacy at a humbler level; a demand which can be linked with Burckhardt's classic interpretation of the Renaissance as 'an awakening of individuality'.[40]

A study could indicate a conscious desire for self-improvement, however small or humble the room: several owners of such a space commented on the fact that it allowed them to use their leisure productively, and sometimes to good moral purpose. Lapo Mazzei retreated into his study at night to give moral counsel as well as practical advice to his friend Francesco Datini. It was the only place where he said he could be 'free and alone' and write to Datini.[41] The freedom which his study afforded him is a common theme in his letters. In 1391 he wrote to his friend: 'I have considered your state a hundred times, on my walks, and in my bed, and in my study, when I was most alone'.[42] This was a preamble to some well-considered advice: he often recommended Francesco to take time away from his business affairs, as he himself sometimes did, in order to cultivate detachment. In 1395 he wrote to Francesco:

> I remain alone at home, in bed and in my study, as happy as the good hermits are on the mountain, and I feel no winds either from left or right. I think you are doing the same, and if this is not the case, you are doing the wrong thing, and if you do not do this you will achieve little and give yourself trouble for nothing.[43]

Mazzei's delightful reference to happy hermits conjures up contemporary paintings of St John the Baptist entering the wilderness (fig. 9) or St Jerome in the desert, reading quietly at a makeshift desk – a kind of study away from home – which was all part of Mazzei's vain attempt to divert Datini away from the single-minded pursuit of material wealth. It conveys the peace, and the human scale, of the study.

A vivid sense of how the study was integrated into the texture of an ordinary householder's daily life is given by a passage in Machiavelli's last play, *Clizia*, which he based on a comedy by Plautus. It is set in Florence in 1506 (as stated in the text), and the characters are recognisable and believable: they people a world Machiavelli knew well. He presents a disgruntled wife, Sofronia, complaining about the changes in her husband since he had become infatuated with a young girl. Talking about his behaviour before the girl appeared on the scene, Sofronia shows how her husband's work in his study on business (he appears to be a merchant from Machiavelli's description) or on family affairs was part of his daily routine:

> Anyone who knew Nicomaco a year ago and came across him today couldn't help being amazed by the great change that's come over him. He used to be thought

9 Lorenzo Monaco (*c.*1730–1425), *St John the Baptist Entering the Wilderness*, tempera on panel. Leicester City Museums, New Walk Museum. Photo: © Leicestershire Museums, Arts and Records Service.

dignified, responsible, sober. He passed his time worthily, got up early in the morning, heard Mass, ordered the day's food, and then saw to whatever business he had in town, at the market, or the magistrate's office. If not, he either discussed some serious topic or other with a few friends or shut himself up in his study at home to balance and tidy his accounts. Then he dined happily with the family and after dinner talked to his son, gave him advice, helped him to understand human nature, taught him how to live, in fact, with examples from past and present. Then he went out and spent the rest of the day either in business or in some sober and respectable recreation. Every evening, he was home by dusk, stayed with us by the fire if it was Winter, then went into his study to look over his affairs, and three hours after sunset he had supper in the best of humours. His way of life, in fact, was exemplary to everyone else in the house, and everyone was ashamed not to imitate him. So things went on, orderly and happy.[44]

The role of the study as an office, writing-room and family archive meant that wedding contracts were sometimes signed there. Mantegna's daughter, Laura, was married in his study on the ground floor of his house in Mantua on 31 August 1486. This room, which adjoined his painting-room, was beautifully decorated with a painted cornice and palmette frieze, and it was the focus for his collection of bronze and marble busts.[45] Laura Mantegna's presence in her father's study shows that women did sometimes enter this typically masculine preserve.

All these considerations gave the study a vital role to play, as a room which answered utilitarian needs as well as providing a space for reflection and solitude. The retreat into one's study was not merely a fashionable literary theme or a philosophical ideal – though it was evidently both of these things – but a practical reality in the lives of many householders. In analysing the way in which studies structured certain types of activity and the demand for particular kinds of art object, this book documents the study both as a private and as a social space. The way in which the room was associated with withdrawal and contemplation, while conferring social honour and worldly status, perhaps appears paradoxical to the modern reader. Yet it was precisely the need to have a degree of privacy and organisation in one's personal, professional and familial affairs, as provided by or formalised in the study, which distinguished an individual and established his social, intellectual or even his business credentials. A number of studies discussed in this book indicate just this representative nature of the room (Helman 1606; Bianchini 1510; Fece 1450; Pasqualigo 1579).

The book examines not only the study itself as a particular kind of space, its construction and fittings, but the range of people who owned these rooms. From the pleasures of ownership afforded by the study, the argument moves to the social role of the room and the way in which it was displayed and viewed. The final chapter narrows the focus in considering the variety of art objects characteristic of the room, their function and significance.

Contemporary terms used to refer to studies, and their various resonances, are investigated in chapter 1. As far as the contents of studies are concerned, this book deals with furnishings in the widest possible sense. Art historians have fast become accustomed to the notion that many surviving Renaissance panel paintings were originally associated with, or even part of, pieces of furniture, but the notion that furnishings could have much the same value as antiquities or what we would call works of art does not have a wide currency. Recent research has shown the extent to which Italian Renaissance hierarchies of aesthetic value were not only very different from our own, but to some extent countered a hierarchy based on financial value alone. The idea that a bronze inkstand might be considered an appropriate use of sculpture and that it might, in combining utility with elegance and literary association, have a dignity of its own, is a radical one to the modern

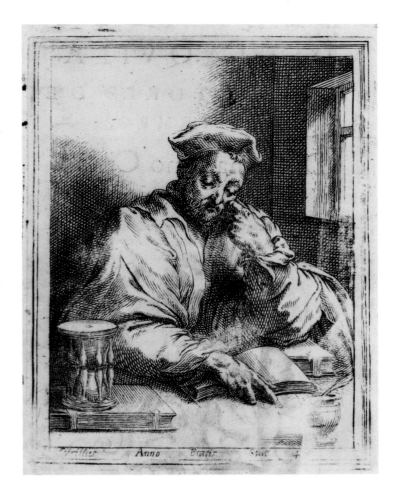

10 Engraved portrait of the historian Bernadino Cirillo at the age of forty, from his *Annals of the City of Aquileia* (Rome 1570). This unusually sensitive and meditative portrait conveys the ambience of the study through the subtle use of chiaroscuro. London, British Library.

reader. Yet a bronze inkstand can be shown to have shared study space with what we would call 'fine bronzes', in other words, works of art (Usper 1601). Similar arguments can be made for mirrors, and it is a proven fact that a collector's cabinet could have only slightly less financial value than a prized antiquity. 'History-painted' maiolica raised the status of Italian ceramics to such an extent that it was thought to bring gentility and civility to the villa, or could even share study-space with imported Chinese celadon (Odoni 1555).[46]

Considerations like these have encouraged me to use the words 'art object' and 'collectable' to bridge the aesthetic gap, as we would now see it, between the prosaic and ill-defined words 'object' or 'furnishing', and the specialised term 'antiquity'. 'Art object' serves to describe the range of furnishings created in the Renaissance with rooms like the study and bedchamber in mind; these include new art forms (like the medal, or the sculptural inkstand). 'Collectable' denotes an item of elegant furnishing which was not necessarily part of a collection or accumulation of art objects or antiquities, but which nevertheless rated in the eyes of contemporaries and had in itself a certain cachet: mirrors and cabinets came into this category, and as such are examined in detail in this book.

1 Sources and Interpretation: The Urban Context

TWO RECENT STUDIES SERVE as precedents for dealing with Italy's urban élites as a single dominant group with regard to the commissioning and consumption of art and art objects: one, written by an economic historian, dealing with wealth and demand, and the other, written by a social historian and museum curator, with production and patterns of consumption.[1] Both cover the same date ranges, and both discuss the Florentine fifteenth-century model in detail (as does a third fundamental work on the social world of art, upon which they both draw[2]) but both compare Florentine experience with that of other cities and chart the quick spread of ideas or shared values between them. As an élite phenomenon, the study-rooms throughout Italy exhibit certain common features, some of which have already been mentioned, justifying a similar approach. The inventories, both published and unpublished, on which these findings are based cover a wide date range; although they derive from a number of Italian cities, as a quick glance at the Concordance at the end of this book indicates, they are principally Venetian and Florentine. Inventories including a room or rooms referred to explicitly as a study or office of an individual are relatively rare in these records, and, where they do appear, their contents cannot be interpreted, analysed or understood in isolation from those of other rooms in the Renaissance house.[3] Work for this book has therefore involved reading through about five hundred inventories in Venice and Florence alone, in order to provide the crucial material and lexicological context to the points made here about studies and their furnishings.[4] Principal sources have been the sixteenth-century Florentine and Venetian inventories which derive from the Office of Wards in each city, known as the Giudici di Petizion in Venice and the Ufficio de' Pupilli in Florence.[5] The system of administration in the Venetian Office is less well known than its Florentine counterpart, although Cardinal Gaspare Contarini describes the responsibilities of the Office, and the standing of the Procurators of St Mark's, associated with it, in his book *La republica dei magistrati di Vinegia*. It is quoted here (in a sonorous contemporary translation) to give a sense of the status of the Procurators of St Mark's with regard to the Office of Wards, and that Office's relations with Venetian society as a whole:

> Their office is to take upon them the defence & tutorship of Orphelins, who being under age, and their fathers deade without making any will, have not any tutor or overseer appointed them: for which cause this charge and office is never given to any, but to such as are throughly knowne to be of singular good conscience and integritie of life, and have passed (in a manner) through all the other offices of the city. [. . .] In times passed, this office was of passing great and honourable estimation, not onely within Venice, but also in forrayne regions, in so much that not onely the subiectes and neere borderers, but also forreners and strangers, made them by testament their executors, and out wholly into their hands the administration of their goodes, during the minority of their children. [. . .] this ofice was at the first instituted, to the end that the heritage and substances of those citizens that should either die in service of their countrey, or on trafficke of merchandise among forraine nations, should not bee by fraude misemplyed or diverted from their heires.[6]

The statutes of the Florentine Office have been published and analysed in some detail in Kent Lydecker's thesis, *The Domestic Setting of the Arts in Renaissance Florence*, and his account is merely summarised here.[7] When a Florentine died intestate leaving dependent minors, and his family were unable or unwilling to take over the estate, the Office acted in the interests of the heirs during their minority. When an estate came into the care of the Office, an *auctore* or administrator was appointed to take care of it; he had full legal and financial responsibility to settle debts by selling off part of the estate or dividing property as he saw fit. His first duty was to compile an inventory of movables within fifteen days of taking on the estate. The original was later copied into the files of the Office by a notary (these *campioni d'inventari* are the principal Florentine sources used here). What makes inventories from these archives so useful is perhaps explained by the regulations of the Florentine Office which stipulate that the two closest paternal and maternal relatives should be present while the inventory was being compiled. They were likely to know the house and its contents well, and to remember details which might otherwise have gone unrecorded, such as the ownership of a particular room or the subject of a portrait. Assessors were officials of the Office, who called out objects as they came to hand, while the notary wrote them down. Inventories in the acts of individual Venetian notaries and in the archive of the Venetian Lower Chancery frequently name the assessors and sometimes their connection with the deceased as relatives, friends or business partners. If this is not stated in the inventory's preamble (*proemio*) it is sometimes clarified by references to the subjects of portraits or to family or business papers.[8] This can be useful in the case of the close-knit community of Flemish merchants in Venice, who tended to use a few notaries for all their needs, making it possible to trace the careers and activities of an individual from his arrival in Venice until his death.[9] The profession, occupation or status of the deceased (as a Venetian *cittadino*, or non-noble holder of certain legally defined privileges, for example[10]) is often given in the *proemio*. If it is not, it usually becomes apparent in the inventory itself, as in that of the Venetian lawyer Ludovico Usper, whose working papers are described as being necessary for his profession.[11]

Post-mortem inventories have well-known limitations. First, the inventories used here generally lack valuations, since they were intended to ensure the preservation of property rather than estimate them for sale.[12] Second, they can only be snapshots of an individual's possessions at a particular moment, making the fluctuating world of goods appear static and deceptively complete. This is not a serious limitation from the point of view of this book, which aims at building up an impressionistic picture of the Renaissance study in general, rather than tracing the entire worldly goods of a number of given individuals within the wider context of their lives and testamentary dispositions.[13] Checking an individual's will against the post-mortem inventory of his movables indicates how bequests in a will would often not appear in an inventory, as relatives or friends who knew that they had been left a specific bequest in a will, or who had been promised something, took care to remove them before an inventory was compiled.[14] Inventories can in themselves include details of bequests: that of Giovan Francesco Buizzi, compiled in Florence in 1594, itemises things belonging to his brother, Niccolò, and the rooms in which they were to be found, which included alabaster sculpture from Giovan Francesco's study (Buizzi 1594). The Venetian inventory of a goldsmith's estate is followed by a note listing works of art which he had bequeathed to his brother and executor, Father Bon Serafin Fontana. The paintings are described in unusual detail in terms of their subject-matter and – unusually – attributions are also given. The works included a Titian, a Palma Giovane, a Giovanni Bellini and 'a copy of a Bassano' (Fontana 1583).[15]

The Venetian and Florentine Offices of Wards had distinct house styles in the format as well as the content of the inventories they compiled. The majority list objects under the room in which they were found by the assessors, though occasionally their lists are

12 A dying man makes his will. A friend leans close to relay his words to the notary sitting at a nearby table, while the dying man's pregnant wife raises one hand as if to emphasise a point. This woodcut appears in the most popular *abbaco* book (textbook of commercial arithmetic) of the sixteenth century, as a way of making a game of proportion vivid and immediate. The text on the preceding page explains the problem: the dying man wishes to leave the residue of his estate, 1400 ducats, to his widow and his future child, and specifies in his will the proportions which each is to receive, depending on the sex of the child. After the man's death, his widow gives birth to twins, a boy and a girl. If the testamentary dispositions are to be honoured, how many ducats will each receive? As Michael Baxandall has explained of a similar problem, 'underneath the costumes of the widow and the twins are three early capitalists carving up a profit according to their relative investment in some trading venture'. The woodcut stresses the practical relevance of the issue by situating the scene in a contemporary interior, faithfully if schematically recorded. Girolamo Tagliente, *Il libro d'abaco*, Venice 1530, GIII*v*. Oxford, Bodleian Library.

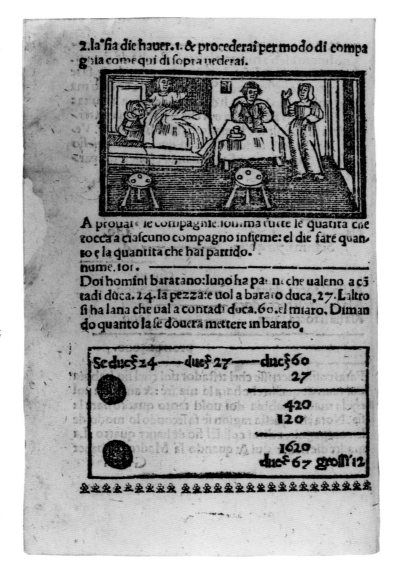

subdivided not by room but by material, arranged in a rough hierarchy according to value. Sometimes an inventory consists merely of a list of apparently unsorted objects, perhaps because movables had been removed from their original rooms and piled up in a heap for the purposes of recording them.[16] A good example is the inventory of the movables of Ottavio Fabbri, compiled in the interests of his widow Ursetta in 1616, in which the contents of the study (which was famous enough to have been described in admiring detail by Stringa in his 1604 edition of Sansovino's guidebook to Venice) can only be recognised in relation to that description, having long ago been removed from the study which had previously contained them (Fabbri 1616; for another Florentine example of an inventory consisting of a single list, see Fancielli 1592).[17] This is not a typical pattern, however, so that it is possible to differentiate between studies and other rooms in the house on the basis of hundreds of inventories.

★　★　★

The Terminology Used for Studies in Inventories

The Italian word 'studio' is the general term used in the documents to describe studies, since it derives from the medieval Latin *studium*, which is consistently used to describe a monk's cell, or the cell and library of the head of a religious house, throughout the Middle Ages.[18] The secular royal study-rooms of the fourteenth century, such as the one constructed by Charles V of France, were known as *estudes* or *estudi*, also derived from the Latin *studium*.[19] The first important study to be constructed by an Italian ruler and collector was that built by Paolo Guinigi in his palace in Lucca in the first two decades of the fifteenth century, which was referred to in an inventory of 1430 as a *studio* (Guinigi 1430). Fifteenth-century documents confirm the use of this word, whether in Emilia-Romagna, the Marches, Tuscany or the Veneto. A sense of the range of meanings given by the word *studio* is best given by John Florio's Italian–English dictionary of 1611, which contains two entries under the term as follows:

> *Studio*, an earnest bending of the minde to a thing, affection to doe good or evill, study, endevour, diligence, industry, laborious desire, mentall exercise.

> *Studio*, a private study, cabinet, closet, or any place to study in. Also an university where studies are profest. Also a Colledge where Students are. Also a standing-deske in a schoole for great bookes.[20]

Florio's definition of the study as a room, 'or any place to study in', is of course the definition concerned here, and it is full of social information. His inclusion within his definition of not only a designated room, but also of a portion of one used for the purposes of study, and a large piece of furniture, is mirrored in the inventories analysed here.[21]

Regional and literary usage make for a more complex picture. Florentines tended to refer to their studies as *scrittoi*, whereas cabinets or desks found in this type of room were known as *studioli*.[22] One wealthy Florentine, Domenico Berti, whose estate was inventoried in 1594, had an inlaid cabinet or *studiolo* 'in the Venetian manner' in his *scrittoio* (Berti 1594). Venetian inventories of the same period generally use these terms with diametrically opposite meanings. One Venetian merchant, for example, had a lacquered cabinet or *scrittor* in his *studio* (Calderini 1597). Sometimes the word *studiolo* or its Venetian dialect form *studiol* is used to describe a room, but this is rare: I have come across only a few examples, and each refers to a collector's study (Helman 1606; Pasqualigo 1579; Odoni 1555; Vendramin 1612).

Other, rarer words used to describe a study have been carefully analysed by Liebenwein in his book on the study as a room-type. He identifies the first use of the word *Museum* (from the Greek *Museon*, or dwelling-place of the Muses) to refer to the collection of Alessandro Maggi da Bassano.[23] Poggio Bracciolini's playful use of a derivative from Greek, *gymnasiolum*, to refer to his study-bedroom, is well documented.[24] Other diminutives include *camerino* (literally 'small chamber') which might serve the same functions as a study: when Ulisse Aldrovandi described the collection of Giovanni Gaddi in Rome he listed 'the most distinguished, but also the smallest things' which were to be found in 'the *camerino*, which serves as a study'.[25] It was this kind of room which was to be the model for the English closet and French *cabinet* of the seventeenth century, and which was to play an important role not only in interior decoration, but also in the pattern of social life within the household.[26]

★ ★ ★

The location of each room described in an inventory is generally given in terms of its position in relation to such structural features as doors, staircases or other rooms. An inventory may indicate the disposition of rooms in a given house, even if it cannot provide an accurate groundplan. Many of the Venetian inventories describe the location of the rooms not only in relation to each other, but also to public spaces which each one overlooked, such as a *campo* (small open space), canal or *rio* (small canal).[27] Once a starting-point had been chosen, the assessors tended to work systematically from room to room, and they specify if they break the sequence. They often start on the ground floor, a fact of particular significance in Florentine inventories since this is where the summer apartments were situated, in order to benefit from the relative coolness provided by insulating walls, whereas in Venice, the ground floor of many of the dwellings documented in inventories was taken up with storerooms and offices. Inventories of Florentine interiors generally start with the all-purpose room, the *sala*; Venetian examples with the *portico* or hall on the main (first) floor, moving down to the ground floor at the end of the inventory.[28]

The Venetian, Florentine and other inventories consulted here give a detailed picture of a wide variety of housing, from substantial, imposing buildings of the kind now referred to loosely as *palazzi*[29] (Gondi 1578; Usper 1601) in Italian, to smaller town houses, single rooms,[30] shops,[31] workshops[32] and villas.[33] Sometimes they move from one family residence to another in the space of a single inventory (perhaps from town house to villa: Buondelmonti 1563; Buizzi 1594). To consider the Venetian records alone, it is evident that many Venetians lived and worked in crowded conditions which must have provided very little contrast to the bustle and activity of the canals in what was, in the sixteenth century, one of Europe's largest cities. This perhaps explains the status attached to private and enclosed spaces, such as halls, roof-terraces, *altane*,[34] gardens,[35] private land and water entrances, and the needs which they answered. Pressure on space in Venice meant that buildings had been adapted and remodelled over centuries; many buildings clearly show the scars of sixteenth-century alterations as doors, mezzanine rooms, corridors and windows were added or removed. Alterations and building work could spark off a lawsuit, as Marcantonio Michiel discovered when he tried to rebuild the windows and balconies over the courtyard which he shared with his Pisani neighbours. He lost the case after expensive litigation in April 1522.[36] The example illustrates some of the social checks operating on development in sixteenth-century Venice, in addition to practical and financial limitations on making structural alterations or building new palaces in the severe classical style of the High Renaissance. Hence the outstanding new building of the sixteenth century which took place on the newly reclaimed and drained islands (*insulae*), which provided rare opportunities to build new palaces (like the Palazzo Grimani at Santa Maria Formosa) or blocks of planned housing (such as the housing development at Borgolocco San Lorenzo in Castello).[37]

Tax returns in the archive of the Venetian magistracy which administered property taxation indicate the variety of rooms and apartments within one housing block: from residences, storage spaces to workshops, owned or rented by a wide range of people, from patricians to servants or tradesmen.[38] Such complexity of social – as well as architectural – conditions needs to be kept in mind when interpreting individual inventories which must often list the contents of a small section of a large building. Many of the inventories cited here indicate that the people whose movable property they document lived in houses of irregular plan, fissured with corridors, mezzanines, landings, attics and other irregular features.

By far the most useful aspect of inventories is that they give indications of room-use,

13 Albrecht Dürer, plan and elevation of an Italian *palazzo*, thought to have been where the artist stayed on his second visit to Venice. This ink sketch is probably a fragment from Dürer's notebook, and is covered with notes identifying the rooms and their furnishings. London, British Library, Sloane MS 5229, fol. 167r.

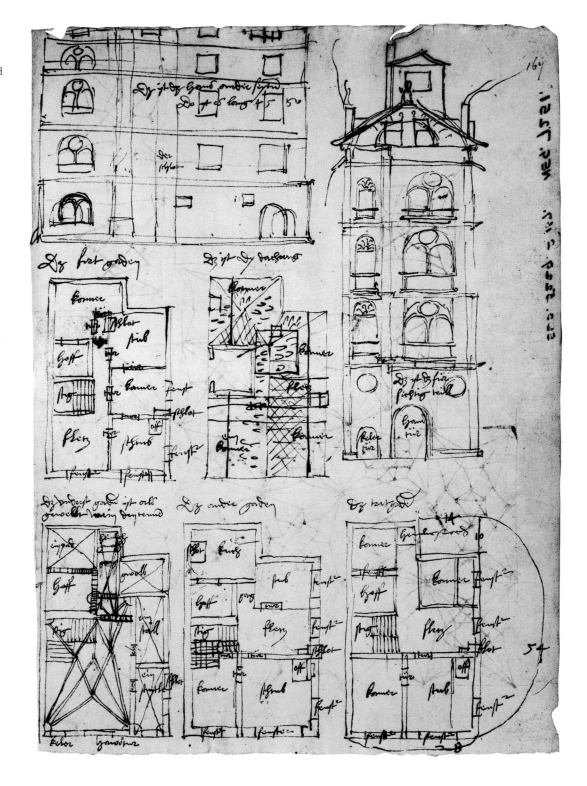

and so act as a useful corrective to architectural plans, which are prescriptive by their very nature. From inventories, one receives the impression that many of the humbler studies and offices referred to here were squeezed into any convenient space – for instance, in a mezzanine or off a staircase that had not been commandeered for better uses. They also indicate an important fact, that studies could be in a corner of your bedchamber and not

14 Part of the section listing the contents of a study in the inventory of the estate of Maestro Bartolo di Tura, 1483. This is a fair copy which would have been retained by the family for reference, and is beautifully written on vellum. Items listed here are discussed below on pages 83–4. Florence, Biblioteca Medicea-Laurenziana, Codice Ashburnhamiano 1768, cc9v–10.

in a separate room, a fact which would not be provided by a plan, but which had considerable significance for the way in which Renaissance people lived.

Memoranda and Patterns of Acquisition

Whereas an inventory can record only one instant in a room's history, memoranda and account books can chronicle room changes over the period of an individual's lifetime so that, for instance, one can follow the study of Andrea Minerbetti in inventories of 1493, 1499, 1502 and 1546, during which time it is evident that it went through a number of vicissitudes. The six cypress-wood chests for papers (*scritture*) are mentioned in 1499 and 1502, but had been jettisoned by 1546, as had the mirror on a stand, and the mezzo tondo relief of the *Pietà* mentioned in the first two inventories. The built-in desk unit with cupboard underneath, first mentioned in the listing of 1502, remained in 1546, but the four exotic inkstands in different materials had gone. Two engraved or inlaid (*alla domaschina*) brass candlesticks and two basins were to be found in 1546. Only one painting,

15 From the account book of the Florentine patrician Andrea Minerbetti: his own inventory of his movables, listed room by room in 1502, showing here the items to be found in his study. The list of furnishings includes a fitted desk unit with bench and shelves, a glass window, and inkstands (*chalamai*) in four different materials: ivory, glass, marble and cypress wood. Florence, Biblioteca Medicea-Laurenziana, Acquisti e Doni 229, vol. 2, 46v.

a *Madonna*, was then to be found in the room (apart from two canvases with 'heads' over the door frame), in contrast to the two panel paintings (a *Pietà* in a gilded frame and a *St Francis*) listed in 1493: no paintings are listed in 1502. Whereas a glass window is proudly mentioned as part of the fittings of the room in 1502, it is not mentioned again in 1546, by which time such a detail would hardly have been perceived as novel (though both glass and linen windows were important enough to have been among the things given to his son and daughter-in-law in 1521).[39] The various devotional objects listed in 1493, such as strings of paternosters, an Agnus Dei of gilded wax[40] and a pax with a relief, are completely absent in the 1546 listing, but the latter does include a papal indulgence in a little chest. The books, so carefully listed in 1502, are merely mentioned as 'Andrea's books' in 1546 (Minerbetti memoranda).

Given that Minerbetti was compiling these lists of property for himself, could it be that the young man was keener at the job than the older one, and should considerations like this not be taken into account in assessing this rare record of changes to a study over time? Or should the diminishing detail of Minerbetti's recording be considered as part of that elusive process by which, as the frequency and number of household acquisitions were made, the accounts listing them became more perfunctory? Such a process can be observed in other account books over roughly the same period, as well as in inventories in the Office of Wards (not only in Florence), which would point to its significance as an index of changing attitudes to material objects and the fact of possession.[41] It will take quantitative analysis of both inventories and account books, however, and careful interpretation of terminology in relation to new types of art object and changing forms and decoration, to take this argument any further.[42] Of its importance, there can no longer be any doubt, after the ground-breaking work of Richard Goldthwaite and others which would now make statistical analysis both possible and valuable.[43] New forms of analysis are all the more needed, since the density and range of furnishings listed in the sixteenth-century records, in comparison with the fifteenth-century ones, makes the evolution of particular rooms (and the demands for certain art objects which they channel) correspondingly difficult to assess. The changes in the nature of the documentation mentioned above increase the necessity of working from the evidence of surviving objects: in themselves, these objects can provide clues about their own status and significance which the other records simply do not provide. Such work is only now being done.[44]

Unlike the bulk of inventories consulted here, memoranda books include expenses on art objects and household items, whether commissioned or bought, and on interior decoration. They reveal both the transmission of collectables between individuals and between generations, and also document the way in which individuals sought to create their own private spaces, even if they re-used fittings from a study set up by another, older family member. A fascinating purchase of the kind of object found in studies is recorded in the memoranda of the sculptor Alessandro Vittoria, who noted in 1563 that he had bought a cast of the foot of Michelangelo's marble figure of *Day* from a Bolognese dealer 'who sells drawings'. The cast would appear to have been similar to those made by Schardt after Michelangelo, which are documented in the collection of Paulus von Praun.[45] Vittoria typically enters the exact price, but atypically adds 'and both were satisfied with it'.[46]

Although invaluable when assessed to appraise the relative values of works of art at the point of purchase, or total spending by an individual on furnishings over his lifetime, the usefulness of this kind of information is limited by the fact that an individual rarely records the information which makes it possible to deduce his total income.[47] Where memoranda score, from the point of view of this book, is in recording the amount of time taken to fit and furnish a study as part of remodelling an apartment, and, as this happened, the evolution of proprietorial feelings and a sense of ownership about the room.

Apart from recording that a room changed over time, memoranda books show how this happened, chronicling patterns of acquisition, exchange, lending and inheritance. The emphasis of much recent research on the origins and development of the art market, particularly in Florence, has obscured the fact that individuals often exchanged and lent objects within their family, kin group and neighbourhood. Those who could not afford an antique piece might persuade a relative to lend one, hence Andrea Minerbetti's exchange of eight objects with his brother for 'a large antique bronze bust' (Minerbetti memoranda). The balance of the exchange indicates the perceived value of the bronze – hardly surprising at a time when bronzes were exceptionally rare according to the evidence of contemporary inventories. From exchanging to lending: Cardinal Bembo's loan request addressed to Cardinal Bibbiena, pleading for the loan of a bronze Venus, is mentioned in the next chapter, but it should be seen within a broader pattern by which lending valued objects was an index of magnanimity. A sixteenth-century biography of Donatello's doctor and patron, Giovanni Chellini, records that

> since he possessed much silver plate, he frequently and indeed almost continuously lent pieces of it to Florentine citizens who were taking up office or celebrating a wedding. So we see that he lent six silver dishes to Neri Capponi when he was sent as ambassador to Milan, and shortly afterwards he lent Giovanni Lorini, who had been made captain of a galley going to Sicily, a silver jug with gilded foliage inside and blue enamelling at the bottom, six silver cups and four silver trenchers or dishes.[48]

Chellini was also continuously lending his books, keeping careful notes of their going out and return by means of paper chits (*polizze*) which were signed on receipt.[49]

Memoranda also record the acquisition of second-hand goods or the remodelling of existing goods. Francesco di Matteo Castellani, who bore the title of Cavaliere, conferring the privilege of wearing a sword, records buying a two-handled sword from a pedlar or traveller (*viandante*) which had formerly belonged to a certain Maestro Ambrogio. He took the sword off to a blacksmith to have it converted to a one-handled sword. Arms as proofs of gentility were often listed among the contents of studies (and represented in pictures as hanging on the wall), along with riding equipment and trappings of office (Castellani memoranda 1441; Tura 1483; Fece 1450; Monticuli 1413; Barzizza 1444).[50]

Just as proofs of gentility and status could be bought from second-hand dealers, so they could also be lost to them. Arms were only one type of possession which fell into this category. Fine furniture had, by the mid-fifteenth century, come to be included in that category of possessions which confirmed and conferred familial honour. Movables in this category, known as *masserizie*, were core possessions which should be preserved in the family.[51] They included plate, as one might expect, but also birth-trays and chests with the family's arms, and fine architectonic sets of furniture such as that made for Giovanni Chellini. Furnishings painted or inlaid with the family's arms represented a family's honour and a great deal of attention was paid by Florentines to ensuring that such pieces did not pass to the second-hand dealers, as Minerbetti's memoranda show.[52] A good description of these attitudes appears in the Castellani memoranda, in which the writer states that in 1439,

> Salamone di ★★★, a Jew from Prato, who has come to live in Florence, had my wall-panel with our family's arms, and sold it on 8 July 1439 with other things to the second-hand dealer Francesco da Nero. It is be discovered from whom the said Salamone bought it and he who took it must be found. Francesco sold it to the Wool-weavers' Guild.[53]

The social dangers of letting property which held associations with family status and honour enter the marketplace are finely nuanced in Castellani's account.

Many antiquities, books and works of art must have been bought at auction; the Florentine Office of Wards, for example, often auctioned an individual's effects in order to settle his estate (Buonaguisi 1462). A white plate of Chinese porcelain which had belonged to Piero di Cristoforo Buonaguisi was listed in an inventory of his estate at 3 florins and sold to Giovanni di Buletta for 4.[54] Such auctions were excellent places to buy books and manuscripts, as Bernardo Bembo described in a note he made in a manuscript of Vitruvius which he had bought at a Paduan auction in 1453:

> This Vitruvius belonged to the distinguished mathematician Jacopo Langusci of Venice, after whose death at Padua it was auctioned and bought by me along with many other things. This was in 1453.[55]

The mention of 'other things' is tantalising, especially when one remembers that two of Isabella's most prized objects for her study – an onyx 'cameo-cut' vase of the late second century and a painting of *The Submersion of Pharaoh* – were bought at auction in 1506. The pieces had belonged to the famous Venetian collector Michele Vianello, and Isabella's agent, Lorenzo da Pavia, who had been Vianello's housemate in Venice, had attempted to negotiate a private treaty sale unsuccessfully. Fortunately, Isabella was able to snap up both pieces at the auction necessitated by the debts on the estate.[56]

Despite the importance of these auctions and sales for the information they yield about owners of books and art objects, we still know little about them, even though they were commonplace occurrences by the mid-sixteenth century. Francesco Sansovino, in a famous passage, mentioned public auctions as a means by which rich furnishings were widely dispersed through Venetian society, making what he called 'polite living' available to many.[57] Florentine records document that property from great households was occasionally auctioned, as Ferdinando di Toledo's furnishings were in 1555, presumably in order to settle his estate.[58]

Lydecker's analysis of the administration of the Office of Wards indicates just how organised their public auctions were by this date, with objects to be sold divided by lot, with estimates and reserves.[59] Since the demand for antiquities and for elegant second-hand furnishings and textiles often shaded into one another, in a way which can hardly be understood today, collectors must have picked up bargains.

A vivid account of luxury goods for sale is given in Montaigne's travel journal. It appears to have been common for such goods to be available for viewing before they were sold, and that this practice had become a form of élite entertainment. Montaigne's diary entry for 10 October 1581 records that

> after dinner, the French ambassador sent a footman to tell me that if I wished, he was coming to pick me up in his coach to take me to see the furniture of Cardinal Orsini, which was being sold, since he had died this Summer in Naples and had left as heir to all his vast property to a niece of his, a little girl. Among other rare things was a taffeta coverlet lined with swansdown. In Siena you see a good many of these swans' skins complete with feathers, and I was asked no more than a crown and a half for one, all prepared. They are the size of a sheepskin, a few of them would be enough to make a coverlet of this sort. I saw an ostrich egg, decorated all over and painted with pretty pictures. Also a square box to put jewels in which contained a certain quantity of them; but since the box was most artfully arranged with mirrors all round, when it was opened it appeared much wider and deeper in every direction, and seemed to hold ten times as many jewels as were in it, since one and the same thing were seen many times by the reflection of the mirrors, and the mirrors were not easy to detect.[60]

It would seem from Montaigne's account, and from what Patricia Allerston has discovered about the five kinds of auctions of second-hand goods in Venice, that Cardinal Orsini's effects were to be sold, so that the cash could be directed to his niece, as stipulated in his will.[61] Auctions funding testamentary bequests, known as *incanti di commissarie*, were frequent events.[62] Inventories of the goods to be sold had to be compiled first by the executor of the estate; such lists, if publicly circulated, must have served as auction lists encouraging likely buyers to view.

Many of the goods sold at auction would be resold and circulated by second-hand dealers (*rigattieri* in Florence, *strazzaroli* in Venice), or by the pedlars who were associated with them and belonged to the same guild.[63] We are now beginning to learn about these tradesmen (and women) thanks to the work of Allerston and others.[64] It is clear from this research that the market in second-hand goods was not marginal, but integral to the functioning of the urban economy, not only in Venice, but also in Rome and in Bologna, where the guild of second-hand dealers was among the top twelve in the city.[65] In Venice, the *strazzaroli* had such a high profile that they were depended upon to hire out furnishings and art objects to deck the Ducal Palace for special occasions, or equip the residences of foreign ambassadors. The English ambassador Sir Henry Wotton resorted to the Jewish second-hand trader Isaac Luzatto to furnish his entire residence, from the gondola at the water entrance to upholstered furniture, beds and bedding as suited to his rank.[66] The surviving list, drawn up for Wotton's successor in 1610, is a reliable index of what rated in furnishings at the time, and can be compared with the post-mortem inventories of wealthy Venetian patricians and Turkey merchants (Helman 1606).[67] Eight years later in 1618 Niccolo Sachetti, resident in Tuscany, was unconcerned about having to furnish his palace in a hurry, knowing that he could rely upon the second-hand dealers: 'the city is big and in two days those still lacking can be obtained for hire'. Nor, he added, would the result be either unsuitable or expensive: 'the textile furnishings are not yet in place, but this is of little concern, for the city is large and in two days one can find for hire whatever is lacking. May Your Illustrious Highness rest assured that all will be carried out to good end, and with every possible saving in expense'.[68]

What is now becoming clear, for the late fifteenth and sixteenth centuries as much as for the eighteenth, is that the flourishing market for second-hand goods complemented that for new furnishings, providing various sources of supply.[69] The research done by Allerston on the organisation and regulation of the second-hand trade in Venice will help to correct our distorted picture of the world of household goods and furnishings, their status and circulation.

2   *Creating a Study*

Architectural Planning and Patterns of Use

THE ROLE OF THE STUDY in the planning and construction of the Italian Renaissance apartment was determined by its status in the eyes of its owner. During the fifteenth century demands for greater privacy were combined with a concern for regularity and symmetry in the planning and distribution of rooms. Studies were one of a variety of smaller, more intimate spaces which came into common use as the concept of the apartment developed.[1] The word 'apartment' does not appear to have been used in this sense until the early seventeenth century, when the French took the initiative from the Italians as leaders of fashion and etiquette in formal planning.[2] Since it has already been analysed elsewhere by architectural historians, the role of the apartment is discussed here only with specific reference to the location and use of studies in the fifteenth and sixteenth centuries.[3]

The nucleus of the fifteenth- and sixteenth-century Italian palace (using the word in its widest and most inclusive sense) was the principal bedchamber or master bedroom (*camera principale*). It served as an informal reception room at the time of a wedding or after the birth of a child. During the fifteenth century a number of small rooms used as studies, lavatories (*agiamenti* or *destri*),[4] bath or bathing-rooms (*stufe*, *stufette* or *bagni*) and store-rooms came to be grouped near the *camera*, and closely associated wih it. The idea of the apartment was to provide a linear sequence of rooms for the use of an individual, which would lead from the more public rooms at the entrance of the house to the more withdrawn ones at its core: this is the scheme of organisation which Alberti and Francesco di Giorgio prescribed in their treatises on architecture.[5] The most public room in the Florentine house throughout this period was the hall (*sala*, derived from the Latin *aula*). Anton Francesco Doni described its functions in his book *I marmi* (1552). The women of the house would sit in the window seats to work at their sewing and look out of the window, while 'one eats at the high table; to that side one plays board games; and so there is space for everyone'.[6] The importance of the *sala*, and the fact that it was situated near the entrance of the house, made it the first room to be described in the majority of sixteenth-century Florentine inventories. The Venetian equivalent was the *portego* (dialect spelling for *portico*) which, like the *sala*, would have other less public rooms opening off it, leading towards the principal bedchamber. The order of progression through the house is best described by Scamozzi in his treatise on architecture, printed in Venice in 1615:

> Let the principal parts of the palace be the *sale*, *salotti*, and large rooms, followed by the medium sized ones, and the smaller ones; so that people who accompany the owner may remain in the first type of room; and his intimate friends in the second. Those who come to negotiate with him may go into the more withdrawn rooms. Let this disposition of rooms be observed not only in Princes' palaces, but adapted in accordance with proportion in the well-governed houses of private gentlemen.[7]

The more withdrawn rooms which Scamozzi mentions were the *anticamera*, *camera*, *studio* and possibly a number of other small spaces. Architectural theorists had little to say about the uses of this complex of rooms, including the *studio* and the *camerini* which were sometimes adjacent to it.[8] A *camerino* might serve the same function as a *studio*: when Ulisse Aldrovandi described the collection of Giovanni Gaddi in Rome he listed 'the most distingushed, but also the smallest things' in 'the *camerino*, which serves as a *studio*'.[9] Both *camerini* and *studii* were forerunners of the seventeenth-century French *cabinet* and the English closet, although the Italian word *cabinetto* or *gabinetto* was rarely used in the sixteenth century. It appears however in Bartoli's translation of 1550 (from Latin into Italian) of Alberti's treatise on architecture, in which the order of rooms in an apartment in a villa is described as leading from the portico 'through the *sale*, and then through the *camere*, and finally through the *cabinetti*'.[10]

The role of the study in the planning of a Renaissance apartment is analogous to that of the bathroom, as described by Nancy Edwards in her classic study.[11] Both room-types were Renaissance creations, based on classical precept and practice as deduced from the interpretation of ancient texts, and both were adapted to modern usage.[12] The aim was to provide greater intimacy and privacy in relatively withdrawn rooms, and to give an elegant, antique form to one's leisure. Studies and bathrooms, it was recognised, had in ancient times been painted with the same kinds of wall decoration. Cellini, railing against the inaccuracy of his contemporaries in referring to this repertory of playful, frivolous ornament as 'grotesques' since they were associated with 'grottoes' (rooms which had long been buried underground), commented how bedchambers, bathing-rooms, studies and drawing-rooms had been decorated alike with what he preferred to call *mostri*: monsters and mythical beasts. His comment applied as much to Renaissance Rome as to the ancient city, as he knew. Like studies, bathing-rooms tended to be close to the principal bedchamber if not adjacent to it.[13] Both rooms gained from this proximity and inter-dependence; bathing-rooms acquired an atmosphere of literary leisure from studies, while the latter gained useful warmth — always important for sedentary readers and writers — and associations with sensuous pleasure from the bath. These qualities can be found in a house designed by Antonio da Sangallo the Younger between 1537 and 1546 for a certain Messer Sebastiano Gandolfo in the ideal city of Castro, which Pier Luigi Farnese had made the centre of his duchy (fig. 16).[14] Both the study and the bathroom were on the ground floor at the back of the house (fig. 17); the study, of which the dimensions are indicated on the plan, measured 6 by 12 palms (1.34 by 2.68 metres). The room would have been heated by the boilers for the bath next door.[15] Sangallo's plan not only illustrates a useful way of heating a study, but also enables a man of scholarly interests to integrate the pleasures of bathing and study into his daily life; an individual's ideal which was in accordance with Castro's planned role as an ideal state.[16]

A close relationship between the functions of the study and the bathroom is also implied in another Sangallo design, the Roman palace of Melchiorre Baldassini, which was admired by Pietro Bembo and later by Vasari.[17] Like the mysterious Messer Sebastiano Gandolfo, Baldassini was a man of scholarly interests (he taught civil law in Rome) rather than great wealth or status.[18] On the first floor was a bedchamber,[19] bearing a frieze depicting scenes from ancient Roman history, appropriate to Baldassini's career as an advocate and orator.[20] Next to this was a study — it has been identified as such on account of its small dimensions[21] — with painted decoration incorporating the Baldassini arms supported by putti, and an acanthus leaf frieze.[22] Interestingly, we know the date by which Baldassini was using his study from the fact that land contracts were drawn up there in May 1521.[23]

Studies were also closely associated with staircases and the landings leading off them; that in Bartolo di Tura's house in Siena is a good example (Tura 1483). Another scholar, Cristoforo Barzizza, had a study 'in a small room, situated in the middle of the staircase' in his Paduan house, which was inventoried in 1444 (Barzizza 1444). Similarly, the Venetian poet Andrea Pasqualigo had a 'study next to the staircase which leads up from

16 and 17   Sketch plan and
detail by Antonio da
Sangallo the Younger for a
house in Castro for a certain
Messer Sebastiano Gandolfo,
between 1537 and 1546. It
includes a bathroom (*stufa*)
and a study (*studiolo*)
adjacent to each other.
Florence, Gabinetto dei
Disegni, U.A.744. Photo:
Florence, Soprintendenza,
Gabinetto Fotografico.

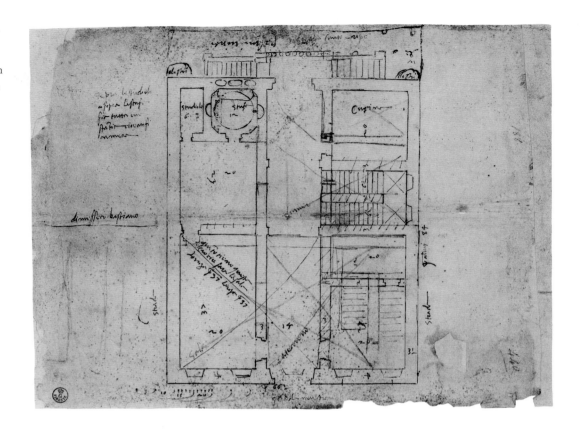

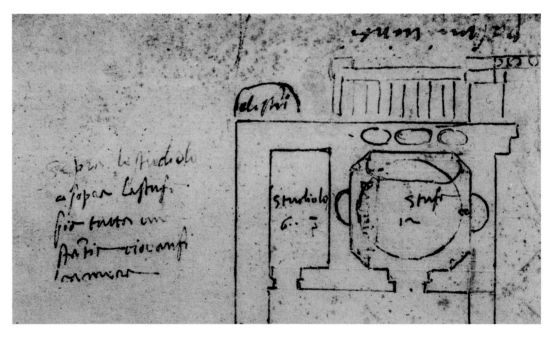

the ground floor' (Pasqualigo 1579). Some Venetians kept their most treasured possessions
in rooms at the tops of their houses, as did the Milanese merchant-collector Andrea Odoni
(Odoni 1555). These far-flung locations tested the stamina of visitors, as Torquato Tasso
described in one of his dialogues. On a hot afternoon, he negotiated the stairs to the study
of a Roman collector, only to collapse, breathless, on a leather-covered chair at the

entrance of the room. Having seen the room, however, he concluded that the collection was so impressive and well organised that it had been well worth the effort.[24]

Felix Platter, a Swiss medical student, enjoyed the fact that his landlord let him use a room at the top of his house in Montpellier as a study. In the summer of 1553 he wrote in his journal:

> I had to move my lodging to another of his [his master's] houses, a veritable palace, which he had inherited from a Doctor Falcon, a Spaniard and a Maran [*Marrano*: a converted Jew] also. At first I was given a vast chamber, but afterwards I installed myself in a little boarded study on the upper floor. I decorated it with my pictures, and my master put in a gilded armchair — for he showed me all sorts of kindness now that his two sons were with my father. At the top of the house there was a fine terrace, or platform, reached by a stone stair. It commanded the whole town, and one could see as far as the sea, the sound of which could be heard when the wind was in the right quarter. This was where I liked to study. I grew an Indian fig-tree there in a vase — my master had been sent a leaf of it from Spain.[25]

There were close links between the study and gardens, particularly in the context of the villa, for it was the villa which offered the greatest potential for making the pleasures of reading, writing and working continuous with the rest of one's existence. The idealised literary perception of the villa had a long history, reaching as far back as the eighth century BC. The fact that real villas of the Roman empire had been celebrated in letters, which were in themselves literary models for Renaissance writers, made the theme yet more fascinating to them.[26] In his treatise on *The Solitary Life* Petrarch articulates the ideal of creative leisure and literary-minded solitude which he saw the villa as providing.[27] This could be a matter of pursuing a systematic programme of study, as envisaged by Petrarch,[28] and suggested by Cardinal Pietro Bembo in a letter of 1505 to a fellow cardinal:

> It has always been my first and most intense desire to be able to live in easy and not dishonourable liberty, in order to advance the study of letters, which has at all times been the vital food for my thinking.[29]

Perhaps this was one reason for Bembo's particular interest in the development of his villa at Santa Maria di Non outside Padua[30] as a place uniquely suitable for study.

Petrarch pictured the solitary man as one who shuttles constantly back and forth between a busy city life and learned rural retreat.[31] Similarly, when Alberti came to write about the villa, he stipulated that it should be situated within walking distance of one's town house. As Richard Goldthwaite has commented, 'the fetish made of *otium* (rural leisure) presupposes an urban point of view'.[32] The tone of Renaissance Italians when writing about life in their villas is one of sophisticated and above all literary nostalgia; a Renaissance humanist was unlikely to forget that Pliny the Younger had written a letter describing his villa, with its study and garden, in some detail.[33] Writing to Bernardo Leoncino, the Vicentine humanist Bartolomeo Pagello described the villa he intended to build at Monticelli di Lonigo, mentioning a garden, portico and courtyard on to which the rooms were to open. The villa would be just large enough to contain his things, and fitted for 'honest pleasure':

> It would be quite sufficient for me to have only one single portico running from the house into the nearby garden, raised above the level of the courtyard by two little steps. On both sides there should be rooms suited for general use, and not luxurious. There should be quite an elegant library, my sole ornament [*unica mia suppellettile*], annexed to the bedchamber.

He added that the gardens should contain many fruit trees and vines, a laurel, trimmed box

18 Valerio Belli, bronze portrait medal of Cardinal Pietro Bembo (1470–1547). On the reverse, Bembo (it is clearly him when compared with his portrait on the obverse) is shown semi-naked in a classical pose, reclining beside a stream. London, British Museum.

19 Bronze portrait medal of Eustachio di Francesco Boiano, an example of which was buried in the walls of the family villa at Ipplis, near Cividale. It has been suggested that the building referred to in the Latin inscription on the obverse, which Boiano began 'in his sixtieth year', may refer to this villa. The rural scene on the reverse, with a greyhound leashed to a tree weighed down with fruit, surely refers to the pleasures of the villa, and the accompanying inscription identifies these as dignified, gentlemanly pursuits: 'Living thus as a means to a long life, he began the study of agriculture at his [advanced] age in 1525'. Venetian, by an unidentified medallist. London, British Museum.

trees and 'a fountain, clearer than glass itself, sacred to the Muses'.[34] All this provided an appropriate literary and pastoral setting for reflection; a place where you could be 'in good humour with yourself', as one of Petrarch's friends wrote.[35]

Scholars liked to turn from their studies to the sensuous delight and relaxation of a garden. A scholar could share figs from the tree outside his study with his friends, as recounted by Angelo Decembrio in his dialogue about literary culture in Ferrara at the time of Leonello d'Este.[36] Decembrio described a delightful, carefully orchestrated outing to the house in Ferrara of one of Leonello's senior courtiers, Giovanni Gualengo. Having demolished the figs in Gualengo's walled garden as a kind of pagan sacrifice, the friends climb a covered staircase to his library. The room is described by Gualengo later in Decembrio's dialogue:

> At my suburban estate there is daily conversation about books, and in this house there is a library – as you see, looking out over the greenest little plot – not perhaps one fortified with such an abundance of books as our Leonello determined ought to be possessed by the most refined owner (nor was I ever as familiar with Greek literature as I am with Latin), but furnished nonetheless with many useful books.[37]

The connection between the delights of a garden and the treasures of the study was worked into a literary topos by Anton Francesco Doni in a dedicatory letter to one of his books, in which he presents his work as 'fruit from my garden, and jewels from my study'.[38]

Night-time Study

Night-time study was a literary ideal with impeccable classical precedent, and its popularity as a topos in Renaissance letters illustrates one way in which, building on classical models, writers sought to emphasise the continuity – even the dialogue – between ancient Roman and Renaissance worlds, a continuity which was best expressed through the study. One of the greatest Roman scholars, Pliny the Elder, had been extolled by his nephew for habits of study to be emulated by all scholars:

> He always began to work at midnight when the August festival of Vulcan came round, not for the good omen's sake, but for the sake of study; in Winter generally at one in

the morning, but never later than two, and often at midnight. No man ever slept more readily, in as much that he would sometimes, without retiring from his book, take a short sleep, and then pursue his studies.[39]

Hence Juan Ludovicus Vives, in his Latin dialogue *The Bedchamber and Studies by Night*, names the main speaker Pliny to make the character fully recognisable to his readers and to identify the classical source on which his playful exercise in colloquial Latin is based. Vives shows Pliny settling down to work at a desk set up in his bedchamber, so that he can best make use of the quiet hours in the night 'when everything rests and is silent'.[40] Erasmus made fun of just this kind of scholarly zeal and its impeccable literary precedent in his dialogue, *The Ciceronian*:

> NOSOPONUS: I have a shrine of the Muses in the innermost part of the house, with thick walls, doors and windows, and all the cracks carefully sealed up with plaster and pitch, so that hardly any light or sound can penetrate even by day, unless it's a very loud one, like quarrelling women or blacksmiths at work.
> BULEPHORUS: True, the sudden boom of human voices and workshop crashes destroy one's concentration.
> NOSOPONUS: I won't allow anyone to use any of the nearby rooms as a bedroom, because I don't want the voices even of sleepers, or their snorts, breaking in on the sanctuary of my thoughts. Some people talk in their sleep, and a good many snore so loudly that they can be heard quite a long way off.
> HYPOLOGUS: When I'm trying to write at night I'm often troubled by mice as well.
> NOSOPONUS: In my house there's no place even for a fly.[41]

Formal retreat into the study is often described in a selfconsciously rhetorical way. Machiavelli, writing to a friend, contrasted the days spent working on his villa estate at San Casciano with the evenings, when he would change his clothes and enter his study in order to read classical texts.

> When evening comes, I return home and go into my study. On the threshold I strip off my muddy, sweaty, workday clothes, and put on the robes of court and palace, and in this graver dress I enter the antique courts of the ancients and am welcomed by them, and there I taste the food that alone is mine, for which I was born. There I make bold to speak to them and ask the motives for their actions, and they, in their humanity, reply to me. And for the space of four hours I forget the world, remember no vexations, fear poverty no more, tremble no more at death: I pass into their world.[42]

On a more practical note (while still recalling classical literature at several removes), Benedetto Cotrugli, author of a fifteenth-century treatise on the business and conduct of merchants, suggested that those who had an interest in books should have a study near their bedchamber, which would be accessible and quiet whenever they had a few moments' leisure. He explained that this was likely to be at night, or in the early hours of the morning before the working day began:

> You ought to have a *scrittoio* in the *solar* on the first floor, suitable for your needs [. . .] which should be separate [from the rest of the house] without causing disturbance to your family on account of the strangers who come to the house to contract business with you. He who delights in letters should not keep his books in the common *scrittoio*, but should have a *studiolo*, set apart in the most remote part of the house. Should it be close to the room in which one sleeps, it is an excellent and most salubrious thing, for it allows one to study with greater ease whenever time allows.[43]

To Cotrugli, the office (*scrittoio*) is obviously the essential public room, while the study is a luxurious extra – a room in which the gains of mercantile activity are evident, rather than the activity itself. He presents the study as a private space in which to pursue leisure interests whenever time permits, hence the importance of its location. He is concerned with literary pursuits, rather than with the study as a repository for works of art or other small ornaments, perhaps because he saw book-ownership as evident proof of culture. This is a definition of the study which is more characteristic of the fifteenth than the sixteenth century, and it has to be remembered that not only was Cotrugli's treatise written a century before it was finally published (in Venice in 1569), but that his book is an amalgam of advice which was for the most part derived from other manuals. His recommendation to place a study next to one's bedchamber may have been derived from a health handbook, the *Tacuinum sanitatis*, which had been translated from Arabic into Latin in the thirteenth century and had consequently enjoyed great popularity.[44] The author, who was an Arabic physician, advocated night-time study to prevent oversleeping, which he considered injurious to the health, since it dehydrates the body. A copy of the *Tacuinum* which was illuminated in Venice around 1480 illustrates how the fifteenth-century Italian reader would have visualised the way in which such precepts were to be applied (fig. 20). The ink drawings in this manuscript were left unfinished. The text on this folio lists the advantages and disadvantages to the human body of particular seasons in the year, and the four illustrations place these comments in a contemporary context. Men are shown chopping firewood in 'Winter', and the companion piece to this activity is '*Somnus*', represented by a bedchamber in which a couple sleep while a maid sits in a nursing-chair minding the baby in its cradle. 'Summer' is suggested by an airy house in a landscape; its neighbouring piece, '*Vigiliae*', shows a man in his study at dead of night. The implication is that this man has gone into his study next to his bedchamber to read his books by the light of the oil-lamp suspended from his rotating lectern. The drawing gives the viewer the sense of being in a pleasant, panelled room, enclosed and private; this scholar is evidently delighted to be there.

Secrecy is the emphasis in Paolo Cortesi's treatise on the ideal Cardinal's palace, in which it is recommended that:

> the room used for study at night and the bedroom [. . .] should be very near to one another; because they serve closely-related activities. Both these rooms should be especially safe from intrusion and so we see why they should be placed in the inner parts of the house. There should be listening devices through which the disputants in the auditorium can be heard, as well as a spiral staircase which provides an inside passage down into the library.[45]

Despite the fact that Cortesi's treatise deals with the needs and neuroses of a princely household, including a range of specialised rooms complete with eavesdropping devices, the essential nature of a cardinal's study is envisaged as being much the same as that of an ordinary householder.

The Study-Bedchamber

Some collectors chose to live with their collections in close proximity, even to the extent of sleeping in the same room. This may have been as much a question of security as possessiveness, which would explain why many merchants and patricians in sixteenth-century Venice did the same, according to the evidence of inventories. The pattern was established well before 1600 however, as can be deduced from Carpaccio's *Vision of St*

Camera Hyemales

atura te perate cal. meli
ex eis. qa ssimilat extmi
tas ueris Iuu. excicat utates so
picas ex frigiditate Nocu. siti et
siaut et faciut descedere cibu
crudum. Remocio nocum.
cum dispositione uersus ae
rem septentrionalem

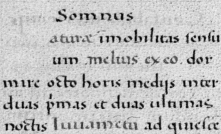

Somnus

atura imobilitas sensu
um melius ex eo. dor
mire octo horis medijs inter
duas pmas et duas ultimas
noctis Iuuametu ad quiesce
du et digeredu Nox. qn mlti
plicat desicat corp. Rem. noc.
cu cibis humectantib

Camera ære ipsius

atura cal. et hum. mj
melius ex eis tem pate
ratione aeris et aque. Iuuame.
sanis consimiles sero. Nocu
tum. syncorizantib et pulsu
cordis. Remoto nocumeti.
cum receptione Ventorum se
ptentrionalium

Vigiliæ

atura exceratum
sensuum. melius ex
eis quibus compleatur dige
stio. Iuuam ad acquisitio
ne cor que sut aduitam
Nocu. tedium sensuum qn
de excedunt. Remo. noc.
cum somno

69

20 From a health
handbook in which the
scene entitled 'Vigiliae'
shows a man at work in his
study at night; next to it is
the scene of sleep ('Somnus').
The illumination is
unfinished: what one sees
here is only the ink
underdrawing. Written and
illuminated in Venice,
around 1480. Vienna,
Österreichische
Nationalbibliothek,
cod. 2396, Tacuinam sanitatis,
fol. 35r.

Ursula (fig. 21). The saint is shown asleep in her bedchamber, in the corner of which is a table with a writing-desk upon it in front of an open bookchest.

Two Venetian incunabula show similar arrangements. A woodcut from the Malermi Bible of 1490 shows the learned King Solomon in his audience chamber, which is also fitted up as a study (fig. 22). The room would have been immediately recognisable to a late fifteenth-century viewer. Solomon is shown reclining on an elaborate daybed with a carved cornice, where he will receive visitors who are entering through the door on the right. He is also shown at work on his books in the study in the left-hand corner of the room. Solomon's study-corner consists of a desk with a table-carpet, a lectern, a convex mirror above to refresh his eyes in writing, and a bookshelf above that. The second is also a late fifteenth-century Venetian woodcut, from the *Hypnerotomachia Poliphili*, which illustrates a man sitting at a desk in a corner of his bedchamber regarding his quill pen critically as he writes a letter (fig. 23). The arrangement is very similar to that in Carpaccio's *St Ursula*. The combination of these illustrations and the later inventory evidence suggests that living like this was relatively common, not just reserved for impecunious scholars and teachers or obsessive unworldly collectors. It could demonstrate good taste in living with one's antiquities; things which were not to be appreciated by the uninitiated. This seems to have been the spirit in which the humanist Poggio Bracciolini set up a study in his bedchamber: he wrote to his friend Niccolò Niccoli explaining how he had had his chamber 'furnished with marble heads' and that though some of these were damaged, they were yet of sufficient quality to 'delight a good artist'.[46] In another letter he described how Donatello had done just that.[47]

Sharing one's daily life with one's collection could also be an elegant arrangement, as it must have been for Cardinal Pietro Bembo. Raphael advised Bembo to write to Cardinal Bibbiena to request the loan of a statuette of Venus which had originally been intended for Bibbiena's famous bathroom.[48] In his letter, Bembo pleaded that he wished to place the Venus in the study in the 'corner of my *camerino*'. The statuette would be placed:

> between Jove and Mercury, her father and brother, so that I may gaze on her ever more pleasurably day by day, which you, because of your unceasing commitments are unable to do. [. . .] I have already prepared that part, that corner of my bedchamber where I can set up the Venus.[49]

Lorenzo Lotto's portrait drawing of a young ecclesiastic in his study-bedchamber, dating to about 1530, demonstrates just how a collector such as Bembo could live with his collection (fig. 24). Berenson's description of the sitter as 'so contented with his possessions' aptly sums up the ecclesiastic's demonstrative gesture as he invites the viewer into his *camerino*.[50] Berenson seems almost to have identified himself with the sitter, as did Philip Pouncey in commenting on the drawing 'we are in the presence of a man who is cultivated and well-to-do, who likes books, tasteful furnishing and comfort'.[51] People have strong responses to Lotto's drawing for just these reasons – the sense of someone at ease with himself, living untidily and harmoniously with his possessions.

One part of his bedchamber is dedicated to his collection. The drawing shows the influence of Flemish depictions of interiors, as a remarkable evocation of a particular way of life. There are spilled coins on the table and large ancient vases and vessels on shelves, rather like scaffolding, which project from the foot of the bed. There is a bust of the Roman Imperial period on the table (possibly an artist's prop belonging to Lotto, since it appears in other paintings[52]) and large folio volumes behind, leaning against the foot of the bed and against the wall. By the cleric's bed on the wall is a devotional painting with folding wooden covers, beneath which hangs a holy water stoup, exactly as in Carpaccio's *Vision of St Ursula*. Made of metal, this is a type mentioned in inventories: one Venetian

21 Vittore Carpaccio, *Vision of St Ursula*, oil on canvas, signed and dated 1495, showing a young Venetian patrician woman's study-bedchamber. Venice, Accademia. Photo: Böhm.

inventory of 1591 mentions 'two small bronze buckets for holy water'.[53] While the X-frame chair alone indicates that the sitter is someone of consequence[54] so does the fact that he has a Near Eastern carpet on the floor by his bed (such a luxury would normally be displayed on a table – indeed, the word 'carpeta' in Italian meant a table-carpet).[55] Similarly, the table bell for calling servants is an accessory listed in the inventories of cardinals and represented in portraits of high-ranking prelates, as well as patricians.

22 King Solomon holding audience, lying on a daybed (*lettuccio*), and, in a separate scene to the left, at work in his study. Note the concave mirror above his desk. Woodcut illustration from the first illustrated bible printed in Italian, the Malermi Bible, Venice 1490. The woodcuts are attributed to a Venetian miniaturist. Photo: author.

23 A man writing a letter at a desk in his study-bedchamber. The bed is at the back, right, with the hangings folded over the coverlet. Woodcut from the *Hypnerotomachia Poliphili*, Venice 1499. Photo: author.

24 Lorenzo Lotto, *An
Ecclesiastic in his Study-
Bedchamber*, brush and brown
wash over traces of chalk,
c.1530. London, British
Museum.

Lotto portrays a patrician way of life, and it is no surprise to find that the Venetian patrician Francesco Duodo, whose movables were inventoried in 1586, had a study in the corner of his bedchamber (Duodo 1586). Here he kept, as head of the household, small objects for occasional use, reference and safe-keeping, as well as for pleasure. These included the family's table knives, a small box containing gold weights, and a mass of letters and accounts. Here too was a devotional image, the *Adoration of the Magi*, in a gilded frame, as well as a dagger, a pistol, one bronze and six lead medals. Family portraits also hung in this corner of his bedchamber: a painting of his father alongside one of himself, and a portrait of Niccolò Duodo. Francesco Duodo seems to have used this study within his chamber as an archive, treasury and family portrait gallery, even if on a small scale.

★ ★ ★

Investing in a Study

To revert from literary prescription and visual representation to actual practice, Kent Lydecker has conclusively shown that when a young Florentine noble wished to furnish his rooms in the latest style in fifteenth-century Florence, he would invest in his bedchamber and the antechamber and study adjacent to it.[56] Two account books of personal expenditure, those of Jacopo di Piero Guicciardini (covering 1503–11) and Zanobi Giocondi, record sums spent on the *camera* and study as a unit in a young noble's apartment within his father's palace (Guicciardini memoranda; Giocondi memoranda).[57] Constructing a new apartment, with bedchamber and study *en suite*, often followed betrothal, since this was where the new bride would be welcomed. Lydecker also identifies this as the moment at which a young Florentine man entered the art market,[58] not only in commissioning new art objects from leading practitioners, but also in exchanging, inheriting and borrowing such objects within his family. Memoranda books show these processes at work in a particularly vivid way, as in the case of Andrea Minerbetti's gifts to his son and daughter-in-law (Minerbetti memoranda). Jacopo di Piero's memoranda are particularly illuminating on the redecorating of his study in 1507. In that year, he invested in wood, panels of wooden inlay, locks, keys and nails for the purpose, apart from paying a woodworker and painter for their work. With typically Florentine thriftiness he also re-used wooden panels from his father's study in creating a private space for himself within his and his wife's apartment in his father's palace on the Via Guicciardini. The expenses on his study were clearly considered with those on other rooms in this apartment – the bedchamber and antechamber – since they were listed together in a single account (Guicciardini memoranda).

The way in which studies were actually constructed clarifies the special significance and distinct character which these rooms held for their owners. The most telling evidence is provided by account books, in which individuals listed expenses incurred in creating or redecorating such a room. The Florentine banker Bernardo Rinieri (1427–1508) recorded in meticulous detail the outlay on his bedchamber on the ground floor of his house, with its adjoining study. Work on his rooms coincided with his marriage, which was followed by the arrival of his wife to live with him in the family palace in 1459. The accounts open two years earlier, in 1457, with the purchase of the blank book in which to record expenses, which he bought from the bookseller Agnolo Tucci (Rinieri memoranda). Work on the study began in June 1458 with the assembly of selected wood for panelling and window-frames; this was the single largest expense. Later that year, in August, a waller was paid for structural work in this and other rooms in the house, after which the walls of the study were plastered by a kinsman of Rinieri. Then a housepainter, Chimenti di Lorenzo, was called in to decorate the walls of the study and other rooms in the apartment to which it belonged. A third, more specialised woodworker was then employed to make the study window itself, with its glass roundels. Finally, the famous furniture painter Apollonio di Giovanni was paid in December 1458 for the work he had done 'in painting the ceiling of the study and for gilding it'.[59] Over seven months, Bernardo Rinieri had constructed himself a splendid study adjoining the principal bedchamber in his apartment, to which he welcomed his bride. Work did not stop there, however, for in 1459 he turned his attention to transforming what appears to have been his summer apartment (given that it was on the ground floor) to a similar standard of elegant decoration. Chimenti di Lorenzo was re-employed to decorate the study in this suite of rooms and was paid for the work he had done in August and September of that year. In 1460 a 'chest with four little drawers to stand on the desk in the study on the ground floor'[60] was commissioned from a third and probably more specialised woodworker, Jacopo di Bastiano, to stand on the

25 Domenico Ghirlandaio, *St Jerome in his Study*, fresco, dated (on the side of Jerome's desk) 1480. The companion piece to Botticelli's *St Augustine*, showing the saint seated at a built-in desk unit with a fine Turkish table-carpet. The saint casts a shadow on the green curtain, which has been drawn back to uncover his books as emblems of his authority as Doctor of the Church. The paper inscriptions in Greek and Hebrew on the edge of the bookshelves presumably point to his role as the translator of the Bible. The horn inkwells – black for writing and red for rubricating – which are wired onto the side of his desk also indicate his role as writer and editor. Splashes of red ink are shown on the side of his desk. Florence, Chiesa degli Ognissanti. Photo: Scala.

26 Sandro Botticelli, *Vision of St Augustine*, fresco, *c*.1480. St Augustine is shown at the moment when he had begun to write to his friend, Jerome, asking advice on an abstruse matter of theology, not knowing that Jerome had just died. At that instant, Jerome appeared to him in a vision accompanied by radiant light and fragrance, pointing to the role of Christian revelation in any kind of spiritual understanding. Botticelli's subtle rendering of the scene, with its carefully delineated armillary sphere, geometrical treatise, clock and table-top desk with drawers places the vision in the study of a learned Florentine patrician. Commissioned by the Vespucci family, whose arms appear on the upper frame, the fresco was intended to complement Ghirlandaio's *St Jerome in his Study*: the two paintings originally flanked the screen of the church and were linked by an inscription. Florence, Chiesa degli Ognissanti. Photo: Scala.

27 Vittore Carpaccio, *Vision of St Augustine*, oil on canvas, *c.*1502. Venice, Scuola di San Giorgio degli Schiavoni. Photo: Böhm.

desk in his study: similar units are shown in Florentine paintings such as Botticelli's *Vision of St Augustine* (fig. 26).

A third set of Florentine accounts record the expenses incurred by Zanobi Giocondi between April and November 1492 in constructing a study as part of an apartment. Giocondi employed the same woodworker as Bernardo Rinieri to construct an entire study unit. Chimenti del Tasso was paid on 30 April 1492 for 'a foot platform, shelves, desk with drawers of walnut [. . .] and walnut window-frames and double doors of walnut for the study which I have received from him'.[61] This work, and further work done in June of that year, was enough to make the study his personal room, for whereas he had referred to the room as 'the study' in his accounts in April, he was calling it 'Zanobi's study' in June. His accounts therefore document not only the development of the room and its fittings, but also his growing sense of ownership and identification with the room (Giocondi memoranda). With this grew the need to secure the study's valuable contents. An obvious resort was to fit a study door with locks, as Marin Contarini did in the Cà d'Oro in the 1430s. He employed a blacksmith, Niccolò Lusse, to make two locks for use in the palace, possibly on the door to his study on the first floor, and to his office on the mezzanine above the storerooms.[62] Locks must have been common on study doors and it is interesting that the study in the back of Carpaccio's *Vision of St Augustine* has a lock on the outside of the door, to secure the books, quadrants and astrolabes within. Shadows cast by iron bars on the window of the room can also be seen. Locks are frequently described as fittings on chests and cabinets, such as a pine chest in Cristoforo's study (Barzizza 1444; Serragli 1576).

42

The *memorie e carte* of the sculptor Alessandro Vittoria give a fascinating account of how
he remodelled and adapted his house near the Pietà in Venice between 1570 and 1595.
There is frequent mention of the study adjoining his bedchamber.[63] As there were
structural alterations to be made, the first craftsmen to be employed were stonemasons. On
13 July 1587 he paid a stonemason for work on eight windows for the apartment which
included his bedchamber, study and a storeroom beyond it. The second stage was to bring
in the house carpenter, which Vittoria did in 1591 when he paid for work done in lining
with wooden panels the ceilings of the study and bedchamber. The final stage was reached
on 16 April 1592, when housepainters were paid for decorating the cornices in the study,
bedchamber and portico (Vittoria memoranda, pp. 158–9, 163). Both Rinieri's and
Vittoria's accounts show how the study and bedchamber were treated as a single unit in
architectural terms, as part of an apartment, and also in terms of the expenses listed in
account books.

Heating

Heating was always a problem in studies. Draughts could be limited by omitting fireplaces
in small rooms. In his Latin dialogue *The House*, Juan Ludovicus Vives states that 'They
say that if bedchambers had no chimney-fire they would be warmer', presumably because
the draw of a good chimney produced a continual draught of cold air to circulate through
a room.[64] Erasmus mentions a technique for blocking a fireplace with wooden panels in

the summer, in his colloquy *The Godly Feast*. A host shows his guests round his house, including a study:

> Adjoining the library is a study, narrow but neat. When the board's removed you see a small hearth to use if you're cold. In Summer, it seems a solid wall.[65]

Chimney-boards could also be painted to form part of the decoration of the room, as mentioned in the inventory of Andrea Odoni (Odoni 1555).[66]

There were other ingenious ways of heating a study, either by planning an apartment so that the room benefited from the proximity of boilers used to heat an adjoining bathroom (as in the house of Messer Sebastiano Gandolfo designed by Antonio da Sangallo the Younger) or through the use of underfloor heating, such as Ercole d'Este used in his palace at the Via Coperta in Ferrara in 1489.[67] The Duke of Ferrara had a stove installed in his study in 1478; a bricklayer was required to set it up.[68] Simpler and more flexible solutions were also found; one Florentine patrician had a brazier in his study (Gondi 1578). Leonello d'Este is cited as saying that 'it is thoroughly noxious, even dangerous, to have live coals brought in without a vent pipe, to generate heat'.[69]

In general, however, studies were rarely heated and it was wise to dress warmly. Bernardo Rinieri listed payments made for cloth and fur for making a warm coat 'for studying in' in his annual expenditure on his study in 1463 (Rinieri memoranda). Furthermore, the heat generated by one's own body and by the flame of a single candle in a small, draught-free room is remarkable.

Lighting

In his dialogue *The Bedchamber and Studies by Night* Juan Ludovicus Vives describes the different kinds of lighting available to the Renaissance scholar and their relative merits. Pliny, the scholar who is the main interlocutor in the dialogue, explains to his servant Celsius who is setting up his worktable, why he prefers a lamp to a candle for working at night:

> on account of the even flame, which is less trying to the eyes, for the flickering of the wick injures the eyes less and the odour of tallow is unpleasant.
> CELSIUS: Then use wax candles, the odour of which is not displeasing.
> PLINY: In them the wick flickers more and the vapour is not healthy. In the tallow lights the wick is for the most part of linen and not of cotton, as the tradesmen seek to make profit out of everything by fraud. Pour oil into this lamp, bring a wick and clean it with a needle.[70]

According to the scholar Comenius, tallow candles were used by poor students who could not afford anything better. The comment appears in his book *Orbis sensualium pictis* which includes a section on the study: 'Richer persons use a taper, for a tallow candle smoketh and stinketh'.[71] Comenius also explains how readers screened the flame of a candle so that it did not harm the eyes in the way Pliny describes. Comenius's scholar puts a green screen in front of a candle for this purpose. Clearly, Renaissance readers who habitually read at night knew the relaxing and soothing properties of green shades on the eye.

Pliny's preferred lamp was probably made of a cord set into a container of oil. The shape of these lamps, which were used thoughout Europe in the Middle Ages, had changed little since Roman times. Elaborate bronze versions were made at the beginning of the sixteenth century – free inventions on a classical theme, such as Riccio's oil-lamps.[72] The printing device of Anton Francesco Doni shows a smoking lamp of classical boat-shaped type above a pile of books and a Greek inscription on a fluttering scroll.

29 Niccolò Pizzolo, fresco, c.1448, showing St Gregory the Great in his study, viewed as if looking up through a lunette. Pizzolo was admired for his perspectival effects, rivalling those of Andrea Mantegna, with whom he briefly worked in Padua. St Gregory sits at a built-in desk unit of solid construction, with two lecterns supported on it, a circular one which enables him to compare texts, and a second one of trapezoidal section, like the larger versions found in contemporary sacristies. This one has a hole in one side to hold a furled-up letter – a detail often depicted by contemporary artists, but here left empty to increase the sense of pictorial depth. The lectern supports a metal arm which swings laterally, from which hang two small oil-lamps which can be hung on a range of vertical hooks. The book cupboard built into the plain desk has doors with locks. The high shelf behind displays a number of ancient and contemporary ceramics, perhaps incorporating local finds. The sense of a small, enclosed space, lit only by a small high window, beyond the mass of the desk in the foreground, is brilliantly conveyed. Formerly Ovetari Chapel, Padua (destroyed in the Second World War).

Small lamps were sometimes set or hung on an articulated metal rod which projected over a lectern or desk. A reader could then direct light over his book as required. This was a common arrangement as shown both by inventories and paintings. One Ferrarese scholar, Francisco de Fiesso, had in his study in 1484 'a brass lectern with a lamp'.[73] Niccolò Pizzolo depicted a lamp on a lectern in his fresco of St Gregory in his study, formerly in the Eremitani in Padua (fig. 29).

The state of a number of surviving Renaissance books testifies to accidents with candles or lamps, leaving oily smears down pages. Leonello d'Este is recorded as saying in Decembrio's dialogue on literary culture in Ferrara that studies ought to be kept clean and free of

> candle drippings – the oily, smelly out-of-place traces of nocturnal study that Pliny calls 'Vulcanalia' (letters 3.5.8.) What may I say about people who, overcome by drowsiness while reading, have burned a book to the centre of the page?[74]

30 (*facing page*) An exceptionally thick tin-glazed floor tile (5.7 cm in depth) from the garden prayer-cell of Maria Benedetti in her convent of San Paolo in Parma. The decoration consists of stylised fruits, subtly shaded in cobalt blue and manganese purple; other tiles in the series to which this belongs are decorated with figurative, chivalric themes. The tiles were ordered between 1471 and 1482, and were possibly made in Pesaro. London, British Museum, Department of Medieval and Later Antiquities.

An exposed flame must have been dangerous in a wooden-lined room. Fires were all too common a hazard in Renaissance and Early Modern cities. The Florentine apothecary Luca Landucci recorded how, on 2 August 1507, fire had destroyed part of his house, including the study which he had built for his son, Maestro Antonio, to study and teach in (his son was teaching medicine at the Florentine Studio, having graduated from Bologna):

> As it pleased God, the house in which I lived, next to the shop (the shop being in the middle of the house) was burnt down, and I lost my rooms, in which were all my things, worth more than 250 gold ducats. I had to buy all my household goods, clothes and furniture afresh, three rooms completely stocked; my son Maestro Antonio alone losing more than 50 or 60 ducats worth; a red cloak, a purple tunic, both new, and all his other clothes [. . .], with all his *studio* and his books which were worth more than twenty-five ducats.[75]

No wonder that Felix Platter records the fury of his landlady when she discovered that he had been cooking eggs over a candle on a thick piece of paper in his study:

> Throughout Lent I collected in my study the shells of eggs that I had cooked there in this manner over the flame of a candle, but a servant discovered them and showed them to my mistress, who was very annoyed.[76]

Floors and Ceilings

A polished floor, laid out on the same principles as the ceiling, was recommended for studies by Leonello d'Este:

> Let one look upon walls and ceiling carefully laid out, and an entire floor highly polished, so much so in fact, that you don't leave cobwebs under the shelves, much less inkblots or candle drippings.[77]

The reference to being 'carefully laid out' would seem to refer to tiled surfaces. This was certainly a way of creating a practical, durable and colourful floor on which the painted motifs could echo those used on the ceiling or elsewhere in the room, for example the owner's arms or devices.[78] The earliest surviving tiled floor is that laid in the study created by Pope Benedict XII in the Papal Palace in Avignon in the first half of the fourteenth century. The tiles are thought to have been of local manufacture, and many of the originals are still *in situ*; recent analysis has revealed fascinating information about the positioning of furniture in the room and passages through it.[79] Tiles laid along the walls were protected from wear by long cupboards or desk units (presumably used for books and treasures) in contrast to the worn and repaired area to the eastern corner of the room, leading to the entrance into the pope's bedchamber.[80] Sooty tiles in the centre of the room may indicate the use of a portable charcoal brazier, used to heat the room.[81] Only some of the designs on the tiles can now be deciphered, but the surviving patterns reveal a sophisticated variety of geometrical motifs and simplified heraldic elements in contrast to the relatively few and crude representations of animals, plants and a single mysterious human figure.[82]

The tiles ordered by Maria Benedetti, abbess of the convent of San Paolo in Parma between 1471 and 1482 for the floor of her prayer-cell-cum-study in the convent garden, are particularly charming examples (fig. 30). Their decoration with her arms or initials, and with a range of chivalric or courtly themes, befitted a woman of aristocratic family who would have brought her own culture, and the expectations of her rank, into the convent

with her. The tiles are boldly drawn and filled in with a variety of colours, many of them pigments only recently developed by Italian potters, which would have been regarded as examples of new, modern technology. The decoration of the tiles is equally novel, in that figurative designs are separated from a densely decorated ground by a 'contour panel'; a device taken from Islamic tradition by Italian pottery painters of the last quarter of the fifteenth century, as they investigated the pictorial possibilities offered by tin-glaze techniques.[83]

31 Floor tile from Isabella d'Este's Studiolo, showing a white hound with a muzzle and twirling leash. Probably made in Pesaro in the workshop of Antonio dei Fedeli, 1494, this, like the Parma tile (fig. 30), is exceptionally thick, but is scooped out on the back to enable the tiles to dry more quickly, prevent warping, and provide ample fixing for cement. Originally intended for the Gonzaga villa at Marmirolo, but used by Isabella in her Studiolo to discourage mice from burrowing under the floor. Cambridge, Fitzwilliam Museum.

Isabella d'Este had considerable problems with the floor of her Studiolo. On 8 July 1494 her daughter's governess reported that

> Today your Ladyship's Studiolo was paved with square tiles painted with the devices of our most Illustrious Lord, which match each other very well, and in truth it was an excellent bit of foresight and almost necessary since under the floorboards were found many rats' nests.[84]

Isabella's choice of these tiles is another example of thrift in using furnishings destined for another room in decorating a study, since these floor tiles had originally been commissioned from Pesaro by her husband for the floor of his villa at Marmirolo (fig. 31).[85]

Not content with renewing the floor in her campaign against mice and rats, Isabella wrote to the Mantuan orator in Venice in 1495 asking him to buy four Syrian cats to patrol her apartments:

> the kind that come from the Levant, for rat-catching, and send them to us since the rats cannot be allowed to live in the house.[86]

Unfortunately the cat destined for Isabella escaped from the balcony of the room where it had been locked up overnight, despite the height of the window, and lost itself in Venice, never to be found again. The story of its escape, and the cover-up which followed, makes amusing reading in a letter to Isabella from one of her agents.[87] Following her trip to Venice seven years later, Isabella hired a Venetian mason to lay *terrazzo* pavements in her apartments in Mantua, in accordance with the practical Venetian custom.[88] Francesco Sansovino's account of the technique of laying *terrazzo* explains succinctly its attractions for a study:

> For the upper rooms and for the Hall [i.e. *portego*, in the Venetian palace] the floors or pavements are built not of brick but of [. . .] *terrazzo*; which lasts for a very long time, is attractive to the eye and easy to clean. It is made with lime and with bricks or tiles that are well crushed and mixed all together. Then there is added one part of small flakes of Istrian stone, well pulverised, and this mixture, fully compacted, is spread over the deck floor of timber planks, which are closely fitted together and nailed down, so that they cannot distort and can support weight. And then, with bars of iron, the mixture is beaten and pressed down over a period of several days. And when it has been completely levelled and hardened, another layer of the same material is laid on top, into which has been incorporated cinnabar or other red colouring. And then, after it has been left to set for several days, it is coated with linseed oil, with which the *terrazzo* achieves such a lustrous finish that a man may see himself reflected in it, as in a mirror. And although this mixture may have a reputation for being unwholesome because of its coldness, there is however no finer material for pavements, none more beautiful or gracious or more durable than this; it is maintained by scrubbing [. . .] and for those who wish to retain its lustrous appearance, it can be covered with rugs or carpets so that it is not damaged by shoes, and in this way when one enters a room thus appointed, one would think that one was entering a fine and beautifully clean Church kept by nuns.[89]

Outside Venice, ceramic was considered suitable not only for study floors: the Studietto constructed for Piero de' Medici in the Palazzo Medici in the 1450s was lined with enamelled terracotta as a structural unit by Luca della Robbia, and concave roundels depicting the Labours of the Months were set into the enamelled vault, following the curve of the ceiling of the room (figs 32a and b).[90] From the curvature of the roundels it can be deduced that they were disposed in three rows of four, probably between heavy white architectural mouldings as used by Luca in other structural units. Allowing for the curvature of the complete ceiling, the floor area of the study measured approximately 4 by 5.5 metres.[91] The tight spatial organisation of the room would have demanded careful planning and it has been suggested that Michelozzo may have designed the room as a whole, in close consultation with Luca.

As the Studietto lacked windows,[92] it must always have been lit by candlelight, reflected off the curved surfaces of the ceiling and heightening the subtle shading in each roundel, in which the number of daylight and night-time hours for each month is indicated within the border. The fact that the sun, subtly shown as the light source in the roundels, is shown in each on the left[93] indicates that this was intended to unify the ceiling decoration and maximise its impact when admired by candlelight. It was the architectural unity of the room, as well as its technical innovation and brilliance, which was admired by contemporaries.[94] An anonymous poem commemorating a visit in 1459 to the Palazzo Medici by Galeazzo Maria Sforza, son of the Duke of Milan, mentions the *lavoro d'intarsia* but omits any reference to the ceramic decoration, either because the latter had not been completed before 1459 (which seems unlikely) or because the Milanese were not particularly impressed by the material or the technical brilliance with which it had been used.[95] Filarete, writing in 1464, however, mentions Piero's 'extremely ornate studietto with the pavement and also the ceiling made of figurative enamelled terracottas, in such a way that it creates

32a and b Luca della Robbia, *c*.1450–56. Two of the twelve enamelled terracotta roundels from the ceiling of Piero de' Medici's study, depicting the Labours of the Months. August is represented by a scene of ploughing; November by a boy picking olives, seated in a tree. The iconography, which is closely based on Columella's Latin treatise on agriculture, provides a reassuring sense of continuity from the ancient Roman world. It also suggests that intellectual work and farming are complementary pursuits: hence the appropriateness of these scenes as study decorations. London, Victoria and Albert Museum.

the greatest admiration in whosoever enters the room'.[96] When Vasari later described the room, he mentioned that the ceramic lining was very useful in the summer, presumably since it was cool to the touch.[97]

Similarly impressive, as a scheme of unified decoration, was the study created by Piero de' Medici's brother, Giovanni di Cosimo. He commissioned Donatello to line it with marble inlay between 1455 and 1457, as part of what Lillie has called 'the creation of a self-image in the guise of an ancient Roman'.[98] Since the second of two letters referring to the commission mentions that 'Donatello will repair many broken things', it is possible that he was working to incorporate ancient marble fragments into one modern unit, creating a suitably antique flavour for the room.[99] Giovanni is known to have had a study in the Medici palace which was shown, with Piero's, to such distinguished visitors as Cardinal Francesco Gonzaga in 1462: Donatello's panelling may well have been installed here, rather than in his other study in the new family villa at Fiesole, since it was in the town palace that such a selfconscious statement, intended to rival his brother's, would have had maximum impact.[100]

3 Constructing the Study: Owners and Craftsmen

Panelling and Fitted Desk Units

THE MOST IMPORTANT ROLE in the construction of the Italian Renaissance study was that performed by various house carpenters, joiners and more specialised woodworkers and carvers. Their contribution was more important than that of either masons or housepainters, according to the evidence of inventories and account books. House carpenters and joiners accepted contracts for a wide variety of work, which included building wooden ceilings and floors, constructing partitions dividing a study area from the rest of a bedchamber, and making window-frames and doors. They could also provide the simplest, untreated panelling for lining the walls of a small study, a feature which was much appreciated by contemporary scholars. Alberti pointed out in his architectural treatise the insulating properties of wooden panelling – he recommended fir and poplar woods especially – from extremes of both cold and heat.[1] When Erasmus wrote to John Fisher, Bishop of Rochester in September 1524, he affectionately took his friend to task for neglecting his comfort to the detriment of his health, particularly in the construction of his study:

> You never consider your poor body. I suspect that a large part of your ill-health is caused by the place where you live (for I propose to play the physician, if you will allow me). Your being near the sea and the mud which is repeatedly laid bare at low tides means an unhealthy climate, and your library has walls of glass all round, the chinks of which let through an air which is tenuous and, as the physicians call it, filtered, which is very dangerous for those who are sparely built and not robust. Nor have I forgotten how you sit continually in that library, which to you is a paradise. Personally, if I spent three hours together in such a place, I should fall sick. You would be much better suited by a room with a wooden floor and wooden panelling all round the walls; some sort of miasma issues from bricks and mortar.[2]

33 Marinus van Reymerswaele (c.1493–1567), *St Jerome in his Study*, oil on panel, showing the room lined with plain wooden panelling. Berlin, Staatliche Museen zu Berlin, Preussischer Kulturbesitz, Gemäldegalerie.

Apart from health considerations, which were never far from the minds of Renaissance scholars, a small study lined with panelling was a comforting and reflective place in which to work. When Felix Platter felt lonely one Christmas Eve, he

> took a lamp and shut myself up in my study, which was at the top of the house and was a plain little closet lined with boards. I stayed there until the others arrived home from Midnight Mass, reading the comedy of Amphitrion in an old copy of Plautus.[3]

Before independent pieces of furniture such as tables and cabinets were in common use, studies were built as a unit with integrated furnishings. Some rooms contained box-type closets with roof, shelves and desk: perhaps this was what a certain Baldassera undertook to construct in Lorenzo Dolfin's *camera* according to a contract drawn up in 1451.[4] The fullest and most detailed description of a desk with chests, cupboard and seat built into one unit appears in the inventory of the possessions of Lorenzo de Pierfrancesco de' Medici. Among the furnishings in one of the Medici houses at Fiesole at the end of the fifteenth century was

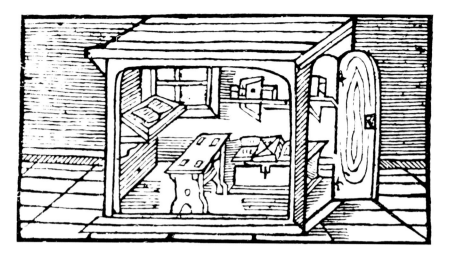

a large writing desk [...] with boards and a backrest, and with a cupboard with a cornice made of walnut, and compartments decorated with inlay. Underneath the desk, where one puts one's feet, is a wooden platform raised above the ground. A valuation is not given here because the unit is firmly fixed to the wall.[5]

In other words, the structure was considered to be a permanent fixture, and so was not assessed in an inventory of movables. A desk and bench were fixed to a platform base, which not only made the unit stable but raised it off the floor so that a reader or writer was less likely to suffer from cold feet and draughts. Many such platforms are mentioned in inventories (Minerbetti memoranda; Serragli 1576; Colombe 1561; Rinuccini 1499). A somewhat breathless account of a complete study in wood, made *in situ* by Chimenti del Tasso for Zanobi Giocondi in fifteen days in April 1492, mentions 'a shelf with a cornice [above] and little shelves, a desk and bench, and compartments of walnut, window frames and a door in my study'.[6]

One of the best and most famous representations of such a hutch appears in Antonello da Messina's *St Jerome in his Study* (fig. 35).[7] Structures like this certainly existed, although Antonello has, for pictorial reasons, left out the ceiling and one wall in order to show a spacious church-like interior with hexagonally tiled floor and an arcade. A delightful miniature from a Florentine manuscript of about 1480, illuminated by Lorenzo Attavante, shows just such a unit, and how comfortable and perfectly adapted for use it could be (fig. 36). A scribe is shown at work transcribing a text; the text for copying is supported at a convenient height on a lectern slotted into his desk. There is a small high window to the scribe's left, so that he does not write in the shadow of his own hand. There is an early clock on the back wall, and a string of bills or letters on the wall; householders did this themselves as a way of keeping order in their studies.

A description given of a desk unit in another inventory mentions that it had been 'made here in the room', showing that a house carpenter had made the unit to measure.[8] This was probably the usual practice, and it explains why stonemasons might resent the role of house carpenters in creating permanent fixtures. A letter from Bartolomeo Marasca, tutor to Francesco Gonzaga, to the Marchesa of Mantua in 1460 shows an argument developing. Marasca describes how he and Francesco had moved into a newly remodelled house, fitted with glass windows (to the latter's delight) so that 'it seemed that we had passed from a state of Limbo into Paradise'. The only thing that remained for Marasca to do was to commission a carpenter to make for his pupil (then a student at Pavia) 'two desks in the *studio*, and to set four book wheels there'.[9] This commission started an argument between the stonemasons (who regarded these desks as part of the fabric and therefore their responsibility) and the house carpenters. It is clear enough what the argument was about, judging from illustrations of desk units. A woodcut from the Malermi Bible, printed in Venice in 1490, shows St Jerome at work on the Vulgate (fig. 38). This bookwheel is built into a solid base, and shares the same platform as the main desk unit. Copied from the larger lecterns to be found in churches, especially in sacristies, this two-sided lectern was considered to be an attribute of scholarship in the late fifteenth century, particularly in association with Jerome as a translator. This type of desk made it easier to compare two different texts, or a text and a commentary.

34 Woodcut showing a box-type study; the front wall has been cut away so that we can see into the room. Illustration from Gilles Corrozet's *Les Blasons domestiques*, Paris 1539.

35 (*facing page*) Antonello da Messina, *St Jerome in his Study*, oil on limewood, *c*.1475. A depiction of a study unit, set in a fictive Gothic interior, clearly modelled on those seen in Netherlandish paintings which were so admired and collected in Venice. London, National Gallery.

36 Lorenzo Attavante, manuscript illumination, *c.*1480, showing a scholar (perhaps the author of this mansucript) transcribing or translating a text in his study. His desk is comfortably built into a corner of the room, beneath the window, leaving room on the back wall for a clock and a string of bills or letters. Inventories of study contents frequently list needles 'for threading papers', and strings of bills are often mentioned. The miniature appears within an initial G in a manuscript of Berlinghieri's Italian translation of Ptolemy's *Geography*, which he presented to Lorenzo de' Medici. Milan, Biblioteca Braidense, MS AC.xiv.44.

A miniature within the initial M in a copy of Donato Accaiuoli's translation of Leonardo Bruni's *Florentine History* shows a particularly fine study (fig. 37). The manuscript was commissioned by the Medici about 1480, and their arms appear on the sheet from which this miniature is taken. It shows Donato Accaiuoli at work. He holds a pen in his right hand and a penknife in his left, which he could use for holding down the springy parchment, for correcting mistakes, or sharpening his quill pen. It is significant that a contemporary Florentine is shown here as if he had the status of a classical author or Christian saint. Donato was a member of one of Florence's most illustrious families, as well as being a diplomat and scholar. His study, with its well-judged and human proportions, its fine coffered and gilded ceiling and its panelling, reflects this status. He wears court

37 Master of the Serafonte Hamilton, miniature within an initial M, showing Donato Acciaiuoli in his study, Florence, *c.*1480. From Donato's translation of Leonardo Bruni's *Florentine History*, which achieved classic status in fifteenth-century Florence. The manuscript was commissioned by the Medici about 1480, and their arms appear on the sheet from which this miniature is taken. Florence, Biblioteca Nazionale, B.R.53, fol. 11r.

dress, as Machiavelli claims he wore when studying. The elaborate and very fine marquetry in this room was the latest fashion when this miniature was painted. Florence was a leading centre for this kind of work, which was in demand throughout Italy from the second quarter of the fifteenth century. As the proud Florentine Giovanni Rucellai wrote, commenting on contemporary craftsmen in his memoranda:

> there have never before been such master craftsmen in woodwork, in inlay or marquetry, capable of such great skill in perspective that it cannot be bettered in painting.[10]

The original model for a study lined with complex *lavoro d'intarsia* appears to have been the unit made by Arduino da Baese for Paolo Guinigi of Lucca before 1414, when

Arduino was paid 199 florins for the work. We do not know whether Arduino was the first master craftsman to create illusionistic effects in wooden panels, and Guinigi's study generally has not yet received the attention it deserves as the first in the famous fifteenth-century line of courtly examples. The inlaid panels and cupboards were important enough to have been removed by order of Leonello d'Este after Guinigi's fall and to have been taken by Arduino to Belfiore in 1434 for use in Leonello's famous study.[11] The fact that Leonello was so keen to use Arduino's work, even though it was by then at least twenty years old, argues for its perceived quality in his eyes. His brother, Ercole, re-used the panels again, though economy seems rather to have been his motive. He had Stefano de Dona Bona move the panels from Belfiore and fit them into his study in the Palazzo del Corte in 1479, along with the iron grilles from the windows. The panelling was customised for Ercole's use by making two doors inlaid with his arms and devices, and the court painter, Tura, was asked to adapt and repaint for the new room four of the Muses which he had made for Leonello.[12]

Whatever the reasons for the long life and visibility of his famous panelling at the d'Este court, Arduino da Baiso's status and renown was considerable. His work in Florence was judged by goldsmiths – no less than Lorenzo Ghiberti and Cola di Niccolò Spinelli – and a contract for work in Ferrara in 1428 included a copyright clause.[13] Niccolò da Uzzano recommended Arduino's craftsmanship and motivation in the highest possible terms to his fellow Florentines in a letter of 1419. Having described someone who was (so Niccolò puts it) spurred as much by desire for his patron's fame as for his own gain, Niccolò added:

> Judging by the experience that I have had of him, and by the appearance of work he has done for me, he is the finest master and his works are as exquisite as they could possibly be; for, knowing his virtue, I pray that he may be recommended to you, for I am most certain that you will receive good service from him and that his works for you will be very well-received, and that you will remain very content with them.[14]

It may have been on the basis of recommendations like these that Arduino was commissioned by Palla Strozzi to construct choirstalls in the sacristy of Santa Trinità in Florence in 1419–20.[15] Not surprisingly, it was to Arduino that Piero de' Medici turned for advice on 'some work in wood' in 1451 when considering his own study in the Via Larga palace.

We do not know who made the panelling for this room, which was constructed before 1459, when it was admiringly described in an anonymous poem commemorating the visit of Galeazzo Maria Sforza, eldest son of the Duke of Milan, to the Medici palace. The poem mentions:

> a door inlaid with *lavoro d'intarsia* on one side/Gives into the chapel so genteel that no-one ever tired of admiring it./[. . .] Likewise one sees on the other side/an exit done with such art that I take it/for true relief – and it's flat *lavoro d'intarsia* – /which gives into the triumphant and lovely study/that has such order and measure/that it represents angelic exultation/with complete art in inlays and painting/in perspective and carvings sublime/and in great mastery of architecture.[16]

The inlay here is both geometric and floral, probably on a walnut base which Florentines favoured for this kind of work – as in the Medici inventory quoted above. Inlaid panels remained in fashion for studies into the first decade of the sixteenth century. Jacopo di Piero Guicciardini re-used pieces from his father's study when redecorating his own in 1507, as part of a general refit of his apartment in readiness for his marriage in that year (Guicciardini memoranda).

Cannibalising other people's studies to furnish one's own had good precedents in Leonello d'Este's re-use of Guinigi's panelling; in Guicciardini's case, he may have saved money on several counts in re-using panels from his father's study, since putting these together in his own room would only have involved the services of a joiner, rather than a craftsman who specialised in inlay.

Venetian woodworkers were subdivided into four groups by the mid-sixteenth century, but the distinction between these categories seems to have corresponded to working classifications observed elsewhere at an earlier date. The Venetians were divided into *marangoni da fabrica* or *da casa*, who worked on structural features such as floor and roof joists; *marangoni de noghera*, who worked in fine woods such as walnut; *marangon de soaze* or *intagliatori*, who did gilding and fine carving on picture frames and tabernacles; and *rimesseri*, who worked on inlay and marquetry (or cabinet-making, as it was later to be known).[17] The inventory of the workshop of one Venetian woodworker shows that he was a maker of chests in walnut, but that he sent these out to another workshop for gilding (Zuanelli 1587).

The same kind of distinction between grades of woodworking skill is shown in Giovanni Chellini's memoranda. He cleverly rented out houses to different types of *legnaiuolo*, in exchange for payments in kind as well as (or in place of) rent. Piero di Strozzi signed a contract in 1446 for renting a house and workshop from Chellini. In return he was contracted by Chellini to make 'a little desk and a backrest entirely at his own expense' every year.[18] From the description this sounds like a built-in desk unit, or something which could be fitted in to a room by another craftsman. Piero fulfilled his contract for seven years, during which he also made a window-opening and frame for the room of Chellini's son, Tommaso, without charge.[19] Since this was fairly low-grade work, Piero was probably a house carpenter who worked on structural features. Chellini also rented a house to Giovanni d'Andrea d'Albola, who paid rent, but made extremely fine sets of furniture for Chellini, presumably at a special price. This included a complete refit of Chellini's son's apartment in 1454, when a matching set of furniture with elaborate wooden inlay was made:

> a *lettuccio* with *cassone* underneath and a hat-rack above, worked in walnut with inlay of spindle wood with a frieze of foliage pattern and an inscription also in spindle wood and a pair of chests with locks, also with inlay of foliage in the same way, and for a frieze of walnut with foliage pattern in spindle wood for a bedstead, all for the room of Tommaso.[20]

Such fine work, with contrasting inlay of pale wood in a darker ground, recalls the luxurious set of furnishings to be seen in Filippo Lippi's *Annunciation* of *c*.1465. The Virgin is shown at her desk for praying and reading sacred texts (*inginocchatoio*), with her *lettuccio* and bed decorated with an inlaid foliage pattern similar to that described by Chellini.[21] Both the painting and the document inform one another in recording fashionable Florentine taste in the middle of the fifteenth century.

Sets of Furnishings

A set of furniture comprising a bedstead and *lettuccio* made of pine with spindle wood inlay, like Chellini's, is for example mentioned in the bedchamber of Giovanni de' Medici (Medici 1492, pp. 72–3). A *lettuccio* was a grand, expensive and dignified piece of furniture of the kind found in bedchambers in their role as reception rooms; their function is clear from contemporary woodcuts such those in Savonarola's *Arte di ben morire* or the Malermi

39a and b   Sketch model (and detail) in limestone for a tomb monument for an unidentified scholar, Bolognese, *c*.1530. Bologna, Museo Civico Medioevale.

40 Tomb monument (dated 1533) to the scholar Giovanni Battista Malavolta. Bologna, San Giacomo Maggiore. Photo: Bologna, Soprintendenza, Gabinetto Fotografico.

Bible.[22] In Florentine houses, *lettucci* might be used to store books, as in the inventory of Giovanni di Benedetto Cecchi da Pescia in 1596. His *lettuccio* contained Caesar's commentaries, Quintilian's *Oratory* and works by Paolo Giovio (Cecchi 1596). The *lettuccio* served as a daybed, so the idea of keeping one's reading matter in the base of it must have been attractive. It was easy to extract a book from the chests underneath the cover before lying down to rest or read.

Something of this idea was taken up in the mid-sixteenth century in the iconography of scholar's tombs and wall-monuments, which often show them reclining on a daybed similar to a *lettuccio* with a book in hand, or surrounded by books (fig. 39). This iconography seems to have been particularly popular in Bologna, where some of the best examples are to be seen (notably at San Giacomo Maggiore (fig. 40) and the Museo Civico). A *lettuccio* could also serve, like a cabinet, as a base for displaying a collection of bronzes. The collector Girolamo Garimberto, who also acted as an artistic adviser and agent to Cesare Gonzaga of Guastalla in the formation of the latter's collection, had 'a *lettuccio alla Toscana* for Summer use'. It was to be inlaid with marble so as to be cool to the touch and refreshing to the eye.[23] The cornice was to be set with an array of bronzes.[24] In this, too, Garimberto was following Florentine custom, since a Medici inventory describes a *lettuccio* being used as a base for a bust (Medici 1492) while a later inventory mentions that four busts were displayed on one.[25] Garimberto's *lettuccio* was made to match his inlaid marble bedstead, which he dreamt up while in his villa. He describes in a letter of 1564 how 'in this state of villa-leisure I have had a design made and shall have it made up the minute I get back to Rome'.[26] He obviously considered the bed to be part of his collection since it is listed in the note of art objects which he offered for sale to Albrecht V of Bavaria in 1569.[27] It was, however, eventually bought by Emmanuel Philibert, Prince of Savoy.[28]

The *lettuccio* could therefore be a suitable piece for a fashionable bedchamber, or alternatively an integral element in a collector's *camerino*.

Desks

Not every study contained a built-in desk unit. The simplest, cheapest and most adaptable form of writing-desk was a trestle table, such as is frequently depicted in pictures of Doctors of the Church. One schoolmaster in Padua had 'a table [. . .] with two trestle supports', while a late fifteenth-century bibliophile owned 'a little table fixed to walnut trestle supports'.[29]

The vital role played by house carpenters and joiners in constructing studies diminished during the sixteenth century, as the independent desk or cabinet evolved. By the mid-sixteenth century, desk units would have been considered antiquated and clumsy, and one inventory, that of Agostino di Piero del Nero, revealingly shows that such a unit with its desk, cupboards and two painted bookwheels, had been removed from his study to the attic of his house by 1576 (Nero 1576). By this date, fitted desk units had been superseded by the cabinet.

A new type of writing-desk evolved around 1500. It was of Spanish Moorish origin, and consisted of a shallow desk with a sloping lid for writing on, which opened to reveal small drawers and compartments for pens, ink and papers. It could be placed on any available table surface. Juan Ludovicus Vives refers to this type of desk in one of his Latin dialogues for schoolboys, *The Bedchamber and Studies by Night*, in which he pictures a scholar (modelled on Pliny the Elder) sitting down to work in a contemporary setting:

PLINY: Set the table up on its supports in the bedchamber.
CELSIUS: Do you prefer the table to the desk?
PLINY: At the moment, yes, but place the small desk on the table.
EPICTETUS: The fixed or the revolving one?[30]

Vives represents Pliny as having a choice between a revolving lectern or one of the small desks described above. The latter is illustrated in Bellano's monument to Pietro Roccabonella in Padua (fig. 42). He sits at a semicircular desk which acts as a frame for the composition, with a small desk with a sloping lid lying to his right. With his left hand he smooths down the page of a large book propped up against the wall of his study.

Because of its size, this was the perfect writing-desk for travellers. The Jesuit missionary

41 (*facing page*) Woodcut illustration from Francesco Torniello's calligraphic treatise of 1517, showing the author writing in his study. Note the convex mirror on the wall, which another calligrapher recommended as a study accessory for those who are continually writing. Francesco Torniello, *Opera de fare le littera*, Milan 1517. By courtesy of the Master and Fellows, Magdalene College, Cambridge. Pepys Library.

¶ Opera del modo de fare le littere maiuscole antique, con mesura de circino: & resone de penna, composita per Francisco Torniello da Nouaria scriptore professo.

42 Tomb monument of the Venetian doctor of medicine and lecturer at the University of Padua, Pietro Roccabonella (d.1491). Made by Bartolomeo Bellano and Riccio. Padua, San Francesco. Photo: Böhm.

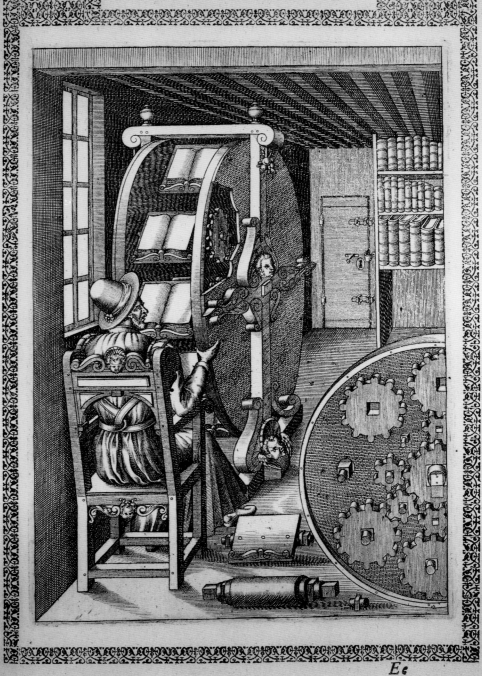

FIGVRE CLXXXVIII.

Eє

43   Design for a revolving
desk, from Agostino
Ramelli, *Le diverse et
artificiose machine del capitano
Agostino Ramelli*, Paris 1588,
chapter CLVXXVIII. London,
British Library.

44a and (*facing page*) b Two ink sketches of an extending table and a desk designed about 1595 for the convenience of the ailing Philip II of Spain. One of several ingenious study fittings intended for the king, including a special oil-lamp and a reclining chair. The drawings are annotated in Spanish or French so as to make clear to the king the comfort and convenience which a particular piece would provide. Brussels, Bibliothèque Royale Albert 1er, Den Gheyn catalogue MS II 1028, fol.151r.

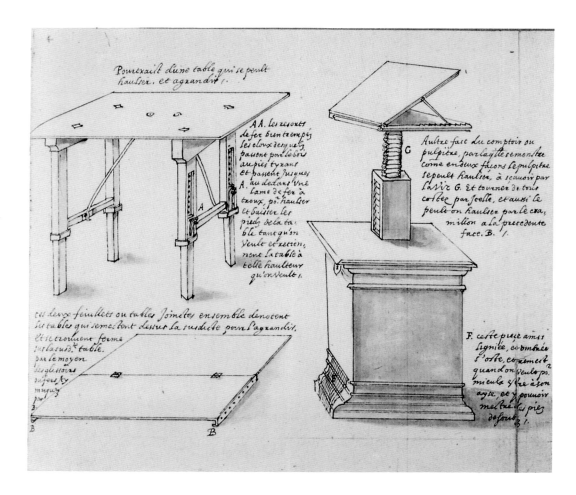

45 Alberto Rusconi, marble relief from the screen of the notaries' chapel in San Petronio, Bologna, dated 1483. A revolving lectern is set into a book cupboard with a lock. Photo: author.

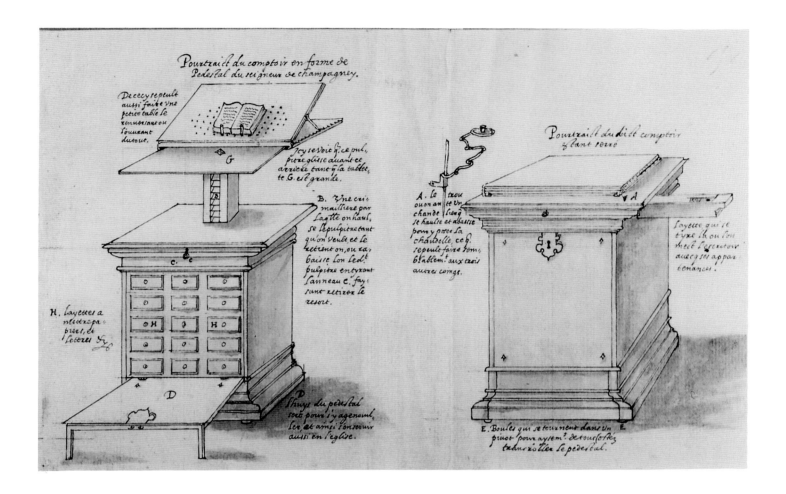

Matteo Ricci nearly lost his when he was shipwrecked on the way to Ganzhou in 1595. Ricci described the scene in vivid detail in a letter to a fellow Jesuit in Macao, in which he told how he had seen his writing-desk bobbing on the water along with his bedding, 'and I was able to stretch out my hand and pull them to where I was', after which some sailors, swimming back to the boat and climbing aboard, helped me to clamber back up'.[31] Since Ricci probably kept papers and letters in his desk, it was a very important possession.

In a fundamental Latin handbook of manners and civility for schoolchildren, Erasmus counselled that 'if anyone should open his writing-desk in front of you, you should leave the room'.[32] Evidently the contents of a portable writing-desk were not just personal, but private. A beautiful example of a writing-desk made for Francesco Maria II della Rovere of Urbino around 1600 is now in the Victoria and Albert Museum. Inlaid with ivory, it opens to reveal compartments for pens and an inkwell, as well as several drawers for seals and papers.[33]

Two designs for a desk unit and a lectern – one manuscript and the other printed – show the technical ingenuity and expertise which could be focused on these pieces of furniture. An ink sketch for a desk to be made to order for Philip II of Spain shows a desk unit with every convenience for the reader, including ledges for folios, pegs to support books of different sizes, and a lamp so flexible that it can be easily angled wherever one wants light on the desk surface (figs 44a and b). Instructions in Spanish and in French explain the advantages of particular features. Even more curious is an engraved design for a lectern published by the royal engineer to the King of France, Agostino Ramelli in 1588 (fig. 43). Ramelli explains the contraption as 'a beautiful and ingenious machine, extremely useful and practical for anyone who loves study', particularly, he adds, for anyone with gout since one can view or read many books without changing position. A large number of books could be supported, open, on individual lecterns. A diagram at the lower right of the engraving shows the mechanism: square bolts for the lectern attachments; a central axle; and cogs which control the rotation of the bookwheel.[34]

Bookchests and Bookshelves

Desks often had cupboards built into them which served as bookchests. Ercole d'Este had a desk which was described in an inventory of 1490 as 'a writing-desk made of walnut supported on four legs, or rather a little table'.[35] It probably consisted of a cupboard with doors at the front, in which were compartments for books. The top of the cupboard served as a writing-desk, hence the assessor's qualification of his original description. A later inventory mentions a large walnut desk unit fitted with cupboards in the base, containing a large number of printed books and papers, and with a shelf above.[36] 'Compartments for papers' (*buche da scripture*) were useful for organising family documents. Bookchests had long been the conventional way of storing books in the domestic interior, and the custom persisted into the sixteenth century. One scholar kept a list, in one of his Latin manuscripts, of books which he owned and which were generally to be found 'in an extremely beautiful bookchest', annotated in such a way that he could keep track of books lent out to his friends.[37]

Some fifteenth-century householders built bookchests into the walls of their studies, as the Romans had done. Pliny the Younger, in a letter to Gallus, described a chest 'like a bookcase' which was set into the walls of one of the rooms in his villa, containing 'a

46   Ink sketch by Vittore Carpaccio showing a scholar in his study. Moscow, Pushkin Museum.

47   Bronze medal of
Galeotto Marzio (d. *c.*1494),
'poet and mathematician',
Bolognese. The reverse
shows a book cupboard
realised in extremely shallow
relief, which yet creates a
superb illusion of depth.
Berlin, Staatliche Museen zu
Berlin, Preussischer
Kulturbesitz, Münzkabinett.

collection of such authors whose works cannot be read too often'.[38] Fifteenth-century
drawings and paintings often show wall cupboards with or without doors, containing
books or other select objects. A sixteenth-century inventory lists 'a chest with two drawers
built into the wall' (Ciampoli 1564) while another describes a cupboard 'fixed to the wall
with an enamelled terracotta figure on one of the shelves' – perhaps the figure was a
product of the Della Robbia workshops (Nero 1576). Bookchests built into the wall
became, like rotating lecterns, attributes of the scholar, as demonstrated by the medal of
Galeotto Marzio of Narni.[39]

Cabinets

By the mid-sixteenth century, cabinets had become indispensable study fittings, objects as
much for display as for use. Luxurious examples were assembled from exotic woods, such
as ebony and ivory, or decorated with mother-of-pearl plaques painted and gilded in
imitation of Far Eastern lacquer. They could be set with silver mounts and fittings, and
with elaborate locks and lockplates; with columns carved from hardstones such as jasper,
serpentine marble or even alabaster. Some were specially designed to show to best
advantage an existing collection of cameos, or a select group of bronze or silver figurines.
Cabinets answered the late sixteenth-century passions for organising collectables according
to systems of classification, as well as for combining different materials, textures and
colours to maximum decorative effect; something which was as important to wealthy
householders as to noble collectors in late sixteenth-century Italy.[40]

The fashion for constructing cabinets to contain and display an existing collection, and
for using their design as a programme for collecting sculpture and coins with which to
decorate them, seems to have originated in Rome in the mid-sixteenth century. One of
the earliest and best-documented collector's cabinets was that made for Cesare Gonzaga
(1536–75), ruler of the principality of Guastalla, in the 1560s.[41] The story of Cesare's
cabinet illuminates his relationship with his archaeological adviser, Gerolamo Garimberto

(1506–75), who commissioned the cabinet in Rome on Cesare's behalf and saw it through its somewhat tortuous progress towards completion in 1564.[42] The following account is taken from letters edited and published by C. M. Brown with A. M. Lorenzoni, which document the story in remarkable detail.[43] Garimberto was himself a collector, who seems to have benefited from his position as adviser first to Cesare, then to Cardinal Alessandro Farnese, in building up his own collection and library.[44] His letters to Cesare show that he was not only a witty and erudite man, but also well able to manage his patron.

Cesare's cabinet was constructed according to a design by Francesco da Volterra, who was both a master craftsman in wood and an architect.[45] Cabinets were often designed by architects, since they provided an opportunity to construct a miniature building or triumphal arch on the Roman model, complete with cornice, columns, pilasters and pediments surmounted with figurines. The interior of a cabinet could be decorated with dramatic perspectival effects in paint or marquetry, imitating contemporary theatre design. All these features of the sixteenth-century cabinet perhaps explain its appeal to such an architect as Palladio. There was also a link with the design of temporary catafalques used in funerary ceremonials; Volterra, apart from providing the design for Cesare's cabinet and for the Galleria dei Marmi in which it was to be displayed, is also known to have designed the catafalque for Cardinal Francesco Gonzaga's funeral in Rome in 1566.[46] Drawings of famous cabinets were eagerly passed round in collecting circles; the dealer Jacopo Strada, who acted as agent to Albrecht V of Bavaria and to the Holy Roman Emperor Maximilian II, commissioned drawings of Cesare Gonzaga's cabinet for each of them in 1567–8.[47] No one was more adept than Strada at profiting from the relentless drift of antiquities and works of art away from Italy to the Northern European courts which began in the 1560s. Pursuing the finest Italian cabinets was to remain a preoccupation among German collectors for over a century. A cabinet's design was, in the eyes of contemporaries, even more important than its workmanship or the prestige of the materials used to make it. This is demonstrated by the proud comment of the Ferrarese collector, Roberto Canonici, who described his cabinet as being

> very beautiful, made of walnut, with many secret compartments and little drawers, some of which are made in cypress wood. The cabinet was made according to my specifications and to my design, which I gave to the Master craftsman who stayed in my house for a year in order to construct it, at a cost of four hundred ducats.[48]

Canonici's method of overseeing the work on his cabinet to his satisfaction, by keeping the craftsman in his own house, was an eminently practical way of getting exactly what he wanted. Cesare Gonzaga did not have this advantage in his dealings with Volterra and Garimberto over the construction of his cabinet, since much of the work was supervised at a distance, involving many delays and setbacks. Garimberto was to supervise the carving of twenty-one alabaster and marble columns in Rome, which were to be sent to Mantua for assembly there into the body of the cabinet. Alabaster was hard to find and difficult to carve, and only some of the finished columns were finally sent to Mantua.[49] Garimberto kept the rejected columns for his use in his own cabinet, which was clearly inspired by Cesare's, as described in a delightfully transparent, manipulative letter to his patron, dated 30 December 1564. He was particularly pleased with the cabinet's design, which was

> very beautiful and rich in fine stones and accompanied by those [alabaster] columns roughed out for Your Excellency's cabinet, which, through the additions of the odd piece, stucco infills and other repairs, have turned out to be very lovely and beautiful, at an honest expense to myself. Put together with the ornament of many ancient figurines, the cabinet has proved a great success, nor could it have been otherwise, given that it is the work of a pupil of Father Volterra, which delights me, but even more I

rejoice in Your Excellency's cabinet as a work of Father Volterra's own hand, and I await its completion with eagerness. With reference to Your cabinet, it has not been omitted to procure bronze figurines with which to ornament it, through the diligence of Giovanantonio [Stampa].[50]

Despite Garimberto's awkward assurances that his cabinet was proceeding well and that attention was being paid to its complement of bronzes, Cesare Gonzaga might well have been furious at Garimberto's rival project, but he was won over by this letter, stating only in reply that his own cabinet was to go on display in his Mantuan apartments at Easter.[51] The two letters reveal the rivalry, as well as the rapport, between patron and adviser. Garimberto's cabinet was important enough to have been valued at 400 scudi in the inventory he prepared of his antiquities offered for sale to Albrecht V of Bavaria in 1569; a value which was only 100 scudi less than one of his most prized Roman sculptures of *Hercules Strangling the Serpents*, and indicates its role as a fashionable Roman collectable.[52]

Roman cabinet design in the 1550s provided the inspiration for two famous examples commissioned for leading Venetian collectors in the third quarter of the sixteenth century. Perhaps the most famous – in that it was documented in three inventories from the sixteenth to the eighteenth centuries – was the cabinet inlaid with ebony which was made for Giovanni Grimani, Patriarch of Aquileia.[53] Designed for his magnificent study in his new, Roman-style apartments in his palace at Santa Maria Formosa (a leading example of its kind, as discussed in chapter 5), the cabinet was transferred after his death, with much of the family collection, to the library of St Mark's.[54] It is known that the cabinet was made by a Flemish craftsman; a common practice, since what was later to be known as 'cabinet-making' was a specialised skill associated with the Low Countries and Southern Germany. The architect who designed Grimani's cabinet is not known, but it would surely have been 'one of the best architects in Italy' mentioned as having been involved in the construction of the study in which it was to stand. Palladio or Scamozzi – both architects in the Grimani circle – are probable choices. It was an extremely complex piece of furniture, an art object in itself, encrusted with fine cameos from the family collection, and set with marble busts and bronze figurines on the cornice, in a manner reminiscent of one of Palladio's palaces.[55] In the 'tribune' or gallery at the centre of the cabinet were two silver-gilt plaques cast by the goldsmith Moderno (now in the Kunsthistorisches Museum, Vienna).[56] Set in the middle of Giovanni Grimani's study, on the chequered marble floor, the cabinet must have been the focal point of the room as a display of small-scale sculpture.

Palladio is known to have provided the design for a cabinet made for Cavaliere Leonardo Mocenigo, which was bought for the Grand Duke of Tuscany in 1578 by Guglielmo Bos. That year Bos described it in a letter to the Florentine collector Cavaliere Gaddi:

> a very beautiful ebony cabinet, made to resemble the Arch of Constantine, as directed by Palladio [. . .] it was made to conserve all the large, medium-sized and small medals of silver, gold and other metal which the said most famous Cavaliere Mocenigo possessed. I am absolutely sure that this cabinet will be to the taste of His Most Serene Highness, for besides the excellence of the architectural design, it has been worked by a man who is extremely skilled in this art.[57]

Mocenigo's cabinet provided in turn the model for a coin cabinet designed for Cardinal Alessandro Farnese for his study in Rome. Farnese would have become acquainted with the sophisticated design of Mocenigo's cabinet while attempting to acquire some of Mocenigo's ancient coins through the agency of Giovanantonio Stampa between 1576 and 1578.[58] Farnese's cabinet was designed by the antiquarian Fulvio Orsini and made by another Fleming, Flaminio Boulanger, in 1578–9. As so often with collector's cabinets, the work went through several difficult stages, recorded in letters from Orsini to his patron. Orsini had designed the cabinet to be made from several woods, principally walnut, comprising thirty-six compartments to contain and organise Farnese's collection.[59] The desirability of a coin cabinet is easily proved by the simple organisation of Farnese's coins at Caprarola up to this date: his coins there were stored in little wooden boxes, labelled with letters of the alphabet running from A to N, offering only a primitive form of classification and location.[60] In the new cabinet, each drawer was to be lined with crimson velvet as a backing for the coins, cameos and figurines, enabling them to be seen to best effect.[61] Boulanger, however, made his own changes to Orsini's design, in that he restricted the wood used for the cabinet to walnut, and used hidden wooden locking devices instead of metal locks. Since he had departed from Orsini's design, his work was also to cost 100 scudi more than Farnese had agreed as the cost for executing the original scheme.[62] Perhaps this was an additional reason for commissioning – and adhering to – an architect's model, in order to avoid troublesome disputes in executing such an expensive and complex piece of furniture.

Grimani's cabinet appears to have influenced lesser collectors in Venice. The lawyer Ludovico Usper had a cabinet in the mezzanine library of his palace at San Stae. The focal point of the room, it was made of walnut with ebony inlay and served as a display stand for his small but unusual collection of bronzes: 'a satyr in bronze, with Venus, tied to a tree', an inkstand with a bronze statuette of a horse, and a bronze figurine.[63] Since Usper is known to have been a patron of Alessandro Vittoria, and to have owned a signed bronze of the Madonna by Jacopo Sansovino,[64] his group of bronzes was likely to have been important, if only as a fitting complement to his large library of ancient and modern Latin and Italian authors. A further tantalising reference to a small array of bronzes displayed on a cabinet appears in the inventory of the patrician Alvise Loredan, whose little study contained 'an olivewood cabinet set with four bronze figurines'.[65]

Palladio's cabinet design, as Palumbo Fossati has shown, may also have had an impact on a Venetian woodcarver in designing and making his own cabinet.[66] Andrea Foscho had worked with Palladio on the Ducal Palace following its damage by fire, and had earned Palladio's praise.[67] His signature appears on a contract drawing, a design of 1578 for a ceiling to be executed in the Sala dei Pregadi – an extremely complex piece of carving.[68] His cabinet is described in his inventory as 'painted green on the outside and with figures and perspective scenes on the inside'.[69] In the cabinet, Foscho kept his most treasured possessions: his architectural library (which included treatises by Palladio, Vitruvius and Serlio)[70] and a medal of himself (fig. 48).[71] His cabinet and its contents express much of his sense of himself as an artist and master craftsman.

The Venetian habit of setting aside a corner of one's bedchamber for use as a study was perfectly served by the cabinet, which could contain all those objects conventionally associated with the study in one piece of furniture. The merchant Gianfrancesco Calderini had a remarkable cabinet in his bedchamber which, judging from its description, was painted in imitation of lacquer and inlaid with plaques of mother-of-pearl.[72] This technique is known to have been practised in Venice in the second half of the sixteenth century for making small boxes, mirror-frames, cabinets, cases for musical instruments and elaborate bookbindings.[73] It was an inexpensive but showy technique for making a display piece for one's bedchamber, as Calderini's certainly was; his was; topped by an alabaster vase. The contents of his cabinet show how small treasures and personal items were stored there. These included silver forks, a diamond ring and a gold chain, two medals, in silver and in gold, of the Holy Roman Emperor Charles V, six spectacle lenses ground from rock crystal, an illuminated breviary in a binding with silver fittings, and eighteen printed, hand-coloured images of saints with thirteen Flemish copper prints.[74]

48 Lead uniface portrait
medal, signed A.A., showing
Andrea Foscho of Faenza.
Emilian school, possibly by
Alessandro Ardenti, a painter
from Faenza. Milan, Civiche
Raccolte Archaeologiche e
Numismatiche di Milano,
Brera, n. 702.

Similar cabinets are described by Fynes Moryson as characterising the bedrooms of
wealthy Venetians. Visiting a woman who had just given birth, he describes 'tables and
Cabinetts of mother-of-pearl, and pearl and Jasper, and other precious stones'[75] which
were to be seen in such rooms.

Cabinets came to be associated with mirrors, hung above them or even made *en suite*,
in the later sixteenth century. One wealthy Florentine had in his study a mirror described
as 'Venetian' (its frame was decorated with painting, probably imitating lacquering as
described above) and a cabinet, also described as being 'Venetian'. It was small, a *braccia*
and a half in length, decorated with inlay, and stood on a table covered with a worn
worsted cloth. Two chests similarly 'inlaid in the Venetian manner' were kept alongside
it (Berti 1594).

A later Venetian inventory shows how cabinets and mirrors were associated, listing 'an
ebony table cabinet [i.e: to stand on a table] with columns made of precious stone, inlaid
with alabaster, agate and other stones: the outside is covered with green velvet with gold
laces, with its mirror' (Formenti 1611). Cabinets were also adapted to perform the function
which Florentine *cassoni* or marriage chests had earlier fulfilled, in that they were used to
contain and organise a young woman's trousseau on her marriage. Hence Eleonora de'
Medici, on her marriage to Vincenzo Gonzaga in 1584, took with her to Mantua an
ebony and silver cabinet which had a mirror set into it, and contained numerous drawers
or *segreti* holding cups, ivory combs and similar toilet articles.[76] The fact that the small
drawers and compartments of a cabinet were sometimes referred to as *segreti* is significant

in explaining the appeal which the cabinet must have had. Florio explains, in his Italian–English dictionary of 1611, that 'La Segreta' was 'the name of a place in Venice where all their Secret Records or ancient evidences are kept as in Westminster Hall'. A 'segretario' was in Florio's definition 'a secret keeper', a service which Anton Francesco Doni claimed to be essential to every individual in order for him to make balanced and considered decisions about his affairs.[77] The cabinet, with its numerous drawers and locked doors, enabled its owner to keep precious objects and papers in an organised and above all private manner; a function which had previously been performed only by the study as a room. Whereas the earlier custom of arranging objects around the walls of a room had licensed disorder and diversity, the cabinet encouraged a more compartmentalised and uniform organisation. This in itself can be linked to intellectual developments of the time, in the move towards more comprehensive, 'scientific' collections which represented the man-made and natural worlds in microcosm, and the wish to systematise knowledge, as in the densely packed handbooks of the late sixteenth century. Thus a cabinet could replace a study, offering all its amenities in microcosm.

This explains why the same words were sometimes used to denote either the study as a room, or a cabinet as a piece of furniture, since the difference (in the mind of sixteenth-century assessors) was primarily one of scale, and not function. Admittedly, the words used varied from city to city, so that Florentines tended (at least in the inventories on which this book is based) to refer to their studies as *scrittoi* and their cabinets as *studioli*, while Venetians did exactly the opposite.

The evolution of the cabinet as a piece of furniture was the single most important development in the history of the study in Renaissance Italy, for it demonstrated the importance of collecting as a form of interior decoration in the second half of the sixteenth century, and not merely as an activity for its own sake. But the cabinet had a greater importance still, which was that it made the amenities of a study more widely available to the urban élite. Quite how it did this within a wider European framework is conveniently summarised in a poem in praise of the cabinet published in Gilles Corrozet's *Blasons domestiques* (Paris 1539). Corrozet came from a family of Parisian mercers, hence the loving and accurate detail with which he described the likely contents of a cabinet owned by the gentry or in an urban household: these items ranged from the dowry of a wife or put aside for a daughter, a woman's make-up and perfume, household plate and cutlery, to arms and armour, the writing equipment of the master of the house, jewellery, trinkets and fashionable accessories. These were the kinds of things which had been kept locked away in a householder's study before the cabinet became more commonly available in the early sixteenth century. Corrozet's description not only matches inventory lists of the contents of cabinets but also suggests how this new form of furniture provided a highly organised display case for the trappings of gentility (Calderini 1597; Cecchi 1596). The cabinet, with all its various niches, secret compartments, drawers and stands, was certainly crucial in shaping and promoting the development of sixteenth-century collecting. In Corrozet's account, however, this quality of the cabinet is mentioned in order to introduce something more significant still, for he shows how the cabinet had a much wider appeal in providing a very visible focus for a new kind of selfconsciousness on the part of urban élites:

> cabinet filled with Paintings and with numerous beautiful images of greater and lesser personages, cabinet embellished with medals and curious antiquities, with marble, with Jasper & Porphyry as much as would satisfy anyone, Cabinet where stands the buffet fully stocked with gold & silver, cabinet supplied with girdles with gold ornaments, & with trimmings with gold chains, with swords, with paintings, with chains, with beautiful buttons, with cuffs, with bracelets, with gorgets & with collars, sewn with

pearls from the Orient: with laundered & perfumed gloves, with musk more precious than gold ducats with fine ambergris and musk-scented soap, with powder from Cyprus & pomade to restore faded colour: with Damascus, pink and Rose water stored in phials of glass, and a hundred other compositions of different mixtures and among such a variety of jewels, are rich & substantial signet rings, crystal paternosters. Seals of paste & Corals, of pearls & of fine Rubies, which are attached to the clothes, next tassels, of gold & silk, to make them appear more prominent, then delicate & well-made knives, forks, and Scissors, the Mirror, the graceful scriptor, the hat the ivory chessboard, in short so many other things are gathered together in this beautiful and confined space that it seems impossible to describe.[78]

4   *Offices and Studies: The Urban Elites*

OFFICES ARE NOT ALWAYS GIVEN a name in inventories, but are instead referred to simply in terms of their location in the house. This is not as vague a description as it might appear, for a room's location in relation to such basic structural features as a staircase would often decide its use. Many offices in the late sixteenth- and early seventeenth-century residences of Venetian merchants (*case fondachi*) are described as being 'in mezà'. This was the term in Venetian dialect for a mezzanine,[1] generally situated on the first landing on a staircase which led up from the ground floor of a house to its principal floor. There would often be several rooms opening off the staircase at this point.

These rooms made well-appointed offices, especially for merchants and lawyers, hence the Venetian word 'mezà' came to be extended in meaning to signify office or *scrittoio*. They formed a kind of cul-de-sac off the principal staircase, separate from the domestic areas of the house, while being easily accessible from the entrance. This was what merchants required, so as to be able to invite partners and clients to their offices to conduct business with ease and efficiency. The office had to be near the ground floor, so that the merchant could organise the arrival and dispatch of goods by water and by land from his storeroom at ground level.[2] It also had to be accessible from the principal living-quarters on the *piano nobile*, so that he could descend the staircase to greet his clients and lead them into his office, their visit causing minimal interference to the household. It was this feature of the *mezà* which made it suitable for all kinds of meeting or assignation. Hence the heroine, Angela, of the sixteenth-century Venetian comedy *La Venexiana*, receives her lover Julio 'nel mezzanino'. She descends from the *piano nobile* to meet him, while he climbs the stairs from the canal entrance of her palace to join her *in mezà*. The servants who have set up the meeting continue up the stairs to the kitchen in the upper regions.[3]

Because of their location, mezzanine rooms tended to be small and cramped, with low ceilings, and hence were not well suited for any use other than as offices. Here merchants could settle correspondence, weigh coin and compile memoranda. Inventories record in detail the mass of business and family papers (*scritture*) which were kept here. These would include marriage contracts, leases and records of payment, all of which are listed in detail so that the executors of the deceased's estate could identify his contacts and settle outstanding debts and disputes.

The office of the merchant Alessandro Borghetti is a classic example of this type of room (Borghetti 1594). The inventory of 1594 begins the list of objects for his room with a painting of the Madonna. A devotional image was a basic piece of household equipment, and such paintings are commonly found in offices and workshops. Next to this was a writing-desk (*cancel*) covered with papers. On this stood two small walnut cabinets (*scrittori*), which were inlaid with *lavoro d'intarsia*, used in Venice for chests of every kind. These cabinets had drawers (*casselle*) for papers. There was also a small counting-table supported on trestles (*cavaletti*), which had a compartment for a pair of balances for weighing coin.

By the mid-sixteenth century studies contained a wide variety of objects, many of which had been accumulated, with the aim of proving gentility, as well as literacy beyond

50 (*facing page*) Plate made of tin-glazed earthenware (maiolica) painted in cobalt blue, manganese purple and lustre with the arms of the Soderini family of Florence at the centre. The design, whereby panels of delicate floral and leaf patterns alternate in blue and golden lustre, is apparently unique. Spanish lustred pottery of this quality was particularly admired in Tuscany, which was closely linked to Valencia by common trading interests in the Western Mediterranean. Several Florentine banks had branches in Valencia, and it was probably through one of them that a special commission such as this would have been made. Valencian lustred plates are listed in the inventory of the estate of Giovanni Soderini among the contents of his study, where luxury display pieces would have been admired and kept for occasional use. Early fifteenth century. London, British Museum, Department of Medieval and Later Antiquities.

that required by an individual in his work. The house of the gem and Turkey merchant Carlo Helman is a good example of a *casa fondaco* in which the *piano nobile* was situated over the mezzanine offices which controlled the ground floor storerooms. Helman also had a study (*studiol*, a Venetian dialect form of *studiolo*); the Italian name given to it indicates that it was accorded the dignity of a collector's study. Like the rest of his house, the room and its contents showed that he was a well-travelled man of taste who had the means to indulge his interests. The principal rooms in his house indicated his dual loyalties to his native Antwerp and to his adopted city of Venice, of which he had become a citizen in 1596.[4] Carlo and his brother Guglielmo operated within an extended network of Flemish merchants trading from Venice. Like many of their compatriots, they had become integrated into the culture of their adopted city, patronising Venetian musicians (Carlo referred to Giovanni Gabrieli as 'mio carrissimo amico' in his will) and assembling an important collection of Venetian paintings including works by Titian, Giovanni Bellini and Veronese.[5] The pictures were important enough in the eyes of Helman's assessors to be given attributions in the inventory of Helman's movables – a rare detail in Venetian inventories of this date despite the numbers and distribution of paintings among Venetians at this date. The Helman example of Titian's *Mary Magdalen* was important enough to receive a mention by Ridolfi, who stated that the family had taken the picture back to Flanders with them on leaving Venice.[6]

Carlo Helman's study showed that he had a marked taste for Turkish artefacts, in that it contained a collection of exotica, Turkish weapons, dress and travelling equipment (Helman 1606). These items appear to have represented the spoils of one of Venice's leading Turkey merchants whose citizenship gave him the privilege of engaging in lucrative trade with the Levant. Perhaps the Helmans had adopted the Venetian custom of sending a son to Istanbul to form trading contacts and gain experience. If Carlo had spent time there, he may well have ordered furnishings to take back with him, like the merchant Antonio Paruta who wrote home in 1592 describing how he was planning to bring home 'the furnishings, most beautiful things' that he had obtained in Istanbul.[7] One of the objects in Helman's study that might suggest he had made a visit to Istanbul was 'a book in the Turkish manner with portraits of Turks in it'.[8] This may have been a little book illustrated with scenes of Turkish life, the personal record of a journey. There is a similar one by an English traveller, brought back from Istanbul in 1588, including portraits of prominent courtiers, among them an Englishman, Samuel Rowlie, briefly annotated.[9] Another example in the genre is the album compiled in Istanbul for another Englishman, Peter Mundy, in 1618 (fig. 52). In response to the increasing interest shown by merchants and travellers, the Ottomans themselves began to produce costume books with illustrations in gouache depicting representatives of a broad range of Ottoman society. These souvenir books are often annotated in a European language, usually Italian or German, a further indication of the market they reached. Carlo Helman's *Libro alla turchesca con effigie de turchi* was surely such a tourist album. Three of the other Turkish objects in his study were scimitars, two of them with damascened blades.

Damascened vessels and arms had long been admired in Italy. Benvenuto Cellini's autobiography, in a passage relating to 1525, describes how he had examined some Turkish poignards with iron blades inlaid with gold wire. In his typically boastful style he states that they were made:

> in the most exquisite Turkish style, neatly filled in with gold. The sight of them stirred in me a great desire to try my own skill in that branch [. . .] and finding that I succeeded to my satisfaction, I executed several pieces. Mine were far more beautiful and more durable than the Turkish, and this for divers reasons. One was that I cut my grooves much deeper and with wider trenches in the steel; for this is not usual in Turkish work.

51 Turkish objects brought back as souvenirs from Constantinople in 1569. From the collection of Stephan III Praun (1544–91), who had travelled as a member of the Embassy of the Holy Roman Empire in that year. Anti-clockwise, from left: a quiver with arrows; a double purse with leather appliqué; a pair of red leather slippers with steel heels; and a bow (lacking its string) with bowcase. Nuremberg, Germanisches Nationalmuseum, lent by the von Praun family.

52 (*facing page*) Leaf from a souvenir album, 'A briefe relation of the Turckes their Kings, Emperours or grandseigneurs', put together in Constantinople in 1618 for the English traveller Peter Mundy. Typically, the owner's annotations are not directly related to the delicate miniature and bold paper-cuts: here, Mundy talks about steam baths as meeting places for Ottoman Turkish women. London, British Museum, Department of Oriental Antiquities, 1974, 6–17, 013, fol. 46v.

Another was that the Turkish arabesques are only composed of arum leaves with a few small sunflowers; and though these have a certain grace, they do not yield so lasting a pleasure as the patterns which we use.[10]

Whatever Cellini's criticisms about the inferiority (as he perceived it) of Turkish work, the technical finesse, fine ornament and associations of Turkish scimitars and weapons made them collectors' pieces in the 1530s.[11]

Describing the collection of the Florentine art lover Bernardo Vecchietti, Rafaello Borghini mentions 'most beautiful knives from the Orient, Turkish scimitars worked in various fashions'.[12] In addition to the scimitars, Helman had in his study a saddle with red velvet housings 'in the turkish manner' (*Una sella alla turchesca di velluto rosso*), perhaps like those mentioned by Francesco Sansovino as being used by Süleyman the Magnificent in his weekly procession to Friday prayers. Sansovino mentions the sultan's retinue of Spahis, courtiers and Janissaries, followed by

There are danceing and Singeing women & women tumblers
actors of playes. but performed by them only among women at
theire festivalls. & times of reioycing. as at Childbearing: circumcision
of theire sons. as fol. sit. 60:

Bathes they us: often where they theire merry meetings as gossopings
with us haueing conuenient roomes for that purpose there they
wash bath & cleans: themselues especially those women that haue
had the company of theire hus... latily: those plunge themselues

fifteen or twenty horses, all with rich head trappings, adorned with carbuncles, diamonds, sapphires, turquoises and great pearls, the saddles not being seen since they are covered with housings of red velvet.[13]

Helman also had 'a quiver and two Turkish bows' (uno valisetta e doi archi turchesi). The shape of the bows must have been distinctively Islamic to identify them as Turkish in the eyes of assessors of Helman's estate, but we know that Venetians were familiar with Turkish bows from a description given by Leonardo Fioravanti in 1564: 'The Turks lacquer their bows and arrows with varnish made of three parts pine resin to one of linseed oil'.[14] Besides Helman's other inventories also mention Turkish bows and bowcases (e.g. Calderini 1597; fig. 52).

More unusual in Helman's inventory perhaps was a woman's dress, 'new, made in the Turkish manner from cloth of silver embroidered with little flowers in silk and lined with green satin'.[15] Turkish clothes, especially women's court dress, fascinated European travellers and had associations with the harem: this was particularly true of the largely fanciful European depictions of Roxelana, consort of Suleyman.[16]

Helman's inventory tells us about the status of Turkish artefacts as curiosities – in fact his collection has the flavour of a Wunderkammer in that it contained a cabinet 'with Turkish and Indian things in it' and 'a rhinoceros horn'.[17] What the inventory does not tell us is how the collection was arranged. As no chests are mentioned, the objects were probably on fixed shelves which would not have been listed in an inventory of movables. Helman would have been interested in making a dramatic impact on anyone to whom he showed his collection. Perhaps he could take the occasional visitor or business partner up from his office to his study. This was his showpiece: an advertisement for his own activities and success as one of Venice's leading Turkey merchants, not only in the Levant, but in his dealings in the East Indies and Persia. It had a representative function.

The demands made by doctors of medicine on their studies were very different.[18] They needed a consulting-room in which to receive patients, where they could also prepare and prescribe medicines, analyse blood and urine samples, and check medical authorities in their frequently large libraries (Tura 1483; Barzizza 1444; fig. 8).[19] Books were essential tools in making and maintaining a doctor's reputation in public disputation. Books one did not own personally could be borrowed: Giovanni Chellini, Donatello's doctor and patron, lent books regularly (Chellini memoranda).[20]

The Sienese doctor Maestro Bartolo di Tura[21] had a built-in desk unit with bookshelves and writing slope (Tura 1483; fig. 8). His desk was also fitted with a rotating two-sided lectern, which made it possible to compare two texts or commentaries at once. The study had formerly contained six large bookwheels which had since been banished to the cellar: these had perhaps been in use when Bartolo taught students at the Studio in Siena. Bartolo's study also contained two bronze mortars, one 'for grinding medicines' and a smaller one 'for making pills'; a pair of balances for spices and herbs, and a number of clyster pipes, all of which were kept in a large chest. His specialised library, kept on shelves and in chests, consisted of over 120 volumes which have been analysed in detail.[22] Two Lucchese doctors, whose possessions were inventoried in 1408 and 1419, also had sizeable libraries. Nicolas Ranuccio Liena, who tended Ilaria del Caretto in her last illness,[23] had an iron bookchest in his study for loading on a packhorse or mule: a doctor's need to carry his library with him on his travels demanded specialised equipment even at this early date (Liena 1419). Ugolino de Nuzio had a leather trunk for transporting books (Nuzio 1408). These were perhaps the precursors of the travelling libraries of late sixteenth-century Italy and early seventeenth-century England, like that of Sir Julius Caesar in the British Library.[24]

A later example of a doctor's consulting-room, library and office is the study in the house of a Jewish doctor, Vital Alatino of Ferrara, in his house in the Ghetto Nuovo in

53 Fine glass-footed dish decorated with gilding and enamelled with the arms of the Colombini family of Siena. Venetian (Murano), *c*.1500. London, British Museum, Department of Medieval and Later Antiquities.

Venice (Alatino 1620). He had a library of 325 Hebrew books and a small chest of surgical instruments[25] which were the only objects in what appears to have been his surgery. Without a special papal licence he could have treated only Jewish patients: recently published documents recount the process by which one Jewish doctor, David de Pomis, acquired a licence enabling him to visit and treat Christian patients.[26]

A doctor's study could serve and represent not only professional, but also social and civic status. Bartolo da Tura's study contained many luxury items, not least two Venetian dishes made of gilded *cristallo* glass (fig. 53) and other high-status glassware such as a salt, a covered cup and goblet; the status of 'a man's straw hat, large, old', which was also kept in the study, is harder to judge.[27] Kept with the glassware, arms and armour and armorial plate, it was not likely to have been a mundane object. It could have been a fine straw, even a courtly accessory, like the one sported by St George in Pisanello's famous *Virgin and Child with Sts George and Antony Abbot*.[28] St George wears his with his armour and furs, giving an impression of the way in which Bartolo, with his evident social pretensions, might have worn his own hat.

Bartolo's study contained three pieces of plate bearing his arms. The latter included a parcel-gilt basin, a silver jug with gilt rim and an embossed silver cup with his arms and those of the Medici at the centre.[29] Since the heraldic tinctures of the Medici *palle* are described, they were probably enamelled on a central roundel. Bartolo had often been sent out as public orator on behalf of the Sienese *commune*, and this would have required him to make a ceremonial, formal entry.[30] As a result he would have acquired various trappings of office to take with him. These are duly listed in his study: a helmet lined with crimson velvet bearing his arms; a short sword and dagger; a standard of crimson taffeta embroidered with his arms in gold, and another of taffeta with his crest and others painted on it.

The preacher Fra Bernardino of Siena, who was always quick to pounce on the snobbery and pretensions of his fellow Sienese in his sermons, mentions both arms and official trappings with heavy irony:

And you, who are in your way to take up office, you carry the standard, which is your sign. [. . .] It is a sign that this man is good and is taking up office, and such a man ought to be good in word, heart and deed. And these nobleman's arms, what do they signify? That this man is noble in his speech, in his heart, and in his actions – and if he is otherwise, those arms are not rightly his.[31]

Bartolo showed a proper Tuscan pride in preserving trappings of office in his study. His son Bandino considered the account books recording his two periods of office in the Sienese Treasury important enough to be preserved for safe-keeping in a nearby monastery (Tura 1483),[32] while another Sienese, who had served as a customs official for the city government, kept the measuring rods used for his official duties as a customs' official (*Uno paio di canne da misurare botti*) and the relevant account books in his study almost as if they were a kind of trophy (Fece 1450).[33]

While Bartolo's room served as study, consulting-room, library and family treasury, it may well also have been used for teaching students from the Sienese Studio. Another example of such a use is provided in the inventory of 1503 of Giovanni Calpurnio, who taught rhetoric – alternating with his rival Raphael Regius – at Padua University.[34] Calpurnio lived in two rooms: a bedchamber (*eius camera in qua iacebat in lecto*) and an adjoining room which served as a study. Both rooms contained chests overflowing with books. The study contained nothing but bookchests, a few clothes and bedlinen, also shoved into chests. Perhaps the sheer number of his books caused them to overflow into his bedchamber. His executors included a friend who was also a Venetian bookseller;[35] they recounted their actions in bending down to open each chest and list every book, which must have been back-breaking work. As with many devoted scholars, Calpurnio's two rooms – which may have been rented, or part of a friend's house – have the character of an academic bedsit of the kind depicted in contemporary portrayals of St Jerome. Like other teachers, he may well have taught in his lodgings, surrounded by the texts he needed for his work.[36] Juan Ludovicus Vives described in an early work a meeting of Spanish students in Paris who discussed theological matters in the lodgings of their teacher.[37]

A very different scholarly study to Calpurnio's is that described in an inventory of books and objects in the study and bedchamber of Frate Franceschino da Cesena, second librarian of the Malatesta Library in Cesena (Frate Franceschino da Cesena 1489). Given that he was a friar, the collection is unlikely to have been perceived as a personal one, even if he had had a considerable role in creating or adding to it. Perhaps this was a collection formed as an adjunct to the convent library and an aid to the study of texts by the friars, who, from the fourteenth century, had had a Studium annexed to their convent.[38] When their library was incorporated into the Malatestiana, it took on the character of a civic collection. The friars had appealed to Malatesta Novello, ruler of Cesena, to develop their existing library, and build a proper library room, in 1447. The reading room was begun in that year and opened in 1452; Malatesta Novello also presented books, established a book grant, and paid the salaries of the *lector* and of the keeper of the collection. For this role, his personal chaplain and scribe, Francesco da Figline, was selected.[39] After Malatesta Novello's death in 1464, the library lost its patron and went through many vicissitudes until, in 1484, a new librarian was selected: Frate Franceschino da Marco da Cesena.[40] He was prior of the convent and taught theology in the Studium there. He is referred to in the inventory consulted here as 'Frate Franceschino', the name by which he was probably known to his fellow friars at San Francesco. As yet, little is known about him, since references to his activities are scarce: a rare mention records his paying Taddeo Crivelli in 1452 for *all'antica* illuminations on a manuscript made for Malatesta Novello.[41] The inventory lists a remarkable antiquarian collection, including fragments of ancient marble sculpture, such as a relief possibly depicting Hercules and the Nemean Lion or a lion hunt,

54 An enamelled terracotta bust of the young St John the Baptist, possibly similar to the unidentified bust in the study of Frate Franceschino da Cesena in 1489. Tuscan, *c*.1500. Oxford, Ashmolean Museum.

such as is frequently portrayed on Roman sarcophagi; serpentine capitals and columns; and a fragment of a Latin inscription.[42] It also lists curiosities: a tortoiseshell, an ostrich egg, a bear's head, and a pig's head displayed as if it were to be presented at a banquet.[43] Contemporary art objects were also kept in the room, including unusual sculptural ceramics. A likely Tuscan product was a half figure of a man in enamelled terracotta (fig. 54). There were also two sculptural ceramic inkstands. Medals of famous contemporaries included Niccolo Fiorentino's of Lorenzo de' Medici and Sperandio's of Camilla d'Aragona, wife of Costanzo Sforza, Lord of Pesaro, with an unidentified medal of Polidore Vergil.[44] Frate Franceschino had also gathered together casts of seals and little reliefs – the latter referred to as such, or as *piastre* or *quadrettini* – which would now be categorised as plaquettes. Occasionally a subject is given for one of these, which enables a tentative identification to be made. One, depicting St George in lead, is likely to have been a well-known plaquette by or in the style of Gianfrancesco Enzola, who was active in Parma, Ferrara and Pesaro in the last quarter of the fifteenth century, the latter in the service of the Sforzas.[45] The plaquette is attributed to him on the basis of comparison with the reverse of a medal by Enzola of Costanzo Sforza himself.[46] If this identification is correct, then the reference is extremely early and therefore valuable in the study of a relatively unknown branch of Renaissance sculpture. Most tantalising of all is the reference in this inventory to the use of paternosters to decorate rooms in combination with other art objects and furnishings. Frate Franceschino's study is described as having strings of paternosters threaded with casts of coins or medals coloured white and red, looped along the top of wall panels around the room, reaching from corner to corner.[47] Accompanied by a large number of books (presumably borrowed from the library) and by his own portrait on panel, the collection was clearly considered by the assessors as an integral part of the Malatestiana, and not merely the creation of its librarian.[48] Whatever the status of the study within the Malatestiana complex, the inventory of 1489 is invaluable as the only indication yet found in the research for this book of a scholarly friar's study-room. Perhaps it was not as exceptional a phenomenon as it would appear, however. When Richard Symonds visited Padua in the late 1640s, he was shown the bedchamber and study of a certain Augustinian friar, 'Padre Quaglino', at the Eremitani, which contained Venetian pictures and a painted panel from a fifteenth-century dowry chest ('Part of a chest guilt in which it was formerly the custome to putt in all the Dowrie of the young bride said this father Quagli').[49]

The study of Bartolomeo Bianchini of Bologna is a much more select and rarefied collection, suitable for that of one of the city's leading humanists (Bianchini 1510). The son of a silk merchant, Bianchini studied under Beroaldus and Codro Urceo, writing the latter's biography in 1502.[50] He was also a friend of the learned Matteo Bosso of Verona, who described the qualities both of Bianchini the man, and of his collection, in a letter of 1497.[51] Bosso, like Codro, was impressed by Bianchini's knowledge of the art of painting and by his critical discernment: it was for this, and for his close friendship with the goldsmith and painter Francesco Francia that Bianchini was principally admired. The paintings by Francia in his study testify to this close relationship, and include the superb portrait of Bianchini (fig. 55), a fine Crucifixion (the municipal collections, Bologna), and a Holy Family (fig. 56).[52] Beyond his interest in contemporary art (which extended to medals, of which he had eighteen) he was also famous for his numismatic collection. Bosso mentions the 'gold and silver coins' in his house, and the inventory of his study lists 138 silver and 8 gold coins. The fact that there were no bronze examples, and no lead casts, points to the quality of Bianchini's collection, and this in a city famous for its ancient coin collections. There were, however, what must have been contemporary medals (on the grounds of their size): 'seventeen medals, large, in lead'. Perhaps these too were portraits by (or of) friends and contemporaries. The inventory of the contents of Bianchini's study gives a fascinating insight into the little-known (and hence undervalued) world of Bolognese humanism (Bianchini 1510).[53]

A later inventory recording the library and collection of Annibale Caro, poet, translator of the classics and artistic adviser to Cardinal Alessandro Farnese, reveals his study in such detail that it appears as an extension of his intellect (Caro 1578). Well known for his inability to provide an iconographic programme without consulting his books, Caro had created a working library of remarkable comprehensiveness.[54] Listed individually here are his manuscript papers – handbooks on ancient coins (for which he had developed his own ideas about classification and study), translations from the classics, letters and study notes (*scartafacci*).[55] His large collection of ancient coins, kept in four large boxes, is listed in a separate inventory dated a day before the rest, as the property of Lepido Caro. The descriptions are precise enough to enable many of them to be identified. Not only the letters, but also the works of art document his professional activities and his friendships in the world of artists and collectors, such as a miniature by Clovio (for whom Caro helped to secure a key commission) and a bronze portrait bust of his friend Michelangelo.[56] The fact that Caro's brothers preserved such a personal study collection and library for twelve years after his death, as recorded in the inventory, shows their regard for him. This respect also prompted their commissioning of a posthumous bronze portrait bust by Calcagni to stand in the hall of their house. The bust was made from a painted portrait, probably that listed among the contents of the study.

Writers of treatises on architecture and other subjects in the fifteenth century gave recommendations as to who needed a study and where it should be situated in the house. In his second treatise, Francesco di Giorgio discusses the artisan's and merchant's need for an office, and the scholar's need for a study. Each of these rooms should be separated from the rest of the household so that the occupant could enter freely and work without being disturbed. This was a standard prescription in contemporary treatises, as we have already seen. He considered the artist's or artisan's need for a workshop under the house, 'and a

55 (*facing page*) Francesco Francia, portrait of the Bolognese collector and scholar Bartolomeo Bianchini, oil on panel. Possibly the portrait listed in the post-mortem inventory of Bianchini's study in 1510. London, National Gallery.

room for doing accounts and writing nearby'. Failing that, 'there should at least be a little room [*stanzietta*] where the craftsman can work at his trade' at home.[57] Perhaps Francesco di Giorgio, like Alberti in his architectural treatise, was giving idealised and formal expression to existing practice, since it is clear from the evidence of inventories and other sources that many artists worked at home, as well as in a workshop elsewhere.[58] Mantegna is known, for example, to have painted the *Madonna of Victory* at home, for he describes in a letter to Isabella d'Este how the painting was taken in procession from the house.[59] Filippino Lippi's study, inventoried in 1504, contained one of his own unfinished devotional paintings, drawings, papers and accounts, lead medals or coins in a box and a porcelain vase, intermingling his own works with a study collection (Lippi 1504). A list of things stolen from Sodoma's study by one of his pupils in 1529 seems to indicate that this was a room in which the painter both worked and displayed his collection of antiquities and casts (Sodoma 1529). It contained not only an unfinished painting, drawings, prepared pigments in boxes and a mortar for grinding them, but also an interesting collection of antiquities incorporating local finds, such as Etruscan terracotta plaques and a bronze figure of Apollo – an accumulation which suggests something more than the usual artist's working collection.[60] Benvenuto Cellini certainly worked at home: he describes in his autobiography how he was working on a model of the fountain in the Piazza della Signoria in Florence when Francesco de' Medici called on him unexpectedly. 'I showed him two little models of different design', Cellini proudly added. He seems to have moved small commissions back and forth between his house and workshop.[61] His domestic working space was probably in the *anticamera* of his house, since this is where he kept his goldsmith's punches in a small olive-wood cabinet, and a plan chest containing his drawings.[62]

On a more elevated level, Mantegna's study, adjoining his painting room, is an excellent illustration of the scholar-artist's dignified sense of self. Similarly Pomponius Gauricus, keen to establish his humanist credentials, describes in his treatise on sculpture how he was visited at home by Raphael Regius, Professor of Rhetoric at Padua University. They talked in Gauricus's domestic working-room (*domestica officina*), where there were bronze and marble figures which soon prompted them to discuss the nature of sculpture. Gauricus uses a modest phrase to describe the sculptures which set off the debate, shrugging them off with the words 'nescio quas effigies', which implies that they were his own work and not pieces from his collection.[63]

Artists might also construct a study as a room to contain a collection, and show off their own works. Mantegna's has already been mentioned, and can still be seen in his house in Mantua. Very different is the artist's study – in the sense of a collection – described in the will of Alessandro Vittoria. Vittoria lists (presumably in his own words) the contents of the bedchamber adjoining his study with some care, reflecting a degree of selfconsciousness in the selection and arrangement of works in the room which must relate to his sense of his own status as a Venetian artist. He starts by listing paintings by contemporary Venetians, then reliefs made by himself. Finally, the room contained a collection of portraits of Venetian artists of his own time, starting with himself:

> Two large portraits and three small ones of the aforesaid Signore Alessandro, portrayed at different ages, and painted by different hands/ the portrait of Titian, most excellent painter, by the hand of Veronese/ The portrait of Maestro Paolo Caliari Veronese, by the hand of his son/ The portrait of Signor Giacomo Palma, by his own hand, small/ The portrait of Maestro Alessandro Maganza, painter from Vicenza, by his own hand./ A portrait of Tintoretto, small, as a young man.[64]

Vittoria's portrait collection clearly established his own credentials among the artists of

56 Francesco Francia, *Holy Family*, oil on poplar wood. Another painting that may have been in Bianchini's study, and was certainly commissioned by him from Francia, as recorded in a Latin inscription on the pedestal at left (barely visible here) which translates: 'painted at the expense of Bartolomeo Bianchini, the greatest of mothers is brought to life here through your hands, O Francia'. Berlin, Staatliche Museen zu Berlin, Preussischer Kulturbesitz, Gemäldegalerie.

his adopted city, where he had been the dominant sculptor after the death of Jacopo Sansovino.

Both fifteenth- and sixteenth-century writers advocated a degree of secrecy for the study within the household. The classic formulation is Alberti's, in the third book of his treatise *Della famiglia*. Modelled on Xenophon's treatise on household management, *Oeconomia*, which had recently been rediscovered in Florence, Alberti's book of 1427 both shaped and served the interests of the Florentine élite.[65] Whereas Xenophon, in prescribing a wife's role in the household, concentrates on the necessity of good order, the careful categorisation of property, and the segregation of men's and women's quarters, Alberti focuses on the shared valuables (*masserizie*) in the marital bedchamber (*camera*).[66] His emphasis on the private world of the household, and on the sense of lineage and patrimony which lies at its heart, gives the study a vital role. One of the speakers in Alberti's dialogue, Gianozzo, comments:

> It pleased me to keep only my books and papers, and those of my ancestors, shut up then and for always in such a way that the woman should never see them, let alone read them. I never kept my papers in the sleeves of my clothes, but always locked up in their allocated place in my study, almost as if they were sacred and religious things. I never gave my wife permission to enter my study either with me or alone, and furthermore I commanded her that if she ever came across any paper of mine, she should hand it over to me immediately.[67]

The resonance of Alberti's prohibition is clear – that no man should let his wife enter his study – as part of a wider limitation on a wife, that she should not aspire to know about her husband's (or indeed current) affairs.[68] Moreover, debarring a woman from knowledge of family papers ('my [. . .] papers, and those of my ancestors') also denied her a part in the building and maintenance of that sense of family dignity, status and memory which was thought to reside in them.[69]

Women very rarely owned studies – a fact which has much to do with the perceived dignity of women, their education and the problematic status of learned women.[70] When a woman did in fact own a study, this was unlikely to be recorded in an inventory listing the movable property of her husband: inventories therefore have little to tell us about this phenomenon.[71] This is just one example of the difficulties of documenting women's experience. Letters, whether written by women themselves or by their male correspondents or relations, provide a few tantalising references. The earliest of these appears in a letter written in 1466 by the recently married Ippolita Sforza to her mother, Bianca Maria Sforza, requesting portraits of her family with which to decorate her study. The letter fairly breathes with homesickness:

> My *studio* for reading and writing in occasionally having been completed, I pray Your Illustrious Highness, as I have written on other occasions, if it would please you to have made for me portraits from life of His Excellency my father and of Yourself, and of all my Illustrious brothers and sisters, for beyond the adornment of my *studio*, looking on them would give me continual consolation and pleasure.[72]

Why would Ippolita wish to construct a study? Her Milanese upbringing provides important clues. Her mother, Bianca Maria Visconti, was renowned as a learned and capable woman, while her father, Francesco Sforza, was a *condottiere* who (contrary to the general pattern) had successfully retained a duchy and founded a dynasty.[73] His cultural policy for Milan, which was an integral part of his success as a ruler, included giving his children an excellent education in Greek and Latin, and Ippolita learnt alongside her brothers.[74] Such were her abilities that she represented her family in addressing a Latin oration to the learned Pope Pius II when she was only fourteen.[75] Betrothed to Alfonso, Duke of Calabria (later King of Naples), at an early age, she was married in 1465.[76] Her study in the Castel Capuano in Naples was therefore one of her first projects on her marriage. She took manuscripts with her to Naples, which included a Virgil illuminated by a Milanese artist who, on account of his work for her, has become known as 'the Master of Ippolita Sforza'. Her portrait appears, with the Phoenix, in an initial P, along with Sforza–Visconti devices, her name and the date on the first folio.[77]

Where did the idea to create a study come from? Her father, Francesco, may have provided a model, since he is known to have created a room in the early 1460s which may have been based on Piero de' Medici's study in Florence.[78] He would surely have been helped by his court architect from 1451 to 1465, Filarete, who had visited Piero's study and gave a good account of it in his treatise of 1465, which was dedicated to Piero.[79] Other elements in her Sforza background were not so promising. Her brother Galeazzo Maria, who received a humanist education similar to Ippolita's, showed no wish to construct a study for himself as part of his ambitious remodelling of the Castello di Porta Giovia in Milan, even though he is known to have seen Piero de'Medici's famous study on a visit to Florence in 1459.[80]

Evelyn Welch has recently suggested that the initiative to create a study was Ippolita's own, and that it should be seen as part of 'her determination to expand beyond the expected forms of female behaviour'.[81] A statement made by Ippolita's secretary and former tutor, Baldo Martorelli, who had travelled with her from Milan to Naples, bears this out:

> At the moment her ladyship is finishing a beautiful study and she has announced that she wishes to study. And she begs Your Illustrious Ladyship [Bianca Maria Visconti] to aid her in adorning it and to send her portraits painted on panels of yourself and her father and all her brothers and her sister. And though I too delight in medals and pictures I swear [. . .] that it was not done at my suggestion – neither the study nor the books nor the pictures. But because of this, I have taken an even greater pleasure in it and already she has announced her intentions to ask for these portraits to her husband the duke and to all these gentlemen and to the count of Maddaloni [Diomede Carafa]; therefore I beg your Ladyship to reply with good effect.[82]

It could have been on the prompting of Martorelli (her adviser and intermediary) that, following her brother's example, she had visited the Medici palace, as recorded in a letter from Piero de' Medici to the banker Filippo Strozzi in Naples, dated 20 July 1465.[83]

Perhaps the impetus to create both a study and a well-stocked library had its darker side, in Ippolita's sense of rivalry with her husband. As a man very much in the Medici orbit, he was also a leading patron of Tuscan artists and knew of the latest artistic developments in Florence.[84] In the early 1440s he had commissioned Agostino di Duccio (who had worked in the workshop of Luca della Robbia) to make the tomb of his brother, a work likely to have incorporated enamelled terracotta decoration of the same technique as the roundels in Piero de'Medici's study.[85] Alfonso's friend Diomede Carafa, Count of Maddaloni, was also closely connected to the Medici and their followers, being godfather to Filippo Strozzi's son. He was to write in 1468 to Piero asking for drawings of the ceiling of the latter's study, and was to create a painted version of his own in Naples.[86] The nature of Neapolitan contacts with Florence suggests that Ippolita, with the help of her secretary, and with the mediation of Filippo Strozzi, created a study on the model of Piero de' Medici's, which was to encourage Diomede Carafa to do the same three years later.

Much has been made of Isabella d'Este's two successive studies, in terms of the sheer tenacity, wilfulness and acquisitiveness with which she designed and decorated her Grotta and Studiolo in the Castello di San Giorgio and the Corte Vecchia in Mantua from the last years of the fifteenth century.[87] Isabella's determination and drive were unique, though she owed much to the example and influence of her mother, Eleonora d'Aragona. Eleonora, daughter of King Ferrando of Naples, had created two studies in Ferrara in the 1480s and 1490s, one in her apartment in the Castel Vecchio (which must have been designed for books since it contained wooden bookshelves) and another in her garden apartment, in which the young Isabella is known to have played.[88] Isabella drew upon her mother's inheritance not just in creating a study of her own, but in the inscription which she had placed around the courtyard of the Secret Garden adjoining it, in which she proclaimed herself to be the granddaughter of a king (Ferrando of Naples, through her mother), daughter of a duke and wife of a marquis.[89] The placing of the inscription again emphasises the connection of studies with status.

Less well known is the study of another Mantuan, the mother of Baldassare da Castiglione, Aloysia Gonzaga Castiglione. She was a cultivated, highly literate woman, to whom her son addressed many letters and one of ten presentation copies of his book *Il cortegiano*, in which the well-read and articulate woman courtier plays an important role.[90] It was to her that her anxious son sent his antiquities for safe-keeping in the hope that she would effectively hide them in her study during his absence from Mantua. He wrote:

> Since I am desired by the court here to send this muleteer to Mantua, I have given him some of my possessions, so as to be less burdened with luggage when I return home. I am exceedingly anxious to know if they arrive safely, and beg Your Ladyship to write the moment they reach you. Please have the case opened at once and the contents placed where they will not be blackened by smoke or seen by anyone. A good place would be Your Ladyship's little study.[91]

The sense of security which his mother's study offered echoes the reference in *Il cortegiano* to Elisabetta Gonzaga's withdrawal, after the lively debate on the status of women, into her 'innermost secret chamber' at the end of Book III: a private room in her apartment into which no one could follow her except by invitation.

Much greater freedom than that which could be claimed by any courtier was sought by those Renaissance courtesans who modelled themselves on the *haeterae* of classical antiquity. Several of the leading courtesans, such as Veronica Franco and Tullia Aragona, were adept at profiting from the expansion of the world of learning through cheaper print and the new status of the Italian vernacular as a dignified language.[92] Women without a classical education could now publish not only their letters, as Latin-educated noblewomen had done in the fifteenth century, but works in poetry and prose. Perhaps the best definition of the pleasures and rewards of literary work appears in Louise Labé's preface, addressed to another learned woman, to one of her poetic dialogues. She was brought up by an indulgent father in the Italian tradition in Lyons, and her cultural formation was arguably as much Italian as French.[93] In her preface, she writes:

> For if there is anything to be praised after fame and honour, the pleasures granted by the study of letters must have its claim on each one of us; for this is a different class of thing from other recreations; for when one has partaken of one's fill of those, one can boast simply of having passed the time. But the practice of study leaves a contentment within oneself, which is longer lasting: for the past is a joy to us, and of greater service than the present; in contrast, the pleasures of the heart are quickly dissipated, never to return, and indeed the memory of them is often as disagreeable as the acts were once delicious. Moreover those other pleasures are of such a nature that no matter what the remembrance which we hold, they can never render us that state in which we once were: and however powerful the image of them which we imprinted on our mind, we know only too well that this is nothing but a shadow of the past which abuses and betrays us. But when it so happens that we should record our thoughts in writing, however much our brain should in aftertimes be incessantly shaken and coursed through by an infinity of troubles, it is nevertheless the case that, taking up our writings, even long afterwards, we return to the same point, and to the same state of mind in which we once were. In this way, we may redouble our content, for we once more find past pleasures, whether they lie in the subject-matter of which we wrote, or in the understanding of the knowledge which we brought to our writings. And beyond this, the judgement which leads us from first principles to further conclusions renders us singular contentment.[94]

It is hard to believe that Louise Labé, no less than her Italian counterparts such as Veronica Franco, did not have a study or something like it in a corner of her bedchamber as a space in which to write.

There is fortunately at least one example of a courtesan's inventory which records a study. Julia Lombardo, a well-known courtesan of Venice, set herself up in style in what she herself called 'a very comfortable house'. From the list of objects in the study it is clear that Julia wished to present herself to her protectors and clients as a cultivated and discriminating woman. Her bronze figurine, possibly that of Cupid or of Apollo,[95] was perfectly appropriate for a courtesan's study. Her inventory (Lombardo 1569) is valuable as a record of one courtesan's cultural pretensions and sense of herself, as expressed through her possessions: 'a portrait through property'.[96]

★   ★   ★

Later in the sixteenth century, Luc'Antonio Ridolfi's *Aretefila* suggests how a gentle-woman with a taste for learning and philosophy in particular might own a study: this example is based on a real woman (see chapter 5). Yet Ridolfi's dialogue, which opens with Aretefila's almost wordless yet courtly reception of her visitors and their gentle attempts to tempt her into speech, establishes the way in which a woman's modesty was thought to be linked to her silence, especially in the presence of men, and hence to her chastity. Chastity was the ultimate feminine virtue and perhaps the only one which a woman could truly and completely attain.[97] The custom of praising an intelligent or well-read woman for her chastity rather than for her wit or learning was established before the Renaissance: a poem and letter from Antonio Loschi to Maddalena Scrovegni, written in 1389, defines the type very clearly. Loschi pictures Maddalena seated not in her study (in which, it is implied, he had seen her in her father's house) but in a glorified temple of Chastity, constructed around his image of her as the personification of that Virtue.[98]

The freedom to read and study was questionable, since a woman alone – and therefore in some measure outside society – was suspect and sometimes feared.[99] The mediation of parents (such as Isotta Nogarola's mother; the parents of a young woman in one of Erasmus's dialogues; or the enlightened husband in Erasmus's colloquy *The Abbot and the Learned Lady*) was always deemed important in preserving the honour not only of an individual woman, but also of her family.[100] If as young girls they had been educated and supported by their fathers or brothers, as were Alessandra Scala and Moderata Fonte, there was not much room for learned women outside their parental home.[101] Few learned women continued their literary studies after marriage; exceptions were Laura Cerreta (who studied at night when domestic responsibilities were less pressing) and Moderata da Pozzo (before her early death in childbirth).[102] For this reason, the decision whether or not to marry could loom large. When Alessandra Scala (1475–1506) debated the question, she approached another learned lady, Cassandra Fedele (1465–1558) for advice. In her reply, Fedele wrote enigmatically:

> and so, my Alessandra, you are of two minds, whether you should give yourself to the Muses or to a man. In this matter, I think you must choose that to which nature more inclines you.[103]

One of four daughters of the Florentine Chancellor Bartolomeo Scala, Alessandra had been educated at home by a private tutor. She was later taught by the humanist Angelo Poliziano, and was admired for her knowledge of Greek.[104] She decided to marry, but, on the early death of her husband, entered a convent and died not long after without fulfilling her early promise.

The story of Alessandra Scala provides the context for the 'book-lined cell' (*cella libraria*)

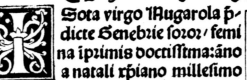

of Isotta Nogarola, which barely qualifies as a study in the same sense as others mentioned here (fig. 57). She retreated to her mother's house, in the same way as late Roman female ascetics had done.[105] Her room exemplifies her feminine role as a mystic and contemplative, hence the use of the word *cella* to describe it.[106] Again, the fact that a word with such inescapable associations with spiritual retreat was used for her study-room shows the ambivalence with which learned women were often regarded by contemporaries.[107]

The developing association of the Virgin with books in late medieval iconography coincided with the rising number of book-owners among lay women (fig. 58). Aristocratic women are known to have had their own libraries, in the sense of an assemblage of books, if not a space in which to house them. Eleonora d'Este's books are for example listed in a larger inventory of Este books, while Margaret of Austria (1480–1530) had 'a well-stocked library for women' in her palace at Mechelen.[108] Like the *libri da donna* ('women's books') listed in household inventories of members of the urban élites, these tended to be devotional works or directed at women in some other way.[109]

Paintings and other visual representations of women reading or studying show why a study (in the sense in which it is considered in this book) was deemed unsuitable for a woman. The Virgin Mary, at the moment of the Annunciation, is often shown with an open book beside or in front of her, but she is rarely shown to be reading, but rather mentally rehearsing her prayers. A text, if shown, serves as a prompt or aid to prayer, pointing the viewer towards meditation on the theme of the Incarnation. Hence these texts are usually taken from the Book of Wisdom or Isaiah's prophecy of the Incarnation, or the salutation made to the Virgin by the Archangel Gabriel. Mary often has a lectern such as the ones depicted in the studies of male scholars and saints, but the context is very different: the lectern is often set up in her bedchamber, at the foot of her bed or in close visual relation to it, rather than in a separate book-lined room.[110] This fits in with the devotional literature, in which the *camera* is the centre of a woman's domestic space – a room in which to seclude herself, an inner sanctum. A prayerbook written for young girls in 1454 and later printed in Venice connects the role of the bedchamber in religious meditation with the theme of Christ's Passion, in which the characters are based on people known to one, and the places situated in a known city. Once these identifications have been made in the imagination, the reader is advised to:

go into your chamber. Alone and solitary, excluding every external thought from your mind, start thinking of the beginning of the Passion, starting with how Jesus entered Jerusalem on the ass. Moving slowly from episode to episode, meditate on each one, dwelling on each single stage and step of the story. And if at any point you feel a sensation of piety, stop: do not pass on as long as that sweet and devout sentiment lasts.[111]

Showing the Annunciation set in an elegant young woman's bedchamber was part of this process of training the visual imagination in the service of devotional meditation. In this connection, women are very rarely depicted in a study as such. A rare exception is a woodcut in Jacopo Foresti's *De Plurimis claris sceletisque mulieribus* (Ferrara 1497), a book on female *exemplae*; it is used twice in the book, once to represent Isotta da Nogarola. A Northern European equivalent is a stained-glass panel in King's College, Cambridge, showing St Barbara writing to Origen from her carefully delineated study.[112]

Nor are women shown reading with any frequency. Pinturicchio's fresco showing the young Virgin Mary reading in a room akin to a study, attended by angels, is exceptional for the impression of concentration and intellectual seriousness with which the young girl is endowed. It exemplifies the way in which a young woman of liberal family might be free to study (fig. 58). It is otherwise unusual even for a woman to be shown with a book other than as an attribute for a female saint, a missal for a laywoman, or in a scene of the presentation of a manuscript or book to a female patron. Rare in a secular context is a much-damaged marble roundel (fig. 59) showing a young woman holding out a book in one hand. She has been tentatively interpreted as a sybil: the interpretation points up the rarity of this kind of iconography for women and the allegorical significance which is thereby given to this sculpture.

Perhaps wives were invited into the study of a male relative on occasion, whether formally or informally. Laura Mantegna's presence in her father's study was surely explained because this was a family treasury, office and archive, and therefore a suitable place in which to sign documents concerning a daughter's marriage and dowry.[113] A rare

59 Marble relief roundel with a young woman holding out a book, Urbino, *c*.1475. Unfortunately damaged before its acquisition by Berlin and again in the Second World War, this delicate relief has conventionally been interpreted as representing a sibyl. The inscription in the book is legible as NESCIO QVIBUS. VERBIS. QVO. Berlin, Staatliche Museen zu Berlin, Preussischer Kulturbesitz, Skulpturensammlung.

northern European reference to a woman being informally invited by her husband into his study appears in a letter of Sir Edward Dering (1598–1644), written in his retirement on his Kent estate just before the outbreak of the English Civil War. The Derings' marriage was particularly affectionate, as Sir Edward's letters to his wife show: their relationship might be taken as an example of the idea of 'companionate marriage' which Stone and others have seen as a new development of post-Reformation society.[114] Writing in 1642, Dering mentions how 'my wife at chosen times came into my studie, and made my stollen commons a feast with her society, while my servants thought me far from home'.[115]

Even in a Protestant culture, in which the cultivation of private conscience might prompt women towards reflection and study, women seemed rarely to have owned studies, though they often created closets as small, intimate rooms.[116] Judging by the titles of books addressed to women, closets were spaces for housewives[117] or for housewifely tasks. When Hamlet bursts into Ophelia's closet, she is sewing quietly there.[118] Inventories recording the contents of a woman's closet tend to list distilling and preserving jars, or devotional works.[119] Lady Margaret Hoby records withdrawal 'to my Closit, wher I praied and writt som thinge for my owne private Conscience', as a contrasting room to her more public bedchamber.[120] Even when a woman's closet was used for study, it was still distinct in character and status, sometimes even in name, from a man's. John Evelyn, lamenting the death of his much-loved studious daughter, Mary, describes in his diary how:

> Nothing was so delightful to her as to go into my Study, where she would willingly have spent whole days, for as I have said she had read an abundance of history, and all the best poets, even Terence, Plautus, Homer, Virgil, Horace, Ovid; all the best romances and modern poems.[121]

His own study, dignified by its initial capital letter, was rather different from her closet, which he describes looking into after her death:

> On looking into her Closset, it is incredible what a number of papers and Collections she had made of severall material Authors, both Historians, Poets, Travells &c., but above all the Devotions, Contemplations, and resolutions upon those Contemplations, which we found under her hand in a book most methodicaly disposed, & much exceeding the talent & usage of young & beautifull women, who consume so much of their time in vaine things.[122]

From this one gathers that a closet could be the property of a man or a woman, while a study was still a masculine preserve, even a misogynistic one, judging by an early seventeenth-century epigram:

> If in his study he hath so much care
> To hang all old dry things, then let his wife beware.[123]

5   *The Collector's Study*

Design and Organisation

WEALTHY COLLECTORS CONSTRUCTED custom-built studies on the latest architectural principles, calling in artists and architects to advise on the design. Given that the interior design of a study – and this seems to have included listings or at least placings of key collectables within the room – was considered to be of such significance, it is not surprising that, at least from the mid-sixteenth century, collectors were exchanging information in the form of *modelli*: drawings or plans. Hence Marco Mantova Benavides, whose famous collection in Padua was well established by mid-century, sent the Venetian collector Andrea Loredan 'a model of the study' on request in 1553.[1] Models of this kind were to become the norm in communicating the latest ideas about studies. Hence when Giovanni Grimani, Patriarch of Aquileia, was having a study constructed in his Roman-style palace at Santa Maria Formosa in Venice from 1568, the room was such a famous project among collectors throughout Europe that it was being talked about even while it was being planned. When Nicolo Stoppio wrote in 1568 to Duke Albrecht V of Bavaria, who was planning a similar gallery space in Munich, he enclosed a sketch of the Grimani study, adding that 'the first architects in Italy' were being consulted in its design.[2] The room was a triumph of planning in the most advanced contemporary taste: a highly organised architectural space designed to hold the bulk of the family collection of two hundred ancient statues and fragments, 'all of them select and of great value', as Francesco Sansovino put it.[3] It is no surprise to learn that the French King Henry III spent a whole day in this room in 1574.[4] He probably entered the apartment in which it was apparently situated by the door in the Ramo Grimani, which gave entrance to the suite of rooms leading to the study, specially built for the use of visitors. Three of the antique busts are still in place, above a dedicatory inscription reading 'to the glory of the city, and for the use of friends'.[5]

Similar sets of rooms to Grimani's were being planned elsewhere. Two sketches of Albrecht V of Bavaria's Antiquarium in Munich survive from 1568, as well as the Antiquarium itself with its superb series of Imperial Roman portrait busts,[6] while Pirro Ligorio's 1571 design for the library and Antiquarium of Alfonso II d'Este also survives.[7]

Apart from exchanging information about studies in the making, collectors also drew up plans of their own rooms and the way in which they had organised them for their own use, or for illustrating their manuscript catalogues. The Bolognese scholar Antonio Giganti drew a plan and elevation of one wall of his study in 1586, by which date the room had become a place of pilgrimage and point of contact for Italian and foreign visitors.[8] The elevation of one wall, named 'A' in the autograph drawing, shows a complex of shelves divided into two blocks or compartments named *caselle* in the drawing. The upper surface of the case of shelves (*sopra le scaffe*) was used to display small objects, and Giganti hung 'various things' from the beams of the ceiling above his shelves. Some objects were also fixed directly to the wall. Giganti's plan of his rooms[9] shows that he separated the books from the rest of the collection, for the room 'where the books are' was situated between the study and his bedchamber.

The Venetian collector Andrea Vendramin showed his pride in the 'extremely honourable decoration' of ancient Greek and Apulian vases in his study. The manuscript

60   Andrea Vendramin's arrangement of his vase collection in his study, using wooden wall compartments (see fig. 61). *De Sacrificiorum et Triumphorum Vasculis*, Oxford, Bodleian Library, MS d'Orville 539, fols v*v*– vi*r*.

61 Elevation of one wall of the study of the Venetian patrician and collector, Andrea Vendramin, showing his collection of vases and other antiquities displayed in box-type wooden compartments. Ink sketch from one of the manuscript catalogues of his collection, dating to 1627. *De Sacrificiorum et Triumphorum Vasculis*. Oxford, Bodleian Library, MS d'Orville 539, fols Vv–VIr.

catalogue of 1627 which details this part of his collection, *De Sacrificiorum et Triumphorum Vasculis*, is prefaced with his sketch of one wall of the room in which the vases were carefully arranged and classified in individual wooden compartments (fig. 61).[10] The catalogue reveals that Vendramin's collection contained several objects that were not ancient, but does not indicate whether Vendramin was himself aware of this. A standing cup of rock crystal is illustrated on folio 31, which, from its engraved decoration, proportions and carving technique, would seem to be a product of the famous Miseroni workshop. It can be compared with a similar vase which dates from the early seventeenth century and is attributed to Dionysio Miseroni, working in Prague (British Museum, London).[11] Significantly, this vase later belonged to Sir William Hamilton, who considered it to be ancient.[12] Vendramin's collection also contained a milk-white (*lattimo*) pilgrim flask of glass which, judging by its proportions, moulding and handles would again seem to be a Renaissance work, in this case, of around 1500 when this type of glass was highly valued.[13]

The renewed interest in the letters of Pliny the Younger from the early fifteenth century onwards stimulated awareness as to how the ancient Romans had intermingled books, paintings and busts in libraries and studies. One of the speakers in a dialogue written by Angelo Decembrio at the court of Leonello d'Este describes how

> he possessed [. . .] a large store of books but had no familiarity of this kind with pictures and statues, for he considered that they had nothing to do with learning or instruction. It was strange, he said, that someone as learned as Pliny the Younger should make so much of a Corinthian figure in his library.[14]

A second speaker in the dialogue cites Juvenal's Second Satire, in which he criticises pretenders to learning:

> Chrysippus' statue decks their library.
> Who makes his closet finest is most Read,
> The dolt who with an Aristotle's head
> Carv'd to the life, has once adorned his shelf
> Straight sets up as a Satgyrite himself.[15]

Reference is also made in Decembrio's dialogue to Juvenal's Third Satire, in which he describes how friends rush to the burning house of a rich Roman with statues 'or bronzes that had been the glory of old Asian shrines' to replace what had been lost in the fire. 'Others will offer books and bookcases or a bust of Minerva'.[16]

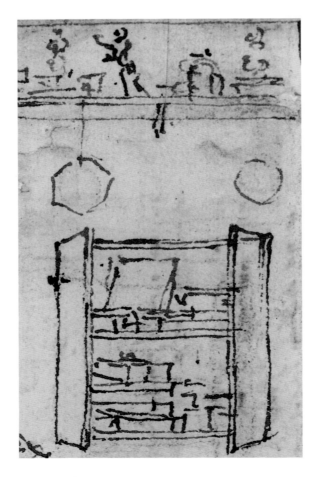

62 Detail from an ink sketch by Vittore Carpaccio of a scholar in his study (see fig. 46), showing a high shelf with ornaments – including what may well be a bronze statuette – and a bookcupboard built into the wall. Moscow, Pushkin Museum.

The aim of many Italian Renaissance scholars, whether conscious or not in following classical precedent, was to crown their bookshelves or other ledges with a bust, either an antique piece in bronze or marble or a modern version. The Venetian poet and patrician Andrea Pasqualigo had an exceptional array of five marble busts of famous men (and one woman) of antiquity in his study: Homer, Caracalla, Brutus the Younger, Socrates and Giulia Mamea (Pasqualigo 1579).[17] The busts must have had painted or carved inscriptions on their bases to enable Pasqualigo's assessors to identify them by name in the inventory of his estate. It is this precision which distinguishes Pasqualigo's busts, for other groups of sculpture mentioned in contemporary inventories may have been just as impressive, but remain mysterious, such as the 'eight large busts of black stone' in the study of another Venetian, Andrea da Brazzo (Brazzo 1587). Marbles are rarely listed in Venetian inventories, and, when they are, they are often mentioned among the contents of *portici* (*porteghi* in Venetian dialect), the open halls which characterised the Venetian *palazzo*. The fact that Pasqualigo restricted the busts in his collection to the less public ambience of his study was atypical: only three out of his eight busts were to be seen in the *portego*. His decision to keep the other five in his study was that of a collector who wished to enjoy his collections in privacy, or in the company of a few close friends or visiting scholars. The busts of Homer and Socrates surely indicate his own sense of himself as a philosopher, writer and poet. That he had something of a contemporary reputation in his own city is shown by Alberici's description of him as

> a celebrated poet, [who] was a man of very prudent and vital invention. He wrote a very beautiful treatise on Eloquence, which contains divers and various things, all beautiful and useful, concerning artificial memory.[18]

Regarding sculpture as part of the interior decoration of a room did not in any way diminish its value or dramatic impact as a work of art in the eyes of contemporaries. Cellini, who had a keen interest in presentation and dramatic effect, clearly saw the potential in placing his works among those by ancient or modern artists in the setting of a study. In his autobiography, he describes the care he took in the arrangement of the bronze figurines which he had made for the base of his Perseus in a small room in the Palazzo Vecchio, 'where I was in the habit of working'.[19] This was a characteristic Cellini boast, for the room was located in the private apartments, and had been allocated to him as a special privilege. His aim in arranging them there for viewing was to make the maximum impact on Francesco de' Medici and his sceptical consort, Eleonora, who had been understandably irritated by Cellini's persistent visits and by his passage through her private apartments. In order to impress his patrons, Cellini arranged his figures of Mercury, Minerva, Danaë and Jupiter 'in a row, somewhat raised above the line of vision, so that they produced a magnificent effect'. Eleonora was, he says, so impressed by his calculated display that she insisted: 'I do not like to let these exquisite figures be wasted on the pedestal down there on the Piazza. [. . .] I would much rather have you fix them up in one of my apartments, where they will be preserved with the respect due to their singular artistic qualities'.[20] As Pope-Hennessy has pointed out, the figures, since removed from their pedestal, are now displayed 'lower than Cellini would have liked' in the Museo Nazionale del Bargello.[21] Cellini could not, however, influence the way in which a patron displayed one of his works, once it had been purchased. He complained that Bindo Altoviti had placed his superb bronze portrait bust, one of Cellini's masterpieces, in his study:

> which was not designed for statues or for paintings, since the windows were too low, so that the light coming in from beneath spoiled the effect they would have produced under more favourable conditions.[22]

Cellini quoted a letter from Michelangelo in support of his claim:

> if those windows were above instead of beneath, the whole collection could show to better advantage, and your portrait, placed among so many masterpieces, would hold its own with great credit.[23]

Apart from being yet another example of Cellini's boasting and self-justification, the passage also indicates that much was known about showing sculpture to its best effect. Vincenzo Scamozzi praised the studies (using the word in the sense of collections) which were to be seen in Venice at the beginning of the seventeenth century, giving recommendations of his own as how best to light sculpture. Rooms designed to contain statues and reliefs should have windows facing north (*verso Tramontana*), since this provided the most constant daylight, and prevented variations and distortions in perceiving colours and relief effects.[24]

Setting off Sculpture

Sixteenth-century Italians developed other means of complementing sculpture, and showing it to advantage. A common device was to make spheres (*palle* or *balle*), which were placed on shelves and other ledges as decorative, colourful objects. *Mischio* or *mistio* was the type of *breccia* marble most often used, on account of its rich intermingled pink and red colours, which appealed to collectors and wealthy householders alike.[25] Not only did Florentines have local supplies of this marble, but the fashion for using it was led by Duke Cosimo de' Medici, as recorded by Vasari, who noted that Cosimo had commissioned door-frames and chimney-pieces in this marble for all the rooms in the new apartments of the Palazzo Vecchio, 'and the effect is most beautiful'.[26] The study in the house of the Caro family at Civitavecchia provides an example of how *mischio* spheres were used to set off independent bronzes and other artworks, ranged along the shelves (Caro 1578). On one high shelf, the fourth up from the floor on a wall of the study, were 'two *mischio* spheres on their stands' next to some antique bronzes and terracotta lamps, small vases and a spearhead; there was also a glass sphere (probably a product of Murano) imitating the effect of *mischio*, which stood on another high shelf next to a marble bust.[27] These are also listed in Florentine inventories (Bambelli 1573; Buizzi 1594; Berti 1594) and were sought after by Florentine collectors: Piero Guicciardini, for example, bought 'a Venetian glass sphere' from the merchant Giovanni Massi in 1622.[28] Venetian collectors were using spheres of coloured stone and marble in their studies from the mid-sixteenth century (Odoni 1555; Vendramin 1612; Fabbri 1616). Francesco Cornaro set off stucco reliefs of the Twelve Caesars with six black spheres in his study (Cornaro 1597),[29] while Lodovico Usper displayed a marble portrait bust of himself on a chimney-breast with three marble spheres in his palace at San Stae (Usper 1601).[30] Information from inventories is complemented by literary accounts of collections. Rafaello Borghini described 'the spheres of fine stones of various kinds which are placed on a shelf inlaid with *lavoro d'intarsia* and set with gold' in the study of Matteo Botti.[31] Torquato Tasso's admiring account of a visit to Vincenzo Malpiglio's study in Rome (written about a year after Borghini's account of Florentine collections was printed in 1584) includes a reference to marble spheres 'of various colours'.[32] Without the evidence provided by inventories, we would not know about the popularity of these ornaments, which demonstrate one facet of the mid-sixteenth-century taste for rich and colourful effects in the study, particularly as an accompaniment to sculpture and other art objects and antiquities.[33]

Display and the Literature of Collecting

The principles of organising studies are made clear in literary descriptions, which show that the arrangement and display of a collection was admired as much as its quality and comprehensiveness from about 1550 onwards. The way in which objects were categorised and massed became a matter for comment and praise. Common features emerge from these descriptions. When Ulisse Aldrovandi recounted his visit to Cardinal Pio da Carpi's three studies in Rome, he mentioned a high shelf 'which runs around the room on all sides' – a common arrangement for displaying small or fragile objects where they could be seen but not accidentally jolted – on which stood ancient terracotta vases. Beneath this shelf were three levels of shelves (*scancie*) and beneath these was a row of marble inscriptions leaning against the wall, forming a continuous band or frieze. Aldrovandi did indeed use the word frieze (*fregio*) to describe the hang of the Cardinal's paintings which ringed the walls of one of his studies.[34] He was not alone in using this term; Borghini also used it in *Il riposo* to describe a continuous panel of decoration made by different objects to create a unified impression. Describing the study of Matteo Botti, Borghini lists the frescoes on the walls of the room, then analyses the arrangement of the room's contents: 'Under the roof, arranged in a frieze, are prints by Albrecht Dürer, placed in between certain brackets on which are placed little wax models'. Under this a frieze of busts of ancient emperors and spheres of different types of stone were arranged along an inlaid wooden shelf. Below this, forming a fictive *spalliera* (a kind of wall-hanging which hung behind the shoulders or *spalle*) were eleven oil paintings.[35]

The sculptor Ridolfo Sirigatti had five elaborate and highly organised studies. The third of these, containing the bulk of the sculpture collection of ancients and moderns, was divided laterally into three richly adorned friezes, the first of which consisted of paintings by Pontormo, del Sarto and others, grouped on either side of wax *modelli* and ancient bronzes. This form of arrangement, by which a row of paintings is punctuated by clusters of statuettes, resembles Matteo Botti's. The second frieze of Sirigatti's third study was composed of eight paintings by Salviati, among which, 'on beautiful brackets, are placed little bronze figures by Giambologna'. From these brackets hung ovoids and spheres of semi-precious stone. The third and last frieze consisted of marbles and bronzes in the midst of which hung paintings by 'ancient masters'.[36]

Borghini's comments on the collections of his friends and contemporaries are valuable less for what they tell us about works of art in private collections as for their precious indications about the conception and planning of custom-built study-rooms, which few architectural plans or inventories could provide. Equally valuable is Giorgio Vasari's account of working for Cosimo de' Medici, who had commissioned the remodelling of a study for his son, Francesco, in the Palazzo Vecchio. Cosimo had daily discussions with Vasari, centring on the proposed changes and how to implement them, in which both patron and artist use the future tense. Vasari recorded the discussions which took place during their walks through the palace in his *Ragionamenti*. The fourth dialogue includes a detailed description of Cosimo's study, in which Vasari emphasises the importance of organised display of fine objects in the Medici collections. The discussion is the perfect illustration of a custom-built study of the period:

> PRINCE: Let us enter the study, to complete the tour.
> VASARI: Let us go in. In this study, Signor Principe, the prince wishes to use the cornice which rings the room and which rests on these pilasters as a shelf for his small bronzes. As Your Excellency sees, there's a large number of them, and they are all antique and beautiful. Between these columns and pilasters will be placed little cedar-wood boxes containing all his medals, so that they can all be seen easily and without confusion. The Greek ones will be here, the brass ones there, the silver ones in this place, and the gold ones will be divided between these places.
> PRINCE: What will you put in this rectangular space between the columns?
> VASARI: All the miniatures by Don Giulio [Clovio] and other excellent masters, and pictures of little things which are gems in themselves. Underneath everything else these little chests will hold gems of various kinds, and in these cupboards beneath them will be oriental crystals, sardonyx, cornelians and cameos. Antiquities will be kept in these larger cupboards because, as your Excellency knows, he has very many of them, and they are all fine.
> PRINCE: It pleases me greatly, and it is well organised.[37]

The same principles of organisation were recommended to Cardinal Alessandro Farnese in his plans to construct a room for the conservation and display of his antiquities at the Palazzo della Cancelleria in Rome in 1566.[38] His adviser, Girolamo Garimberto, suggested to the Cardinal that the room could also be used for private pleasure and public instruction:

> It would greatly enhance your *camerini* in the Cancelleria, if you made a *studiolo* with all your small objects, such as medals, cameos, inkstands, and clocks, but of course giving pride of place to that outstanding *cassetta*, which deserves a tabernacle of emerald. You could have a fine cornice running around the internal wall, accompanied by several niches, and you could adorn it above with a fine order of little bronze or marble figurines, such as the two remarkable Fauns that you have, and the unsurpassed figurine which belonged to Corvino, the Hercules with the Goddess of Nature of Pietro Paolo. [. . .] But above all, you should try and acquire a little Bacchus by Signor Giangiorgio Cesarini, to adorn such a place, as much because it is in proportion with the above-mentioned figures, as for its unusualness; so by gathering together an ensemble of so many gems and objects of extraordinary beauty and richness, and not omitting to put in their places some little vases of agate and other precious stones, you will give pleasure to yourself regularly and to others on occasion, besides it serving as an antidote to all your worries.[39]

Garimberto's prescription is invaluable as a complement to the inventory of the study, drawn up after Farnese's death in 1589, for the two sources corroborate one another in every detail, except that the casket which Garimberto praises so much was not finally kept in this room.[40] The inventory alone, however, would have given an impression of a densely crowded room rather than a carefully designed unit: hence the importance of the letter in clarifying the spirit and intention of this study.

Both Vasari and Garimberto describe carefully planned ensembles built around existing collections, leaving room for *desiderata* and other future purchases as long as they fitted into the spaces available and were in keeping with the whole. Even the most dedicated collector, such as Isabella d'Este, who in a memorable phrase described 'this our insatiable desire for antiquities',[41] was known to refuse great treasures if they did not fit into the spaces she had in mind for them. Her artistic agents were kept very busy on this score, as her correspondence with Lorenzo da Pavia clearly shows.[42]

The accounts by both Vasari and Garimberto cover rooms which were very similar in content and arrangement: each contained bronze statuettes arranged along a cornice shelf, and both contained the same classes of small antiquities. The aim of such a carefully calculated display was not only decorative, but to enable the learned and cultivated visitor to appraise a collection – its range and its component categories, from gems to bronzes, each in their expected location – and discern its quality.

Garimberto continued the theme in his own study-library (referred to as a *galleria*), as described in a letter to another patron, Cesare Gonzaga in 1572. He writes:

> In this library I have placed around two thousand books in order, with all the sciences and arts distinct in their sections, with cornice shelves above on which I have placed according to the said subjects, many antique busts of philosophers, mathematicians, poets and historians, such as Plato, Aristotle, Solon, Hesiod, Socrates, Seneca and others which I will not mention so as not to spin you a story to set Your Excellency wondering how it has been possible for me to make such a fine and large arrangement (*concerto*). I have enriched it with a quantity of beautiful pictures and portraits of famous men of our time, interspersed with some tablets of antique marble with figures in half relief, some of them history subjects, and others fables, and also round reliefs. I have had three of these fables placed on three large tablets of the blackest Indian stone, polished

to an extraordinary degree, so that they appear to be cameos of infinite beauty, particularly those telling the fable of Phaeton, which are very large and rare.[43]

Taken together, these three descriptions illustrate the ideal of the collector's study in the sixteenth century, emphasising the importance of arrangement and dignified display in creating the maximum impression on the visitor to a collection.

Owners and Visitors: The Pleasures of Ownership

Sixteenth-century descriptions, in contrast to their fifteenth-century predecessors, are usually written from the viewpoint of a visitor rather than an owner. This literary development was intimately connected with the perceived status of collecting as an activity. Fra Sabba di Castiglione (c.1480–1554) stands at an important point in this shift in what one might call literary sensibility, for no one describes the pleasure of owning a study with greater penetration or delight.

Sabba's account demonstrates the way in which works of art, books and antiquities stimulated a fierce pride of possession, which included the room which contained them. Studies are often referred to as personal property – 'il mio studio' – and inventories often record them as the property of a particular individual. The inventory of the lawyer Andrea de Monticuli refers to the study in his house as being 'Andrea's' (Monticuli 1413). Owners sometimes used a diminutive to describe their study: Sabba refers to 'il mio piccolo studiolo'.[44] The affection and pride which he felt for the room is clearly shown in the famous description he gives of it in his *Ricordi*, in a chapter entitled 'On the Suitable Decoration of Grand Interiors'.[45] Sabba's comments reveal his experiences both as an agent on behalf of that insatiable collector Isabella d'Este, and as a collector on his own account, and they include appraisals of many Renaissance artists, many of whom were friends of his.[46] Since Sabba's description of his own study is a unique document, it is worth quoting in full:

> Even though I am only a poor knight, I adorn my little study with a bust of John the Baptist at the age of about fourteen, sculpted in the round from Carrara marble by the

63   Detail of a lunette painted in grisaille above Fra Sabba's memorial tablet, showing him kneeling in the presence of the Holy Family. The melancholy Latin inscription on the tablet itself, which is only partly legible, records his presence at La Commenda: 'Solitary and little content I lived, little content and solitary do I lie here.' Commissioned from Francesco Menzocchi, before 1554. La Commenda di Santa Maria Maddalena della Magione, Borgo Durbecco, Faenza. Photo: Bologna, Soprintendenza, Gabinetto Fotografico.

64 Girolamo da Treviso, fresco representing the Virgin with saints (detail), 1533, in the apse of the church of La Commenda, Faenza. Fra Sabba di Castiglione as patron is dressed in his robes as a Knight of the Order of St John; the portrait profile here is closely comparable with that on an intaglio which is also inscribed with his name, possibly from his signet ring (fig. 76). Faenza, La Commenda. Photo: Bologna, Soprintendenza, Gabinetto Fotografico.

hand of Donatello, which is very beautiful. Its quality is such, that, if one could find no other work by him, this alone would be sufficient to make him eternal and immortal in the eyes of the world. I adorn my study with a figure of Saint Jerome [fig. 65], made of terracotta, but finished so as to imitate bronze, in three-quarters relief and about a cubit high, which is by the hand of Alfonso di Ferrara. It could easily be compared with his most famous works. I adorn my study with a little board [fig. 66], and with two portrait panels, one of Saint Paul, the other of Saint John the Baptist, which are worked

66 Writing surface of Fra Sabba's desk, made for him by his friend Fra Damiano da Bergamo, as mentioned in the *Ricordi*. This inlaid walnut panel was once very fine, but has been damaged by generations of schoolboys in the school at La Commenda which Fra Sabba himself set up. At the dissolution of the school at the suppression of religious orders in 1866, this and other relics of Fra Sabba were transferred to the local Comune. Fra Sabba's arms are at the centre; four Latin inscriptions appear on cartouches, framed by panels inlaid with arabesques. The elegance and sophistication of the panel must closely reflect Fra Sabba's own tastes. Faenza, Pinacoteca. Photo: Bologna, Soprintendenza, Gabinetto Fotografico.

65 (*facing page*) Attributed to Alfonso Lombardi, terracotta relief showing St Jerome in penitence in the desert. The relief belonged to Fra Sabba di Castiglione and is described by him among the contents of his study in his *Ricordi*, at which time it was painted to imitate bronze; no pigment remains. Faenza, Pinacoteca. Photo: Bologna, Soprintendenza, Gabinetto Fotografico.

in *lavoro d'intarsia* by the hand of my venerable friend, Fra Damiano da Bergamo. All three panels are most excellent works. In my opinion, the good father excelled himself in the portrait of Saint John, showing the final and ultimate proof of everything he knew. Similarly, I adorn the room with an antique urn of alabaster [fig. 67], oriental, with some veins of chalcedony, which certainly does not yield precedence to any other alabaster vase which I have seen until the present hour, though I have seen many of them in Rome and elsewhere. I would continue to praise the objects in my study as their quality deserves, but as they are my things, I would not wish anyone to think that, deluded by the feeling which one naturally has for one's own things, I had overstepped the bounds of Truth. I adorn the room with many other little things, which, because they are not of the same dignity and excellence of the others, I do not mention or refer to here. If by chance you were to ask me, which ornaments I would desire in my house above all others, I would reply without much pause for reflection, Arms and Books. The arms should be fine, fit for every test, by an excellent hand such as a good Italian or German master. I would wish them to be kept limpid, burnished, shining and polished, as the arms of a noble knight should be, and not rusty like those of a tipstaff or sergeant. I would wish the books to be those written by serious, mature and approved and prescribed authors, and I would want the books to be used and studied,

and not so dusty that one could write on the boards with one's finger. For to have books, and not use them, is as good as not having them. And if by chance you were to ask me which item of furnishing or which ornament it would please me most to have in my house, I would immediately respond: a steel mirror. It would be one of the large and beautiful ones made by the German Giovanni della Barba, most excellent at making mathematical instruments such as solid spheres, globes, astrolabes and mirrors. I would hold it more dear, because it represents reality more than the others.[47]

Among the 'other little things' was probably a Dürer print, such as the one Sabba describes in another passage in his book. His account shows the extent to which objects kept in a

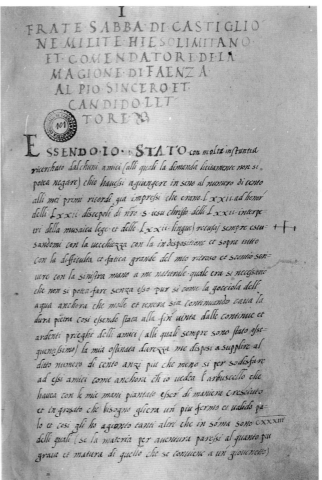

study were lived with and known, so that they became a continual source of pleasure to their owner. Sabba admired his print as an excellent work by a modern master, as well as being a new acquisition.

> Some years ago, during the heat of July, towards the hour of None, I found myself in the rustic and poorly tended garden at La Magione, at the foot of the ever-verdant Mount Formicone, under the fresh shade of trees which I can boast of having planted myself. In this retreat, designed to evade the heat as much as the mid-day sun, I set myself to looking at a print by Albrecht Dürer, which is certainly divine, and which had recently arrived from Germany. With delight and great pleasure I admired and considered the figures, animals, perspectives, houses, distant views and landscapes, and other marvellous depictions which would astonish Protogenes or Apelles.[48]

This expensive print was, like Mantegna's mythological prints, designed for a collector's study, where it would be admired as a work of art in its own right.[49] Sabba was not alone in the way in which he scrutinised Dürer's work; Vasari's admiring description of Dürer's famous *St Jerome in his Study* refers to the extraordinary skill with which light falling through the window into the room is represented, a quality which is particularly evident in the British Museum's early impression of the print.[50] One wishes that Sabba had described his response to Dürer's depiction of a humanist's study, given his joy in his own. What his account reveals, however, is the way in which he had created in his study, and

69 (*above*) The inner courtyard of La Commenda in Faenza as it is today. As recorded in the inscription dated 1525, which is spelt out in terracotta tiles above the arches, it was lovingly restored and revitalised by Fra Sabba di Castiglione. (Little remains of his improvements beyond the fresco which he commissioned from Bartolomeo da Treviso for the apse in the small church, and the grisaille decorations by Francesco Menzocchi for his monument there. His presence at La Commenda, which lies on the ancient Roman Via Emilia near the city gate, attracted fellow collectors there. Photo: Bologna, Soprintendenza, Gabinetto Fotografico.

71 (*facing page right*) Detail from a memorial painting in grisaille (see fig. 63) showing Fra Sabba di Castiglione kneeling before the Virgin and Child. Unlike the more public portrait in fig. 64, this captures the meditative and reflective quality evident in Fra Sabba's description of himself and his way of life in the *Ricordi*. La Commenda di Santa Maria Maddalena della Magione, Borgo Durbecco, Faenza. Photo: Bologna, Soprintendenza, Gabinetto Fotografico.

70 (*above left*) Johann Gregor van der Schardt, terracotta bust of the Nuremberg patrician and collector Willibald Imhoff (1519–1580), 1570. The artist here combines Netherlandish and Venetian traditions of portraiture in a particularly forceful and original bust, which is more than life-size. Imhoff looks intently down at a small object held in his left hand; although the present fingers holding the ring are restorations, he must have originally held a similarly small object. The very private, reflective quality of this portrait provides the perfect visual parallel to Fra Sabba di Castiglione's description of his study collection, and conveys a similar sense of someone who lives with their things. Berlin, Staatliche Museen zu Berlin, Preussischer Kulturbesitz, Skulpturensammlung.

in his garden at La Magione, spaces in which to sit quietly with his art objects and scrutinise them with discrimination and knowledge built up over years. It is this quality of 'retiredness' which Francis Junius was later to define as a necessary precondition for aesthetic understanding and appreciation, which gives Fra Sabba's writing its excitement and vividness.[51]

Sabba's fond pride in his collection is echoed in the will of the Venetian Jacopo Contareno, who exemplified a particularly Venetian desire for co-existence with his things, whether art objects, books or mathematical instruments:

> My study is one of the dearest things that I have, or could have had, and from it have proceeded all the honours and respect which I have gained. By the study I mean not only the room in which the books are to be found, but all those things contained in the four mezzanine rooms in which I ordinarily live. There are in these rooms exquisite things, beyond the belief of anyone who considers them well, such as manuscript and printed books, mathematical instruments, stones, secrets and other things, all of which have been gathered together by me with the greatest studiousness and care.[52]

The concept of the honour, virtue and fame conferred on an individual by a study and its contents had already been expressed by Cardinal Pietro Bembo, who charged his son in his will

> not to sell, pawn, or give away for any reason whatsoever any of my antiquities, whether of stone, copper, silver or gold [. . .] but to keep them on account of his honour and my memory.[53]

Such ideas became commonplace in sixteenth-century Venice, as collectors congratulated themselves and complimented each other on their discrimination. Within this élite circle, the study had considerable status and prestige. Literary descriptions show how collecting was promoted as a generous and public-spirited, rather than a selfish and introverted, activity or merely private indulgence. Paolo Manuzio provided a justification for the large sums and energy invested in amassing a collection in a letter to Andrea Loredan, in which he describes visiting the latter's museum:

> You could never leave your sons any land, palace or treasure which could equal the value and excellence of these antiquities of yours. These are not material goods, which one may acquire with simple labour; the collection is not a gem which one may obtain at a price: these are virtuous riches, which do not fall to the lot of the uneducated, which one may only collect with judgement, with infinite knowledge over a long period of time. These antiquities of yours will bear good witness to your fine mind, and to your very noble thoughts, in future centuries. On account of them, your house, as much as the city itself, [. . .] will be visited and honoured by strangers, eager to see rare and excellent works.[54]

Manuzio went even further in declaring that he was looking out medals in Rome which would 'increase the ornament of your very beautiful *studio*, and in consequence that of our city'.[55]

The Visiting Circuit

Art collections were publicised by those who visited them, particularly by writers seeking patrons among the great contemporary collectors. By the middle of the sixteenth century a clearly established visiting circuit of studies had come into existence. Groups of collectors can of course be traced back to the early fifteenth century, particularly in the Veneto, and dedicated collectors even earlier. Ambrogio Traversari described in two of his letters how several young Venetian patricians had shown him their ancient coins.[56] Marin Sanudo mentions in his diary a visit made by several learned patricians to his house in 1505:

> I make note that Signor Alberto da Carpi came to see my study and the worldmap along with the following learned men, Signor Alvise Bembo, Signor Maffeo Lion, Signore Daniel Barbarigo.[57]

He proudly asserted that another of his visitors had been the first to view Andrea Loredan's collection, as if he fondly hoped that his own collection would become similarly well known. Marcantonio Michiel's manuscript notes on collections imply that the private houses he visited, owned by patricians, merchants and others, were open to interested viewers and other collectors.[58] Cardinal Pietro Bembo appears to have kept a kind of open house for visiting scholars, making his collection available (with the help of a custodian referred to as 'Gerolamo') even when he himself was absent from Padua.[59] The collection was a known meeting-place for like-minded antiquarians.[60] Later in the century, Francesco Sansovino's comprehensive gazetteer and history of Venice included notes on what he called the 'case aperte' of the city: presumably well-appointed and furnished palaces which could be visited. He also gave listings of *studii d'arme*, *studii di musica*, private libraries, art collections and gardens, and the parish in which they were to be found.[61] This was one way in which private collections in Venice were drawn into the public sphere: a development culminating in the bequest of the Grimani collection to the Signoria by Cardinal Domenico in 1523, which however was not formalised until the death of Giovanni Grimani in 1593.[62] Sculptures from the study of Federico Contarini were added before the Statuario Pubblico was constructed in the Marciana Library and opened in 1596.[63] This date was therefore an important one in the history of collecting, for it marked the point at which a private collection became indisputably public.

The fact that collecting was publicly promoted must have stimulated collectors to advertise the qualities of their own studies. The architect Vincenzo Scamozzi claimed that 'the studies of Venice can be compared in their number, quality, price and importance to all the other studies [in the sense of collections] in Europe, not excluding those of antiquities in Rome'.[64] His friend Bartolomeo della Nave had 'gathered together almost thirty statuettes [. . .] and terracotta models [. . .] and placed them in one of his rooms which he proudly shows to all the most important people in Venice'.[65] Even outside a city famous for its art and antiquities, such as Venice, Rome and Florence, a collection could add to the fame of a region and act as a magnet for learned people travelling through it. When the goldsmith and collector Valerio Belli died in Vicenza, one of his executors wrote to the Archbishop of Antibari at Trent to request that the study (again in the sense of a collection) could remain in Vicenza, instead of being sold to the Cardinal of Trent, on account of its cultural value as an ornament to the city.[66] It was well known on the collecting circuit, and had been visited by the Paduan collector Marco Mantova Benavides and by Giorgio Vasari, who mentions his visit in the *Vite*.[67] Generally, it was local historians and topographers who would promote a collection: Vittorio Ranieri of Bologna described Sabba di Castiglione's study at La Magione as that of

> a man of great integrity of life, and of great wit, and no less a *curioso* of antiquities, as one can easily discern from the works which he has composed and from the antiquities which he keeps in his house.[68]

Ranieri writes as if he had actually visited La Magione. It was important enough for such dignitaries as Fra Sabba's old friend Pope Clement VII to have been attracted there from Bologna in 1529 and 1530.[69] It would of course have been possible for Ranieri to have based his brief account on Sabba's own description, which was frequently republished in the course of the sixteenth century.

A sense of immediacy in describing a collection was considered one of the desirable features of literary depictions, which are always written as if the writer had actually seen them. Accounts of studies and their contents came to be set pieces in the collected letters of literary individuals which began to be printed in the mid-sixteenth century, and details of the appearance, organisation and contents of famous collections began to appear. Written in the vernacular as selfconscious rhetorical exercises in the cultivation of reputation and favour, the letters in which such descriptions appear are 'private in address but public in purpose', and were calculated to create an audience.[70]

We do not know how a visit to a collection was generally organised; whether it was always at the personal invitation of the owner, or by presenting a letter of introduction or whether it took the form of élite tourism.[71] Ulisse Aldrovandi, publishing an account of a visit to the palace of Niccolò Gaddi in 1550, added that it was easy enough to make an appointment to view the collection: 'If any gentleman wishes to visit his [Gaddi's] rooms, everything will be courteously shown him by the above-named Messer Hieronimo, as he did for me'.[72]

Paolo Manuzio's account of visiting Andrea Loredan's collection while the latter was absent from Venice is another example of such an arrangement.[73] Two letters published by Anton Francesco Doni in 1544 also show how visits were set up. Both letters describe a visit to Paolo Giovio's museum in his house at Lake Como, following their meeting at the Florentine Academy. Doni worked as a printer for the Academy, but was seeking a powerful patron; when Giovio invited him to his house, Doni must have had hopes of employment. He described the plan and decoration of the villa in detail in a letter to Count Agostino Landi, a fellow-member of the Accademia Ortolana in Piacenza, and in a second letter to his friend, the painter Tintoretto, recording in each details calculated to interest and amuse his correspondents. In his letter to Landi he concentrates on the learned inscriptions over the lintels of the doors of the villa, whereas the letter to Tintoretto concerns a fresco of Parnassus in the villa. Doni understood what he saw and described it accurately, for his account is backed by Giambattista Giovio's *Elogio* and a letter of Benedetto Giovio's describing the museum. When Doni visited Giovio in 1544 the museum had only recently been completed, and Giovio must have been delighted by the publicity Doni gave it when his appreciative accounts were published in 1544.[74]

In his book on contemporary and ancient dress, which was published in Venice in 1599, Cesare Vecellio described Odorico Pillone's villa at Casteldardo near Belluno as a magnet for virtuosi. Vecellio knew the villa well, for Pillone had employed him to paint the fore-edges and covers of some of the books. Vecellio's admiring account of his patron and his collection appears in his introduction to the section on Bellunese dress. It is an excellent example of the custom of presenting the study as visible, lasting proof of an individual's wit, honour, wordly success and discernment:

> An admirable Doctor of the utmost integrity, whose virtue is worthy of being praised, proclaimed and honoured with all the honours of the world. For he is very learned, grave and witty in his speech, and there is nothing trivial in his judgements and opinions, in such a way that all his actions (which proceed from his very sharp wit) are by long experience directed towards virtue, enriched by various doctrines, and resolved by his perfect judgements. Above all, his actions are begun with very regular disposi-tions, and are followed through and conducted to their conclusion: these are true testimonials to his valour, which he has shown in many magistracies and offices of great importance, and repute. He has taken nothing other than praise and glory from these offices: all in all, he is a man who possesses all the virtues, of all types and species, who enjoys many gifts of fortune and many possessions. [. . .] He has a study which contains many different kinds of book, and is crammed with every kind of antiquity that one could desire. There are many ancient medals and portraits of heroes, and sculptures in marble and bronze, and there are also fine natural marvels, so that the study is appropriately known in that region as the Ark of Noah, a name given to it by that most illustrious Cardinal della Torre. So that there is no-one who passes nearby in the region who does not want to visit it, as something marvellous and singular.[75]

Conversation and Sociability in the Study

Satirising collectors as obsessive individuals seems to have been part of the literature of collecting. Those who collected coins or medals were often singled out for humorous treatment. An example of a teasing portrait of a collector of ancient coins appears in a book by a leading Bolognese humanist, Giovanni Philoteo Achillini.[76] Achillini describes a dream-like vision of the ideal collector's house, decorated with artworks by contempo-rary Bolognese artists in rare materials, such as a pair of doors cast in silver relief by the writer's friend Francesco Francia. The house contains comprehensive collections of books, arms and armour, riding equipment, and dress both ancient and modern, in addition to a coin collection, and in describing them in his Italian text, Achillini seems to wish to prove the flexibility and range of the vernacular. His principal aim is to amuse that small circle of young Bolognese artists and collectors to which he belonged: a select group which included the printmaker Marcantonio Raimondi, Francia and Amico Aspertini, Fra Leandro Alberti and Bartolomeo Bianchini.[77] The last mentioned certainly had a collection of ancient coins (Bianchini 1510); could he be the butt of Achillini's satire in his account of how the fictional character Ombruno (his name perhaps refers back to the shadowy, visionary quality of Achillini's description) spends his evenings in this ideal collector's residence?

[The room also contains] boxes of precious coins [. . .] in high relief, perfectly round, with smooth surfaces, select and with perfect proportions, made of yellowish brass, [. . .] of copper, silver, gold, and other extremely subtle metals, and worked with the greatest artifice, so as to make even Nature want to hide herself for shame in a privy. The aforesaid [. . .] Ombruno, in contemplating these coins, speaking with reverence of the abbreviations and the significance of the legends upon them, affirms that he spends and consumes ten ducats on candle ends [*moccoli*] every evening in order to illuminate them for study.[78]

Fra Sabba di Castiglione, who saw collecting as a dignified activity, criticised the medal-mad collector in his *Ricordi*:

I tell you that I have known many great men; great men, I say, in riches and dignity, but for the rest, ignorant, gross, and stupid. [. . .] these men, in order to demonstrate their wit and spirit to the common people, used to make a great show of delighting in antiquities, especially in medals of men who have been worthy and famous in the world, though their taste and understanding in these matters was like that of an ass faced with music played on the lyre. Among the others I knew was a great lord, who, merely because of his reputation for gentility and wit, used to present himself as someone who delighted in medals, of which, by the Grace of God, he had a study-ful, whether of bronze, tin or lead examples. Among these were many papal bulls in lead, from the time of Pope Gianni; however, as long as they made a good number he did not care whose Bulls they were. Among the others were four lead medals, even thicker than he was. One was a medal of Ugolone della Faggiola, who [. . .] was the most voracious military commander that one could find in Italy in his day, for in one morning and in one sitting he ate up Pisa and Lucca. There was a medal of Boldrino da Panicale [. . .] and of the other two, one was of Niccolò Piccinino and the other of Gattamelata.[79] When anyone came to have audience or negotiate with him, even if it were only a peasant, this man would show off the four medals, which were his favourite and most prized ones, and begin to recount the deeds of these great captains, famous in their own times [. . .] and he would not stop until darkness overtook him. One day a very beautiful ancient coin was presented to the same lord; it was gold, featuring Alexander the Great, with the Winged Pegasus on the reverse, and if I said I had seen it myself I would not be lying. When someone asked him whose portrait it was on the coin, he answered 'Alexander's', and showed that he had great regard for it. Thanking the donor, he sent for his secretary (who, if not more ignorant than his master, was thicker still) and said to him: 'This fine coin is of Alexander, but I would like to know if it is of that Alexander [de Villedieu] who wrote the *Doctrinale* [an elementary Latin grammar in verse[80]], for having a good memory he remembered having learnt by heart as a child the *Doctrinale*, whose author was called Alexander. The good secretary answered 'I will look in the Cornucopia [. . .] and see if he is mentioned there'. As Seneca replied when, having spent ten years studying Virgil continuously, he was asked if he understood the author: 'very well, but even now I am not very clear as to whether Aeneas was male or female', showing that those ten years had indeed been well spent.[81]

Sabba does not say who this collector was, though his later characterisation of him as someone who indulges in chivalric notions in reading *Il Morgante* at night, and who is easily provoked into violence,[82] suggests that he is satirising a contemporary type: the military professional or *condottiere*, a man of questionable social rank and little education, who wished to assume the learned collecting culture of the day and take on the prestige and dignity which this conferred.[83] Sabba's satirical portrait of an upstart, would-be collector, obsessed with the military exploits of famous *condottieri* but ignorant of Alexander the Great and of classical culture in general, is a portrait of failure. It makes a sharp contrast to the subtle but triumphant success of Federigo da Montefeltro's study at Urbino, in which the learned Federigo presents himself as someone who combines military and chivalric prowess with literary culture.

In the course of the sixteenth century, satires directed against collectors became even sharper and more focused as collecting came to be seen as an expression of power.[84] In Venice, for example, a single critical voice contradicted not only Giovanni Grimani's view of himself, but also satirised the greed which lay behind his public façade. The critic was Alessandro Caravia, an outspoken goldsmith who had been investigated for heresy by Grimani. He was well connected in literary circles, and appears to have been a friend of Aretino's; perhaps it was through the latter that he obtained a description of the famous study in Palazzo Grimani.[85] This he uses as a preamble to his criticism of collectors in his dialect poem *Il Naspo Bizaro*, narrated by a dockyard worker from the Arsenal.[86] All that is missing in the Grimani study, he says irreverently, is a marble statue depicting his girlfriend, Blond Kate (a perfect Venus) with himself and Cupid. Even then, he refers to collectors as greedy individuals (*avari*) and to their accumulating passion in the pursuit of *virtù* as a form of miserliness.[87] Caravia's outspoken and well-informed critique still shocks today, since it follows a straight and conventional description of Grimani's study and its contents, without any warning of the biting satire which is to come.

One of the most unusual fictional accounts of visiting a study – which could profitably have been taken as a lesson in how not to talk to a collector – appears in a book by the prolific and widely read author Anton Francesco Doni, *I marmi*, printed in Venice in 1552. Apart from having an important medal and print collection himself, Doni knew several famous collections, and his writings show that he was familiar with the characteristic tastes, foibles and failings of collectors as well as with the objects they collected.[88] He used this knowledge to mock the contemporary habit of collecting 'bits of stone' as precious relics of antiquity, and to caricature the collector as deluded and foolish in his misplaced passions. The account quoted here is highly coloured, but it reveals how collections were viewed, displayed and appraised in sixteenth-century Italy in literary and antiquarian circles:

> A few days ago, I went to see a collection of antiquities, and he who showed it to me is in my opinion madder than I am myself, given that I am not like the majority of people, who think that they alone are wise. He began by showing me a marble head, praising it to me (for these things are all like vanities which establish themselves in mens' fantasies) as the most stupendous thing in the world. Then he showed me various busts, feet, hands, and fragments, a sack of medals, a little chest of bizarre things, a stone crab and a shell converted to stone, a piece of wood which is half wood and half the most solid rock [i.e. fossilised]; certain vases known as *lacrimarii*, into which the ancients poured their tears when they mourned their dead, certain terracotta lamps, cinerary urns, and a thousand other novelties. When I had been there for four hours, and when I saw that he was so deeply in love with these bits of stone, I said to him with a sigh:
> 'Oh, if you had been the owner of these things when they were complete, eh?'
> 'Oh God, what pleasure I would have had', he replied.
> 'And if you had seen them as they are now?'
> 'I would have died', said the noble man.

The narrator then suggests that the collector should repair or remake plaster statuettes out of the jumble of fragments remaining. Better still, he should go to Rome:

> so that in a month you may satiate yourself, and when you return home and see these things of yours, you will laugh as I do now. As for myself, I can find nothing which

delights me for more than a day: I am a most unstable and restless man, and I don't understand myself. See now, Doni, if you know how to find some receipt that will still my blood.[89]

This extraordinary description appears at the end of a one-sided dialogue between a restless, loquacious character whom Doni calls Inquieto ('the restless one') and Doni as narrator. Doni presents Inquieto as a young, educated man of means, and the collection described here is a good example of what contemporary virtuosi wanted in a study well stocked with antiquities. Inquieto's dismissal of the collection is not one of mere boredom but stems from a deeper malaise or *noia*, and this section of *I marmi* as a whole is an excellent example of Doni's skill as a moralist as well as stylist.[90]

Inquieto's vivid account of a long guided tour received from the nostalgic, engrossed collector shows the way in which a visitor would be led from one object to another as the owner discussed its quality and provenance. Inquieto's response is unexpected; he starts by addressing the collector formally as 'voi' but ends by giving him a few friendly words of advice. The parting note is that the collector should remember that the sun is a fine antiquity, worthy of his attention.

Doni's account of a visit to an existing collection, that of Gabriel Vendramin in Venice, makes an interesting contrast in that it demonstrates the way in which a visitor was expected to behave. Doni knew Vendramin, and considered his collection to be one of the glories of Venice. His visit, as recounted in *I marmi*, evokes a conversation prompted by a sculpture in the collection as owner and visitor looked round the study.

> Among other things, he [Vendramin] showed me a lion with a Cupid above it. We talked for a long time about this fine conceit, and finally I praised it for this quality, that Love conquers all ferocity and violence in men.[91]

As Jaynie Anderson has pointed out, Doni did not invent this piece of sculpture in order to illustrate a literary commonplace referring to the taming power of Love, for a bronze sculpture of *Cupid Trampling a Lion* is listed in the inventory of Vendramin's collection which dates from 1567.[92] Even if Doni used the conceit to introduce a fable about a marble lion, his description is based on the study as it actually was, and illustrates the way in which Doni interweaves fact and fantasy in *I marmi*.

Sculpture in the study was often used in treatises and other writings as a literary device introducing a philosophical argument. Pomponius Gauricus used this means in introducing his treatise on the nature of sculpture, in describing how Raphael Regius, the Professor of Rhetoric at Padua University, had come to visit him at home. Seeing his collection, Gauricus continues, 'we soon fell to talking of sculpture'.[93]

Luc'Antonio Ridolfi used a similar means to introduce a discussion on the nature and progress of Love. Ridolfi's dialogue is entitled *Aretefila*, 'She who loves learning' – a name derived from Plutarch – after the learned lady who conducts the debate between two visitors to her study. The book is dedicated to Marguerite du Bourg, the model for Aretefila. Her 'ornate and excellent' study in Lyons was decorated and furnished in the Italianate manner – Lyons being one of the principal points of entry into France for Italian customs and art in the sixteenth century – and Ridolfi described it twice in his works without specifying whether it was to be found in her town house or in her château.[94] One of his accounts however mentions 'elegant inscriptions' in Latin, French and Italian, painted in gold on the walls of the room, which would answer to remnants of similar inscriptions on the walls of a room of her town house as described in the nineteenth century.[95] Apart from the inscriptions, there were 'very many books in Tuscan and Latin as well as French, infinite numbers of geometrical and astrological instruments' and art objects such as a silver statuette of Pallas. Aretefila receives her two courtly visitors and leads them into

> her very ornate and most copious study. She made them sit with her by the fire, as the season demanded. While all four of them were sitting quietly there, Federigo, looking round the room with great pleasure, happened to see a small statuette, which appeared to be made of silver, among all the other beautiful and rare ornaments which were there.[96]

Federigo delicately tempts Aretefila into speech by commenting on this statuette of Pallas, and so the dialogue begins by setting the scene. Federigo provides a model of formal, courteous behaviour for visitors and owners of studies, which is very different from Doni's account of lively, informal and irreverent conversation. Using a fictive or real study to introduce an argument was a convenient ruse – a kind of indoor equivalent to the use of gardens and meadows which often set the scene in Renaissance dialogues – but it perhaps points to that fact that some studies may have been intended not only to offer pleasure to visitors as well as to their owners, but also to stimulate and shape discussions which were intimate yet formal, in providing a dignified and appropriate setting for intellectual exchange.

The Convivial Study: The Courtly Context

Reading aloud and studying could flow into other, more obviously sociable activities, especially in the right company. The Florentine humanist Angelo Poliziano described in a letter to Clarice de' Medici how he and his companions had spent a delightful evening:

> At San Miniato yesterday evening we began to read a little Saint Augustine. And this at last turned into making music, leaping up and polishing a certain model of dancing practised here.[97]

The convivial study as an elegant space to be shared was well represented by Leonello d'Este's at Belfiore. Ludovico Carbone records visiting 'the very beautiful study' at the villa but adds that Leonello's intention was not to create this in the country, but to move it into Ferrara, into his apartment and near his bedchamber in the Castello at the very centre of the city, so that it could more easily be visited by orators and poets.[98]

A similarly sociable and representative function for a study which housed the Muses, a room which would be appreciated by orators and poets, must have been intended for Federico da Montefeltro's famous room in Urbino. It has been suggested that the room was not created until the Sala delle Udienze was constructed: that it was, in other words, intended to serve less as a secret study than as a small reception room of a more intimate kind.[99] Luciano Cheles's exhaustive study of the room's iconography has shown that the decorations allude playfully to all the expected qualities, functions and contents of the ideal courtly study, without actually providing for any of them.[100] Federico's extensive library was kept elsewhere,[101] and the room was not designed for reading in – the small desk made by a panel unfolding from the wall is a fragile fixture, more of a stage prop or temporary lodging place than a lectern proper.[102] The impression is heightened by the study-within-a-study effect represented in the recess of the room, consisting of a fictive alcove into which the inlaid inscription running under the ceiling of the real study is continued.[103] The fictive room contains a lectern set on a desk as one would expect to find it in such a room. This imaginary room, and the benches invitingly placed against the wall, wittily deny every expectation as to what a study should be, yet the room is perfectly furnished, since the cupboards contain every collectable, from instruments of the speculative sciences to clocks and plate, including armour carelessly strewn over benches which (it is suggested) Federico has just removed.[104] The room is intended to represent the accomplishments, taste and learning of the owner, but does so in a way which includes and compliments select visitors to the room.[105] The remarkable unity of the design and the complexity of this very personal Pantheon of Federico's suggests the work of one designer, providing models for the da Maiano brothers, who are believed to have done the inlaid work.[106] We know that Francesco di Giorgio was present in Gubbio in 1477, when he was documented as being in charge of the decoration of a room there which may well have been Guidobaldo da Montefeltro's study.[107] This would seem to argue in favour of Francesco di Giorgio's role in the creation of Federico's study at Urbino.[108]

What was the room for? Surely not (as has recently been suggested) for the most secret negotiations of Federico's government, which would properly have taken place in his bedchamber.[109] As a small reception room lined with panelling, it was perfectly adapted for intimate sociable and musical gatherings. A sketch by Carpaccio shows musicians playing in a study (fig. 72), with the same garlanded cornice shelf as rings the scholar's study in three of his other sketches relating to studies.

Musical instruments, like those used for the study of geometry and astronomy or for casting horoscopes, were appropriate to the study, being both decorative and instructive. The Udinese lawyer Andrea de Monticuli had a lute and two armillary spheres in his room,[110] while the Lord of Lucca, Paolo Guinigi, had an armillary sphere[111] and a small organ in his study (in addition to a considerable library). More explicitly, Leonello d'Este (as characterised in Angelo Decembrio's dialogue *De politia litteraria*) associated different kinds of instrument in his recommendations as to how to decorate private libraries:

It is not unseemly to have in the library an instrument for drawing up horoscopes or a celestial sphere, or even a lute if your pleasure ever lies that way: it makes no noise unless you want it to.[112]

72 Vittore Carpaccio, ink drawing showing musicians playing in a study, watched by a monk. Note the viol and bow hanging from the shelf against the wall and the string of what may well be paternoster beads looped decoratively beneath the shelf, similar to the arrangement recorded in the inventory of the study of Frate Franceschino da Cesena (see above, p. 85). This drawing appears on the reverse of another ink sketch showing a single scholar in his study (fig. 28). London, British Museum.

73 A gilt-bronze medal by Giovanni Boldù depicting the lutenist Pietrobono, signed and dated 1457. This celebrated musician was a key figure in musical life at the court of Leonello d'Este of Ferrara. The inscription around his portrait describes him as surpassing Orpheus himself. Oxford, Ashmolean Museum.

Leonello played the lute himself – in a letter to Giambattista Guarino he mentions turning from his books to his lute and to singing 'for the relaxation of the spirit and as a pastime' – and he employed one of the most famous lutenists of the day, Pietrobono, at his court (fig. 73).[113] Having created a court chapel (with an organ which he himself occasionally played) he built up a *capella di corte* of distinguished singers against intense competition from other courts.[114] Appropriately, his study at Belfiore was one of the first to be decorated with paintings of the Muses according to a programme devised with the help of Guarino da Verona.[115] The theme was repeated by Federico da Montefeltro in his Tempietto delle Muse in the Ducal Palace in Urbino, while Apollo playing his lyre to accompany the Dance of the Muses featured in the *lavoro d'intarsia* panels of the study.[116] Individual musical instruments also feature in the illusionistic cupboards represented in the panels, as objects which were as suitable to the room as mathematical instruments.[117] Isabella d'Este's Studiolo in Mantua included a number of musical references, not least in the iconography of Mantegna's *Parnassus*, in which the Muses are shown dancing and singing to the imagined music of Apollo's lyre.[118]

Representations of musical instruments and performance indicate that studies were likely to have been used as private music rooms for chamber ensembles and singers, numbering up to four performers. This has been suggested for Isabella's Studiolo and Grotta, given her known proficiency as a performer on the lute, *lira da braccia* and keyboard instruments, and her skill as a singer.[119] Isabella did not improvise settings of lyric poetry, but, like other noble amateurs, she wished to imitate this tradition of performance, as can be seen in her promotion of the *frottola* as a new musical genre. The *frottola* was a solo song setting of a poem, with string or keyboard accompaniment.[120] Not only did Isabella demand manuscript and printed *frottole* from which to perform, she also elevated the tone of the poetry set in these songs, suggesting a poem by Petrarch as a suitable text in 1504.[121]

Born into the d'Este family, in which musical accomplishment and patronage were highly rated, Isabella was yet exceptional in the intensity of her musical interests. Many of her letters to the man who doubled as her artistic agent and maker of musical instruments, Lorenzo da Pavia, include requests for elegantly decorated musical instruments for her own use. Isabella was well aware of the sensuous and intellectual attraction of beautifully made instruments and their appropriateness for her Studiolo. Her contemporary, Sabba di Castiglione, best explains this attraction:

I very much commend them [musical instruments] because they greatly delight the ears, and refresh the spirits, which, as Plato said, recall the harmony which is produced by the movements of the celestial spheres. They greatly please the eye, too, when they are diligently worked by the hand of excellent and ingenious masters such as Lorenzo da Pavia or Bastiano da Verona.[122]

Typically, Isabella's love of rich and unusual materials and her instinct for elegance and display led her to ask for a lute to be made in her favourite wood, ebony. Lorenzo refused to do this in a letter, writing that:

it is not possible to make the lute from ebony because it would be hideous to look at, but, what is worse, it would lack tone [*vose* or *voce*], no less than if one were to sound a slab of marble, but if I make the lute out of cypress wood, it will be very beautiful and excellent for giving the instrument tone.[123]

Isabella's insistence on the elegant appearance of her instrument indicates that this and others may well have been intended for her Studiolo, as a room in which she could show off her accomplishments. This she would have done only before a select few, such as Pietro Bembo, who recorded 'that happy evening' in July 1505 when she had sung in his presence – perhaps performing one of the new *frottole*.[124] Music was recognised as a social art in the exclusive world of the Renaissance court,[125] and as such was integrally connected with the ideal of the study as a place which would give its owner pleasure 'regularly, and to others on occasion'.[126] This prescription of Gerolamo Garimberto's in a letter to his patron, Cardinal Alessandro Farnese, indicates the kind of urbane sociability which the room could both stimulate and serve.

★   ★   ★

Much of the contemporary literature on the study is prescriptive in nature (such as architectural or other treatises) and it is always necessary to distinguish real rooms from the literary framework and conventions used to describe them. Writing on the Renaissance villa, Amanda Lillie has suggested:

Rather than assuming that literary texts can explain buildings, it may be more helpful to turn the argument round and discover whether buildings and their physical environment can shed light on the construction of literary models [. . .] [and] the nature of invention and imitation in the literary reconstruction of Renaissance pastoral.[127]

A fascinating example of how real collectors' rooms and the conventions governing their arrangement could structure a literary account appears in a remarkable discussion of Torquato Tasso's style, written by Galileo Galilei around 1589:

it has always seemed to me that this poet [Tasso] is beyond all words cramped, poor and wretched in his inventions, by contrast with Ariosto, who is magnificent, rich and admirable. When I turn to considering Tasso's chivalric heroes, their deeds and fortunes [. . .] it seems that one has entered the little study of some curious hermit, who has delighted in adorning his room with things, either on account of their antiquity, or rarity [. . .] which are however little things in terms of the impact they produce, such as to say a fossilised crab, a dried chameleon, a fly and a spider petrified in amber, some of those *fantoccini* of earth which they say are found in ancient tombs in Egypt. As regards painting, such a room might include some little sketch by Baccio Bandinelli, or Parmigianino, or a thousand other little things. When I enter the world of Orlando Furioso [by Ariosto] it seems in contrast that one sees opening out before one a

Guardaroba, a Tribuna, a royal gallery, ornamented with a thousand ancient statues by the most famous sculptors [. . .] and by the best of illustrious painters, with a large number of vases in rock crystal, agate, lapis-lazuli and other hardstones, and finally replete with rare, precious and remarkable things of the greatest excellence.[128]

Galilei's criticisms take us from the cramped and heterogeneous antiquarian's study of the fifteenth and early sixteenth century – the kind revealed in the inventory of Frate Franceschino of Cesena and illustrated by Carpaccio – into the dazzling vista of the great galleries of the sixteenth-century courts: his mention of the Tribuna is a clear reference to the Medici collections as transferred to and displayed in the Uffizi by Francesco I de' Medici.[129]

The literary theme of the study had nothing like the pervasiveness or grip on the Renaissance mind as that of the villa, but, extending Lillie's argument, real study-rooms tell us much about the literary and visual construction of scholarship, learned and elegant leisure, individualism and comfort in the fifteenth and sixteenth centuries.

74   Parmigianino, *Portrait of a Man*, oil on wood. Probably painted in Parma before 1524. The relief showing Mars, Venus and Cupid, the figurine of Ceres and the ancient coin point to collecting interests, but the nature of the landscape is unclear: is it a painting or a view from a window? London, National Gallery.

PINXIT QVEM NON VIDIT

CORPORIS EFFIGIEM ISTA QVIDEM BENE PIC
EXPRIMIT, AST ANIMI TOT MEA SC
M.D.LXII.

6   *Instruments and Ornaments for the Study*

THE PREVIOUS CHAPTERS HAVE BEEN concerned with the relationship between certain individuals among the urban élites and the spaces they inhabited. This chapter concentrates on objects typically found in studies, including implements related to writing, such as pens, penknives, inkwells; boxes of sand for scattering over freshly written sheets; stationery boxes and paperweights. The evolution of the sculptural inkstand in metal or ceramic was a development of the Italian Renaissance which was intimately connected with the humanist and selfconscious ideal of the study as a dignified space created by or for an individual. Seal-dies and signet rings, bearing an individual's arms and often accompanied by a personal motto or device, were often kept in studies and were used to seal correspondence. Mirrors, apart from their beauty, the mysterious fascination of their technology, and their perceived value in enhancing any room in which they were placed, were also thought to refresh the eyesight. For this reason they were considered useful accessories for anyone who was constantly reading and writing. Small hand-mirrors were also used as reading aids in deciphering illegible or merely faded script. Lenses and spectacles were prized not just as reading aids, but for close work or for examining precious, small-scale or detailed objects, such as ancient coins or illuminated manuscripts.

All these objects became in some way emblematic not only of the study but of the kind of person who owned such a room. The aim of this chapter is to show how this happened in the course of the Renaissance, examining a wide range of evidence, from inventories and account books to paintings, bronzes, medals and maiolica. The evolution of art objects which were closely if not exclusively associated with the study, and the proliferation and refinement of their form and decoration, illustrates a development which has often been overlooked by art historians. As the economic historian Richard Goldthwaite describes:

> In inventing all kinds of new furnishings ranging from pottery to paintings, in elaborating their forms, in refining their production, and in organising them into new spatial arrangements within their homes, Italians discovered new values and pleasures for themselves, reordered their lives with new standards of comportment, communicated something about themselves to others – in short, generated culture, and in the process created identities for themselves. In this cultural development there was a dynamic for change that resulted from the interaction between people and physical objects.[1]

The following examples illustrate the working of that dynamic in the context of the Italian Renaissance study.

75   Detail from Gianbattista Moroni's posthumous portrait of Giovanni Bressani (see frontispiece) with still-life details: a sander and an inkstand in the form of a sandalled foot. Edinburgh, National Gallery of Scotland.

Pouncepots, Penknives and Scissors

Pouncepots, which were used to scatter sand over wet ink in order to dry it, could be integral to inkstands or made separately. Just as much ingenuity went into the search for the perfect pouncepot as for the appropriate inkstand, as the correspondence between Ercole d'Este and his agent in Buda demonstrates. In 1501 Ercole requested his agent to find him 'one of those pouncepots [*spolverini*] of the kind that comes from Cracow'. His agent replied saying that he had ordered a dozen, but that they might not materialise since

> the maker of these instruments [. . .] was a friar [. . .] who is now very ancient and lives in Vienna, one hundred and sixty Italian miles away. And they have told me that they doubt that he makes them still, on account of old age.[2]

Penknives, used to temper quill pens (hence their name, *temperatoi*) were also useful accoutrements for writing. The calligrapher Gianbattista Palatino described the qualitites they should have and how they should be used:

> The knife used to temper pens should be of steel, well-tempered, well-ground and with a fine edge, and the handle should be fat and rectangular in section, so that it does not turn about in one's hand as one uses it.[3]

One should not use a penknife to cut paper, since this blunted the blade.[4] Perhaps this is why penknives are so often listed in inventories along with small pairs of scissors intended for that specific purpose. A gilded penknife and a gilded pair of scissors appear in the study of Andrea Minerbetti in 1502 (Minerbetti memoranda) while an inkstand in the study of Mario Seghieri contained a pair of scissors (Seghieri 1592). Scissors were elegant objects for the study. Isabella d'Este wrote to one of her agents in 1505:

> For furnishing our study, we pray you or rather we desire you to have made a little pair of scissors and one of those little penknives, fine and neat, which should be good and very handsome. In doing this you will give us great pleasure.[5]

Scissors could be hung on nails on the side of one's writing-desk, as frequently shown in paintings. In Ghirlandaio's *St Jerome* (fig. 25), scissors are leaning on their points against the side of his portable writing-desk, which has two small inkhorns for different coloured inks and a pair of spectacles attached to it. A small pouncepot can also be seen on Jerome's desk, next to his ruler. A portable inkwell hangs from the edge of the overcrowded shelf above his head. Tomaso da Modena's *St Jerome* has an even more practical arrangement, in that the penknives and other writing equipment are stored in a leather pouch pinned to the side of the desk unit.[6] Scholars who were continually writing must have customised their desks and working areas as shown in these pictures. The artists convey the authority of the saint or scholar depicted by illustrating their familiarity with the processes of writing and editing.

Seal-dies and Signets

Seal-dies, used to seal letters with an heraldic or personal device, were often to be found with writing equipment in the study. Many examples have survived of the type itemised by Giovanni del Chiaro: 'a box with several seal-dies' and another box specifically for seals, decorated with gesso reliefs.[7] Andrea Minerbetti's seal-die was made of ivory (Minerbetti memoranda) while a later Florentine inventory mentions a seal-die cut with the arms of the owner, kept in an inkstand with a pair of scissors and a table bell (Seghieri 1592).

Signet rings could also be kept in the study when not being worn by their owner: they were very much regarded as personal property. A signet could be made entirely of gold, engraved in intaglio on the bezel, or could be set with an antique or modern intaglio gem. The latter became increasingly popular in the course of the fourteenth and fifteenth centuries, as superb examples in the British Museum demonstrate.[8] A fascinating reference to a signet ring appears in the memoranda of the Florentine Francesco di Matteo Castellani, who records that in July 1490:

> I gave Meo del Lavachio, goldsmith, my ring of a sapphire intaglio cut with my arms, for him to reset [*el mio anello del zaffiro intaglato coll'arme perché mi rilegassi*]. The setting with the stone weighed nine and a half *onzie*, and I gave him [amount of payment left blank] for adding to the setting and making it bigger, and the ring heavier. And he must engrave for me the inscription on it [. . .] that is to say, 'Semper consilii plenus esto' ['Always full of counsel']. I fetched back the ring on 8 August. It weighed 16d, *grani* 20, as I wrote Meo on his receipt. He is to have [amount left blank] *lire* for workmanship and gold.[9]

The sapphire may have been surrounded by an inscription on the bezel recording Castellani's name, as often appears on surviving signets, while the inscription intermingling Latin and Greek would appear to have been engraved on the enlarged hoop of the ring. This was again in line with contemporary Italian practice as signets became heavier from the early fifteenth century.[10]

Ancient intaglios could also be set in heavy and elaborate gold mounts for use as seal-dies (fig. 76), as in the case of the superb cornelian gem by Dioscorides showing Apollo and Marsyas which was in the collection of Lorenzo de' Medici (Medici 1492). Listed among the contents of Lorenzo's study along with other precious gems from the Medici collection,[11] the gem is described as being 'set in gold' (*leghato in oro*); the mount does not survive, but we know about its design, workmanship and lettering from plaquettes[12] which reproduce the inscription placed around the gem, and from Lorenzo Ghiberti's description in his *Commentaries* of the gold mount which he had made for it.[13] Ghiberti set the gem so that it was held between the wings of a dragon, and surrounded by an inscription taken from a coin of the Emperor Nero (the seal was thought to have been the Emperor's seal-die, hence its remounting for Lorenzo's use, and its reputation in the Renaissance). The

76 Three gems (reproduced slightly larger than actual size) from Renaissance collections. Top left: a cameo with a lion (in a later ring setting) inscribed with the ownership inscription, LAUR.MED., possibly from the collection of Lorenzo de' Medici and similar to one mentioned in the Medici inventory of 1492. Top right: the Noah cameo of onyx in a heavy gold pendant setting, showing Noah and his family leaving the Ark. Inscribed LAU .R. MED on the open doors of the Ark. The date of the gem is uncertain: it has been thought to be ancient, or to have been made in the court workshop of Frederick II Hohenstaufen (d.1250). The cameo is mentioned in the 1492 Medici inventory. Bottom left: a sard intaglio with profile portrait of Fra Sabba di Castiglione, labelled SABBA CAST. The gem is finely cut, even indicating the stubble on Fra Sabba's chin. It is tempting to attribute it to the latter's great friend, the gem-engraver Giovanni Bernardi da Castelbolognese (1496–1553), who is praised in the highest terms as 'my Giovanni of Castello' in Fra Sabba's *Ricordi*. Bernardi retired from Rome to Faenza, where he died only a few years before his friend. This gem was possibly intended for Fra Sabba's signet ring, which would date it to the first half of the sixteenth century. London, British Museum, Department of Medieval and Later Antiquities.

conceit of the dragon mount sounds far from classical, being more chivalric and heraldic in inspiration, while the lettering, which Ghiberti described as being in carefully executed *lettere antiche*, appears distinctly Gothic from the plaquettes which record it. For all his antiquarian expertise, Ghiberti was also unable to identify the subject of the gem. His description conveys his pride and excitement in the task of resetting such a fine antique gem, restoring it (as he would have seen it) to its original role as a seal-die. Ghiberti's work would therefore have increased its worth as a study object, even though the valuation given for it (1000 gold florins) in the Medici inventory is less (despite its gold mount) by 500 florins than that given for the chalcedony intaglio of Diomedes and the Palladium, another work by Dioscorides, which was thought to have greater intrinsic value on account of its composition (Medici 1492).[14]

Paper Storage and Paperweights

A stationery box in which to keep writing-paper was also a desirable study piece. Isabella d'Este asked Lorenza da Pavia to find her one made of damascened iron to place in her study, like the box he had found her daughter, the Duchess of Urbino, after a year of looking in Venice.[15] Such a box made it easier to transport paper from one place to another, useful for travellers. Fra Sabba di Castiglione recommended in his notes for travellers that one should always carry 'a little inkwell with a little paper so that one can write should the need occur'.[16]

One method of keeping papers was to tie them up in bags known as *tasche* or *sacchetti*, which are frequently mentioned in inventories (Battaghini 1572; Fece 1450). Some householders gave bags of papers to monasteries for safe-keeping in times of plague or war, in which case the inventory includes them after listing the contents of the house, as in the inventory of Maestro Bartolo di Tura (Tura 1483).

Papers could also be sewn into books, in the manner of notarial acts (as many householders would have learnt at the vernacular schools) or letters threaded on string. One inventory mentions 'a needle for threading papers together' in a study (Seghieri 1592), a rare reference to a common practice, since it was not only notaries who made manuscript books of their papers. 'A string of bills' is listed in another Florentine inventory (Battaghini 1572).

77 Detail from a woodcut from the Malermi Bible (Venice 1490) showing a string of bills hanging on the wall of a study (see fig. 49). London, British Library.

Depictions of saints and scholars show other methods of keeping papers in studies. Carpaccio included a tape holding papers against a wall in a *trompe l'oeuil* panel (fig. 78) on the reverse of his painting *Hunting on the Lagoon*. It has recently been suggested that the panel, attached to another missing panel by hinges, may have served as the door to a study, painted with a particularly appropriate subject.[17] Carpaccio's preliminary drawing for his *Vision of St Augustine* depicts a door leading into the study at the rear left which has a batten or cleat attached top and bottom (fig. 28 above). If the *trompe l'oeuil* panel had had such attachments, it would explain the original lack of paint at the top section of the scene on the front.[18] Seen from inside the room, the letter-rack would have formed a wall of the room and an integral part of its decoration, alluding to the expected contents and arrangement of a contemporary study.

The definition of the word 'scartabello' in Florio's dictionary suggests that not all writers were so organised and neat, for he glosses it as 'an od[d] corner to cast writings in'.[19] Could this be a record of student slang of a kind which does not survive anywhere else? Botticelli's panel painting of *St Augustine* (Uffizi, Florence) shows discarded pens and paper scraps on the floor of his study, illustrating not only a saint's false starts but also Botticelli's delight in 'optical virtuosity'.[20]

Fascinating references in the correspondence of Philipp Hainhofer and Duke Augustus the Younger of Brunswick specify the use of small bronzes as paperweights in the early seventeenth century, such as 'a portrait of Attila in bronze, used for weighing down writings' (fig. 79)[21] and 'a gilded lizard and a snake which fight together and are beautifully intertwined, cast from life by the artful Gottfried Münderer and used for weighing down papers' (fig. 80).[22] Mention is also made of frogs in lead (sometimes painted), lizards and snakes in silver, all cast from life.[23] Such curiosities have traditionally been thought of as Paduan in origin,[24] but there now appears to be good documentary evidence for assigning at least some of them to Augsburg. Whether Italian or a German import, the lizard on the scholar's desk in Lotto's portrait of a scholar in the Accademia would appear to be a bronze cast from life, used as a paperweight.[25]

79 Bronze relief of Attila. Identifiable as the paperweight offered to Duke Augustus the Younger of Brunswick by the dealer Philipp Hainhofer in 1645. Italian, sixteenth century. Brunswick, Herzog Anton Ulrich-Museum.

In his book in praise of Venice, Marcantonio Sabellico mentioned small spheres of *millefiori* glass which may have been used as paperweights, or pierced and set in silver mounts to hang from a shelf as decorative objects:[26]

But consider to whom did it first occur to include in a little ball all the sorts of flowers which clothe the meadows in Spring. Yet these little things have been under the eyes of all nations as articles of export.[27]

Just this kind of object is listed in a Florentine document recording a division of property between the male heirs of Filippo Strozzi in 1494. Porcelain and glass bought by Filippo from Venice included 'two spheres of multicoloured glass with flowers'.[28]

80 Two lizards fighting a snake, cast from life in lead. Perfectly designed so that the joined heads form a handle for lifting the piece, making it a useful paperweight as well as an impressive sculpture. Italian, sixteenth century. Florence, Museo Nazionale del Bargello. Photo: Florence, Soprintendenza, Gabinetto Fotografico.

Reading-cushions

Perhaps the strangest of all pieces of study equipment (though not Italian) is the mention of a specially designed cushion in the collection of Prince Augustus which he kept in the drawer of a cabinet:

> a cushion made of coloured Spanish silk very artfully and minutely embroidered and with a gold edge on which can be seen on one side *de arte optica* [i.e. in distorted perspective] embroidered the story of Judith and Holofernes, and on the other side the story of Jael and Sisera; and when you set up a round looking-glass in the centre of these stories you can see the stories on the cushion quite perfectly. And this cushion is for the studying gentleman or lady, to prop their arm (when they are holding their head in their hands) or to kneel upon in prayer.[29]

Nothing of this elaboration could be shown in a painting showing a scholar or collector in his study, though melancholic individuals are sometimes depicted leaning their elbow on one cushion or several, like the silk taffeta cushions in Moretto da Brescia's portrait of a young man (figs 82 and 106).[30] These were status objects as well as study props.

The Care, Binding and Display of Books

A considerable amount was known about how best to preserve books, judging by information given in Decembrio's dialogue *De politia litteraria*. Leonello d'Este is quoted as saying:

> Keep the books free of household dust, as people do who shut them up in cupboards or chests, and never take them out to read or put them back except one at a time – which is to keep them inside a private and secret library – not an open one and for one's friends. Household dust sticks stubbornly to books soiled just in the course of being taken out and put back, no matter how often the floor of the room is washed – which is why washing one's hands counters the trouble to begin with, and which ought

81 Attributed to Guglielmo
della Porta, tomb monument
in marble showing a scholar
with his books, late
sixteenth century. Berlin,
Staatliche Museen
Preussischer Kulturbesitz,
Skulpturengalerie.

82 (*facing page*) Moretto da
Brescia, *A Young Man*, oil
on canvas, *c*.1542. The
man's melancholic pose,
leaning on his study
cushions, is underlined by
the Greek inscription on his
hat-badge which translates as
'Alas, I desire too much'.
London, National Gallery.

to be seen even more carefully, whether you have the books standing one after the
other, fore-edges out on the bookshelves, or chained like slaves, as is the case in
monastery libraries. Also some people shut them up behind glass or canvas panes, on
account of the dirt, and to protect them from too much direct sunlight and dust in
the air.[31]

The curtains shown in several paintings – as in Ghirlandaio's *St Jerome* (fig. 25), where they
hang over the book ledge on one wall of the study – were perhaps designed to protect
books from dust and light. Leonello adds that a paste of bay and other herbs 'prevents
bookworms within the covers of the books, and is thought to greatly benefit not only
books but also clothing particularly, and all domestic furnishings'.[32]

Further information about the care of books is given in a set of instructions sent from
the Neapolitan ambassador in Buda, Antonio Probi, to his chaplain Mathias during his
absence abroad in 1479. Probi asks that his chaplain should:

Take the time one day to rearrange all the books, taking them one by one and shaking
off the dust and cleaning the bindings with a cloth [*pigla tempo un jorno remascolareli tucti,
aprendoli un per uno scotolandoli da la polvere et nectandoli de fora con un panno*]. Then put
them back in the bookchest, which should be locked [. . .] so that neither Cola nor
Constanti nor anyone else can handle them. And make sure that the chest containing
the aforementioned books does not stand in a humid place, nor anywhere where there
is water.[33]

During the fifteenth century, many studies began to be fitted with shelves. Whereas
bookchests had ensured that books were easy to move, the custom of storing on shelves

gave a library greater permanence. This could cause difficulties when the owner had to move house, as the archpriest of Mantua, Benedetto Mastino, complained in a letter to Lodovico Gonzaga in 1477. He had adapted an audience chamber in his house as a study with iron bars on the windows and shelves laden with books (*con le asse intorno piene di libri*). There were so many books that he feared there would not be enough room in the new house 'in which one could lodge so many books in each discipline, such as I have'.[34]

The shelves in Mastino's study were not permanent fixtures, but were made of boards (*assi, assides tavole*) such as are frequently mentioned in fifteenth-century inventories. One inventory lists shelves as movables: 'many boards which used to be fixed up in the study of the said master Francesco as tables, benches and shelves for books' (Fiesso 1484). Shelves which followed an architectural feature of the room which contained them were permanent fixtures, however, and were often painted to fit in with the decoration of the room. One Florentine had a study in his bedchamber in which the shelves (*cornici*) were painted yellow and green, as were the chests and bedstead, matching the green hangings. On the shelves marking the mouldings lay a number of Greek and Latin books (Portigiani 1571). Books in this period rarely stood vertically on shelves, but lay flat, fore-edge outwards,[35] as shown in many manuscript illuminations of Doctors of the Church. Later in the fifteenth century large folios are often shown propped at an acute angle on a shelf or ledge, leaning against the wall of the study (fig. 8). This may be a result of artistic licence, an excuse to depict elaborate bindings. It could also have been a device to emphasise books as religious texts, and so demonstrate the authority of the saint or scholar depicted. St Jerome is often shown in this manner in the fifteenth century, with books as attributes of his authority as translator of the Bible (fig. 25). It was also a practical device for propping up large, heavy books in a small cramped space, so that they stood at an angle

83 Ink sketch by Vittore Carpaccio showing a scholar in his study. Note the high shelves – the lower one with instruments suspended from it – and the iron window grilles and door lock for securing the room's contents. British Museum, London.

to accommodate easy reading. Perhaps artists recorded a contemporary custom among those who habitually used books in their work.

Books could be stood on shelves with their fore-edges facing outwards (fig. 84). One bibliophile, Odorico Pillone, commissioned Cesare Vecellio to paint the fore-edges of his books with appropriate portraits of scholars in their studies (fig. 85). Vecellio probably painted over the name of the author, written in ink, which had already been inscribed on the edges of each book for easy identification. The degree of Pillone's involvement as patron becomes evident from the instructions which he wrote on particular books for Vecellio to follow.[36] Lined up on the shelves of Pillone's study, they must have proved the point that books do indeed furnish a room, and Pillone's commission shows the importance of interior decoration and organisation to the sixteenth-century collector. When a bibliophile wished to furnish his study, he might turn to a fellow scholar for advice as to which books he should buy and how they should be displayed. When Giovanbattista Grimaldi began to furnish his study in his palace in Genoa in 1544, he asked his tutor and mentor Claudio Tolomei for guidance.[37] Tolomei summarised the contemporary ideal of a well-furnished study when he stated that

84   Detail of Antonio Fabriano's *St Jerome in his Study* (fig. 3) showing books lying fore-edge outwards and flat on shelves. Note the paper markers tipped into the books for easy reference: these sometimes survive in Renaissance books. Baltimore, Walters Art Gallery.

if Grimaldi followed his advice, 'it will form a complete library, which will ornament first your study, and then, to a much greater degree, your soul'.[38] The study was arranged to show the equal achievements of ancient and modern authors, with the moderns bound in red, and the ancients in green.[39] Using different coloured leather bindings in this way appears to have been a mid-sixteenth-century custom, which was sometimes thwarted by the scarcity of dyed skins of suitable quality (fig. 86). When Cardinal Alfonso Carafa wished to distinguish the classes in his library, his agent complained that this had not been possible, since 'the only skins that are any good are red or violet-coloured'.[40]

The Grimaldi study was divided into two complementary sections. The quarto and octavo volumes in the library are titled on the front boards, showing that they were intended to lie flat on shelves or lean up against ledges or walls, while other books in other formats stood upright on shelves in the modern style.[41] As John Hale has pointed out, the significance of the Grimaldi project was that it was a colour-coded library designed to show at a glance that the moderns were at least a match for the ancients in every branch of learning. The library was also complete and finite, representing the sum of human knowledge within a carefully selected group of core texts.[42] As so often with grandiose design schemes, we do not know what Grimaldi himself made of it. Anthony Hobson has drawn attention to the fact that the newly married Grimaldi marked a passage in his copy of Marsilio Ficino's *Della vita sana* (book II, chapter 6) which states that the three enemies of study are making love, eating and drinking to excess, and staying up late.[43]

85 Three of the books from the library of Odorico Pillone of Casteldardo, with fore-edges decorated by Cesare Vecellio between 1581 and 1594. Here, the complete works of St Jerome are painted according to Pillone's instructions, with two scenes showing the saint in his study, flanking a third showing him in penitence in the desert. Facing outwards from the bookshelves, as here, Pillone's library must have proved the point that books do indeed furnish a room. Jerome, *Opera Omnia*, Basel 1536. Pillone Collection, courtesy of Pierre Berès.

86 (*facing page*) Binding on Pico della Mirandola's *On the Providence of God*, one of about 140 surviving volumes bound as a set for the library of the young Genoese patrician Giovanbattista Grimaldi. The books were gathered together and bound in Rome by binders of the Pontifical Court between 1540 and 1548. All of them are decorated with the same device or *impresa*, stamped on the front board, showing Apollo in his sun chariot approaching Parnassus. The image is strengthened by the Greek inscription, ORTHOS KAI ME LOXIOS, which translates as 'Straight and not crooked'. Purple morocco, decorated with blind and gold tooling; the impression gilded, silvered and painted. Copenhagen, Kunstindustrimuseet.

Grimaldi's library shows how a study could have a representative function. Too much attention to the appearance of a study, with elegantly bound books neatly lined up on shelves, could prevent one from having any wish to read. Such an interest in superficials came to be used as a literary topos denoting a pretender to learning. In the brilliant *Letters of Obscure Men*, written to defend the humanist scholar Reuchlin against the obscurantist Cologne theologians, a satirical mention is made of the chief protagonist's well-furnished study:

you must not believe that I disparage you in that you possess but few books, for I know that you have many. Indeed, when I was in your study at Cologne I could see well

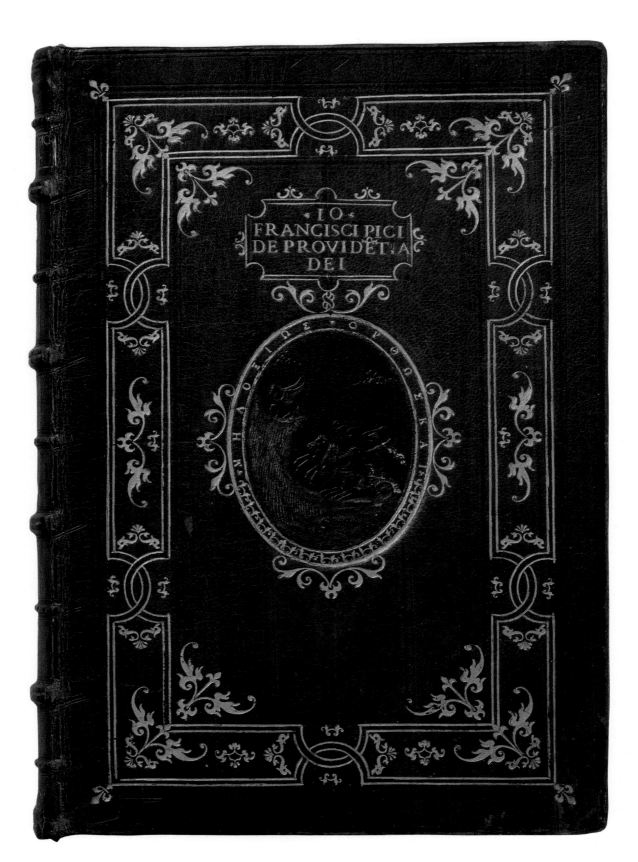

enough that you had a multitude of volumes both great and small. Some were clad in wooden boards, and some in parchment bindings – some were covered all over with leather, red and green and black, while some were half-bound. And there you sat with a fly-whisk in your hand, to flap away the dust from the bindings.[44]

The idea clearly conveyed is a that a self-regarding concern for books as proof of one's own learning has taken the place of intellectual curiosity or a lively concern for knowledge. As the satirist John Earle in his *Microcosmography* put it, describing a 'young gentleman of the University':

His study has commonly handsome shelves, his bookes neat silken strings [. . .] which [. . .] he is loth to untie or take down, for feare of misplacing. Upon foule days for recreation hee retyres thither.[45]

When Fra Sabba di Castiglione wrote a book of advice for his great-nephew on how to become a perfect knight of the Order of St John, he described the kind of study which he should create for himself, in which books were an essential ingredient. Fra Sabba was well aware that vernacular literature, particularly chivalric romances and the works of Ariosto, held a greater attraction for at least some of his readers than the kinds of book which he recommended. He blamed printers, binders and booksellers for the way in which they printed and presented the works of the Doctors of the Church, making them even less attractive to potential readers. It pained him to see such books printed in

ignorant, deep, ugly and graceless type so as to put off even a studious reader from wanting to read them. Apart from the villainous characters [type] the pages are black, smoky, rotten and filthy like paper packages used to wrap rotten tunny fish, or like Bolognese almanacs. On the other hand, one sees Ser Morgante, Ser Orlando, Messer Decameron, Donna Fiametta and other similar works [. . .] which are vain, unfruitful and totally useless works, printed with great care, with great solemnity and patience. They are printed on very delicate paper using the finest type, as if they were the Law written by the finger of God, which was given to the great Moses on Mount Sinai. While the other books, which provide virtuous food of greater substance, nourishment and vigour than these do [. . .] are rejected and without value in the streets, like Sicilian biscuit, mossy, verminous, and covered with spider-webs. Orlando, Rinaldo, Messer Decameron and Monna Fiametta, and others like them, are continually dressed up in snakeskin and precious purple, like kings, while the poor holy organs and trumpets of the Holy Spirit go about covered in humble, rough and austere russet homespun, like Capucin friars.[46]

Sabba's words show that he was aware of the powerful hold which chivalric romances or 'battle books' had for his contemporaries, whether they read them themselves, learnt them at the vernacular schools, or heard them declaimed in public places.[47] Principally valued for their role in children's and school culture, romances continued to attract adults. An inscription in a manuscript of Andrea da Barberino's *I Nerbonesi* indicates that it was a fair copy of a children's book made by a Florentine banker for his own pleasure in 1534.[48]

Sabba's denunciation of popular books was part of his attack on men's credulity and false values, for it is in the same spirit that he denounces a sentimental man, who, having heard the story of Orlando declaimed in the marketplace, went home to his family in tears, 'like a well-beaten child', scarcely able to tell his wife what the matter was in the face of her fear that he had been beaten up on the way home.[49] Perhaps Sabba's critique of the ways in which secular books were bound and marketed, for all its bluster, best indicates his keen sense of the aesthetic appeal of books, despite his concern for content in recommending works suitable for the study.

87 Attributed to Gerolamo da Carpi, *A Gentleman in his Study*, *c*.1526. The study accessories, like the dignified dress, the gold chain and the sword that he wears, serve to identify his high social rank. The animal which lies on his gold-tooled books (is it a dog or a rough-haired cat?) may allude to the sitter's identity. The emphatic gesture with which he places his hand on its back would suggest that it has some such significance, although it is worth noting that small dogs are frequently shown as companions to scholars in their studies from representations of Petrarch onwards (see Corio's portrait, fig. 7, and Lorenzo Lotto's portrait, fig. 24). A literary reference to dogs as being far from ideal study companions appears in a dialogue from the court of Leonello d'Este, in which the latter is cited as saying that playful dogs should be kept out of these rooms. Oil on canvas. Rome, Galleria Nazionale d'Arte Antica a Palazzo Barberini. Photo: Alinari.

Lenses and Spectacles

Spectacles appear to have been in common use in Italy by the mid-fourteenth century, judging by literary and pictorial evidence.[50] A letter from the master woodworker Arduino da Baese to Piero di Cosimo de' Medici in 1451, asking him for a replacement pair of spectacles for close work,[51] fascinatingly indicates that craftsmen making *lavoro d'intarsia* used optical aids in order to do precision work in wooden inlay.

The use of spectacles would have spread quickly in a mercantile society with relatively wealthy and developed urban centres. The overall literacy rate of Florence and Venice in the 1480s has been estimated at between 30 and 33 per cent.[52] There was a guild of spectacle-makers in Venice by 1320,[53] but Florence took the lead, appropriately for a centre of optical experiment, from the beginning of the fifteenth century. A letter written in 1462 from Francesco Sforza, Duke of Milan to his ambassador in Florence, Tranchedin da Pontremoli, asks for three dozen pairs to be sent in boxes to Milan:

> Many people are demanding those spectacles which they make over there in Florence, seeing their fame and that they make them to greater perfection there than anywhere else in Italy.[54]

Of the three dozen ordered, he asked for lenses to correct long sight and others described as 'normal' (commune) lenses. The order was fulfilled within ten days, so there must have been a ready stock in Florence.[55]

Eye-glasses as well as spectacles were used for reading, but also for magnifying coins, cameos and manuscript illumination so as to appreciate details of workmanship. Millard Meiss long ago suggested that just as illuminators might have used lenses for their work, so patrons too may have taken up lenses when looking at a manuscript.[56]

Cardinal Francesco Gonzaga's inventory lists three lenses or eye-glasses (occhi) probably made of rock crystal since they are listed with other rock-crystal objects (Gonzaga inventory 1483, pp.91, 477). Francesco is known to have appreciated books as visual objects as well as for their contents.[57] He certainly owned a pair of spectacles since his inventory lists a superb enamelled gold case for them (Gonzaga inventory 1483, p.91). One Florentine, whose movables were inventoried in 1493, kept no fewer than one hundred pairs of spectacles in a box in his study (Panuzio 1493). Someone who needed spectacles may well have thought it wise to lay in supplies in case of breakage, and this was a well-stocked study, with large quantities of glass, silver-mounted cutlery and leather-bound books, as well as a steel hand-mirror to help with reading.

Other inventories list rock-crystal lenses as visual aids, including a mention of one mounted in silver in a Florentine inventory of 1462.[58]

A Venetian merchant kept six lenses of ground mountain rock crystal in a cabinet, along with an assortment of small, precious objects. These included eighteen painted depictions of saints, thirteen Flemish copper engravings, his own portrait in stucco and an illuminated breviary with silver clasps; he also had two medals (one silver, one gold) of the Holy Roman Emperor Charles V (Calderini 1597).

Inkstands

Of all the rooms in an Italian Renaissance apartment, the study was the perfect place in which to display small objects of fine workmanship associated with literacy and learning. Inkstands were useful objects to those who needed to write, and like many objects made with the study in mind, they were decorative as well as being ostensibly functional. They could have a representative role, for they demonstrated an individual's taste and literacy. They could also make references to the classical or chivalric past which were enjoyable to recognise and identify, and which carried associations of gentility. An inkstand could be made out of an exotic, luxurious or unusual material, such as silver or ebony. Made of coloured glass or tin-glazed pottery, it could bring vivid colour into the study; disguised as a box or a book, or taking the form of desk-top sculpture imitating dignified classical models in miniature, an inkstand was the quintessential study object in that it combined playfulness with decorum. Perhaps reduced copies of famous antique sculpture in marble had the same status and associations as facsimiles of famous antiquities in twentieth-century Britain, giving their owners a sense of contact with the past.[59]

All these characteristics explain why the decorative inkstand, as a new kind of art object

88 Detail of Franciabigio's
oil portrait of a scholar (fig.
91) showing an inkwell
made of two truncated
cylinders soldered together.
The deeper container is for
ink, the shallower one for
sand. Berlin, Staatliche
Museen zu Berlin,
Preussischer Kulturbesitz,
Gemäldegalerie.

89 Inkwell and penholder
consisting of two pairs of
truncated cylinders made of
cast metal sheet, crudely
soldered together. A
simplified version of the
same design can be seen in
Franciabigio's portrait
(fig. 88). Probably a very
common type, of which
it is a rare survival. Late
sixteenth or early
seventeenth century.
Florence, Museo Horne.
Photo: Florence,
Soprintendenza, Gabinetto
Fotografico.

designed for a domestic setting, answered a new type of demand among the urban élite of Renaissance Italy. Like the sandboxes, oil-lamps, table bells and seal-dies which are so often listed with them in inventories, inkstands were turned out and assembled in quantity in workshops and foundries, enabling a wide group of patrons to imitate the tastes of leading scholar-collectors. The simplest and most functional inkwells are not described in any detail in inventories. Paintings and woodcuts are often the best sources of information about the writing equipment used by those for whom writing was a daily activity, such as merchants, doctors, lawyers, notaries and clerics.

An inkwell was an essential accoutrement, since it kept ink black and lustrous, ready for use: this was particularly important for those who took the time and trouble to make their own ink, rather than buy it. A sixteenth-century calligraphic manual gives a receipt for iron gall ink in a section on writing equipment. The author, Gianbattista Palatino, was clearly a perfectionist, unusually concerned with the quality of materials required by the calligrapher and others who were continually writing. To make ink that was neither too thick nor too thin, he stipulates, one should pound three ounces of gall nut – derived from oak apples – and set it to soften in a half-beaker of wine for one or two days, allowing the mixture to infuse in the heat of the sun. One should add two ounces of ferrous sulphate (*cuperosa*) or strongly coloured green vitriol from Rome, finely pounded. Presumably these ingredients were available from apothecaries. Stirring the mixture with a fig-wood stick, one should add an ounce of gum arabic, 'so that the ink should be lustrous and clear'. Then the ink should be heated over a slow flame. Finally, the ink should be stored in a glass or lead vessel, 'to keep the ink fresh and black'. He explained that wooden inkwells were not to be recommended since they dried out the ink and made it too viscous. Ideally, an inkwell should consist of a squat drum set on a wide, stable base, 'so that one does not knock over the inkwell whenever one takes ink from it'.[60] Another calligraphic manual by Giovanantonio Tagliente includes a woodcut showing this type of inkwell and other writing equipment arranged in a decorative pattern, framed by set square and ruler (fig.90).[61]

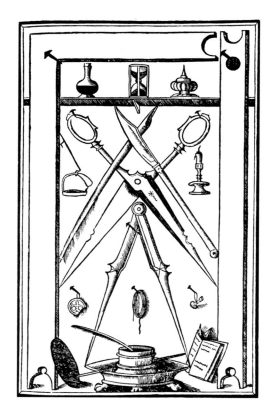

The simplest inkwells available in the fifteenth century were of a type that had been used for centuries, usually made of lead. The inkwell could often be attached to a leather pencase with a thong, so that it could be hung off one's belt or from a shelf in the study. Ghirlandaio's fresco of *St Jerome in his Study* shows a pencase with inkwell hanging from a shelf (fig.25). Pencases with inkwells of this type are listed in inventories as 'un pennaiuolo col calamaio', as in a Sienese inventory of 1450 (Fece 1450).

Although Palatino recommended glass inkwells, inventory references to them are few. As so often with Muranese glass production in the fifteenth century, important information comes from legal records, since glassworkers were particularly litigious. One glassmaker from Murano, Giorgio Ballarin, declared to the Venetian Chancery on 7 October 1487 that 'a glass inkstand, half of which was blue and the other half white' had

been stolen from his workshop. Presumably the cover was of one colour and the body of the other.[62]

At the top end of the market, the pattern was set by the inkstands made in precious metal, which had unique status among collectors in the second half of the fifteenth century. Three cardinals are known to have commissioned or owned fine examples. The post-mortem inventory of movables belonging to Cardinal Ludovico Trevisan, compiled in Florence in 1465, included 'A silver inkstand with four small figures of angels on top, and with an angel on the cover'.[63] Judging by later surviving figurative inkstands in bronze, Trevisan's inkstand probably consisted of a round or square base containing the inkwell, which was perhaps supported by the four angels. The angel, either fixed to the cover or cast in with it, would have been used as a handle. This magnificent inkstand must also have had a compartment or drawer built into it, for the inventory lists with it 'a pair of scissors and two iron penknives', which the Cardinal would have used to temper his pens ready for use.

Cardinal Francesco Gonzaga also had 'a large silver inkstand' among the objects in his study, which he bequeathed to his secretary and executor, Giovan Pietro Arrivabene (Gonzaga will 1483). A third cardinal known to have had a silver inkstand was Giovanni of Aragon, who had reputedly offered its maker, the leading Milanese goldsmith Caradosso Foppa (1452–1527), 1500 gold pieces for it in the early 1490s.[64] Caradosso appears to have been part of Giovanni's household at the time. The inkstand seems to have stayed in Milan after Caradosso's death: Sabba di Castiglione mentioned in his *Ricordi* that it was to be seen there and that it represented twenty-six years' work.[65]

It may be this object, or another variant made by Caradosso, that is described in an inventory compiled in Milan in 1586 in the interest of Francesco di Giovanni Battista di Lucio Foppa, who is thought to have been Caradosso's great-great-great-nephew. It was not then assembled, and its component parts were listed in the inventory as follows: a cast upper section in the form of a little turret or tower worked with Roman triumphs in relief; a little silver door or lid – probably to cover the inkwell – which was decorated in relief with one of the Labours of Hercules; three small reliefs also decorated with the Labours of Hercules; and four larger reliefs with unspecified subjects. The inventory states that these elements 'are all part of the said inkstand'.[66] The subjects of three of the reliefs which decorated the sides of this square inkstand are known from the description in Ambrogio de Leone Nola's *De nobilitate rerum natura*, which was printed in Venice in 1525. Leone was a physician and scholar of some reputation. His account of the history and archaeology of his home town of Nola,[67] which was illustrated with engravings by Mocetto and published in Venice in 1514, testifies to his humanist interests, while he is perhaps best remembered for having earned the praise of Erasmus for his learning as a physician and his membership of the household of Aldus Manutius.[68] Leone's account of Caradosso's reliefs takes the form of an *ekphrasis*,[69] a rhetorical description which, through a vivid, appraising account, attempts to bring them before our eyes:

> On one side [of the inkstand] nude men are seen riding on horses, who are coming to the assistance of a certain boy, whom an eagle has snatched into the skies; whereby through these figures is represented the Rape of Ganymede. Those men catching up with the eagle carrying off the boy display spirit and purpose as they seem to call to him and strain after him with their horses. On the other side [of the inkstand] is the Battle of the Centaurs with the Lapiths.[70]

Leone also mentions two of the Labours of Hercules; his account of Hercules killing the Nemean Lion includes such vivid details as the spectator almost being able to hear the lion groaning in its death agony.[71] Leone's description does not give a sense of the inkstand as a three-dimensional object, but as a set of reliefs, which perhaps suggests that he was

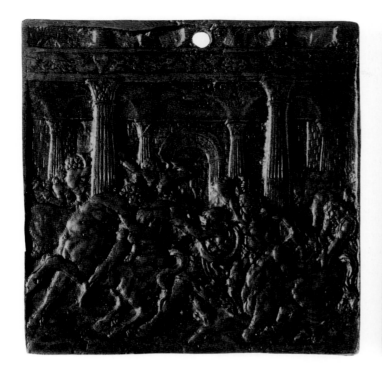

92a and b Caradosso Foppa
(1452–1527), two bronze
plaquettes showing (a) the
Battle of Lapiths and Centaurs
and (b) the *Rape of
Ganymede*, *c*.1485–95.
London, Victoria and Albert
Museum (*left*); British
Museum (*right*). Photos:
British Museum.

writing from copies of the reliefs – sulphur impressions – of the kind which he mentions as circulating at the time of writing in 1505.[72]

More permanent records of Caradosso's reliefs survive in the form of bronze plaquettes after the Rape of Ganymede and the Battle between Lapiths and Centaurs which, although they lack the crispness of the silver originals, still convey the dramatic charge of Caradosso's brilliantly compressed designs.[73] The example depicting the *Rape of Ganymede* (fig. 92b) measures only 5 by 4.9 centimetres, yet gives a compelling sense of pictorial depth even though it is executed in shallow, flattened relief.[74] Horsemen and dogs turn into the picture plane in sudden fear and amazement, guiding the eye to the focal figure of Ganymede as he is wafted into the air. The companion piece, the *Battle of Lapiths and Centaurs* (fig. 92a), is often represented by plaquettes of poor quality: late casts from worn moulds; this example, however, is a clean cast straight from the mould.

Leone's description is vivid enough to suggest that he had seen the inkstand, or copies of the reliefs set into it, shortly before writing his *ekphrasis*. His appraisal belongs to a literary and rhetorical tradition and certainly contains all the expected elements, but for all that, it should not be dismissed, since it represents one observer's response to an extremely fine study object which was thought to merit this kind of attention. For one thing, its reliefs were experiments in the latest Milanese style of figure design:[75] their miniature scale, the fact that they were made of silver and the way in which they were incorporated into an inkstand would only have made them more appealing in contemporary eyes.

In 1500 Caradosso made it known to Isabella d'Este's artistic agent that he would sell her a similar inkstand for 1000 ducats.[76] Isabella was anxious to take the inkstand on approval – though the asking price was well beyond her means – and in 1505 she petitioned Charles of Amboise in Milan for a patent exempting Caradosso from any duty which he might incur in bringing the inkstand from Milan to Mantua and back. 'I have a great desire', she wrote,

> to see a silver inkstand worked by Caradosso, the Milanese jeweller, which he has in Milan. Since he may be liable for customs duty in taking it out of Milan, I pray you,

for my especial pleasure, that it may please you to grant the aforesaid Caradosso a patent exempting him from any duty incurred in bringing and taking back the said inkstand throughout the Duchy of Milan.[77]

Isabella had at least two silver inkstands in her Grotta. One of them weighed over 59 ounces and was 'shaped in the form of a box, somewhat large, with the arms of Gonzaga impaling Este on the middle of the lid, standing on four little feet'.[78] This and other silver went missing from her Camerino during a visit by the Duke of Bourbon's retinue to her apartments in July 1509, proving that even well-born courtiers could be light-fingered. Once Isabella had discovered the theft, she wasted no time in sending descriptions of the missing pieces to her agents, asking them to circulate not only bankers but goldsmiths – who often acted as bankers and financial agents – to whom the silver might be turned in as bullion or metal for remodelling.[79] Isabella's silver inkstand was just the kind of luxury object that might find its way into a banker's hands as security for a loan: perhaps the wealthy Roman banker Agostino Chigi got hold of the silver inkstand listed under silver in the 1497 inventory of his movables through just this kind of transaction.[80]

Those who could not afford silver reliefs to decorate their inkstands could opt for reliefs in a relatively inexpensive metal, such as copper, which could then be silvered. One inkstand by an artist known as the Master of Coriolanus is set with silvered copper plaquettes showing scenes from the life of Coriolanus; they are surrounded by a moralising Latin inscription testifying to the virtue of Coriolanus's mother Volumnia, when she dissuaded him from marching on Rome, and his filial piety in desisting (figs 93a, b and c).[81] The inkstand provides a context for the myriad plaquettes of Roman history and mythology which are otherwise so difficult to place. Pope-Hennessy defines the cultural significance of this inkstand:

> as a child, you learnt about the Siege of Troy or the story of Lucretia from *Cassoni* [. . .] as you crawled over the floor of your parents' bedroom, and when you grew up, you had on your desk inkstands and candlesticks with reliefs by Master IO.FF or Moderno or Riccio though which images were repristinated in a form that was applicable to the conduct of your life.[82]

This inkstand is the kind of object that a young man might have chosen when decorating his bedchamber and the adjoining study in order to maintain exactly this type of cultural continuity.

Bronze sandboxes were also set with plaquettes to match or complement inkstands: the triangular box supported on lion's paws, each side of which is faced with a plaquette attributed to the Paduan sculptor Riccio, is a superb example; the reliefs draw on classical mythology and Christian chivalric legend, including St George and the Dragon, Nessus and Deianira, and Cupid with his quiver of arrows (figs 94a, b and c).[83] Examples of the first two plaquettes in the British Museum were clearly made as a pair to decorate such a sander since they are identical in size, colour of alloy, and the casting marks on the reverse, as well as having bevelled edges on the back of the rim fillet showing how they were intended to fit together to cover the angles of the box.[84]

The pairing of these two vivid and sophisticated reliefs as suitable decorations for a sandbox show the way in which chivalric themes popularised by the widely read *libri di battaglia* or 'battle books'[85] could co-exist with classical mythology in the context of the study.

Brass was not despised as a medium for inkstands, especially if it was engraved and inlaid with gold or with silver wire. Cardinal Francesco Gonzaga had a second inkstand listed in his inventory as 'An inkstand made of brass, in the form of a compass, decorated with damascening'.[86] This was probably a Mamluk export piece from Syria, since Italian

craftsmen were not working in this technique at this date.[87] The 1549 post-mortem inventory of Isabella d'Este's Grotta lists an elaborate inkstand made of damascened iron which contained a complete set of writing equipment: 'An inkstand of iron, which is engraved and inlaid with gold with four penknives, a pair of scissors worked in the same manner, with two pens inside, one of which has an ivory handle and the other an iron handle worked in the same fashion, with a seal mounted in the form of a signet ring which makes an impression of the musical rests, the personal device [*impresa*] of our mistress of excellent memory'.[88] This *impresa* cut in intaglio on Isabella's signet consisted of a clef for contralto voice (like Isabella's own), nine rests of varying length, and a repeat sign. It was one of her favourite decorative devices, appearing on the stucco reliefs which punctuate

94a, b and c Triangular bronze sander with pierced lid, set with three plaquettes attributed to Riccio: Cupid afloat on his quiver (*below left*), Nessus and Deianira (*below right*), and Saint George and the Dragon. Paduan, early sixteenth century. London, Victoria and Albert Museum.

the barrel-vault of her first Grotta, and on the walls and ceiling of the second. It also features on two of the surviving dishes from the Urbino maiolica service commissioned for her in 1524 by her daughter, and was embroidered on the gown she wore at the wedding of her brother, Alfonso d'Este, to Lucrezia Borgia at Ferrara in 1502.[89] The use of the same device in so many different media points to the consistency and continuity of Isabella's passionate concern for visual and intellectual refinement.

Bronze was one of the most highly valued materials for inkstands on aesthetic grounds, and a few sculptors were able to produce inkstands which deserved the same status as fine statuettes in the antique manner for their technical ingenuity, quality and finish. Objects like these may have answered the demand for small-scale bronzes among those who could

95 Bronze inkstand with a sleeping nymph, Veneto, first half of the sixteenth century. Daniel Katz Ltd.

not afford the independent works of ancient or modern sculptors which were snapped up so quickly by collectors. This is indicated by the fact that some inkstands imitated the reduced miniatures of well-known antique marbles which were made by the Mantuan court sculptor Antico between about 1484 and 1528. Severo da Ravenna, for instance, made a copy of the famous ancient Roman bronze of the *Spinario*, screwed onto a base plaque along with a globular container or whelk shell for ink.[90] The Ashmolean's example (fig. 96) is interesting in that the figure is shown with his right leg crossed over his left, contrary to the ancient original.[91] Perhaps Severo copied the composition from a print, which reproduced the statue in reverse.[92] An example of an inkstand based on the *Spinario* appears in a grand and dignified context in a portrait of Cardinal Antonio Pucci by Pierfrancesco Foschi, which is dated 1540 (fig. 99). Beautifully patinated, standing on a Timurid table-carpet from Anatolia next to an elegant bookbinding, the inkstand is clearly an object of significance. This is underlined by the fact that Foschi has taken the liberty of adding an inscription to the base of the inkstand which dates the portrait to the first day of December 1540: KAL[ENDIS].DECEM[BRIS.M.D.XL.][93]

Severo was only one of a group of craftsmen who can now be individually identified as producers of a wide range of small domestic objects cast in bronze, such as inkstands.[94] Northern Italian foundries did good business, judging by the destinations of signed and dated works by Giuseppe de Levis of Verona which are decorated with the arms of patrons from Mantua, Genoa and Milan.[95] Brescia and Venice had foundries which were largely occupied in making cannon and other weapons, and there were foundries in other centres, such as Padua. In these larger production centres, figurines, plaquettes and ready-made inkstands seem to have been turned out or assembled from elements in stock as requested by a patron.[96]

A good example of this practice is a humble inkstand (fig. 100) in the form of a boy

96 (*above left*) Workshop of Severo da Ravenna, Ravenna, *Spinario*, bronze inkstand, *c.*1510–30. The separate inkwell is made from a cast shell. The trunk on which the boy is seated is hollow, and served as a penholder. Oxford, Ashmolean Museum.

97 (*above right*) Detail of Pierfrancesco Foschi's portrait of Cardinal Antonio Pucci (fig. 99) showing a bronze inkstand with the *Spinario*, set on a Timurid table carpet. The inkstand is a significant enough element in the composition to bear the date, 1 December 1540. Florence, Galleria Corsini. Photo: Alinari.

99 Pierfrancesco Foschi, *Cardinal Antonio Pucci*, 1540. Note the inkstand based on the *Spinario* (fig. 96). Oil on canvas. Florence, Corsini Gallery. Photo: Alinari.

98 (*left*) Inkwell and sander in bronze. The sander, with its drilled top, is beautifully shaped as a shaker: the breasts and wings of the harpies on the sides help the user to maintain a firm grip. The well-designed inkwell on the left has a broad, flat base to give it stability, with a curved lip on which to drain away excess ink from one's quill pen after filling. This fits on top of the sander, and has its own fitted lid with a knop. The whole unit, apart from its quality as a desk-top sculpture, is remarkably practical to use and is surprisingly stable. Probably Italian, sixteenth century. Berlin, Kunstgewerbemuseum.

holding up a candle socket, standing on a log pierced with holes designed for quill pens. The log is attached to a triangular base plate, with two globular containers at two of the corners. One of these is a lidded inkwell, screwed to the base, while the other is a sander, today fixed with a modern screw to the base, but perhaps more easily removable for use originally. It fits snugly into the hand; the lid can be raised with the thumb in order to scatter sand over a page of wet ink. Cast in eleven pieces, including pieces found on other composite objects originating from Severo's workshop (such as the screws, the pierced log and the containers), the inkstand illustrates a point made by Pope-Hennessy, that a client could choose elements from stock and have an inkstand assembled to order.[97]

153

100 Inkstand from the workshop of Severo da Ravenna, Ravenna, second quarter of the sixteenth century. Oxford, Ashmolean Museum.

Founders were quite capable of casting to their own designs,[98] as well as pirating other people's. There seem to have been three basic forms for inkstands: an inkwell with a lid mounted with a figurine which served as a handle (as in the case of Cardinal Trevisan's silver inkstand described above), or a base plate onto which a separately cast figurine and an inkwell were screwed (as in the case of Severo's *Spinario*). The third type consisted of a box with compartments. A very early description of a box-type inkstand made of copper-alloy appears in the 1497 inventory of the movables of the Florentine scholar Pierfilippo Pandolfini. In his study was 'a square inkstand made of copper with certain masks and centaurs, mounted on four feet'.[99] Given the relatively detailed description, it must have been a fine and unusual object which deserved to share the study with a silver-mounted branch of coral listed after it which, from the evidence of contemporary paintings, may have been an amulet of the kind seen worn by the infant Christ.[100]

The style of bronze inkstands varied as much as their form. Some of those produced in Venice used classical themes, adapting them freely to suit the function and scale of their objects. A particularly fine and elegant example is an inkstand which consists of a seated female figure holding a tablet and stylus – perhaps a personification of Clio, Muse of History (fig. 103). The figure, the seat on which she sits and the tablet she holds are cast in one piece, fixed to a square plate. Using the figure as a finial, this entire plate can be

101 Bronze inkstand in the form of a triton seated on a turtle, with sander in the form of a drawer, hidden in the turtle's body. Possibly Venetian, late sixteenth century. Oxford, Ashmolean Museum.

lifted to reveal a tray underneath, containing compartments for the inkwell, seals and quill pens.[101] Another striking inkstand features a triton riding on a tortoise, with one shell supported on his scaly tail as an inkwell and a small whelk shell held above his head (fig. 101). The latter – which is cast from a real whelk – is fitted with a slot for a lamp wick at the narrowest point of the lip, showing that this inkstand was intended to double as a lamp. Similarly ingenious is the way in which the tortoise's head serves as the handle for a drawer, which pulls out to reveal a sandbox. When the lamp was lit, highlights and shadows on the lower part of the bronze would have emphasised the contrast between the triton's gelatinous flesh and the ridged shell of the tortoise. Seen by this light on a table-carpet in a collector's study, this bronze would have come into its own as a piece of desk-top sculpture which could also be used, at least on occasion. It is not surprising to find that a very similar inkstand, 'A satyr with an inkwell [supported] on its shoulders' (*Un satiro cum un canomal in spalla*) is listed among the bronzes in the study of one of Venice's leading collectors, the patrician Marcantonio Michiel (Michiel *c.*1552).

Roman bronze lamps could be reproduced either as lamps or – with minimal adaptations – as inkstands in the North Italian foundries and sculptors' workshops.[102] A good example of a Roman prototype is a lamp in the form of a sandalled foot, probably dating to the first century AD (British Museum, London). This example is designed to be

102 The base of the inkstand depicted in fig. 103 with the figure lifted away, showing compartments for inkwells, sander and other writing equipment. On the right, the underside of the lid showing the hollow cast figure. The inkwell sits in the hollow core of the figure. Oxford, Ashmolean Museum.

103 (*facing page*) Bronze inkstand with a female figure holding a tablet. Venetian, late sixteenth century. Oxford, Ashmolean Museum.

suspended from a lampstand, and even the hobnails on the sandal's leather sole, which would therefore be visible, are faithfully imitated in the bronze.[103] This type of bronze lamp in the form of an inkstand with a hinged lid was occasionally imitated (fig. 104).[104] Originating in the collection of Marchese Ferdinando Cospi, this, with the rest of Cospi's Museum, joined the Aldrovandi collection in the University Library in 1657 before being donated to the City in 1667.[105] Perhaps Cospi had included it in his collection in the belief that it was a Roman object, as we know happened with other Renaissance bronzes in the seventeenth century. In 1652 the Paduan antiquary Fortunius Licetus published two late fifteenth- or early sixteenth-century lamps of this type (fig. 105), suspended from a foliate handle projecting from the Achilles tendon on each lamp. Both the lamps and the lampstand from which they hang appear fancifully Renaissance rather than classical to the modern viewer, but by the time Licetus was writing, much of the culture which had created such exercises in the antique had changed. Some pieces had even had spurious archaeological provenances invented for them.[106]

An inkstand of identical form to the one in Bologna appears in Moretto's portrait of a Brescian nobleman, which provides a dating of around 1535–45 and a social context (fig. 106).[107] A variant of this type, with a built-up base, appears in Giovanbattista Moroni's portrait of Giovanni Bressani, which is dated 1562 (frontispiece and fig. 75). As with the Severo da Ravenna inkstand of the *Spinario*, the artist has added an inscription to the base, in this case referring to the fact that Moroni had not taken the portrait from life: 'Giovanni Battista Moroni painted him whom he did not see' (IO.BAPT.MORON.PINXIT/QUEM NON VIDIT). This cryptic phrase refers to the fact that the portrait was posthumous: Bressani had died in 1560, two years before the date recorded in the painting. Perhaps this explains the emphasis given to the still-life of objects on Bressani's desk, referring to his work as a prolific poet.[108] The monumental inkstand, from which he has just drawn ink to write the letter in his hand, conveys dignity and learning. Similar inkstands of the early sixteenth century had built-up bases: an example in the Louvre has a strip of acanthus leaf ornament, containing two drawers for sand and seal-dies around the base.[109]

104 Bronze oil-lamp in the form of a foot. Sixteenth century. Bologna, Museo Civico Medioevale.

105 Seventeenth-century engraving from a book on ancient oil-lamps, showing a composite bronze stand with two pendant bronze oil-lamps in the shape of sandalled feet which, even though they are of Renaissance type, were then thought to be ancient. Fortunius Licetus, *De Lucernis antiquorum reconditis libbri sex*, Udine 1652, pl. VI chap. XIV, p. 667. London, British Museum, Department of Medieval and Later Antiquities.

106 (*facing page*) Detail from Moretto da Brescia's portrait of a young man (see fig. 82) showing coins in turned wooden or bone boxes and a bronze lamp in the form of a sandalled foot. The sitter leans reflectively on two silk taffeta cushions—elegant study furnishings at the time the portrait was painted (*c*.1542). London, National Gallery.

Inventory references to inkstands of this type confirm that they were collectors' pieces. In the 1570s the sculptor Pompeo Leoni settled in Madrid, where he was working on sculptural commissions with the Habsburgs, and he presumably took with him from Milan his collection of bronzes. An inventory of 1609 lists two small bronzes in the form of a foot: one in the form of a candlestick (*Un pie de bronze que sirve de candil*) and another, described as being hollow, which was probably an inkstand (*Un pie de bronzo*).[110] That similar pieces remained collectors' items into the eighteenth century is demonstrated by a printed sale catalogue of 1764, which records the auction in London of bronzes from three major Florentine collections: that of the Pitti-Gaddi, Francesco Marucelli and Baron Stosch. Marucelli had in his collection three lamps, 'Two in the shape of feet and another, antique, in fine preservation'. The distinction between the antique example and the other two, which were by implication considered to be 'modern' pieces of sixteenth-century date, show the degree of interest and knowledge which Renaissance bronzes inspired in eighteenth-century London.[111]

Given the status of these bronzes over several centuries it is not surprising that they were copied in relatively inexpensive materials. An inkstand in the British Museum, which is dated 1569 on the sole, is made of red earthenware covered with a transparent glaze (fig. 107).[112] There is a round hole pierced through the upper instep beneath the unidentified arms, which must have been intended for a quill pen; the two carefully shaped holes cut into the ears of the monster mask which gapes open to form the ink compartment at the ball of the foot may have also been intended for dipping and draining excess ink from quill pens. The impaled arms (which might signify that the object was commissioned to commemorate a marriage) and perhaps the inscription on the base customise the object.[113] This playful and allusive object would surely have been designed for only occasional use as an inkstand, but would otherwise have served as a piece of table sculpture or desk weight.[114]

Similar pieces were also made in tin-glazed earthenware into the seventeenth century.[115] The ceramic copies are clearly based on bronze prototypes, but it is interesting to note that there were also Roman ceramic lamps of this form to copy.[116] Whether made of bronze or earthenware, copies of Roman bronze lamps suggest that founders or sculptors had access to the originals in contemporary collections and that there was a demand for them. Inventories show that collectors classified sculptural inkstands as works of art suitable to be shown alongside antiquities and fine bronzes which had been made as independent works of art.

During the sixteenth century some studies were designed around existing collections which included inkstands. Girolamo Garimberto advised his patron Cardinal Alessandro Farnese to build a study to house 'all your small objects, such as medals, cameos, inkstands and clocks'.[117] The 1542 inventory of Isabella d'Este's Grotta lists two bronze inkstands displayed on a shelf above the cornice of the room in approved contemporary fashion. One inkstand consisted of 'a little head, with a figure above, which serves as an inkstand'; the other is described as 'A figure with an inkwell at its feet and holding a staff in its hand'.[118]

Venetian collectors tended also to intermingle their bronze inkstands with bronze figurines. Marcantonio Michiel's inkstand in the form of a satyr, which has already been mentioned, co-existed in his studies with bronzes which may have been made by his friend Riccio. The Venetian lawyer Ludovico Usper concentrated all his bronzes on a cabinet in a mezzanine room in his palace which contained his fine library. The bronzes are described as being 'above the cabinet' (*sopra il scrittoio*) and may have been set into the cornice of the cabinet, since this became the standard way of displaying figurines in Venice in the second half of the sixteenth century. The pieces included 'A satyr of bronze with Venus, tied to a tree, A statuette of a horseman in bronze with an inkstand, A cast bronze figurine'.[119] Usper, as mentioned earlier, was a discriminating collector of means, a patron of Alessandro Vittoria, and an owner of a signed bronze of the *Virgin and Child* by Sansovino:[120] he did not regard his inkstand as a purely functional piece of writing equipment, but as an art object, suggesting that it was a piece of high quality.

The fact that there was often more than one inkstand in a single study certainly suggests their decorative value. The Florentine patrician Andrea Minerbetti, who inventoried the contents of his study in his account book in 1502, listed four inkstands in the room. They were made of ivory, crystal, marble and cypress wood.[121] The humanist scholar Annibale Caro had four inkstands in his study in the Caro family house outside Rome, which was inventoried in the interests of his nephew in 1578. One was of terracotta, with a figurine of a male nude; another was of multi-coloured marble in the form of a classical sar-cophagus – a popular shape for chests and boxes of every kind in the first half of the sixteenth century as furniture became more monumental and classical; and the third was mounted with a bronze statuette of a horse.[122] Statuettes of horses *all'antica* were popular among collectors in the early sixteenth century, particularly in Venice (fig. 108). Small bronze examples can be seen in paintings (fig. 109) and are occasionally listed in inventories in the later sixteenth century; one reference to a 'small and fine' example appears in an inventory dated 1587 (Brazzo 1587). Fra Sabba di Castiglione ridiculed collectors who paid large sums for antique statues or statuettes of horses which could serve no useful function and cost five times as much as the real thing:

What can we say about the vanity of the man who spends five hundred or a thousand ducats on a statue of metal or marble which serves him nothing, yet this man cannot serve himself in any way, and does not dare buy a living and true servant for twenty-

108 Bronze statuette of a pacing horse, Venetian, *c.*1500. One of many small reproductions of the famous bronze horses of San Marco. Oxford, Ashmolean Museum.

ITALIAN ABOUT 1500
Reduced copy of one of the antique
bronze horses brought in 1204 from
Constantinople and placed upon
the front of St. Marks at Venice.
Chambers Hall Bequest 1855

five ducats, by whom he could have been served and helped in many things? And what can one say about the man who goes on foot so as not to spend ten ducats on a horse, and then spends five hundred ducats on a silly little antique horse of bronze only a palm high, which not only cannot carry him, but is itself a load to carry.[123]

Given the demand for such statuettes (despite Sabba's typically vigorous critique of the false values which he took them to represent), copies such as the one mounted on Caro's inkstand must have proved popular. The fourth of his inkstands took the form of a leather-covered chest with a lock and key.

Box-type inkstands of wood were favoured in the sixteenth century. They could be decorated with marquetry inlay known as *lavoro d'intarsia*, like the example in the study of the Florentine Baccio Martelli,[124] or they could be covered with leather to look like books. Two Florentine inventories of the early 1560s mention inkstands 'in the form of a book', which must have been considered particularly apposite for a study as a room in which one wrote, and which often contained a small library.[125] A wooden inkstand earned a special mention in a poem praising the amenities and contents of the Villa Campeggi, especially the study: 'In this room [...] is a writing table with an octagonal walnut inkstand standing on it, a very choice object'.[126]

162

109 Detail from Vittore Carpaccio's *Vision of St Augustine* (see fig. 27) showing a shelf-ful of collectables: ancient vases (possibly Apulian, fifth – fourth centuries BC), a bronze statuette of Venus and another of a horse, and an array of what have been taken for neolithic flint instruments – possibly local finds. Venice, Scuola di San Giorgio degli Schiavoni. Photo: Böhm.

Least of all is known about the appearance and quality of terracotta inkstands, since they have not apparently survived. Terracotta was the perfect medium for miniature sculpture, and therefore for inkstands, and the medium had a good classical precedent for small-scale sculpture – such as antique Roman oil-lamps – which would have added to its appeal. The visual excitement generated by one terracotta inkstand is conveyed by Guarino of Verona's letter to a friend thanking him for this gift – it is interesting to note that an inkstand was considered a suitable gift between scholars. Like Leone's description of Caradosso's silver inkstand, Guarino's letter takes the form of an *ekphrasis*, suitable for a Latin letter written by one humanist to another:

> Not to speak of countless other things, how could I find words and style worthy of the inkstand you sent me? Though certainly its form is most beautiful, elegant and apt, this is over-shadowed by the truly Phidian skill and workmanship on which I feast my eyes. If I fix my gaze on the leaves and little branches and look at them attentively, shall I not think that I am looking at real leaves and real branches and that they could safely be bent this way and that? So does the diligence of Art seem to rival the ease of Nature. Often I cannot have enough of the pleasure I find in examining the little figures and the living faces in the clay. What has not been represented to the life here by imitation of Nature the creator? Nails, fingers and hair, soft even though earthen, take me in when I behold them. When I look at an open mouth I expect a voice to come from the dumb; when I see the putti hanging from the tree I forget that they are made of earth and fear that they may fall and injure their small bodies, and I call out in pity. Just as childhood and changeable souls make for varied feelings of the soul, so here you see varied expressions on their faces: one is grinning, another is a little sad, this one is carefree, that one meditative, and here too are postures immodest through the wanton- ness of childhood, for parts of the body which should in natural prudence be hidden are here exposed to view.[127]

Guarino's subtly literary and Latinate account tells us little about the inkstand as an object, other than that it is made of terracotta and is moulded with naked putti tumbling about in a landscape. There is humour in the use he makes of it all, in using an inkstand on his desk as the starting-point for a formal literary exercise. Michael Baxandall has taken Guarino's letter to exemplify a humanist's literary response to a particular work of art.[128] It also surely illustrates the way in which sculptural inkstands embodied social values – ideas about literacy, refinement, comportment and cultivated leisure.

Potters appear to have followed the lead of bronze sculptors and founders in the forms and types of inkstand they produced. This is clearly shown by the imitation of bronze forms – as in the case of inkstands in the shape of a sandalled foot which were mentioned earlier – and by the attempt made by fifteenth-century potters to create polychrome desktop sculpture. The inkstand in the form of St George and the Dragon (fig. 110) has been attributed to Giovanni di Nicola Manzoni of Colle (Acole).[129] It is skilfully constructed so as to imitate the effects of a cast bronze, despite the difficulties of using earthenware as a medium: the weight of the equestrian figure of St George is borne by the dragon's scaly wings, forelegs and curled tail. Perhaps the composition was adapted from the woodcut illustrations in one of the 'battle books' or illustrated histories which were available in particular maiolica workshops, as is suggested by the scenes painted on the front of 'story-painted' plates and the inscriptions on their reverses.[130] Alternatively, the model may have been full-scale sculpture, as in the case of some of the bronze inkstands discussed earlier. The visored helmet or *celata* is accurately observed and helps to date the inkstand to around 1500, as does the way in which an edge of mail is visible below the breastplate.[131]

This inkstand deserves to be considered an attempt at sculpture: certainly the cylindrical inkwell standing on the base plate, like that on the grander bronze examples it copies, would not have held much ink or kept it liquid, even if it had had a stopper. A contemporary inventory of 1489, that of the study of Frate Franceschino da Cesena, suggests that this type of inkstand (whether decorated with slip or tin-glaze) was a collector's piece. This inventory lists 'A large inkstand with a Saint George' which is likely to have been made of glazed earthenware, since it appears with other examples. The two other inkstands in the room were definitely made of maiolica: 'Another inkstand with a fountain and various figures and another, square, both of polychrome glazed earthenware'.[132] These were probably high-quality local products from Faenza workshops, made at a time when Faenza had the artistic and technical initiative in maiolica manufacture.

Figurative maiolica inkstands continued to be made in the sixteenth century in Faenza and elsewhere. The inventory of the workshop of Virgiliotto Calomelli of Faenza, which is dated 1556, lists different grades of inkstand within a hierarchy. High-quality products include 'Six large white inkstands' of the so-called *bianco di Faenza* ware for which his workshop was famous, and 'Seven inkstands with lions'. There were thirty-two terracotta inkstands 'with figures, large', and another forty-two with 'satyrs, horses and fishes' which must have been intended to imitate the crude and bizarre bronzes produced in Northern foundries and workshops. These had been criticised in 1504 by the Paduan scholar Pomponius Gauricus in his treatise on sculpture for their frivolity: he railed at his contemporaries for their preoccupation with satyrs, hydras, chimerae and other monsters 'as if they had nothing better to do'.[133] Clearly potters, like bronzeworkers, were impervious to such criticism in their wish to produce attractive wares. Calomelli's stock also included 'twenty-seven asses, lions and trifles for use as inkstands, painted' and, at the bottom of the list, plain inkwells (Calomelli 1556). Perhaps it is one of the latter type, liberally splashed with ink, which appears on the right of Lorenzo Lotto's double portrait of the physician Giovanni Agostino della Torre and his son Niccolò.[134]

Sculptural inkstands came into fashion again at the end of the sixteenth century. An indication of their high status is given by the fact that Cardinal Ferdinando de'Medici bought 'An inkwell made of earthenware from Urbino made in the form of a casket, in seven sections' from the Urbino potter Flaminio Fontana, in October 1573. He seems to have given the same inkstand to Archbishop Veralli two years later.[135]

An exceptional surviving example of Urbino style of the later sixteenth century is an inkstand from the Patanazzi workshop in Urbino which can be closely dated by the arms it bears (figs 111–13). It comprises several elements: a sculptural group of the *Pietà* on a lozenge-shaped base, in which the Virgin holds the Dead Christ on her lap, flanked by

110   Inkstand in the form of St George and the Dragon, made of tin-glazed earthenware (maiolica). Attributed to Giovanni di Nicola Manzoni of Colle (Acole), probably Faenza, *c.*1510. This potter specialised in ceramic sculpture, usually inkstands or cribs. He signed nine of his inkstands. Washington, In the Collection of The Corcoran Gallery of Art, William A. Clark Collection.

111 Patanazzi workshop, Urbino, quadrangular inkstand of tin-glazed earthenware with figure group of a *Pietà*, *c*.1596–1605. The kneeling boy on the right supports the arms of Cardinal Baronius. Faenza, Museo Internazionale delle Ceramiche.

112 (*below left*) Back view of the inkstand depicted in fig. 111, showing the inkwell attached to the back of the figure of Virgin Mary.

113 (*above right*) The inkstand (fig. 111) taken apart to show its various components: the figure group which serves as a handle for the lid; a tray with built-in inkwells and space for pens and penknives; a compartment with two drawers, one with a further inkwell.

two angels bearing candles. On the outer edges are two kneeling putti, one of whom bears a shield with the arms of the Aldobrandini – the family of Pope Clement VIII (1592–1605) surmounting those of the Baronius. This angel also holds a palm, the device of the Baronius family. A second putto humbly offers a cardinal's hat to the Virgin. The iconography and arms suggest that this inkstand commemorates the elevation of the historian Baronius to the Cardinalate in 1596. The inkstand must therefore date to between 1596 and 1605, when the Aldobrandini Pope died. It has been suggested that the inkstand was perhaps a gift from Baronius's fellow Oratorians to commemorate his elevation: if so, it would be a second case of an inkstand as a gift between friends.[136] The inkstand would have been a perfect gift for Baronius, in that it combines devotional references with a practical function. The sculptural group is backed by a container for pens, and the middle section of the inkstand, which is revealed when the figure group is lifted away, contains two inkwells built into the outer edges of the lozenge-shaped tray, and a central compartment painted on the base with the objects which one might wish to keep there – two pens, scissors and a penknife. A third base section holds two triangular drawers, one with an inkwell, the other intended for use as a sandbox. This base is supported on scrolled feet at the four corners, beneath four moulded figures of winged harpies. The fronts of the two drawers are painted with figures of St Luke in his study, and St John writing in the wilderness, derived from woodcuts in an Italian Bible of the last quarter of the sixteenth century.[137] Potters and painters did not only copy woodcuts in this way in decorating inkstands; they also translated them into three dimensions.[138]

Inkstands, even when made in inexpensive materials such as maiolica, could function as desk-organisers which conveyed *gentilezza* as well as literacy. As with the cabinet, so with the inkstand: both came to represent the functions of the study on a smaller scale, making its amenities more widely available in the second half of the sixteenth century.

Mirrors

Writing at the end of the fourteenth century, the notary Lapo Mazzei mentioned the comforting reflection of a mirror in his study in a letter to his father. Ser Lapo was keen to show off 'the new house to which I have returned, and my library, or *studiolo*, where I am writing. It has a mirror or ray of sunlight which comforts me'.[139] Mazzei is perhaps referring to the refreshing qualities of the reflection which Palatino mentions as a means of avoiding eye-strain. Five years earlier Mazzei had not been so keen on having a mirror in his study for he had written to his friend Francesco Datini presenting him and his wife with a mirror for which he had not been able to find a place in his house. He had tried hanging it in the main reception room (*sala*), then in the bedchamber and finally in the study. In a charming compliment to his friends' house, and as an encouragement to them to accept such a grand present, he ends: 'but I thought it did not look well in any place – indeed, it seemed that it complained of the rough lodging I had given it'.[140] His new house was to provide a better setting for a mirror.

Mirrors were often to be found in studies, hanging on a wall above a desk or cabinet, or set on a small wooden stand. There were several reasons why contemporaries thought them eminently suitable – even useful – in a study. First, a mirror could be used as an optical glass in reading, despite the fact that they reflected script in reverse. The *Roman de la rose* mentions the properties of mirrors 'which have such marvellous powers' that they magnify small letters and illuminate ancient, faded script so that it could be read more easily.[141] A small convex hand-mirror, such as the one illustrated in Tomaso da Modena's fresco of Isnardo da Vicenza in his carrel or cell, could be taken down off its shelf, brought to a text and angled as one wished.[142] This is why a small convex mirror is included in a woodcut showing the calligrapher's equipment in Giovanantonio Tagliente's treatise on the art of writing (fig. 90 above). Small mirrors which could be hung on a wall or stood on a writing-desk or shelf until needed became scholarly attributes because of their association with writing, as in Francia's medal of the Bolognese scholar Ulisse Musotti (fig. 114).[143] This depicts a scholar's writing equipment, grouped around an open book which is leaning on a stand fixed with an armillary sphere at the top, and supporting a set square and a pair of compasses. A small convex mirror on a triangular frame hangs above the open book, in which one can read a Latin inscription claiming that Musotti had, in his legal career, fulfilled various Old Testament injunctions: 'He did not forsake the orphan and stranger; he was a helper to orphans and to the widow'.[144] In front of the book is an inkwell and quill, a penknife, a penner and inkhorn threaded on a thong, a flask for ink, a candlestick, an hourglass, a ruler with a plumbline attached for ruling lines and establishing margins, and a pair of scissors.

Second, a mirror was thought to focus and concentrate light, and reflect it on to one's

114 Attributed to Francesco Francia, bronze portrait medal of Ulisse Musotti, 1515. Note the small convex mirror on a triangular frame above the open book. London, British Museum.

desk to help one in one's reading. The calligrapher Gianbattista Palatino stated in his treatise that mirrors 'preserve the sight and comfort it during constant writing'.[145] A woodcut showing the calligrapher Francesco Torniello in his study at his writing-desk with all his equipment around him includes a convex mirror on the wall behind his head, with its protective curtain drawn back behind pegs (fig. 41). Palatino's comment indicates that the mirror here is not just an elegant fitting. Certainly, inventories record that mirrors often hung near writing-desks packed with papers, as in the house of one Florentine in 1563 (Buondelmonti 1563). By the sixteenth century a mirror was almost obligatory in the study. The Florentine patrician Andrea Minerbetti had 'a mirror with a base' in his study in 1493, when he listed in his account book the contents of the rooms in his palace. It was still there in 1502 (Minerbetti memoranda). The librarian of the Malatestiana Library had in his study 'a round mirror with a wooden base' (probably for use in writing) and a showpiece; 'a round steel mirror' attached to the wall panels of the room (Frate Franceschino da Cesena 1489). Both must have been convex mirrors, differing only in size and frames according to their intended functions. Perhaps the use of mirrors as instruments declined gradually with the common use of optical lenses and spectacles.

Many of the mirrors mentioned among the contents of a study in inventories of the fifteenth and sixteenth centuries were made of polished steel (*azzal*, *accaio* or *accio*).[146] The

168

quality of the reflection depended on the alloy used, which was highly polished so as to give a sharp image: clarity depended on whether this corroded or could be repolished. Renaissance householders knew about protecting the steel from scratches or fly spotting by hanging a small veil over the mirror when it was not being used or shown off, as listed in inventories and shown in many paintings.[147] Metal mirrors had of course been in continuous production since classical antiquity, whereas glass mirrors did not come into use until the fourteenth century. Invented in Germany, they were imported into Venice though the Fondaco dei Tedeschi. In 1446 the city's Mercers' Company claimed

> that all mercers' wares which come into the German exchange house shall be subject to our trade, and that our mercers may stock and sell these goods, such as basins and brassware, iron and tin, locks, mirrors, mirror-glass.[148]

All such goods should be regarded as being 'subject to our trade', thus enforcing their monopoly against foreign competition. It was only towards the end of the fifteenth century that German craftsmen were settled in Venice, bringing with them the art of 'silvering' glass as we would now call it.[149] This was a closely guarded trade secret of the Mirror-makers' Guild (*Specchieri*) and it was a source of fascination to the uninitiated, so much so that the traveller Pietro della Valle records how he met a Jewish doctor in Kashan who was keen to learn the skill and offered to teach Pietro the secret of 'the fixation of mercury' in exchange.[150] It was generally known that it was the backing of the glass which determined the sharpness and brilliance of the reflection: lead or combinations of lead and tin were fixed with mercury to the back of the glass plate which gave a sharp but dark or shadowy reflection very different from that in modern mirrors. A carnival song of the Florentine Mirror-makers' Guild hinted at the crucial importance of silvering, playing up the popular fascination with mirrors and their properties. Having acknowledged with uncharacteristic modesty that the art of making glass mirrors was German in origin, they boasted:

> First of all our trade demands experience and adroitness in managing the blown glass forms, and then in knowing the fineness of glass [presumably avoiding trapping air bubbles in the process]. But worth more than this or anything else is the secret of the substance which one places behind the glass with great skill.[151]

Early mirror technology was, however, far from perfect. Isabella d'Este's letters to Lorenzo da Pavia document her problems both with glass and steel mirrors. Lorenzo encouraged her to reject a glass mirror owing to a defect in the *cristallo* glass which created a shadow in the reflection.[152] Efforts to repolish one of her steel mirrors in 1536 were unsuccessful. As another of Isabella's agents, Benedetto Agnello, explained: 'the master craftsman who polished the mirror said he was not able to make the surface smooth because of a very poor metal alloy'.[153]

A mirror was not only costly and desirable, but was thought to enhance the room in which it hung. As Leonardo Fioravanti astutely observed:

> A mirror can be a fine ornament in a room, on account of the bizarre effect of seeing everything which is in the room reflected in it: this is why it is so much valued.[154]

This effect would have been particularly pleasing in a study full of small precious objects. By the time Fioravanti was writing, large flat sheets of mirror glass were common, but the earlier, smaller convex mirrors must have produced even more bizarre effects on account of the distortions they produced. The lure of reflecting the whole room and its contents in one focused image may explain why Isabella d'Este pursued large steel mirrors, referred to as 'specchi da camera', from the 1490s into the 1530s.[155]

Something of the visual fascination of convex mirrors is suggested in contemporary

115 Parmigianino,
*Self-portrait in a Convex
Mirror*, oil on panel, 1523–4.
Vienna, Kunsthistorisches
Museum.

paintings and woodcuts. A disturbing self-portrait of about 1523–4 by Parmigianino depicts the distorted image of the artist delineating himself in front of a large convex mirror (fig. 115). The sculptor Alessandro Vittoria recorded in his memoranda that he had bought this painting through the agency of Andrea Palladio for the sum of 10 scudi in 1560. Vittoria bequeathed the painting, which had formerly belonged to the goldsmith and collector Valerio Belli, to the Holy Roman Emperor Rudolf II in his will, on account of the fact that the latter's father, Maximilian II, had long desired the picture.[156]

It is hardly surprising that mirrors were of particular interest to artists. One of the earliest references to an artist possessing one documents the public auction in Venice in 1440 of Iacobello del Fiore's household furnishings. The sale included 'a glass mirror' – it must have been a German export at this date rather than a Venetian product – which fetched 2 lire and 1 soldo.[157] The painter Sodoma – who included a particularly large and richly framed convex mirror in his fresco *Alexander Visiting Roxana* in the Villa Farnesina in Rome in 1511 – kept a large mirror in his study in his house in Siena (Sodoma 1529).[158]

Additional interest in mirrors among artists was stimulated by the *paragone*, the contemporary debate on the relative merits of painting and sculpture in which the presumed superiority of sculpture on account of its potential for showing figures in the round was challenged by painters, using mirrors to show various aspects of their subject.[159] Perhaps the best illustration of the theme is Gian Gerolamo Savoldo's signed portrait,[160] painted around 1531–2 as a witty present for a friend in Florence (as one can read in the reflection of the letter in the far mirror; fig. 116).[161] Not content with mirror reflections alone – the little room in which he depicts himself contains two large flat mirrors reflecting his bed, a green wall-hanging (*spalliera*) and the table at which he sits – Savoldo also plays with reflections on armour. The image is that of a thoughtful, well-dressed protagonist in a primarily literary argument about art; but it is also the portrait of someone who aspires to *gentilezza*. The inclusion of armour suggests high social status: Fra Sabba di Castiglione, writing about the ornaments which above all others he would desire in his study, mentions arms, books and a steel mirror as fitting for 'a noble knight',[162] a reference which gives Savoldo's painting a rather different resonance.

Collectors, too, had a particular interest in pursuing mirrors. Cardinal Francesco Gonzaga's tutor, Bartolomeo Marasca, complained to Francesco's mother about her son's acquisitiveness and cupidity in an amusing letter of 1463. Francesco's collecting tendencies showed themselves early. Marasca wrote that Francesco was:

always buying things which are neither necessary or useful to him. [. . .] one of his household says 'I saw such mirrors', another says 'I found pine-martens' skins or furs at

116   Gian Gerolamo Savoldo, *Portrait of a Man in his Study-Bedchamber*, oil on canvas, Venice, *c.*1531–2. Paris, Louvre. Photo: © R.M.N.

a good price'; another this; another that. As you shall hear, he buys them straight away.[163]

Francesco later laid his hands on a remarkable square steel mirror in a silver-gilt frame set with eight cameos, and with a silver back with his arms executed in niello.[164] This has been identified as the mirror listed as a pledge in a loan negotiated between Piero de'Medici and the banker Agostino Chigi in 1486. This would indicate that it was a vehicle for part of the cardinal's precious and covetable collection of gems, many of which were seized by the Medici in settlement of an outstanding loan from the Medici bank.[165]

Steel and glass mirrors could have elaborate frames, carved walnut (often parcel-gilt) being the most often listed both in Venetian and Florentine inventories of the sixteenth century. Fioravanti recommended ebony as being particularly suitable for mirror-frames, and ebony is occasionally listed, as in the case of the mirror in the study of Hortensio da Mula (Amulio 1590). Lorenzo da Pavia used ebony to make the frame on a glass mirror which, after a great deal of subtle negotiation, he gave to Isabella d'Este in 1506.[166] He had made one the previous year for the Cardinal of San Pietro in Vincoli in Rome.[167] He sent Isabella the mirror on approval as

> the most beautiful thing that I have ever made, so that I value it highly, even though it is not finished, since it lacks a cover on account of my not finding ebony with which to make it, so that I could not finish it.[168]

Finding suitable ebony to make a protective cover for the mirror was difficult, but once that had been done, he wrote to Isabella – who was anxious to know his price – saying that it was a gift:

> God would not wish that I should seek anything for it beyond the fact that it gives you pleasure, and, on my account, I should like to make you a present of it but, seeing that I have to earn my bread, I am forced to be an ignoble fellow [*sono constreto a esere vilan*].[169]

She promptly sent him 20 ducats as a return gift 'per amor nostro', but added a list of demands, tying him to her yet more closely as her agent.[170] This exchange of letters illuminates the complex psychology of that aspect of Renaissance patronage known as *clientalismo*, as well as the status of a fine mirror to a collector.

Householders furnishing a new apartment would also go to considerable lengths to acquire a mirror in a decorative frame: one young Florentine traded in to two painters a small gesso statuette of Hercules in part payment for a mirror-frame painted in gold and blue on his marriage in 1472.[171]

Some frames were so decorative that they were converted to use as picture-frames. The Venetian patrician Camilla Malipiero bequeathed 'a picture of Our Lady, round, which used to be a mirror, which remains in the hands of the said Mistress Camilla' to the monastery of Santa Maria Maggiore in Venice.[172] In the sixteenth century mirrors were often fitted with wooden covers which slid over the mirror or hinged shut on it, and these could be painted. Well-known artists worked in this format: Alessandro Vittoria owned a mirror with 'a small portrait of a lady by Titian' on the frame which he kept in his study.[173] Portraits made particularly appropriate decorations for mirrors. Marcantonio Michiel had two small portraits, 'one [. . .] of my father/Another portrait of Ariosto', painted on mirror-frames in his study (Michiel *c*.1552). Both portraits were again described as being 'in the form of a mirror' in the Michiel inventories of 1595 and 1601.[174] As mirrors improved in quality, new glasses were set into old frames, which explains why so few of the Renaissance frames which survive contain their original glass. Similarly, the painted covers or insets into mirrors have been preserved out of context, for example the

117 After Caravaggio, *Repentance of Mary Magdalen*, oil on canvas, early seventeenth century. Oxford, Christ Church Picture Gallery. Photo: courtesy of The Governing Body, Christ Church, Oxford.

toilet-set (*restello*) painted by Bellini which was mentioned in the will of the painter Vincenzo Catena in 1525.[175]

The fact that mirrors were so desirable sharpened objections to them on moral grounds as instruments of vanity and worldliness. There was a countercurrent to this tradition however, in that late medieval and Renaissance allegory included a mirror as an attribute of Prudence, since it revealed truth.[176] The sixteenth-century iconography of the Repentance of Mary Magdalen depended on these complex associations. Caravaggio's superb painting on this theme shows the Magdalen resting her hand on a large, convex steel mirror at the moment of her conversion: the mirror (as Susan Haskins has pointed out) points both to the Magdalen's former vanity and to the truth revealed to her.[177]

Some writers still felt the need to justify themselves in their fondness for mirrors, as Fra Sabba di Castiglione did in mentioning that he would prefer a mirror to any other object in his study. Fra Sabba describes how Socrates – who was famed for the disparity between his ugly body and his fine mind – had encouraged his disciples to view themselves in a mirror as a means of self-knowledge: 'Because you must know that vanity and frivolity are not inherent in the mirror but derive from our use of them'.[178] He was sensitive to the contemporary view that mirrors were luxuries, but he used the contemporary interest in mirrors to score moral points, and to play on a secondary meaning of the word 'specchio' as 'a patterne of Virtue or Vice', as defined in Florio's dictionary of 1611.[179] At one point in his book, Fra Sabba uses the imagery of mirrors to show how the worldly man, motivated by his sinful nature, wilfully distorts reality to suit his own ends:

> For when he (the worldly man) is moved by love or affection, he uses a convex mirror, which gives such a magnified reflection of the natural object that his eyelashes, hair and the hairs of his beard look like the bristles of an old wild boar, or the twigs of a besom, and his teeth like those of an old Turkish horse, older than mine, which was fifty years old. But when a man is moved by envy, and by hate, he uses another mirror, made of glass, but very small, which reflects the object so much diminished from its real size that it makes it tiny, so that it reduces a man's face from its actual size to that of a child.[180]

As so often, one is aware of the way Fra Sabba scrutinised objects and recorded what he saw in his discursive, vital style which conveys so vividly the way in which he must have spoken. He also tells us that he was familiar with what another writer called 'monstrous mirrors', which produced bizarre and distorted images.[181] Used rightly, however, he believed that a mirror could strengthen a man's will in his pursuit of virtue and spiritual detachment. A scholar benefits from seeing the marks of fatigue etched on his face as a result of study,

> so that the learned man, seeing himself in it, refreshes and comforts the virtue apparent there, which has long been wearied and weakened as a result of many vigils and long hours of study.[182]

Very different advice to the scholarly was given by the physician Cardano, who recommended that scholars keep lascivious paintings of nude women in their bedchambers as an antidote to dry and esoteric study and the unhealthy demands it made on the body.[183] An appropriately light-hearted version of Sabba's ascetic philosophy was turned out by another scholar, Giambattista Gelli, in a carnival song for the Florentine Mirror-makers' Guild, in which he claimed that gazing in a mirror stimulated selfconsciousness and spurred people on in the pursuit of virtue:

> Perceiving his faults when looking in the mirror, (faults which are not so easy to perceive in oneself as in others), a man can then take stock of himself and say 'I will be a better man then I was'.[184]

On a less sophisticated level, another Florentine carnival song for the same guild reminded their audience 'we give general notice that we make mirrors, not faces'.[185] Parmigianino's claustrophobic self-portrait in a convex mirror demonstrates one facet of the selfconsciousness which these writers mention in defence of the mirror as a valued household ornament.

Conclusion

THROUGH THE MEDIUM OF THE STUDY, this book has been concerned with three sets of relationships: between individuals and the spaces which they inhabited; between individuals and the art objects with which they surrounded themselves and lived; and between individuals and their friends or the artists whom they patronised. These relationships and their characteristic patterns have determined the structure of the book. Working outwards from the kinds of people who created studies for themselves, to the nature of the spaces they constructed and the kinds of art objects they demanded for these rooms, attempts have been made to view what is often called 'material culture' in terms of Burckhardt's emphasis on the Renaissance discovery of the individual, of private and domestic life.[1] The study did not only have a private role to play in the life of its owner, however: the book has shown how inviting friends, fellow collectors and rivals into one's study was a particular form of social communication, one which became increasingly significant in the course of the sixteenth century.

The inventories on which this book is based are unique in recording the changing density, as well as types, of furnishings in particular rooms over time. Noting of the early Renaissance study that it often contained treasured possessions, a recent commentator adds:

> There would normally be a concentration of objects in such rooms (this being so striking that it was often depicted); the density of loose objects elsewhere was generally less great.[2]

118 Detail of an ink sketch by Vittore Carpaccio showing a scholar in a study situated near a staircase. This was a common pattern (see Barzizza 1444). Collectors often placed their studies at the top of their palaces for maximum security: Torquato Tasso complained about having to climb a staircase to visit a Roman collection on a hot summer's afternoon, though he admitted afterwards that it had been worth the effort. Moscow, Pushkin Museum.

Perhaps the most significant development over the two hundred years surveyed here is that this concentration of special art objects and treasures, found previously only in the nucleus of bedchambers and studies, spread out into other more public rooms in the later Renaissance house, giving them the kind of dignified, comfortable and well-furnished character which had formerly been restricted to the more private rooms.[3]

Whereas inventories up to the last quarter of the fifteenth century (Barzizza 1444; Fece 1450; Tura 1483) document a clear distinction between the nature and contents of the study (and the master bedchamber to which it was closely allied) and all other rooms, this gap had been largely eroded by the late sixteenth century (Buizzi 1594; Berti 1594; Helman 1606; Usper 1601). Inventories from the latter period list a profusion and variety of elegant fittings and furnishings, not just in the study and bedchamber, but in the rooms which had generally had less defined functions and which were now emerging as spaces with distinct characters of their own. The Venetian *portego* had always been treated as a gallery and display space, but in the sixteenth century it focused demand for a certain large-scale format of portrait (*ritratti in piedi*, Calderini 1597) which was suitable to be shown there, or for the kind of genre scene painted by Bassano, as thought suitable for a dining area.[4] This more defined sense of how a particular all-purpose room should be furnished extended to particular collectables, such as *restelli* or wall-racks for displaying arms and armour (Contareno 1606).[5]

Portraits, clocks and arms and armour had all previously been thought suitable for the more private world of the study and, to a lesser extent, the bedchamber: now they had spilled out into the wider arena of the household. The evolution of the cabinet had a crucial role to play in this development. Seen within the context of the Renaissance domestic interior as a whole, the study serves as a lens through which to observe changes in the highly evolved and diversified material culture which bound Italians together.[6]

It was the quest for greater comfort, privacy and commodity (*commodità*, a fusion of convenience and elegance perfectly adapted to one's needs) that characterised the development of Italian thinking about domestic arrangements from the fifteenth century onwards. Italians themselves believed that they had made considerable advances in this direction, and within a few generations. Something of these processes can be seen at work in the recorded comments of the aged Isabella d'Este, when she made a visit to the Palazzina constructed by her son Federico Gonzaga for his bride, Margerita Paleologo, in 1531. Federico clearly sought Isabella's approval, for he had had a special handrail constructed along a difficult staircase for her, though she proved unable to use it. Federico's act was not only one of filial piety, for Isabella's discriminating taste in creating and furnishing her own rooms was renowned. Her comments are therefore fascinating in revealing her own sense of the building's comfort, as being superior to anything which she herself had been able to create in her thirty years in Mantua. She admired the distribution of rooms in the new apartments, their comfort, privacy and elegance, seeing them as superior to her own.[7] Elegant, urbane architectural planning was considered to be a feature of modernity: in the second edition of his *Vite* Vasari praised Michelozzo for his advanced distribution plan in the Medici palace as providing for 'utility' and 'commodity'; for comfort 'in the modern manner'.[8] Here again, in the words of a recent commentator, the study had a key role, for

> it was in such small rooms [as the study] that personal comfort in many guises was first evolved, as those who owned a study tended to spend long hours there.[9]

Much of this book, in elaborating the idea and nature of the study in Renaissance Italy, has centred on the room as a virtuous space of unique moral and aesthetic worth. This property resided in the room itself as much as in its owner, and did not therefore necessarily depend on the rank or social status of the person who created it. The study rooms of the urban élites which are the subject of the book had a dignity in the minds of their owners which could stand comparison with the grandest examples: a belief exemplified by Vieri's comments on the quality of his small but select library in his villa study, or Fra Sabba's delight in his collection and his discriminating tastes. Vieri explicitly compares his library with that of the Medici and Sassetti, with a just sense of its quality and proper standing. The way in which Fra Sabba situates his own collection modestly but firmly within his discussion of contemporary collecting habits and artistic achievement is a clear indication of how he rated it: as something built up with limited means, but with taste and discrimination. He intended his audience to read from the study to the man, and in doing so, he set himself up as a model of those qualities he most admired: wit, politeness, civility and good manners (*ingegno*, *politezza*, *civilta*, *cortigiania*).

The concept of *virtù* residing in a collection of select antiquities and works of art, or in a library, is a Renaissance topos, one which is implicit in Fra Sabba's account of his study, but which is developed by a number of Renaissance writers. It was not however just through its contents, as proofs of urbanity or good taste, that the study derived its virtue, but also through its nature as a philosophical space. The Renaissance debate about the proper uses of solitude focused on the need for a private space, a need uniqely fulfilled by the study. In his essay 'On Solitude', Montaigne advised that we should

choose treasures which no harm can corrupt and [. . .] hide them in a place which no one can enter, no one betray, save we ourselves. We should have wives, children, property and above all, good health [. . .] if we can: but we should not become so attached to them that our happiness depends on them. We should set aside a room, just for ourselves, at the back of the shop, keeping it entirely free and establishing there our true liberty, our principal solitude and asylum. Within it our normal conversation should be of ourselves, with ourselves, so privy that no commerce or communication with the outside world should find a place there; there we should talk and laugh as though we had no wife or children, no possessions, no followers, no menservants, so that when the occasion arises that we must lose them it should not be a new experience to do without them. We have a soul able to turn in on herself; she can keep herself company; she has the werewithal to attack, to defend, to receive and to give.[10]

Much of Montaigne's argument derives from the moral epistles of his beloved Seneca: a source used by other Renaissance writers in advocating the physical demarcation of personal space within the household. What was new in this Renaissance elaboration of classical ideas was the wish to map this plea for what was essentially an inner sanctuary onto a particular room, the study. While Pliny the Younger had referred to his study-library at his villa, as all Italian Renaissance letter-writers knew and echoed in their own letters written to like-minded friends from their villas, the emphasis on the study-room as a dedicated space for managing one's affairs and the practice of reflection was essentially an emphasis of their own, and it was distinctly modern. Significantly, when the Authorised Version of the Bible came to translate the injunction from the Sermon on the Mount to construct an inner sanctuary in the soul, the word 'closet' – one of the English equivalents of the Italian *studio* – was used to denote it: 'When thou prayest, enter into thy closet, and when thou hast shut thy door, pray to thy Father which is in secret; and thy Father which seeth in secret shall reward thee openly' (Matthew, 6:6). Doni, Cotrugli and Montaigne, to name just a few of the writers on the theme, imply that this 'room [. . .] at the back of the shop' or near one's bedchamber was not reserved for the few, but should be – and was – available to a wide range of people in their daily lives. Both the room, and the demands which it was uniquely qualified to answer, were familiar to their readers.

While the French royal model of the fourteenth century was undoubtedly important in the history of the study, it was Renaissance Italians who gave the room-type its associations with civility, learned leisure and urbane culture. In doing so, they made it available to a wider social group, subtly and permanently changing its character. It was as an important feature of a well-appointed, gentlemanly residence that the Italian Renaissance study was to be exported to the rest of Europe in the course of the sixteenth century.[11] Perhaps this is best illustrated by a poem in praise of the study which appears as part of Gilles Corrozet's *Blasons domestiques*, printed in Paris in 1539. Corrozet's middle-class credentials were impeccable: born into a well-to-do family of mercers in Paris, he worked as a writer, anthologist, poet, translator and publisher. That he was well aware of Italian models is evident in his emblem book, published a year after Alciati's, in 1540.[12] His poem in praise of the study as a necessary, worthy feature of the gentleman's town house articulates so many of the themes of this book that it is worth quoting in full:

LE BLASON DE L'ESTVDE.   THE BLAZON OF THE STUDY.

Le corps humain qui est d'e-
    sprit deliure.
Ne va, ne vient, ne faict &
    ne peult viure
Et n'a vertu, force, ne sentement.
Vne maison qui est semblablement
Sans posseder l'estude fructueuse,
Est d'ung grand bien (pour vray) deffe-
    ctueuse.
Et n'a en soy aulcune vtilité,
Pour cest esprit, car à la verité,
La seullé estudé est de l'esprit viande,
S'il trouué aumoins la lecture friande,
Et n'est au corps viande si plaisante,
Commé à l'esprit l'estude bien duysan-
    te :
Mais quel plaisir plus grand peult on
    auoir,
Que d'enseigner, d'apprendré & de
    scauoir?
Que plus grand bien peult vng mor-
    tel eslire,
Que composer, chanter, escripre &
    lire?
Il n'en est point apres l'amour de dieu.
Celebrons doncq en tout temps & tout
    lieu,
La bonné estudé, ou la philosophie
Son throne tient, & la se glorifie,
Auec l'esprit. Les princes anciens,
Les Grecz, Hebrieux, & les Egyptiens
Ont celebré & estimé les lettres,
Qui ont esté tát en prose qu'en metres.
N'est cé vng plaïsir de lire en vne hy-
    stoire?
N'est ce vng soulas de veoir l'art d'o-
    ratoire?
N'est ce doulceur de veoir la poisie,
Pour l'imprimer dedans sa fantasie?
N'est cé vng grand bien à toute crea-
    ture,

The human body which is devoid of mind. neither goes, nor comes, does nothing & cannot live, and has neither virtue, strength, nor feeling. A house which likewise is not in possession of a fruitful study, is lacking (to tell the truth) a great benefit. And contains nothing useful to that mind, for in truth, solitary study is the nourishment of the mind, at least if it relishes the delights of reading, and there is no meat as pleasing to the body as study is fitting to the spirit : but what greater pleasure could one have, than to teach, to learn & to know? What greater good can a mortal choose, than to compose, to sing, to write & to read? Except the love of god there is none. So at all times & in all places let us celebrate the good study, where philosophy sits on its throne, & is in its glory, with the mind. The princes of antiquity, the Greeks, Hebrews & the Egyptians celebrated & prized letters, both those in prose and in verse. Is it not a pleasure to read a history book? Is it not a solace to observe the art of oratory? Is it not sweet to look at poetry, to imprint it in one's imagination? Is it not a great benefit to every created being to study the holy writ? Is it not a very profitable occupation in every situation, to study & read every law? I declare the same of every discipline. Is it not a joy & a divine pleasure to compose in prose & in verse, rondeaus, verses of ten lines, & many varied treatises, in flat

D'estudier en la saincte escripture?
N'est ce proffit bien grand en tout en-
     droict,
D'estudier & liré en chascun droict?
I'en dy autant de toute discipline.
N'est ce vné ioyé & plaisance diuine
De composer & en prosé & en vers,
Rondeaulx, dizains, & maintz traïctez
     diuers,
En Rithme platé & en Rithme croi-
     sée?
O saincte estudé, O Estude prisée,
Repos sacré des Muses Pernasines
Seiour tant doulx des Nymphes Caba-
     lines.
Chambre de paix, de siléce & concorde,
Ou le doulx Lucz & taisant manicorde,
Rendent leurs sons tant souefz & pa-
     ciffiques;
Estude bellé entre les magniffiques.
Ou est comprinsé vne Bibliothecque,
Autant latine Hebraicque, que Grec-
     que :
Estudé ou sont d'ung costé les docteurs
En lettre saincte, en l'aultre les au-
     theurs,
Hystoriés, traictátz du faict des armes :
En l'aultre part sont les metres & car-
     mes,
Des bons facteurs, en l'uné & l'aultre
     langue :
Les orateurs bien formantz la harágue,
Ont aultres reng, & les loix & decretz,
Monstrét aussi en ce lieu leurs secretz.
La sont Grammaire, & subtile Logic-
     que,
Puis Rethorique auec Arithmeticque,
Doulce Musicque, auec Geometrie,
Et la secreté & haulté Astrologie,
Qui les espritz de scauantz resiouys-
     sent :
Quand de leurs fruictz sauourent &
     iouyssent.
Et briefuement Estude sainctê & belle,
Estude bonné, Arche spirituelle,
Puis que tu as si grande dignité,
Tant d'excellencé & tant d'authorité,
Et qu'en toy gist si tressouuerain bien,
Que la maison (sans toy) ne seroit rien.
Tu as donc mys en honneur ce pour-
     pris.
Parquoy sur tout tu doibs auoir le pris.

Rhythm & in crossed Rhythm? Oh
blessed study, Oh cherished Study,
sacred resting place of the
Parnassian Muses sweet retreat of
the Caballine Nymphs. Chamber
of peace, of silence & harmony,
where the sweet Lute & quiet
clavichord give forth their sounds
so sweet & peaceful; study of a
beauty to compare with the most
magnificent. Where is included a
Library, both latin, Hebrew, and
Greek : study where on one side are
the doctors of sacred scripture, on
the other authors, historians,
treating of exploits of arms : in
another part are verses & songs, by
good poets, in one language or
another : orators who can form
speeches well, occupy other
shelves, & the laws & decrees, also
display their secrets in this place.
There are Grammar, & subtle
Logic, next Rhetoric and
Arithmetic, sweet Music, with
Geometry, and secret & lofty
Astrology, all of which delight the
minds of learned men : when they
taste & enjoy their fruits. To
conclude briefly blessed & beautiful
Study, good Study, spiritual Ark,
because you possess such great
dignity, so much excellence &
authority, and because you are a
store of such sovereign goods, that
the house (without you) would be
nothing. You have therefore made
this abode honourable. On which
count you deserve to be prized
above all else.

Notes

Introduction

1 On the evolution of civility as a social virtue, see Richard Goldthwaite, *Wealth and the Demand for Art in Renaissance Italy, 1300–1600*, Baltimore and London 1993, pp. 162–76, 243–55. John Hale, *The Civilisation of Europe in the Renaissance*, London 1993, pp. 355–413, 489–90.

2 J. Burckhardt, *The Civilisation of the Renaissance in Italy* [1860], trans. S. G. C. Middlemore, London 1944, p. 81. *The Renaissance*, ed. Peter Burke, London 1964, p. 16. On the impact this might have had on materialism and patterns of consumption as a theme for historians, Goldthwaite, *Wealth and the Demand for Art*, p. 238. On the primacy of learning, Hale, *Civilisation*, pp. 392–8; on education and its role in social cohesion, Paul Grendler, *Schooling in Renaissance Italy: Literacy and Learning, 1300–1600*, Baltimore and London 1989, p. 410 for summary.

3 F. W. Kent summarises the familial bonds of Renaissance Florentines, and the way in which these have recently been studied, in 'Individuals and Families as Patrons of Culture in Quattrocento Florence', *Language and Images of Renaissance Italy*, ed. Alison Brown, Oxford 1995, pp. 176–82, esp. notes 30 and 32.

4 'Poi ne venni alle masserizie [. . .] un bicchiere, una guastada, una saliera, un rinfrescatoio, una ampolla, una tazza (questi son vetri), e un fiasco. Volete voi altro? [. . .] tutti i danari che batte la zecca non mi bastavano a comprar la metà d'una cosa per cosa'. Anton Francesco Doni, *I marmi*, ed. S. Bongi, Florence 1863, vol. 4, p. 256.

5 Inventory of the estate of Lorenzo d'Orlando, glassworker, 14 January 1546. Gabriella Cantini Guidotti, *Tre inventari di bicchierai toscani fra cinque e seicento*, Florence 1983, pp. 107–22, p. 107 for gold rings.

6 Hale, *Civilisation*, p. 171 and plate on p. 172.

7 Many of the inventories of the contents of studies list small or large private libraries (for which see the Concordance below) but analysing and classifying these is not the aim of this book. Much of the work has already been done by earlier editors of published inventories (cited in the Concordance); in general studies of book-ownership, e.g. Christian Bec, *Les marchands écrivains: Affaires et humanisme à Florence, 1375–1434*, Paris 1967, Bec, *Les livres des Florentins, 1413–1608*, Florence 1984, and Bec, *Cultura e società nell'età della Rinascenza*, Rome 1981; or in accounts of libraries owned by particular individuals (see Concordance). A useful bibliography of booklists is provided by Gianetto Avanzi, *Libri, librerie, biblioteche nell'umanesimo e nella Rinascenza*, Rome 1954 (of which there is an offprint in the Warburg Library, London).

8 Isabella Palumbo Fossati, 'L'interno della casa dell'artista e dell'artigiano nella Venezia del cinquecento', *Studi veneziani*, VII, 1984, p. 116.

9 E. Rice, *Saint Jerome in the Renaissance*, Baltimore and London 1985, p. 99.

10 Letter from Michele Vieri to Pietro Ridolfi, quoted and translated by Eve Borsook, *The Companion Guide to Florence*, London 1979, p. 328.

11 Giovanni Rucellai, *Zibaldone*, ed. A. Perosa, London 1960, p. 2. Peter Burke, *The Historical Anthropology of Early Modern Italy*, Cambridge 1987, p. 118.

12 Lauro Martines, *The Social World of the Florentine Humanists*, London 1963, p. 56, n. 140.

13 On Minerbetti, see Attilio Schiaparelli, *La casa fiorentina ed i suoi arredi*, Florence 1908 (reprinted 1983), pp. 184–7, Joseph Alsop, *The Rare Art Traditions: The History of Art Collecting and its linked phenomena wherever these have appeared*, Princeton 1982, p. 378.

14 'Tondo da parto dipinto con cornice messo d'oro': G. Biagi, *Due corredi nuziali fiorentini 1320–1493, da un libro di ricordanze dei Minerbetti*, Florence 1899, p. 18. D. C. Ahl, 'Renaissance Birth Salvers and the Richmond Judgement of Solomon', *Studies in Iconography*, VII–VIII, 1981–2, pp. 157–74, p. 164, n. 43.

15 Roberta M. Olsen, 'Lost and Partially Found: The Tondo, a Significant Florentine Art Form in Documents of the Renaissance', *Artibus et historiae*, XXVII, 1993, pp. 31–67, p. 34, p. 56 and n. 34.

16 Lydecker, *Domestic Setting*, p. 66.

17 Goldthwaite, *Wealth and the Demand for Art*, pp. 211 and 230.

18 Angelo Poliziano, *Detti piacevoli*, ed. T. Zanato, Rome 1983, no. 45, p. 51; quoted and analysed by Alison Brown in 'Cosimo de' Medici's Wit and Wisdom', *Cosimo 'Il Vecchio' de' Medici 1389–1464*, ed. Francis Ames-Lewis, Oxford 1992, pp. 95–113, p. 108. Brown situates Cosimo's witticisms in a long history of Florentine jokes (*beffe*) which created a sense of collective urbane culture in the city, pp. 101–2.

19 On the sense of dignity, comfort and aesthetic value embodied in the Renaissance house and its contents, see Matteo Palmieri's treatise, *Della vita civile* (1430s), as paraphrased and interpreted by Richard Goldthwaite, 'The Economic and Social World of Italian Renaissance Maiolica', *Renaissance Quarterly*, XLII, 1, 1989, pp. 1–32, p. 30, n. 91.

20 *Le Muse e il Principe: Arte di corte nel Rinascimento padano*, exhibition catalogue, ed. Andrea di Lorenzo, Alessandra Mottola Molfino, Mauro Natale and Annalisa Zanni, Museo Poldi-Pezzoli, Milan 1991, for analysis of Leonello d'Este's Belfiore study and comparisons with Federico da Montefeltro's at Urbino; the latter is described in detail in Luciano Cheles, *The Studiolo of Urbino: An Iconographic Investigation*, Wiesbaden 1986.

21 This is the classic argument of Wolfgang Liebenwein in *Lo Studiolo: Die Entstehung eines Raumtyps und seine Entwicklung bis um 1600*, Berlin 1977, pp. 30–128, also Liebenwein in *Le Muse*, pp. 135–45, from which all later views have developed.

22 On Urbino, see Luciano Cheles, '"Topoi" e "serio ludere" nello studiolo di Urbino', *Federico da Montefeltro: Lo stato, le arti, la cultura*, ed. G. Cerboni Baiardi, G. Chittolini and P. Floriani, 3 vols, Rome 1986, vol. 2, pp. 269–86; Cheles, *Lo studiolo di Urbino: Iconografia di un microcosmo principesco*, Modena 1991; L. Guidobaldi, 'Court Music and Universal Harmony: Federico da Montefeltro's *Studiolo* in Urbino', *Hamburger Jahrbuch für Musikwissenschaft*, XII, 1994, pp. 111–20; Nicoletta

Guidobaldi, *La musica di Federico: Immagini e suoni alla corte di Urbino*, Florence 1995. On Gubbio, see Cecil Clough, 'Lo studiolo di Gubbio', *Federico da Montefeltro*, pp. 278–87; Cheles, *Lo studiolo*, pp. 27–35; E. Winternitz, *La scienza del Quattrocento nello studiolo di Gubbio*, Turin 1982, chap. 3; Olga Raggio, 'Lo studiolo nel palazzo ducale di Gubbio', *Piero e Urbino: Piero e le corti rinascimentali*, exhibition catalogue, Urbino 1992, pp. 349–60; Olga Raggio with Antoine Wilmering, 'The Liberal Arts Studiolo from the Ducal Palace at Gubbio', *The Metropolitan Museum of Art Bulletin*, Spring 1996 (complete issue); M. L. Evans, '"Uno maestro solenne": Joos van Wassenhove in Italy', *Nederlands kunsthistorisch jaarboek*, XLIV, 1993, pp. 75–110; F. P. Fiore and M. Tafuri, eds., *Francesco di Giorgio architetto*, Milan 1993, pp. 74–125, 475–585; Margaret Haines, 'Giuliano da Maiano capofamiglia e imprenditore', *Giuliano e la bottega dei da Maiano* (Atti del Convegno Internazionale di Studi, Fiesole 1991), ed. D. Lamberini, M. Lotti and R. Lunardi, Florence 1994, pp. 131–42. For a fascinating insight into the technical skills of *lavoro d'intarsia*, see Robert Blanchette, Antoine Wilmering and Mechtild Baumeister, 'The Use of Green-stained Wood Caused by the Fungus *Chlorociboria* in Intarsia Masterpieces from the Fifteenth-century', *Holzforschung*, XLVI, 1992, pp. 225–32. Olga Raggio and Antoine Wilmering are preparing a major publication on the conservation, history and display of the Gubbio room in New York.

23 A point made by Liebenwein in *Le Muse*, p. 144.

24 On Cosimo de' Medici's study, see Liebenwein *Lo Studiolo: Die Entstehung*, p. 58; for Piero de' Medici's, pp. 74–5. The inventory of the contents of Piero de' Medici's study of '1456' (in fact compiled a year or two later) included books from Cosimo il Vecchio, which can be checked against an inventory of 1418, where they are listed *nello scriptoio di cosimo*. For books which went from Cosimo to Piero, see A. C. De La Mare, 'Cosimo and his Books', *Cosimo il Vecchio de Medici 1389–1464*, ed. Francis Ames-Lewis, Oxford 1992, p. 116. Ames-Lewis, *The Library and Manuscripts of Piero de' Cosimo de' Medici*, New York and London 1984, Appendix 1, 'Inventory of Piero de' Medici's Library' (*studietto*) refers to gems, 'silver for my own use', other precious objects and porcelain. For Spanish and Italian ceramics collected by the Medici in the fifteenth and early sixteenth century, see Timothy Wilson, 'Maioliche rinascimentali armoriate con stemmi fiorentini', in *L'araldica, fonti e metodi* (Atti del Convegno di Campiglia Marittima, 1987), Florence 1989, pp. 128–38. On Lorenzo, see Liebenwein, *Lo Studiolo: Die Entstehung*, pp. 75–7. On early Medici collecting, see E. H. Gombrich, 'The Early Medici as Patrons of Art', *Italian Renaissance Studies*, ed. E. F. Jacob, London 1960, pp. 279–311; Marco Spallanzani, *Giovanni di Bicci, Cosimo e Lorenzo di Giovanni, Piero di Cosimo, Inventari Medicei 1417–1465*, Florence 1996; Antonio Morassi, *Il tesoro dei Medici, oreficerie, argenterie, pietre dure*, Milan 1963; *Il tesoro di Lorenzo Il Magnifico*, vol. 1: *Le gemme*, ed. Nicole Dacos, Antonio Giuliano and Ulrico Pannuti, Florence 1973, vol. 2: *I vasi*, ed. Detlef Heikamp and Andreas Grote, Florence 1975; Luigi Tondo and Franca Maria Vanni, *Le gemme dei Medici e di Lorena nel Museo Archaeologico di Firenze*, Florence 1990; Ulrico Pannuti, 'La collezione glittica medicea', *Le gemme farnese*, ed. Carlo Gasparri, Naples 1994, pp. 61–74; *Il giardino di San Marco, maestri e compagni del Giovane Michelangelo*, exhibition catalogue, ed. Paola Barocchi, Casa Buonarroti, Florence 1992. *Renaissance Florence: The Age of Lorenzo de' Medici, 1449–1492*, exhibition catalogue, ed. Cristina Acidini Luchinat, Accademia Italiana, London 1993–4, pp. 113–41.

25 For general introduction on Isabella, see Liebenwein, *Lo Studiolo: Die Entstehung*, pp. 103–27, 134, 141, 145; '*La Prima Donna del Mondo': Isabella d'Este, Fürstin und Mäzenatin der Renaissance*, exhibition catalogue, ed. Sylvia Ferino-Pagden, Kunsthistorisches Museum, Vienna 1994, with extensive bibliography. On Alfonso, see D. Goodgal, 'The Camerino of Alfonso d'Este', *Art History*, I, 1978, pp. 168–74; Charles Hope, 'The *Camerini d'alabastro* of Alfonso d'Este', *Burlington Magazine*, CXIII, 1971, pp. 641–50, 712–21.

26 Clare Robertson, '*Il Gran Cardinale': Alessandro Farnese, Patron of the Arts*, New Haven and London 1992; C. Riebesell, *Die Sammlung des Kardinal Alessandro Farnese: Ein 'Studio' für Künstler und Gelehrte*, Weinheim 1989; Clifford M. Brown and Anna Maria Lorenzoni, '*Our Accustomed Discourse on the Antique': Cesare Gonzaga and Gerolamo Garimberto, Two Renaissance Collectors of Greco-Roman Art*, New York and London 1993. Irene Favaretto, *Arte antica e cultura antiquaria nelle collezioni venete al tempo della Serenissima*, Rome 1990. Martha Macrory's and Clifford Brown's study of the collecting activities of Leonardo Mocenigo is in preparation. Bertrand Jestaz is writing a survey of all antiquities mentioned in Venetian sixteenth-century inventories: as part of this, see his article 'Les antiquités dans les inventaires vénitiens du XVIe siècle', *Venezia e l'archeologia: Un importante capitolo nella storia del gusto dell'antico nella cultura artistica veneziana* (Venice 1988), ed. Gustavo Traversari, Rome 1990, pp. 35–40.

27 Liebenwein, *Lo Studiolo: Die Entstehung*.

28 Goldthwaite, *Wealth and the Demand for Art*, p. 198.

29 Goldthwaite, *Wealth and the Demand for Art*, pp. 188, 193–4, n. 64. For two – sometimes contradictory – accounts of this process in Lucca, Verona and Vicenza, see Martino Berengo, 'La città di antico regime', *Quaderno storici*, XXVI, 1974, pp. 668–71, and James S. Grubb, *Firstborn of Venice: Vicenza in the Early Renaissance State*, Baltimore 1988, chap. 8. F. W. Kent, 'Individuals and Families as Patrons of Culture in Quattrocento Florence', *Language and Images*, ed. Alison Brown, Oxford 1995, pp. 170–92, for commentary, p. 176, n. 30.

30 Gene Brucker, *Florence 1138–1737*, London 1983, p. 56.

31 One that has been traced by Richard Goldthwaite in successive articles and books: *The Building of Renaissance Florence: An Economic and Social History*, Baltimore and London 1980; 'The Empire of Things: Consumer Demand in Renaissance Italy', *Patronage, Art and Society in Renaissance Italy*, ed. F. W. Kent, P. Simons and J. C. Eade, Oxford 1987, pp. 153–77; 'The Economic and Social World of Italian Renaissance Maiolica', *Renaissance Quarterly*, XLII, I, 1989, pp. 1–32; Goldthwaite, *Wealth and the Demand for Art*.

32 A definition of the composition of the ruling class of Florence between 1390 and 1460 made by Lauro Martines, *The Social World of the Florentine Humanists*, London 1963, pp. 270–71, and p. 267. His study is based on the fortunes and aspirations of fifty-five individuals.

33 Peter Burke, *The Italian Renaissance*, new edition, Cambridge 1986, p. 79 for the criteria for his selection of the 'artists' and 'writers' making up the 'cultural elite' discussed in his book.

34 Liebenwein, *Lo Studiolo: Die Entstehung*, pp. 30–36.

35 Peter Burke, *The Renaissance Sense of the Past*, London 1969.

36 Vittore Branca, introduction to Giovanni di Pagolo Morelli, *Ricordi*, Florence 1956, p. 51.

37 Iris Origo, *The World of San Bernardino*, London 1963, p. 191.

38 Morelli, *Ricordi*, ed. V. Branca, pp. 51–2. Paula Findlen, 'Humanism, Politics and Pornography in Renaissance Italy', *The Invention of Pornography, Obscenity and the Origins of Modernity*, ed. Lyn Hunt, New York 1993, p. 82. Stephanie Jed, *Chaste Thinking: The Rape of Lucretia and the Birth of Humanism*, Bloomington 1989, p. 119. Cristof Wienand, '*Libri di famiglia' und Autobiographie in Italien zwischen Tre- und Quattrocento*,

Tübingen 1993, pp. 85–99, on Morelli's place in the *ricordi* tradition.

39　L. Gargan, *Cultura e arte nel Veneto al tempo di Petrarca*, Padua 1978, pp. 36–9 on his collection, pp. 142–88 on his library. Favaretto, *Arte antiqua e cultura antiquaria*, pp. 33–7.

40　Burckhardt, *Civilisation*, p. 81. See also *The Renaissance*, ed. Burke, p. 16.

41　C. Guasti, ed., *Lettere di un notaio ad un mercante*, 2 vols., Bologna 1880, vol. 1, p. 118. Liebenwein, *Lo Studiolo: Die Entstehung*, p. 57, n. 11.

42　'E a cammino, e nel mio letto, e nel mio studio quando più solitario sono stato': Guasti, *Lettere*, vol. 1, p. 12.

43　'Io mi sto solo in casa nel letto e nello studio in quella letizia che stavano i romiti buoni nel monte, e non sento venti nè da man dritta nè della manca. Così penso fate voi costà: e se non ène il vero, mal fate; e poco senno operate, a darvi travaglio di nulla': Guasti, *Lettere*, vol. 1, p. 87.

44　*The Literary Works of Machiavelli*, ed. and trans. John Hale, London 1961, pp. XXI and 84–5. See also Hale, *Civilisation*, p. 388.

45　Ronald Lightbown, *Mantegna*, Oxford 1986, p. 122, notes 14 and 15. Paul Kristeller, *Andrea Mantegna*, Berlin 1902, p. 557, doc. 131.

46　The famous Isabella d'Este maiolica service painted by Nicola d'Urbino is thought to have been commissioned in 1524 by Isabella d'Este's daughter, Eleonora della Rovere, as a gift for her mother which she deemed suitable for the latter's villa at Porto. For the identification of the maiolica set with this description of *cose da villa* see Carmen Ravanelli Guidotti, 'Un singolare ritrovamento: Un piatto del servizio di Isabella d'Este-Gonzaga', *Italian Renaissance Pottery*, ed. Timothy Wilson, London 1991, pp. 13–23, p. 15, n. 15. For further contemporary comment on the suitability of maiolica in the villa, see Peter Thornton, *The Italian Renaissance Interior, 1400–1600*, London 1991, p. 106. On the status of *istoriato*, see also Timothy Wilson, *Italian Maiolica of the Renaissance*, Milan 1996, introduction.

Chapter 1

1　Richard Goldthwaite, *Wealth and the Demand for Art in Renaissance Italy, 1300–1600*, Baltimore and London 1993. Peter Thornton, *The Italian Renaissance Interior, 1400–1600*, London 1991.

2　John Kent Lydecker, *The Domestic Setting of the Arts in Renaissance Florence*, PhD thesis, Johns Hopkins University, Baltimore 1987, Ann Arbor Microfilms 1987.

3　Lydecker, *Domestic Setting*, analyses the *camera* as the principal focus within an apartment for art objects; P. Thornton, *Italian Renaissance Interior*, considers all major groups of furnishings, including textiles, and their distribution through the house; Isabella Palumbo Fossati, *L'intérieur de la maison vénitienne dans la deuxième moitié du XVIe siècle*, PhD thesis, Ecole des Hautes Etudes en Sciences Sociales, Paris 1982, considers the Venetian interior as a whole, concentrating on the period 1570–1600 and drawing upon more than five hundred inventories. This has been the basis of a number of subsequent articles, including 'L'interno della casa dell'artista e dell'artigiano nella Veneziana del cinquecento', *Studi veneziani*, VII, 1984, pp. 109–53; 'La casa veneziana di Gioseffe Zarlino nel testamento e nell'inventario dei beni', *Nuova rivista musicale italiana*, IV, 1986, pp. 633–41; and 'Livres et lecteurs dans la Venise du XVIe siècle', *Revue française d'histoire du livre*, XLVI, 1985, pp. 481–513.

4　P. Thornton, *Italian Renaissance Interior*, has been invaluable both for published inventories and for analyses and interpretations, drawn upon at many points here.

5　On the Giudici di Petizion as an Office responsible for orphans and their estates, and its role in running auctions, see R. C. Mueller, 'The Procurators of Saint Mark's in the Thirteenth and Fourteenth Centuries: A Study of the Office as a Financial Trust Institution', *Studi veneziani*, XIII, 1971, pp. 105–220. Inventories from the files of the Office have long been used by historians, such as Cesare Augusto Levi, *Le collezioni veneziane d'arte e d'antichità dal secolo XIV ai nostri giorni*, Venice 1900. For recent research based on these inventories, see Palumbo Fossati (references as at n. 3 above) and Fritz Schmidt, 'Zur Genese kapitalischer Konsumerformen im Venedig der frühen Neuzeit', *Siegener Studien*, XLVII, 1990, pp. 23–40, p. 23, n. 1. I am grateful to Patricia Allerston for the last reference. For the Florentine Office, the principal source is Lydecker, *Domestic Setting*.

6　Gaspare Contarini, *The Commonwealth and Government of Venice*, trans. Lewes Lewkenor, London 1599, pp. 122–3. Quoted by Brian Pullan, *Rich and Poor in Renaissance Venice*, Oxford 1971, pp. 209–10, n. 40.

7　Lydecker, *Domestic Setting*, pp. 17–23.

8　On the nature of Venetian inventories and the opportunity they give for reconstructing the biography, family-ties, economic and business world, see Palumbo Fossati, 'L'interno della casa', esp. pp. 113–14.

9　The notarial acts of one notary in particular, Giovanni Andrea Catti (active 1577–1621) trace the activities of the principal Flemish merchants: for him and his clients, see Wilfred Brulez, *Les marchands flamands à Venise*, Brussels 1965, pp. X and XIX–XXIX. On the Venetian notary Antonio Marsilio and his connection with Venetian collectors such as Marcantonio Michiel, Ramusio and Gabriele Vendramin, see Vincenzo Mancini, *Antiquari, 'vertuosi' e artisti*, Padua 1995, p. 97, n. 192. Some notaries were themselves collectors or writers with scholarly interests to compare with their clients: Gian Niccolo Doglioni (active as a notary 1573–1611) was an historian of his native Belluno, while Cesar Ziliol (active 1566–88), official in the lower Chancery and notary to Andrea Pasqualigo, who had created a famous garden mentioned by Sansovino, had himself created a garden with rare plants from the Levant. On Doglioni and his works, see E. A. Cicogna, *Delle inscrizione venetiane*, vol. 2, Venice 1827, p. 530. On Ziliol's and Pasqualigo's gardens, see Francesco Sansovino, *Venetia*, Venice 1581, p. 137. Notaries could obtain a high degree of social status: see for example Pietro Cogollo of Vicenza, a friend of Andrea Palladio's, who obtained the privilege of citizenship in 1559 on condition that he ornamented the façade of his house on the main street in Vicenza. On Cogollo and his housefront (perhaps the work of his friend Palladio), see Howard Burns, 'Le opere minori del Palladio', *Bollettino del centro internazionale di studi di architettura Andrea Palladio*, XXI, 1979, pp. 12–14. I am grateful to Howard Burns for this reference.

10　On the status and definition of the citizenry in Venice, see *Venice: A Documentary History, 1450–1630*, ed. D. S. Chambers and Brian Pullan, Oxford 1992, pp. 261–2.

11　The inventory (Usper 1601) mentions a cupboard with 'sumarii, et scritture da diversi per la professione dell'Avocato'.

12　Lydecker, *Domestic Setting*, chap. 1, p. 3, notes that valuations tend to appear when a sale of property was imminent, as in the case of the post-mortem inventory of Cardinal Francesco Gonzaga (Gonzaga 1483).

13　As in David Chambers's detailed study, *A Renaissance Cardinal and his Worldly Goods: The Will and Inventory of Francesco Gonzaga, 1444–1483*, London 1992. Sixteenth-century Florentine wills have been made more accessible by the publication of indices by Elaine Rosenthal, 'Testaments: A Note on Three Unknown Indices in the Florentine Archives', *Renaissance Quarterly*, XXXIV, 1981, pp. 356–8. I am grateful to Kent Lydecker for this reference.

14 A scene from Ben Jonson's *Volpone* (Act I scene 4) illustrates the pressures exacted by interested parties upon assessors to give an incomplete record when compiling an inventory: see Alvin B. Kernan's edition of the play, New Haven and London 1962, pp. 53–61. See David Vaizey, 'Probate Inventories and Provincial Retailers', *Probate Records and the Local Community*, ed. P. Riden, Gloucester 1985, pp. 91–113. I am grateful to Giles Mandelbrote for this reference. See also Palumbo Fossati, 'L'interno della casa', p. 114.

15 The paintings collection is mentioned by Palumbo Fossati, 'L'interno della casa', p. 129, n. 42.

16 Inventories of this kind make up 40 per cent of the total number of Venetian sixteenth-century inventories surveyed by Palumbo Fossati in *L'intérieur de la maison vénitienne*. I am grateful to her for showing me her thesis and for discussing her work with me.

17 The Sansovino reference to this study-collection is cited in Levi, *Le collezione veneziane*, pp. LXVI–LXVII.

18 Liebenwein, *Lo Studiolo: Die Entstehung eines Raumtyps und seine Entwicklung bis um 1600*, Berlin 1977, p. 34. Entries for 'estude' in the *Glossarium mediae et infimae latinitatis*, ed. Du Fresne, 1886, for 1375 and 1447, taken from the Registre du Trésor des Chartes; as the published calendar for this stops at 1350, a more precise reference is impossible. I am grateful to Pierre-Yves Le Pogam for checking this for me.

19 For Charles V, see Liebenwein, *Lo Studiolo: Die Entstehung*, pp. 37–43.

20 John Florio, *Queen Anna's New World of Words*, London 1611.

21 Interpretations of the word 'studiolo' or 'scrittoio' as a cabinet rather than as a room have sometimes caused difficulties to scholars. P. Thornton, *Italian Renaissance Interior*, p. 233, suggests that the two walnut cabinets listed in the study of Annibale Caro contained all the contents of the 'shelves' listed in the room: I do not think this could have been possible, given the objects which are listed. J. Burckhardt, 'Die Sammler', *Beiträge zur Kunstgeschichte in Italien*, Berlin 1911, pp. 341–573, suggested that the *scrittoi* of Rafaello Borghini were cabinets rather than rooms. This is unlikely, given that the word 'scrittoi' invariably referred to a study in contemporary Florentine usage, and that Borghini himself used the word 'studiolo' in describing a cabinet. A cabinet is also rarely described without the materials of which it was made being mentioned, since this is what was perceived to create a cabinet's distinction: no such information appears in Borghini's description of his friend's collection. See also Michael Bury, 'Bernardo Vecchietti, Patron of Giambologna', *I Tatti Studies*, I, 1985, pp. 13–37, for similar interpretation.

22 Interestingly, Florio, *New World of Words*, defines 'scrittoio' not only as an office but also as 'a writing deske', picking up usage which was more Venetian than Tuscan.

23 Liebenwein, *Lo Studiolo: Die Entstehung*, p. 145. Paula Findlen, 'The Museum, its Classical Etymology and Renaissance Genealogy', *Journal of the History of Collections*, I, 1, 1989, pp. 59–78; Marcin Fabianski, 'Iconography of the Architecture of Ideal *Musea* in the Fifteenth to Eighteenth Centuries', *Journal of the History of Collections*, II, 2, 1990, pp. 95–134.

24 Liebenwein, *Lo Studiolo: Die Entstehung*, pp. 65–6, also pp. 13, 28, 29, 34.

25 Liebenwein, *Lo Studiolo: Die Entstehung*, p. 159.

26 P. Thornton, *Italian Renaissance Interior*, p. 296. See also P. Thornton, *Seventeenth-century Interior Decoration in England, France and Holland*, New Haven and London 1978, pp. 77–81,

296 and 303 on the closet and its role in interior decoration. On the closet and study in the medieval house in London (up to c. 1600) see John Schofield, *Medieval London Houses*, New Haven and London 1994, esp. p. 81 (with cross references to his gazetteer, nos. 15, 55 and 62 listing specific sites). Schofield sees studies as 'developments in taste and arrangement of the sixteenth century', perhaps echoing the continental model, although this has yet to be demonstrated.

27 On the reconstruction of groundplans from inventories, see Palumbo Fossati, 'L'interno della casa', pp. 138–45.

28 On the nature of the *sala* and *porteghi*, see P. Thornton, *Italian Renaissance Interior*, pp. 290–91.

29 A *palazzo* in Italy today can be any large imposing building, but there were social controls of sorts in the use of the term in the Renaissance: it meant a large building owned and occupied by a member of a prominent family; see P. Thornton, *Italian Renaissance Interior*, p. 17. Sansovino, *Venetia*, p. 140, claimed that buildings other than the Doge's Palace should rightly be referred to as houses; as Norbert Huse has pointed out, however, Sansovino entitled one of his chapters 'Palazzi di Venezia', 'highlighting the persistent tension between an ideology that idealised the social order of Venice, and the reality of building as a means of self-aggrandisement' (Norbert Huse, *Art of Renaissance Venice*, trans. Edmund Jephcott, Chicago and London 1990, p. 16). Even if not a palace, some inventories list the contents of what Sansovino called elsewhere *case aperte* – well-appointed and furnished houses which could be visited. Other inventories list the contents of *case di statio*, substantial town houses (Lombardo 1569) and yet others list the contents of the merchant's residence which doubled as warehouse and offices, the *palazzo fondego* (Helman 1606). On this building type, see Richard Goy, *Venetian Vernacular Architecture, Traditional Housing in the Venetian Lagoon*, Cambridge 1989, pp. 123–49.

30 A single room, occupied by Daniela Danini, is described in an inventory of 28 November 1585. She lived at a charity hospital, the Cà di Dio: her inventory thus provides an unusual record of an institutional interior. See Palumbo Fossati, 'L'interno della casa', p. 114. On Sansovino's remodelling of the Cà di Dio forty years before the inventory was compiled, see Deborah Howard, *Jacopo Sansovino, Architecture and Patronage in Renaissance Venice*, New Haven and London 1975, pp. 114–19.

31 To list one published example, the stock in the shop of a parfumier (*muschier*) at the Sign of the Angel, 'Francesco da l'Anzolo', is listed in an inventory of 2 April 1547. Gustav Ludwig, 'Das Verschwinden des Restello und die selbständige Ausbildung des Spiegels', *Italienische Forschungen*, IV–V, 1906, pp. 310–14, 320. Apothecaries were surveyed by the Venetian authorities in 1567–8; the resulting documents give a detailed picture of the trade. See Richard Mackenney, *Tradesmen and Traders: The Role of the Guilds in Venice and Europe*, London 1987, pp. 89–90.

32 Fiorentino 1585.

33 Inventory of the estate of Inghiramo di Girolamo Inghiramo da Prato, 8 May 1579, listing contents of his villa at Piemonte. A.S.F., P.D.P. 2712.

34 On *altane* as a Venetian vernacular feature, see Goy, *Venetian Vernacular Architecture*, pp. 53–4.

35 The status of gardens in Venice is evident from Pietro Busello's book, *Il giardino di agricoltura di Marco Bussato da Ravenna*, Venice 1592.

36 Biblioteca Correr, Venice, MS Dandolo PD c. 1007; see J. M. Fletcher, 'Marcantonio Michiel's Collection', *Journal of the Warburg and Courtauld Institutes*, XXXVI, 1973, p. 383, n. 11.

37 Giorgio Gianighian and Paola Pavanini, *Dietro i palazzi: Tre secoli di architettura minore Venezia, 1497–1803*, Venice 1984, p. 136. On the trend towards investment in property in late sixteenth-century Venice, see Brian Pullan, 'Wage Earners and the Venetian Economy 1550–1630', *Crisis and Change in the Venetian Economy in the Sixteenth and Seventeenth Centuries*, ed. B. Pullan, London 1968, pp. 146–74, and 'The Occupations of the Venetian Nobility in the Mid and Late Sixteenth Century', *Renaissance Venice*, ed. J. R. Hale, London 1973, pp. 379–408. Gianighian and Pavanini, *Dietro i palazzi*, passim, and Gianighian, 'Scarichi veneziani in epoca moderna: "Canoni d'acqua, canoni da necessario"', *Studi veneziani*, VII 1984, pp. 161–82. I am grateful to Giorgio Gianighian for this reference.

38 Gianighian and Pavanini, *Dietro i palazzi*, p. 48.

39 On cloth and glass windows, their workmanship and cost in Ferrara under Ercole d'Este, see Thomas Tuohy, *Herculean Ferrara, Ercole d'Este 1471–1505, and the Invention of a Ducal Capital*, Cambridge 1996, pp. 207–8.

40 On Agnus Dei pendants in the late Middle Ages and Renaissance, see R. W. Lightbown, *Medieval European Jewellery*, London 1992, pp. 228–30.

41 Goldthwaite, *Wealth and the Demand for Art*, p. 231, for summary.

42 A point made by Lydecker, *Domestic Setting*, pp. 24–5 and notes 20–21, and by Gabriella Cantini Guidotti and Alessandro Guidotti, 'Proposte per una schedatura elettronica di fonti d'archivio utili per la storia delle arti: Gli inventari di beni mobili', *Centro di elaborazione automatica di dati e documenti storico-artistici, Bollettino d'informazioni*, IV, Pisa 1983, pp. 93–143.

43 See Goldthwaite, *Wealth and the Demand for Art*; Lydecker, *Domestic Setting*; and P. Thornton, *Italian Renaissance Interior*.

44 P. Thornton, *Italian Renaissance Interior*; Jacqueline Musacchio, *Art and Ritual of Childbirth in Renaissance Italy*, PhD thesis, Princeton University, Cambridge (Mass.), 1995; Lydecker, *Domestic Setting*. Chapter 6, in particular, of this book is intended to supplement these.

45 Katrin Achilles-Syndram and Rainer Schoch, eds., *Das Praunsche Kabinett, Meisterwerke von Dürer bis Carracci*, exhibition catalogue, Germanisches Nationalmuseum, Nuremberg 1994, cat. 182. I am grateful to Jeremy Warren for this reference.

46 R. Predelli, 'Le memorie e le carte di Alessandro Vittoria', *Archivio trentino*, XXIII, 1908, p. 131. I am grateful to Bruce Boucher for this reference.

47 Lydecker, *Domestic Setting*, pp. 85–6, part of a general introduction on the use of account books for details about furnishings, pp. 80–88.

48 Ronald Lightbown, 'Giovanni Chellini, Donatello and Antonio Rossellino', *Burlington Magazine*, CIV, 1962, pp. 102–4, p. 103.

49 M. T. Sillano, *Le ricordanze di Giovanni Chellini da San Miniato*, Milan 1984, p. 31.

50 On arms as proofs of gentility, see F. Mutinello, *Lessico Veneto*, Venice 1851, p. 32, for a comment made by the Venetian patrician Maria Soranzo da Mula in 1461, in which he notes the custom of hanging arms in the *portico* or *sala*. Sansovino, *Venetia*, p. 139, later listed *studi d'arme* to be found in *case nobili* in the city.

51 Goldthwaite, *Wealth and the Demand for Art*, p. 211, n. 93.

52 Giovanna Ciapelli, *Francesco di Matteo Castellani, Ricordanze*, vol. 1, Florence 1992, p. 46, n. 42.

53 'Salamone di ★★★ [blank in text], ebreo da Prato che venne a stare in Firenze, ebbe la mia spalliera con l'arme nostra, e vendélla a dì 8 di luglo 1439 con altre cose a Francesco del Nero rigattiere. Bisogna intendere da chi detto Salamone la comperò e troverassi chi la tolse. Francesco la vendé all'Arte della Lana': Castellani memoranda, p. 64.

54 Marco Spallanzani, *Le ceramiche orientali a Firenze*, Florence 1978, pp. 163–4, 50 and 100.

55 Eton College Library, MS 137: 'Olim ex bibliotheca Clarissimi Mathematici Iacobi Langusci Veneti Post eius cansum patavii: sub astatione multis cum aliis in nostratium cetum deductus est. Anno salvatoris M.cccc.Liiio'. N. Ker, *Medieval Manuscripts in British Libraries*, London 1977, vol. 2, p. 758. I am grateful to Paul Quarrie for this reference. For more information on late fourteenth- and early fifteenth-century book auctions in Venice, see Susan Connell, 'Books and their Owners in Venice 1345–1480', *Journal of the Warburg and Courtauld Institutes*, XXXV, 1972, pp. 163–86, esp. pp. 173 and 177–82.

56 Clifford M. Brown, 'An Art Auction in Venice, 1506', *L'arte*, XVII, 1972, pp. 121–36. Irene Favaretto, *Arte antica e cultura antiquaria nelle collezioni venete al tempo della Serenissima*, Rome 1990, p. 59, n. 89.

57 Palumbo Fossati, 'L'interno della casa', p. 111, n. 6.

58 Lydecker, *Domestic Setting*, pp. 214–18.

59 Lydecker, *Domestic Setting*, pp. 216–17.

60 *Montaigne's Travel Journal*, trans. D. Frame, San Francisco 1983, p. 164.

61 The account of the second-hand market in Venice which follows is based on Patricia Allerston, *The Market in Secondhand Clothes and Furnishings in Venice circa 1500–1650*, PhD thesis, European University, Florence 1996, pp. 234–52. I am grateful to her for making her thesis available to me, and for a number of discussions we have had on this subject over several years. See also her articles, 'Le marché d'occasion à Venise aux XVIe e XVIIe siècles', *Echanges et cultures textiles dans l'Europe pré-industrielle*, CNRS, Rouen 1993, pp. 1–15. 'L'abito come articolo di scambio nella società dell'età moderna: alcune implicazioni', *Le trame della moda*, Centro Studi Europa delle Corti e Centro Italiano per la Storia del Tessuto, Rome 1995, pp. 109–24.

62 Allerston, *Market in Secondhand Clothes*, pp. 236–7.

63 Allerston, *Market in Secondhand Clothes*, pp. 4–17; chap. 4 for the composition of the Arte della Strazzaria (pp. 166–96); on pedlars within the Guild, pp. 179–81.

64 Allerston, *Market in Secondhand Clothes*, pp. 185–9 on women. Gian Ludovico Masetti Zannini, 'Ebrei, artisti, oggetti d'arte, documenti romani dei secoli XVI e XVII', *Commentari*, Rome, n.s. 25, July–December 1974, pp. 281–301. I am grateful to Patricia Allerston for this reference.

65 Allerston, *Market in Secondhand Clothes*, pp. 4, 164–5. On Rome, see Zannini, 'Ebrei, artisti'.

66 Allerston, *Market in Secondhand Clothes*, p. 205. Logan Pearsall Smith, *Life and Letters of Sir Henry Wotton*, 2 vols, Oxford 1907, vol. 1, pp. 56–7, 498–9, 501–2, vol. 2, pp. 96, 101–2, 207–9. I am grateful to Patricia Allerston for this reference.

67 Allerston, *Market in Secondhand Clothes*, p. 206, n. 129. Public Record Office, State Papers Venetian, vol. 6, part II, fols 211r, 215–216v. Pearsall Smith, *Wotton*, vol. 1, pp. 498–502. I am grateful to Patricia Allerston for the reference to the PRO documents.

68 'Non essendo per ancora fatti tutti i drapi ma q[ue]sto poco importa, la città è grande et in due giorni quel'che manca si troverà a nolo, et il tutto sia V[ostra] Ill[ustrissima] sicura che si farà con ogni buon'termine, et anche con ogni conveniente modestia ello spendere': Allerston, *Market in Secondhand Clothes*, p. 177, n. 44.

69 For new interpretations of the eighteenth-century evidence, see Carolyn Sargentson, *Merchants and Luxury Markets: The Marchand-merciers of Eighteenth-century Paris*, London 1996, pp. 105–7 on old and second-hand textiles and their value.

Chapter 2

1 Peter Thornton, *The Italian Renaissance Interior, 1400–1600*, London 1991, pp. 282–320. See also *Architecture et vie sociale, l'organisation intérieure des grandes demeures à la fin du Moyen Age et à la Renaissance*, Actes du Colloque, Tours, ed. Jean Guillaume, Paris 1994.

2 Peter Thornton, *Seventeenth-century Interior Decoration in England, France and Holland*, New Haven and London 1978, esp. pp. 57–8.

3 For a primarily architectural analysis of the study, see Wolfgang Liebenwein, *Lo Studiolo: Die Entstehung eines Raumtyps und seine Entwicklung bis um 1600*, Berlin 1977. *Architecture et vie sociale*, ed. Guillaume, pp. 33, 38, 51, 55, 101, 146, 196, 197, 222.

4 Liebenwein, *Lo Studiolo: Die Entstehung*, p. 68.

5 P. Thornton, *Italian Renaissance Interior*, p. 301.

6 'Le Donne si stanno in piedi delle finestre, si per veder a lavorare con l'Agole cose sottili & ricami, si per potere essere commode a farsi alla finestra; alla tavola intesa si mangia, a quello lato si gioca, alcuni passeggiano, altri si stanno al fuoco, et così v'è luogo per tutti': Anton Francesco Doni, *I marmi* (Venice 1552), ed. S. Bongi, Florence 1863, p. 168; see also P. Thornton, *Italian Renaisance Interior*, p. 389, n. 2.

7 Vincenzo Scamozzi, *L'idea dell'architettura universale*, Venice 1615, p. 307. Translated by an anonymous English reader in the seventeenth century: see P. Thornton, *Italian Renaissance Interior*, p. 312.

8 Liebenwein, *Lo Studiolo: Die Entstehung*, p. 69.

9 Liebenwein, *Lo Studiolo: Die Entstehung*, p. 160.

10 *L'architettura di Leonbattista Alberti*, translated from the Latin into Italian by C. Bartoli, Florence 1550, p. 153.

11 Nancy Elizabeth Edwards, *The Renaissance Stufetta in Rome: The Circle of Raphael and the Recreation of the Antique*, PhD thesis, University of Minnesota, 1983, Ann Arbor Microfilms 1985.

12 Edwards, *Renaissance Stufetta*, esp. pp. 3–14, 74–5.

13 Edwards, *Renaissance Stufetta*, p. 77.

14 Edwards, *Renaissance Stufetta*, pp. 152–3. On Castro, see Clare Robertson, *'Il Gran Cardinale': Alessandro Farnese, Patron of the Arts*, New Haven and London 1992, p. 22.

15 Liebenwein, *Lo Studiolo: Die Entstehung*, p. 136.

16 Liebenwein, *Lo Studiolo: Die Entstehung*, p. 136.

17 Edwards, *Renaissance Stufetta*, pp. 35–8, 17.

18 Edwards, *Renaissance Stufetta*, p. 94 on Baldassini's career and reputation, pp. 76–7 on patrons for *stufe*.

19 Christoph Frommel, *Der Römische Palastbau der Hochrenaissance*, 3 vols, Berlin 1973; vol. 2, p. 29 for identification of room functions, vol. 3, pl. 14a for plan.

20 For Baldassini's career, see Frommel, *Der Römische Palastbau*, vol. 2, p. 26.

21 Frommel, *Der Römische Palastbau*, vol. 2, p. 29.

22 Edwards, *Renaissance Stufetta*, p. 36, and fig. 43 for plan.

23 Edwards, *Renaissance Stufetta*, p. 76, n. 78.

24 Torquato Tasso, 'Il Malpiglio secondo overo Del Fuggir la moltitudine', *Dialoghi*, ed. E. Mazzali, 2 vols., Turin 1959, pp. 125–6. Claudio Franzoni, 'Le collezioni rinascimentali di antichità', *Memoria dell'antico nell'arte italiana*, ed. Salvatore Settis, vol. 1, Turin 1984, p. 316.

25 *Beloved Son Felix: The Journal of Felix Platter*, ed. and trans. Sean Jennett, London 1961, pp. 63–4.

26 Amanda Lillie, 'The Humanist Villa Revisited', *Language and Images of Renaissance Italy*, ed. Alison Brown, Oxford 1995, pp. 193–215, pp. 193–4; a development of Lillie's *Florentine Villas in the Fifteenth Century: A Study of the Strozzi and Sassetti Country Properties*, PhD thesis, Courtauld Institute, University of London 1986.

27 Douglas Radcliffe-Umstead, 'Petrarch and the Freedom to be Alone', *Francis Petrarch, Six Centuries Later: A Symposium*, ed. Aldo Scaglione, Chicago 1975, pp. 236–48.

28 Radcliffe-Umstead, *Petrarch*, p. 237.

29 Introduction to Pietro Bembo, *Prose e rime*, ed. Carlo Dionisotti, Turin 1960, pp. 30–31; quoted in Leonello Puppi, 'Le residenze di Pietro Bembo "in Padoana"', *L'arte*, VII, 1969, pp. 30–66, p. 44 and n. 92.

30 Puppi, 'Bembo', pp. 30–66.

31 Radcliffe-Umstead, *Petrarch*, p. 241.

32 Richard Goldthwaite, *Wealth and the Demand for Art in Renaissance Italy, 1300–1600*, Baltimore and London 1993, pp. 217–18. Lillie, *Florentine Villas*, talks of the role of the Florentine *contado* in patrician culture and life, pp. 24–5 and 302.

33 Ursula Hoff, 'Meditation in Solitude', *Journal of the Warburg and Courtauld Institutes*, I, 1937, pp. 292–4.

34 'Mi è abbastanza se un sol portico corra dalla casa sino all'ameno giardino, salendovi dal cortile con due soli gradini; di qua e di là vi siano delle camere non di lusso, ma accomodate agli usi communi. Alla camera da letto vi sia annessa la biblioteca abbastanza elegante, unica mia suppellitile': Puppi, 'Bembo', p. 52, n. 30.

35 Hoff, 'Meditation', pp. 293–4.

36 Alessandra Chiappini, 'La Biblioteca dello Studiolo', *Le Muse e il Principe: Arte di corte nel Rinascimento padano*, exhibition catalogue, ed. Andrea di Lorenzo, Alessandro Mottola Molfino, Mauro Natale and Annalisa Zanni, Museo Poldi-Pezzoli, Milan 1991, pp. 155–65, p. 163, n. 32.

37 John Pearson Perry, 'Practical and Ceremonial Uses of Plants Materials as "Literary Refinements" in the Libraries of Leonello d'Este and his Courtly Literary Circle', *La Bibliofilia*, XCI, 1989, pp. 122–73, p. 150.

38 'Ho pigliato di quel thesoro ch'io ho, di quei frutti, che sono nel mio giardino, & di quelle gioie che sono nel mio studio': Anton Francesco Doni, *La Fortuna di Cesare, tratta da gl'autori Latini*, Venice 1550, preface (unpaginated). I am grateful to Jeremy Warren for this reference.

39 Pliny the Younger, *Letters*, ed. W. Melmoth, London 1915, vol. 1, book III, letter v, p. 199.

40 Foster Watson, *Tudor Schoolboy Life: The Dialogues of J. L. Vives*, London 1908 (reprinted 1970), pp. 110–16, p. 111.

41 Desiderius Erasmus, *The Ciceronian*, ed. A. H. T. Levi, *The Complete Works of Erasmus*, Toronto 1986, pp. 350–51.

42 *The Literary Works of Machiavelli*, ed. John Hale, Oxford 1961, p. 139.

43 Benedetto Cotrugli, *Della mercatura e del mercante perfetto*, Venice 1569, Brescia 1602, p. 86; *Il libro dell'arte di mercatura*, ed. Ugo Tucci, Venice 1990, p. 230 for *scrittoio*, p. 231 for *studiolo*.

44 *The Painted Page: Italian Renaissance Book Illumination*, exhibition catalogue, ed. J. G. Alexander, Royal Academy, London 1994, cat. 57.

45 'Idemque prope est de lucubratorii dormitoriique cubiculi ratione dicendum quae quidem triclinia, eo quod in his sit coniunctus vitae partiendae usus, recte erunt finitima propinquitate nexa, et quod utrorumque usus maximae esse debeat interventorium interpellatione liber, non sine causa utrumque triclinii genus erit in intermedia domus descriptione situm. Itaque iure in lucubratorio non modo tubolos asculatorios sed etiam coclearias scalas esse debere censernus, ex quorum alteris in auditorio disputantes audiantur, ex alteris intestinum sit discendendi in bibliothecam iter': *The Renaissance Cardinal's Ideal Palace: A Chapter from Cortesi's 'De Cardinalatu'*, ed. Kathleen Weill-Gariss and John F. D'Amico, Studies in Italian Art and Architecture 15th through 18th Centuries, Cambridge (Mass.) 1980, p. 84. The translation quoted here appears on p. 85.

46 Poggio Bracciolini, *Epistolae*, 3 vols, Florence 1832–61, ed. T. Tonelli, vol. 1, book 1, letter 10, pp. 42–5. Roberto Weiss, *The Renaissance Discovery of Classical Antiquity*, Oxford 1969, p. 201. Joseph Alsop, *The Rare Art Traditions: The History of Art Collecting and its linked phenomena wherever these have appeared*, Princeton 1982, pp. 349–50, n. 61. Franzoni, 'Le collezioni rinascimentali', p. 309.

47 Bracciolini, *Epistolae*, vol. 1, book 4, letter 12, pp. 322–4. Alsop, *Rare Art Traditions*, p. 340, n. 67.

48 Edwards, *Renaissance Stufetta*, pp. 48–51 for the room's decoration.

49 *Lettere di M. Pietro Bembo*, Rome 1548, vol. 1, 25 April 1516. Ernst Gombrich, 'Hypnerotomachiana', *Symbolic Images*, London 1972, p. 107.

50 *The Genius of Venice 1500–1600*, exhibition catalogue, ed. Jane Martineau and Charles Hope, Royal Academy, London 1983, cat. D23. *The Study of Italian Drawings: The Contribution of Philip Pouncey*, exhibition catalogue, ed. Nicholas Turner, British Museum, London 1994, cat. 59. See also P. Thornton, *Italian Renaissance Interior*, fig. 318.

51 Turner, *Italian Drawings*, cat. 59.

52 Irene Favaretto, *Arte antica e cultura antiquaria nelle collezioni venete al tempo della Serenissima*, Rome 1990, p. 77.

53 'Doi secchi de bronzo de acquasanta piccoli': Ram inventory of 1591; see P. Thornton, *Italian Renaissance Interior*, p. 364.

54 P. Thornton, *Italian Renaissance Interior*, fig. 318.

55 P. Thornton, *Italian Renaissance Interior*, pp. 216–18, 64.

56 John Kent Lydecker, 'Il Patriziato fiorentino e la committenza artistica per la casa', *I ceti dirigenti nella Toscana del Quattrocento*, Impruneta 1987, pp. 209–11. I am grateful to Bill Connell for this reference.

57 Lydecker, 'Patriziato fiorentino', p. 218 and n. 51.

58 Richard Goldthwaite, 'The Empire of Things: Consumer Demand in Renaissance Italy', *Patronage, Art and Society in Renaissance Italy*, ed. F. W. Kent, P. Simons and J. C. Eade, Oxford 1987, pp. 153–75, p. 170. See also Goldthwaite, *Wealth and the Demand for Art*, pp. 227–8.

59 'Per dipintura di uno Cielo dello scrittoio e per fornire d'oro': Rinieri memoranda. On Apollonio di Giovanni, see P. Thornton, *Italian Renaissance Interior*, pp. 97, 196 and figs 123, 219, 371, 314.

60 'La chassetta chon 4 cassettine per tenere in sul descho dello scrittoio terreno': Rinieri memoranda.

61 'Uno palcho & palchetti & descho & cassette di nocie [. . .] & finestre di nocie & uscio di nocie doppie do lo schrittoio avuto da llui': Giocondi memoranda.

62 '2 seradure da studio': Richard Goy, *The House of Gold: Building a Palace in Medieval Venice*, Cambridge 1992, p. 222, n. 23. Also personal communication of 2 May 1993 on the matter of Contarini's accounts, for which I am most grateful.

63 'Il studietto che confina questa camera': Vittoria memoranda, p. 159.

64 Watson, *Tudor Schoolboy Life*, pp. 93–100, p. 98.

65 *Ten Colloquies of Erasmus*, trans. Craig R. Thompson, New York 1957, p. 171.

66 P. Thornton, *Italian Renaissance Interior*, p. 24.

67 Graziano Manni, *Mobili in Emilia*, Modena 1986, p. 76.

68 P. Thornton, *Italian Renaissance Interior*, p. 27, n. 7.

69 Perry, 'Practical and Ceremonial Uses', p. 131.

70 Juan Ludovicus Vives, 'Cubiculum et Lucubratio', *Lingua Latina: Ludovicus Vives, Scenes of School and College Life*, ed. W. H. D. Rouse, Oxford 1931, pp. 66–70; see also Watson, *Tudor Schoolboy Life*, pp. 111–12.

71 Comenius, *Orbis sensualium pictis*, London 1679, pp. 200–201.

72 Anthony Radcliffe, 'Bronze Oil Lamps by Riccio', *Victoria and Albert Museum Yearbook*, III, 1972, pp. 29–58.

73 'Unum fulcimentum de octono a cesenderio': Fiesso 1484.

74 Perry, 'Practical and Ceremonial Uses', p. 132.

75 Luca Landucci, *A Florentine Diary from 1450–1516*, trans. Alice de Rosen Jervis, London 1927, pp. 225–6.

76 *Beloved Son Felix*, ed. and trans. Jennett, pp. 52–3.

77 Perry, 'Practical and Ceremonial Uses', p. 132.

78 On the importance of wooden ceilings and their decoration in Ferrarese palaces under Ercole d'Este, see Thomas Tuohy, *Herculean Ferrara, Ercole d'Este 1471–1505, and the Invention of a Ducal Capital*, Cambridge 1996, pp. 201–5.

79 H. Amouric, G. Demians d'Archimbaud, J. Thiriot and L. Vallauri, *Petits carrés d'histoire: Pavements et revêtements muraux dans le midi méditerranéen du Moyen Age à l'époque moderne*, exhibition catalogue, Palais de Papes, Avignon 1996, esp. pp. 59–66.

80 *Petits carrés d'histoire*, p. 62 and fig. 140.

81 *Petits carrés d'histoire*, p. 62.

82 *Petits carrés d'histoire*, pp. 63–6; figs 141–3, 145–8 for heraldic and geometric designs, fig. 144 for fish, fig. 141 for human figure.

83 Paride Berardi, *L'antica maiolica di Pesaro dal XIV al XVII secolo*, Florence 1984, pp. 207–8, fig. 123. Lucia Fornari Schiandri, *Ai piedi della Badessa*, Parma 1988, for the range of designs on the tiles. For the 'contour panel', see Timothy Wilson, *Ceramic Art of the Italian Renaissance*, exhibition catalogue, British Museum, London 1987, p. 34, and Arthur Lane, *Early Islamic Pottery*, London 1947, p. 16 and pl. 23b. On pigments developed by Italian Renaissance potters, see Wendy M. Watson, *Italian Renaissance Maiolica from the William A. Clark Collection*, exhibition catalogue, Corcoran Gallery of Art, Washington, published London 1986, p. 14.

84 Mariarosa Palvarini Gobio Casali, 'Ceramic Tiles for the Gonzaga', *Splendours of the Gonzaga*, exhibition catalogue, ed. David Chambers and Jane Martineau, Victoria and Albert Museum, London 1982, p. 44 and n. 10, cat. 127.

85 Julia E. Poole, *Italian Maiolica and Incised Slipware in the Fitzwilliam Museum, Cambridge*, Cambridge 1996, cat. 357.

86 Clifford M. Brown and Anna Maria Lorenzoni, *Isabella d'Este and Lorenzo da Pavia*, Geneva 1982, p. 245.

87 Brown and Lorenzoni, *Isabella and Lorenzo*, p. 245.

88 Brown and Lorenzoni, *Isabella and Lorenzo*, p. 209, docs 61, 63–5.

89 Richard Goy, *Venetian Vernacular Architecture, Traditional Housing in the Venetian Lagoon*, Cambridge 1989, pp. 47–8, for this quotation.

90 John Pope-Hennessy and R. W. Lightbown, *Italian Sculpture in the Victoria and Albert Museum*, 3 vols, London 1964, vol. 1, pp. 704–8.

91 Pope-Hennessy, *Luca della Robbia*, Oxford 1980, p. 241.

92 Eve Borsook, 'A Florentine *Scrittoio* for Diomede Carafa', *Art in the Ape of Nature: Studies in Honor of H. W. Janson*, ed. Moshe Barasch and Lucy Freeman Sandler, New York and Englewood Cliffs 1981, pp. 91–3.

93 Pope-Hennessy, *Luca della Robbia*, p. 44.

94 On the innovative pigments developed by Luca della Robbia for application to sculptural terracotta, see W. David Kingery and Meredith Aronson, 'The Glazes of Luca della Robbia', *Faenza*, LXXVI, 1990, pp. 221–5.

95 Rab Hatfield, 'Some Unknown Descriptions of the Medici Palace', *Art Bulletin*, LII, 1970, pp. 232–49, p. 236. Pope-Hennessy dates the *studio*'s ceramic decoration to before 1456, on the grounds that Filarete's description of it dates to 1464, and his last recorded visit to Florence was in 1456. Pope-Hennessy also suggests that the ceramic work, being structural, must have been done prior to the fresco decoration in the late 1450s. Pope-Hennessy, *Luca della Robbia*, p. 43.

96 'Il suo studietto, hornatissimo [con] il pavimento et così il cielo di vetriamenti fatti a figure degnissime in modo che a chi v'entra dà grandissima admiratione': Hatfield, 'Some Unknown Descriptions', pp. 235–6 on *studio*.

97 'Che fu cosa singolare, e molto utile per la state': Giorgio Vasari, *Le vite* (1550), ed. Gaetano Milanesi, Florence 1906 (reprinted 1981), 9 vols, vol. 2, p. 174. See also Pope-Hennessy and Lightbown, *Italian Sculpture*, vol. 1, pp. 704–8.

98 Amanda Lillie, 'Giovanni di Cosimo and the Villa Medici at Fiesole', *Piero de' Medici, 'Il Gottoso' (1416–1469): Kunst im Dienste der Mediceer*, ed. Andreas Beyer and Bruce Boucher, Berlin 1993, pp. 189–205, p. 192. I am grateful to Amanda Lillie for this reference.

99 Lillie, 'Giovanni di Cosimo', p. 201, n. 24 for the letter and for this interpretation.

100 Lillie, 'Giovanni di Cosimo', p. 201, n. 25 summarises the literature on Giovanni's study and the debate over the destination of Donatello's marble panelling. On Cardinal Francesco Gonzaga's visit, see David Chambers, *A Renaissance Cardinal and his Worldly Goods: The Will and Inventory of Francesco Gonzaga (1444–1483)*, London 1992, esp. p. 56, n. 49 for a letter to the Cardinal's mother explaining that he had been shown 'li studii di Pietro e Giovanni belissimi, e gran copia di bei libri'.

Chapter 3

1 Leon Battista Alberti, *L'architettura*, ed. G. Orlandi, 2 vols, Milan 1966, book x, chap. xiv, vol. 2, p. 981. Quoted in Luciano Cheles, *The Studiolo of Urbino: An Iconographic Investigation*, Wiesbaden 1986, p. 24, n. 32.

2 *The Correspondence of Erasmus, 1523–1524*, trans. R. A. B. Mynors and Alexander Dalzell, Toronto 1992, p. 368, letter 1489.

3 *Beloved Son Felix: The Journal of Felix Platter*, ed. and trans. Sean Jennett, London 1961, pp. 52–3.

4 Susan M. Connell, *The Employment of Sculptors and Stonemasons in Venice in the Fifteenth Century*, PhD thesis, Warburg Institute, University of London 1976, p. 159.

5 'Uno desco in detto scriptoio grande da scrivere, con asse et spalliere, e uno armario con le sue cornice di noce e cassettine con tarsie, e di sotto dove se tiene i piedi uno palcho di lignamo d'albaro soxpesa da terra, che non li dà stima perche tutto e fermo nel muro': Medici 1498.

6 'Uno palcho e chornicioni e palchetti e descho e pancha e chasette di nocie, e finestre e uscio di nocie del mio schrittoio': Giocondi memoranda.

7 Penny Howell Jolly, 'Antonello da Messina's Saint Jerome in his Study: A Disguised Portrait', *Burlington Magazine*, cxxiv, 1982, pp. 27–9, figs 30–34. Bernhard Ridderbos, *Saint and Symbol*, Groningen 1984, pp. 52–62.

8 'Fatto qui nella stanza': Nero 1576.

9 'Ne pare essere passati da lo limbo al paradiso'; 'havendo io conducto uno marangone per fare due banchoni in lo studio e mettere quattro rote': letter from Bartolomeo Marasca to the Marchesa of Mantua, from Pavia, 17 July 1460. A. S. Mantua, Archivio Gonzaga B.1621 c488. I am grateful to David Chambers for this reference. On Marasca and the Gonzaga, see *Splendours of the Gonzaga*, exhibition catalogue, ed. David Chambers and Jane Martineau, Victoria and Albert Museum, London 1982, pp. 112–13.

10 'Non ci sono stati simili maestri di lengnami, di tarsie e commessi, di tanta arte di prospettiva che con penello non si farebbe meglio': Rucellai memoranda.

11 Graziano Manni, *Mobili in Emilia*, Modena 1986, p. 77.

12 Thomas Tuohy, *Herculean Ferrara, Ercole d'Este 1471–1505, and the Invention of a Ducal Capital*, Cambridge 1996, pp. 81–2 and doc. 59 for Stefano de Dona Bona's work, pp. 208–9 on Ercole's motives.

13 Pier Luigi Bagatin, *La tarsia rinascimentale a Ferrara, il coro di Sant'Andrea*, Ferrara 1991, p. 17, n. 21, p. 18.

14 'Per experientia di lui avuta et vista in alcuni lavori che m'ae facti, è finissimo maestro et li lavori suoi exquisitissimi quanto possino essere; perchè, conoscendo la virtù sua, vi prego vi sia racomandato, rendendomi io certissimo che di lui avete si buono servigio et li lavori suoi ve saranno tanto grati, che contentissimo rimarrete': L. Fumi and E. Lazzareschi, *Carteggio di Paolo Guinigi, 1400–1430*, Lucca 1925, p. 91.

15 Roger Jones, 'Palla Strozzi e la sagrestia di Santa Trinità', *Rivista d'arte*, xxxvii, i, 1984, pp. 9–106, p. 63 for document recording the work.

16 Rab Hatfield, 'Some Unknown Descriptions of the Medici Palace', *Art Bulletin*, lii, 1970, pp. 232–49, pp. 235–6. I have slightly altered his translation.

17 Peter Thornton, *The Italian Renaissance Interior, 1400–1600*, London 1991, p. 101.

18 'E piu me dee dare ogni anno uno deschetto colla spalliera a tutte sue spesi': Chellini memoranda, p. 198.

19 'Delle quale cose disse non ne voler niente per servigi recevuti da me': Chellini memoranda, pp. 172–3.

20 'Uno lettuccio a cassone di sotto e uno capellinaio a detto lettuccio, lavorato di noce cum fogliame e lettere di silio, e per un paio di casse a due serami ciascuna, prima cum fogliame di silio a detto modo, e per un fregio di noce cum fogliame e di silio a una lettiera, tutto per la camera di Tomaso': Chellini memoranda, p. 177. On the use of *silio* see P. Thornton, *Italian Renaissance Interior*, p. 89, n. 3.

21 P. Thornton, *Italian Renaissance Interior*, pl. 90 and pp. 90, 94.

22 P. Thornton, *Italian Renaissance Interior*, pl. 162 and 167, pp. 149–53. Richard Goldthwaite, *Wealth and the Demand for Art in Italy, 1300–1600*, Baltimore and London 1993, p. 229.

23 Clifford M. Brown and Anna Maria Lorenzoni, *'Our Accustomed Discourse on the Antique': Cesare Gonzaga and Gerolamo Garimberto: Two Renaissance Collectors of Greco-Roman Art*, New York and London 1993, p. 170, item 126 in the 1569 inventory of his possessions, valued at 400 scudi.

24 'Composto di varie et bellissime disegno, varii ornamenti di figurine di marmo et di bronzo': Brown and Lorenzoni, *Gonzaga and Garimberto*, p. 170.

25 'Tre teste di sopra ala chapelinaio di letucio': Florentine inventory of 1512. See also John Kent Lydecker, *The Domestic Setting of the Arts in Renaissance Florence*, PhD thesis, Johns Hopkins University, Baltimore 1987, Ann Arbor Microfilms 1987, p. 71, n. 99.

26 'Mi ha fabricato già nella cervelliera una lettiera di pietre singularissime et in quest'otio della villa ne ho fatto fare il disegno per mettersi in opera come prima sarò giunto in Roma': Brown and Lorenzoni, *Gonzaga and Garimberto*, letter 63.

27 Brown and Lorenzoni, *Gonzaga and Garimberto*, p. 156, item 3.

28 Brown and Lorenzoni, *Gonzaga and Garimberto*, p. 59.

29 'Unam tabulam [. . .] cum duobous trespidibus': Leniaco 1427; 'una tabuleta affixa tripodi nucis': Fiesso 1484.

30 Foster Watson, *Tudor Schoolboy Life: The Dialogues of J. L. Vives*, London 1908 (reprinted 1970), p. 113.

31 Matteo Ricci, letter of 4 November 1595 to Edoardo de Sarde, in Ricci, *Opere storiche*, ed. P. Tocchi Venturi, vol. 2, *Le lettere dalla Cina*, Macerata 1913, pp. 193–4; quoted in Jonathan Spence, *The Memory Palace of Matteo Ricci*, London 1985, p. 92.

32 Erasmus, *De Civilitate Puerorum*, London 1532 (unpaginated).

33 Peter Thornton, 'Capolavori lignei in formato ridotto', *Arte illustrata*, XLVII, 1972, pls 13–14.

34 'Ceste cy est une belle & artificieuse machine, laquelle est fort utile & commode à toute personne qui se delecte à l'estude': Agostino Ramelli, *Le diverse et artificiose machine del capitano Agostino Ramelli*, Paris 1588, chap. CLXXXVIII. Such book-wheels appear to have been constructed: Per Kalm, visiting Sir Hans Sloane's house and museum in Chelsea in 1748, describes a similar structure: see *Sir Hans Sloane: Collector, Scientist, Antiquary, Founding Father of the British Museum*, ed. Arthur Macgregor, London 1994, pp. 33–4.

35 'Uno studiolo di nogaro posto suso quatro piede, o vero descheto': Manni, *Mobili in Emilia*, p. 92.

36 'Un desco grande di noce con sua armari e cornice drentovi piu libri stampate et scritture': Serragli 1576.

37 'In pullcherrimo studiolo': Fregoso 1425.

38 'Parieti eius in bibliotecae speciem armarium insertem est, quod non legendos libros sed lecitandos capit': Pliny the Younger, *Letters*, ed. W. Melmoth, London 1915, letter to Gallus, book II, XVII, p. 151.

39 Unattributed medal of Galeotto Marzio of Narni (poet and pugilist who taught rhetoric at Bologna in 1464–5), with, on the obverse, a book cupboard with books and hourglass. Another medal has a variant of this design on its obverse. G. F. Hill, *A Corpus of Italian Medals of the Renaissance before Cellini*, London 1930, nos 1131–2.

40 Monique Riccardi-Cubitt, *The Art of the Cabinet*, London 1992, pp. 24–46. P. Thornton, *Italian Renaissance Interior*, pp. 229–34. Simon Jervis and Renier Baarsen, 'An Ebony and Ivory Cabinet', *Victoria and Albert Museum Bulletin*, IV, 1985, pp. 48–56. Simon Jervis, 'Tipologie: Stipi: Storia di un mobile-microcosmo', *Casa vogue antiques*, March 1988, suppl. 194, pp. 70–77, nine illustrations.

41 Brown and Lorenzoni, *Gonzaga and Garimberto*.

42 Brown and Lorenzoni, *Gonzaga and Garimberto*, pp. 39–62.

43 Brown and Lorenzoni, *Gonzaga and Garimberto*, pp. 39–62.

44 Brown and Lorenzoni, *Gonzaga and Garimberto*, pp. 39–62. See also Clare Robertson, *'Il Gran Cardinale': Alessandro Farnese, Patron of the Arts*, New Haven and London 1992, p. 50 and docs. 63 and 85 on Garimberto's role with reference to Farnese, and p. 50, n. 209 on his own collection.

45 On Volterra, see Brown and Lorenzoni, *Gonzaga and Garimberto*, pp. 237–40.

46 Brown and Lorenzoni, *Gonzaga and Garimberto*, p. 239, n. 3.

47 Brown and Lorenzoni, *Gonzaga and Garimberto*, p. 24.

48 'Un scrigno bellissimo di Nogara con molti segreti, e cassettini parte sono di cipresso, fattura del mio giudicio per il dissegno, che ho dato al Mastro, che mi stete in casa un anno a farlo, scudi quattrocento': inventory of Roberto Canonici, Ferrara 1632, in Giuseppe Campori, *Raccolta*, Modena 1870, p. 128. I am grateful to Jeremy Warren, who is preparing an article on Canonici's collection, for this reference.

49 On the work on the alabaster columns for the cabinet, see Brown and Lorenzoni, *Gonzaga and Garimberto*, letters 1, 5, 9, 11, 13, 16, 18, 22, 24, 25, 31, 32, 34, 36, 39, 40, 41, 46, 53.

50 Brown and Lorenzoni, *Gonzaga and Garimberto*, letter 73, p. 101.

51 Brown and Lorenzoni, *Gonzaga and Garimberto*, letter 76.

52 Brown and Lorenzoni, *Gonzaga and Garimberto*, pp. 170–71: it would seem to have been the second of these that was the one constructed out of rejected columns from Cesare's cabinet.

53 Anna Maria Massinelli, 'Lo studiolo "nobilissimo" del Patriarca Giovanni Grimani', *Venezia e l'archeologia: Un importante capitolo nella storia del gusto dell'antico nella cultura artistica veneziana* (Venice 1988), ed. Gustavo Traversari, Rome 1990, pp. 41–50. I am grateful to Anna Maria Masinelli for an offprint of this article, and to John Reeve for getting it to me. R. Gallo, 'Due placchette del moderno e il busto di Francesco Novello da Carrara delle Sale delle Armi del Consiglio dei X', *Archivio Veneto*, XLVI–XLVII, 1950, pp. 69–95.

54 Irene Favaretto, *Arte antica e cultura antiquaria nelle collezioni venete al tempo della Serenissima*, Rome 1990, pp. 86–92.

55 For the three inventories listing the objects incorporated into the cabinet, see Massinelli, 'Lo studiolo del Grimani', pp. 41–4.

56 Gallo, 'Due placchette', pp. 69–95. Manfred Leithe-Jasper, *Renaissance Master Bronzes from the Collection of the Kunsthistorisches Museum, Vienna*, London 1986, pp. 125–31. Douglas Lewis, 'The Plaquettes of "Moderno" and his Followers', *Italian Plaquettes*, ed. Alison Luchs, Studies in the History of Art, 22, National Gallery of Art, Washington 1989, pp. 105–43, pl. 1–2, pp. 129–30.

57 '[Un] bellissimo arco d'ebano, fatto a somiglianza di quello di Constantino, così ordinato dal Palladio [. . .] questo fu fatto per conservare tutte le medaglie, grandi, mezzane e piccole, d'oro, d'argento e di metallo che si ritrovava al detto Clarissimo Signore Cavaliere; il quale [studiolo] sono certissimo che sarà molto a proposito di Sua Altezza Serenissima per essere oltre l'eccellenza dell'architettura lavorato da uomo rarissimo in tal magistero': Gallo, 'Due placchette', p. 72, n. 3. Anna Maria Massinelli, *Bronzetti e anticaglie nella Guardaroba di Cosimo I*, Bargello Museum, Florence 1991, p. 84.

58 On his bid to buy Mocenigo's coins, see Brown and Lorenzoni, *Gonzaga and Garimberto*, p. 235, n. 18. On his cabinet, see Robertson, *'Il Gran Cardinale'*, pp. 50–51, fig. 37, pp. 307 and 308. Clifford M. Brown and Martha Macrory are preparing an article on Mocenigo's important collection.

59 Robertson, *'Il Gran Cardinale'*, letter 103 (1578), p. 307.

60 Robertson, *'Il Gran Cardinale'*, letter 48, p. 298.

61 Robertson, *'Il Gran Cardinale'*, letter 103, p. 307.

62 Robertson, *'Il Gran Cardinale'*, letters 103 and 108, pp. 307 and 308–9.

63 'Un scrittorio di noghera con le sue casselle con soazette d'ebano'; 'Sopra il scrittoio uno sattiro de bronzo con Venere legato a un albero/Una figura a cavallo de bronzo con un callamaro/ [. . .] Una figura de getto de bronzo': Usper 1601.

64 Bruce Boucher, *The Sculpture of Jacopo Sansovino*, New Haven and London 1991, 2 vols, vol. 2, cat. 17 and n. 2 for reference to 'Una Nostra Donna de Bronzo opera di Sansovin': Usper 1601.

65 'Un scrittor di olive con quattro figure di bronzo': Loredan 1610.

66 Isabella Palumbo Fossati, 'L'interno della casa dell'artista e dell'artigiano nella Venezia del cinquecento', *Studi veneziani*, VII, 1984, pp. 109–38, pp. 118–38 for this inventory and its contents, and p. 122 for the cabinet.

67 Palumbo Fossati, 'L'interno della casa', p. 119, n. 20.

68 P. Thornton, *Italian Renaissance Interior*, fig. 62. See also *Venice: A Documentary History*, ed. David Chambers and Brian Pullan, Oxford 1992, pp. 402–3 and illustration. W. Wolters, 'Zu einem wenig bekannten Entwurf des Cristoforo Sorte für die Decke der Sala del Senato im Dogenpalast', *Mitteilungen des Kunsthistorischen Instituts Florenz*, X, 1961, pp. 137–44, illustrated p. 139; Peter Ward Jackson, *Italian Drawings*, vol. 1, London 1979, cat. 321; *Andrea Palladio*, exhibition catalogue, ed. Howard Burns, Hayward Gallery, London 1978, cat. 280. I am grateful to Michael Snodin for his comments on this contract drawing.

69 'Un scrittoio d'Albedo dipinto di verde di fuora e di dentro con figure e prospettivi': Foscho 1582.

70 On his library, see Palumbo Fossati,'L'interno della casa', pp. 134–5.

71 G. F. Hill, *Portrait Medals of Italian Artists of the Renaissance*, London 1912, no. 46; the medal would appear to be Emilian and the signature, A.A., to stand perhaps for Alessandro Ardenti, a painter from the subject's native town of Faenza. See Graham Pollard's revised edition of Hill as *Medals of the Renaissance*, London 1978, p. 180, n. 271. I am grateful to Philip Attwood, who is preparing a catalogue of sixteenth-century Italian Medals in British Collections, for his comments on this medal, and for helping me acquire a photograph of it.

72 'Un scrittor dorado et miniado remesso drento di madre perle': Calderini 1597.

73 Alvar Gonzalez-Palacios, *Il Tempio del Gusto*, 2 vols, Milan 1986, vol. 2, figs 693–4 and vol. 1, pp. 307–8. On lacquering in Renaissance Italy, see P. Thornton, *Italian Renaissance Interior*, pp. 99–100.

74 'Disdotto carte de santi colorade et miniade/tredese carte de stampa de Fiandra in rame': Calderini 1597. On the prints, see David Landau and Peter Parshall, *The Renaissance Print, 1470–1550*, New Haven and London 1994, pp. 81–6, 92–3.

75 P. Thornton, *Italian Renaissance Interior*, p. 233, n. 8.

76 Daniela di Castro and Peter Thornton, 'Some Late Sixteenth-century Medici Furniture', *Furniture History*, XX, 1984, p. 7 and pls. 8–9c.

77 John Florio, *Queen Anna's New World of Words*, London 1611.

78 Simon Jervis, 'Les Blasons domestiques by Gilles Corrozet', *Furniture History*, XXV, 1989, pp. 5–35, pp. 30–31.

Chapter 4

1 G. Boerio, *Dizionario del dialetto veneziano*, Venice 1856, entry for 'mezà'.

2 Francesco Sansovino, *Venetia*, Venice 1581, p. 142.

3 Anon., *La Venexiana* (c.1518), trans. M. V. Pfeiffer, New York 1950, Act III scene 3, p. 85.

4 On Carlo Helman and his brother Guglielmo see G. Devos and W. Brulez, *Les marchands flamands à Venise*, 2 vols, vol. 1: Brussels 1965 (Brulez sole author); vol. 2: Rome 1986. Ugo Tucci, 'La psicologia del mercante veneziano nel cinquecento', *Mercanti, navi, monete nel cinquecento veneziano*, Bologna 1981, pp. 43–94, trans. in *Renaissance Venice*, ed. John Hale, London 1974, pp. 357–70, on their Venetian citizenship, p. 363; for an explanation of the system, see Brian Pullan, *Rich and Poor in Renaissance Venice*, London 1971, pp. 101–2.

5 For the will of 1605, see Brulez, *Marchands flamands*, vol. 1, pp. 656–61, esp. p. 658. Among the pictures listed were a Titian *Danaë*, a Veronese *Ecce Homo*, a painting of a concert by Frangipane, and a picture of Adam and Eve by Mabuse.

6 On the importance of Titian's image of Mary Magdalen and various versions of the painting, see Susan Haskins, *Mary Magdalen: Myth and Metaphor*, London 1993, pp. 239–41; Carlo Ridolfi, *Le meraviglie dell'arte* (Padua 1648), ed. D. F. von Hadeln, 2 vols, Berlin 1914, p. 190 for the story of how one version, formerly the property of Silvio Badoaro, came into the hands of the 'Elmani, mercatanti Fiamenghi [...] e mancando quella famiglia in Venetia, fu poscia mandata in Flandra'.

7 Tucci, *Renaissance Venice*, p. 369.

8 'Un libro alla turchesca con effigie de turchi': Helman 1606.

9 Susan Skilliter, *Life in Istanbul*, Oxford 1977, based on MS Or. 430, Bodleian Library, Oxford: see fol. 47r for Rowlie.

10 Benvenuto Cellini, *The Autobiography* (1538–62), trans. J. Symonds, ed. Charles Hope and Alessandro Nova, Oxford 1983, p. 39.

11 Julian Raby and Linda Klinger, 'Barbarossa and Sinan', *Venezia e l'oriente vicino*, ed. Ernst Grube, Venice 1989, pp. 47–56.

12 Rafaello Borghini, *Il riposo*, Florence 1584, pp. 14–15.

13 Francesco Sansovino, *Historia universale dell'origine et imperio de'Turchi*, Venice 1564, fol. 306b. *Süleyman the Magnificent*, exhibition catalogue, ed. Michael Rogers and Rachel Ward, British Museum, London 1988, cat. 3.

14 Leonardo Fioravanti, *Il libro dei segreti*, Venice 1564, chap. 69, book v. F. Gibbs, 'A Historical Survey of the Japanning Trades, 1: Eastern and Western Lacquer', *Annals of Science*, VII, 1951, p. 407.

15 'Una veste nova da donna alla turchesca de panno d'argento con fioretti de sede fodrato in raso verde': Helman 1606.

16 Jennifer Scarce, 'Ottoman Turkish Costume', *Costume*, XXII, 1988, pp. 13–32. Susan Skilliter, 'The Letters of the Venetian Sultana Nur Banu and her Kira to Venice', *Istituto Universitario Orientale, seminario de'studi asiatici*, XIX, 1982, pp. 520–21. *Süleyman the Magnificent*, ed. Rogers and Ward, cat. 46b.

17 'Un armer d'albeo con dentro diverse cosette turchesche et indiane'; 'Un corno di rinoceronte': Helman 1606.

18 Katherine Park, *Doctors and Medicine in Early Renaissance Florence*, Princeton 1985.

19 For inventories of three doctors' libraries see the list of 120 titles left by Giovanni di Marco of Rimini in his study at his death in 1474 (L. Tonini, *Storia di Rimini: Appendice al VI volume*, Rimini 1882, pp. 566 and 262 for the inventory) and the books left by G. Ferradi Grado of Pavia, some of which were sold at auction in 1472 (T. G. Lesporace, 'Due biblioteche mediche del quattrocento', *Bibliofilia*, LII, 1950, p. 205).

20 Park, *Doctors and Medicine*, pp. 193–4.

21 Curzio Mazzi, *La casa di Maestro Bartolo di Tura*, Siena 1900. He was doctor to Pope Pius II in Spring 1460, when he counselled a trip to the baths near Siena and the wearing of an adamant stone in a ring to ward off evil influence: Ludovico Zdekauer, 'Un consulto medico dato a Pio II', *Bollettino di storia patria senese*, V, 1898, p. 100.

22 Curzio Mazzi, 'Lo studio di un medico senese del secolo XV', *Rivista delle biblioteche e delle archivi*, V, 1894, pp. 27–49.

23 E. Lazzareschi, 'Le richezze di due Medici Lucchesi della Rinascenza', *Rivista di storia delle scienze mediche e naturali*, VII, 1925, pp. 112–39.

24 H. Nixon and W. Jackson, 'English Seventeenth-century Travelling Libraries', *Transactions of the Cambridge Bibliographical Society*, VII, 1979, pp. 294–322. I am grateful to Giles Mandelbrote for this reference.

25 'Un armaretto con diversi ferri da cirurgie': Alatino 1620.

26 *Venice: A Documentary History, 1450–1630*, ed. David Chambers and Brian Pullan, Oxford 1992, p. 341.

27 'Una Taza christallina orata, Una scudella christallina, con orlo orato'; 'Uno capello di pagla da homo, grande, vecchio': Tura 1483.

28 Martin Davies, *National Gallery Catalogues: The Earlier Italian Schools*, London 1961, cat. 776. On the nineteenth-century restoration, see Jill Dunkerton, 'L'état de restauration des deux tableaux de Pisanello de la National Gallery de Londres', a paper given at the Pisanello conference held at the Louvre on 26–8 June 1996 (publication in preparation). I am most grateful to Jill Dunkerton for discussing the problem of NG 776 with me and for giving me a copy of her paper, which notes that even though much of the straw hat is repaint, 'the design of the famous straw hat is Pisanello's and some of his paint can be seen on the crown, but on the brim Molteni reinforced the concentric rings of straw'. On the figure of St George as 'a gauger's field-day in its own way', see Michael

Baxandall, *Painting and Experience in Fifteenth-century Italy*, Oxford 1972, p. 93.

29 'Uno baccino d'argento scanellato et in parte dorato, con un'arme di vitelli rossi, et una di maestro bartalo in mezo'; 'Uno bochale d'argento, con l'arme di maestro bartalo; dorato li orli'; 'Uno nappo d'argento lavorato per tutto ad rilievo, con due armi in mezo, cioè un'arme con sei palle rosse et un'arme di maestro bartalo': Tura 1483.

30 He had also held the office of Gonfaloniere of his Terzo in Siena, the Terzo di Camollia, and had served as *capitano del Popolo*. See Mazzi, *La casa di Maestro Bartolo*, p. 35.

31 'E tu uomo che vai a ufficio, e porti lo stendardo, che è il suo segno, no'l portare a piccone [. . .] Che segno è quello della bandiera? E segno che costui è buono e va in uffizio; e debba essare buono con parole, con cuore e con opara. O queste armi di gentiluomini che significano? Che egli è gentiluomo con bocca con cuore e con opara; e se altrimenti è, quell'arme non è veramente sua': San Bernardino di Siena, *Prediche volgari*, 2 vols, Siena 1884, vol. 2, quoted by Mazzi, 'Lo studio di un medico senese', *Rivista delle biblioteche e degli archivi*, VI, 1896, pp. 27–48, p. 35.

32 Bandino had served as *Camarlingo della Biccherna del Commune di Siena* in 1475 and 1476. See Mazzi, *La casa di Maestro Bartolo*, p. 47, n. 200.

33 Giovanni di Pietro di Fece had served as *Camarlingo delle Some*, collecting gabelles at the City gate. See Mazzi, 'Una casa senese nel 1450', *Bollettino senese di storia patria*, XVIII, 1911, p. 166, line 169. On gauging, see Baxandall, *Painting and Experience*, pp. 86–93.

34 Vittorio Cian, 'Un umanista bergamasca del Rinascimento, Giovanni Calfurnio', *Archivio storico lombardo*, XIV, 1910, pp. 221–48.

35 Cian, 'Un umanista bergamasca', p. 222.

36 A. Segarizzi, 'Inventario dei beni e dei libri di un maestro di scuola del secolo XV', *Bollettino del Museo Civico di Padova*, VIII, 1906, pp. 32–4.

37 'In eius vero cubiculum': *Christi Jesu Triumphus*, 1514. Joannis Ludovici Vivis Valentini, *Opera omnia*, vol. 6, Valencia 1782, pp. 110–12, p. 110.

38 A. Domeniconi, *La Biblioteca Malatestiana*, Cesena 1982, for the following summary of the foundation of the library.

39 A. Domeniconi, 'I custodi della Biblioteca Malatestiana di Cesena dalle origini alla seconda metà del Seicento', *Studi romagnoli*, XIV, 1963, pp. 385–96.

40 A. Domeniconi, 'Un inventario relativo a un custode della Biblioteca Malatestiana: Frate Franceschino da Cesena', *Studi romagnoli*, XVI, 1965, pp. 172–89, p. 172, n. 5.

41 *Libraria Domini: I manoscritti della Biblioteca Malatestiana, testi e decorazioni*, exhibition catalogue, eds. Fabrizio Lollini and Piero Lucchi, Cesena 1995, p. 146.

42 'Dui pezzi de marmoro biancho in uno e uno stincho, in l'altro a meza gamba da homo et mezo liono'; 'Dui capitelli de serpentino i quali dixe Zulliano Fantaguzo haver inteso dal dicto maestro Francheschino esser de Ser Jacomo dal Salle'; 'uno pezo de marmoro cum certe lettere grande scolpite videlicet Naz.E': Frate Francheschino da Cesena 1489.

43 'Un ovo de struzo'; 'Una testa de orso'; 'Una testa de porcho cinghiaro cum 4 denti grandi cum una palla de vedro cum fiuri de seda dentro': Frate Francheschino da Cesena 1489.

44 'Una medaglia cum la immagine de Lorenzo di Medisi de bronzo granda'; '2 medaglie grande de piombo una con la testa de la Madonna de Pesaro et l'altra de messer Pollidoro': Frate Francheschino da Cesena 1489. Both medals identified as such by Domeniconi, 'Un inventario', pp. 174–5.

45 No fewer than four plaquettes of this subject were listed by Bange as being by or in the style of Enzola: E. F. Bange,

46 Bange, *Die italienischen Bronzen*, cat. 607.

47 '83 medaglie de piombo fra pizzole et grande coverte di stagnoli rossi et bianchi attachate alla spallera del studio al canto mancho allo intrare cum uno filzo de peltrinostri de piu collori da uno canto al altro cum molti altri paltrinosti grossi de piu collori': Frate Francheschino da Cesena 1489.

48 The books are the focus of the publication of the inventory in Domeniconi, 'Un inventario'.

49 Mary Beal, *A Study of Richard Symonds, his Italian Notebooks and their Relevance to Seventeenth-century Painting Techniques*, New York and London 1984, p. 33. I am grateful to Jeremy Warren for this reference, and for showing me the Bodleian Library MS Rawlinson D 121, fol. 125, for the full acount of Symonds's visit.

50 R. Sighinolfi, 'Note biografiche intorno a Francesco Francia', *Atti e memorie della Reale Deputazione di storia patria per le Romagne*, vol. 6, 1916.

51 Sighinolfi, 'Note biografiche', p. 10. Matteo Bosso [Bossus], *Familiares et secundae Matthei Bossi Epistolae*, Mantua 1498, letter CLVI, dated 5 May 1497.

52 Sighinolfi, 'Note biografiche', pp. 12–13 for these identifications.

53 *Bologna e l'umanesimo, 1490–1510*, exhibition catalogue, ed. Marzia Faietti and Konrad Oberhuber, Pinacoteca Nazionale, Bologna 1988, pp. 1–42; Peter Parshall and David Landau, *The Renaissance Print 1470–1550*, New Haven and London 1994, p. 99.

54 Clare Robertson, 'Annibale Caro as Iconographer: Sources and Method', *Journal of the Warburg and Courtauld Institutes*, XLV, 1982, pp. 160–81, p. 164, and notes 20–21 on his manuscripts left in his study.

55 Robertson, 'Caro as Iconographer', p. 164, n. 21. Compare Caro's papers as listed in the inventory with Vasari's, left in the study in his house in Borgo Santa Croce until 1687: Patricia Rubin analyses these and places them into the Florentine context in her book *Giorgio Vasari: Art and History*, New Haven and London 1995, pp. 39–41.

56 Clare Robertson, *'Il Gran Cardinale': Alessandro Farnese, Patron of the Arts*, New Haven and London 1992, p. 217, n. 76.

57 Francesco di Giorgio Martini, *Trattati di architettura, ingegneria ed arte militare (c. 1480)*, ed. O. Maltese, Milan 1967, vol. 2, Second Treatise, pp. 343–4.

58 Dora Thornton, *The Study Room in Renaissance Italy 1400–1600 with Particular Reference to Venice*, PhD thesis, Warburg Institute, University of London 1990, pp. 193–4.

59 P. Kristeller, *Mantegna*, London 1901, doc. 39.

60 G. F. Hill, 'Sodoma's Collection of Antiquities', *Journal of Hellenic Studies*, XXVI, 1906, pp. 288–9. Roberto Weiss, *The Renaissance Discovery of Classical Antiquity*, Oxford 1969, p. 182, n. 4.

61 Cellini, *Autobiography*, ed. Hope and Nova, p. 199.

62 'Trenta due pezzi di punzoni [. . .] da stampare'; 'Uno Zabarno': Cellini 1571.

63 'Quodam vero die quum in − id enim domesticae officinae nomen, me convenisset, ibique nescio quas expressas aere ac marmore effigies contemplatus esset, de sculptura mox loqui occepimus': Pomponius Gauricus, *De sculptura (c. 1504)*, ed. A. Chastel and R. Klein, Geneva 1969, p. 40.

64 Vittoria will 1608.

65 Richard Goldthwaite, *Wealth and the Demand for Art in Renaissance Italy, 1300–1600*, Baltimore and London 1993, p. 210.

66 *Xenophon, Oeconomicus: A Social and Historical Commentary*, ed. Sarah B. Pomeroy, Oxford 1994, pp. 153–9, esp. p. 154. Alan

Stewart, 'The Early Modern Closet Rediscovered', *Representations*, L, 1995, pp. 76–100, p. 78.

67 'Solo e'libri e le scritture mie e de'miei passati a me piacque e allora e poi sempre avere in modo rinchiuso che mai la donna le potesse non tanto leggere, me ne vedere. Sempre tenni le scritture non per le maniche de'vestiri, ma serrato e in suo ordine allogate nel mio studio quasi come sacrata e reliogiosa, in quale luogo mai diedi licenza alla donna mia ne meco ne sola v'intrasse, e più gli commandai, se mai s'abatesse a mia alcuna scrittura, subito me la consegnasse': Leon Battista Alberti, *I libri della famiglia* (1427), ed. R. Romano and A. Tenenti, Turin 1969, p. 266. Goldthwaite, *Wealth and the Demand for Art*, p. 228.

68 Constance Jordan, *Renaissance Feminism: Literary Texts and Political Models*, Ithaca and London 1990, pp. 47–51.

69 Stephanie Jed, *The Rape of Lucretia and the Birth of Humanism*, Bloomington (Ind.) 1989, pp. 81–2; Stewart, 'Early Modern Closet', p. 79. Alberti was keen to reassert patriarchal values at the centre of Florentine households in his treatise *Della famiglia*, but the extremity of Gianozzo's argument might perhaps be linked to the fact that women were acknowledged to be responsible for many aspects of domestic management, as often recorded by men in their account books, or even by women in theirs. Elaine Rosenthal, 'The Position of Women in Renaissance Florence: Neither Autonomy nor Subjection', *Florence and Italy: Renaissance Studies in Honour of Nicolai Rubinstein*, ed. Peter Denley and Caroline Elam, London 1988, pp. 369–81, p. 375, n. 27.

70 On women's education and the status of learned women, see Paul Grendler, *Schooling in Renaissance Italy: Literacy and Learning, 1300–1600*, Baltimore and London 1989, pp. 93–6. Margaret King and Albert Rabil, Jr., *Her Immaculate Hand: Selected Works by and about Women Humanists of Quattrocento Italy*, Binghampton 1983, pp. 11–25. This discussion is part of a wider debate about the role and status of women in Renaissance Italy, best summarised in Rosenthal, 'Position of Women', p. 369, n. 1.

71 A point made by Peter Burke about female book-ownership in *The Fortunes of The Courtier*, Cambridge 1995, p. 49.

72 Letter of 6 January 1466. Archivio di Stato di Milano, Archivio Sforzesco, B.215. I am grateful to Evelyn Welch for this reference, which she has published in 'Sforza Portraiture and SS Annunziata in Florence', *Florence and Italy*, ed. Denley and Elam, London 1988, pp. 235–40, p. 237, n. 18.

73 King and Rabil, *Her Immaculate Hand*, p. 20, on Bianca Maria. On Francesco Sforza, see Margaret King, *The Death of the Child Valerio Marcello*, Chicago and London 1994, pp. 134–5, 197–200.

74 King and Rabil, *Her Immaculate Hand*, p. 21.

75 King and Rabil, *Her Immaculate Hand*, doc. 5. The following account of Ippolita, her aspirations and her problems in her life in Naples, is largely taken from Evelyn Welch, 'Between Milan and Naples: Ippolita Maria Sforza, Duchess of Calabria', *The French Descent into Italy, 1494–1495*, ed. David Abulafia, Aldershot 1995, pp. 113–36. I am extremely grateful to her for this reference and for discussing Ippolita with me.

76 *Dizionario biografico italiano*, vol. 2, Rome 1960, p. 330.

77 *The Painted Page: Italian Renaissance Book Illumination, 1450–1550*, exhibition catalogue, ed. J. G. Alexander, Royal Academy, London 1994, cat. 11.

78 A letter of 13 October 1460 from Marsilio Andreasi to Ludovico Gonzaga (Archivio di Stato, Mantua, Archivio Gonzaga, B.1621) records a visit that month to the Palazzo d'Arengo in Milan, where the Gonzaga party was shown Francesco Sforza's apartments. The latter included a loggia fitted with *quadri di maiolica* – probably tiles. Evelyn Welch, to whom I owe this reference (personal communication, 28 July 1996), has suggested that the model may have been Florentine.

79 Evelyn Welch, *Art and Authority in Renaissance Milan*, New Haven and London 1995, pp. 146–8 on Filarete in Milan; on his account of the Medici study, see John Pope-Hennessy, *Luca della Robbia*, Oxford 1980, p. 240.

80 On his visit, see Rab Hatfield, 'Some Unknown Descriptions of the Medici Palace', *Art Bulletin*, LII, 1970, pp. 232–49, pp. 235–6 on the study. Evelyn Samuels Welch, 'The Image of a Fifteenth-century Court, Secular Frescoes for the Castello di Porta Giovia', *Journal of the Warburg and Courtuald Institutes*, XLIII, 1990, pp. 163–8 on Galeazzo Maria; p. 168 on his visit to Florence.

81 Welch, 'Between Milan and Naples', p. 127.

82 Quoted in Welch, 'Between Milan and Naples', p. 127. See also Evelyn Welch, *Art and Society in Italy 1350–1500*, Oxford 1997, pp. 305–06. On Martorelli, see Welch, *Secular Fresco Painting at the Court of Galeazzo Maria Sforza, 1466–1476*, PhD thesis, Warburg Institute, University of London 1987, p. 16, and personal communication, 5 May 1996.

83 Eve Borsook, 'A Florentine *Scrittoio* for Diomede Carafa', *Art in the Ape of Nature: Studies in Honor of H. W. Janson*, ed. Moshe Barasch and Lucy Freeman Sandler, New York and Englewood Cliffs 1981, pp. 91–6; p. 92 for Ippolita's visit and n. 14. See also Archivio di Stato, Florence, *Strozziane*, III, 131, c.159 for letter of Piero.

84 Welch, 'Between Milan and Naples', pp. 125–6, and *passim* for Ippolita's difficulties with her husband.

85 Giancarlo Gentilini, *I Della Robbia: La scultura invetriata nel Rinascimento*, Florence 1992, p. 105 for the commission, p. 111 for the Medici study.

86 Borsook, '*Scrittoio* for Diomede Carafa', p. 92, n. 15.

87 C. M. Brown, '"Lo insaciabile desiderio nostro de cose antique": New Documents for Isabella d'Este's Collection of Antiquities', *Cultural Aspects of the Italian Renaissance: Essays in Honour of Paul Oskar Kristeller*, ed. Cecil Clough, Manchester 1976, p. 324; Brown and Anna Maria Lorenzoni, 'The Grotta of Isabella d'Este', *Gazette des Beaux-Arts*, May 1977, p. 155. See also Gonzaga 1542.

88 Thomas Tuohy, *Herculean Ferrara, Ercole d'Este 1471–1505, and the Invention of a Ducal Capital*, Cambridge 1996: for her Castel Vecchio apartment in which a study is documented next to an oratory in 1485, p. 210; for the garden apartment documented in 1491, pp. 210 and 104–14.

89 Tuohy, *Herculean Ferrara*, p. 18.

90 Burke, *Fortunes*, p. 48.

91 Baldassare Castiglione, *Lettere*, ed. Guido da Rocca, Mondadori 1978, vol. 1, p. 665, letter 480 line 8. Julia Cartwright, *Baldassare Castiglione, the Perfect Courtier: His Life and Letters*, 2 vols, London 1908, vol. 2, p. 97. I am grateful to Doris Fletcher for these references.

92 Grendler, *Schooling in Renaissance Italy*, p. 95.

93 Madeleine Lazard, *Images littéraires de la femme à la Renaissance*, Paris 1985, pp. 48–9, and p. 51 on her upbringing. Linda Timmerman, *L'accès des femmes à la culture 1598–1715: Un débat d'idées de Saint François de Sales à la Marquise de Lambert*, Paris 1996, pp. 46–7.

94 Jordan, *Renaissance Feminism*, p. 176. Louise Labé, *Oeuvres complètes*, ed. Enzo Guidici, Geneva 1981, pp. 18–19. The translation given here is one provided by Jeremy Warren and Ann Thornton.

95 'Una figura de bronzo, con un arco in man': Lombardo 1569.

96 C. Santore, 'Julia Lombardo, "Somtuosa meretrize": A Portrait by Property', *Renaissance Quarterly*, XLI, Spring 1988, pp. 44–83.

97 Jordan, *Renaissance Feminism*, p. 47.

98 Margaret King, 'Goddess and Captive: Antonio Loschi's Poetic Tribute to Maddalena Scrovegni', *Medievalia et humanistica*, X, 1980, pp. 103–27. King and Rabil, *Her Immaculate Hand*, pp. 11–13.

99 Christiane Klapisch-Zuber, *Women, Family and Ritual in Renaissance Italy*, Chicago 1985, p. 119, n. 9.

100 Jordan, *Renaissance Feminism*, p. 59, n. 64. King and Rabil, *Her Immaculate Hand*, p. 29 on Erasmus; p. 17 on Isotta Nogarola.

101 Grendler, *Schooling in Renaissance Italy*, p. 93 on Alessandra, pp. 94–5 on Moderata.

102 On Moderata, see Grendler, *Schooling in Renaissance Italy*, pp. 94–5; on Cerreta, see King and Rabil, *Her Immaculate Hand*, p. 23.

103 King and Rabil, *Her Immaculate Hand*, p. 87.

104 Grendler, *Schooling in Renaissance Italy*, p. 93.

105 Gillian Clark, *Women in Late Antiquity: Pagan and Christian Lifestyles*, Oxford 1993, p. 102.

106 Margaret King, 'Book-lined Cells: Women and Humanism in the Early Renaissance', *Beyond their Sex: Learned Women of the European Past*, ed. Patricia Labalme, New York 1980, p. 74.

107 King, 'Book-lined Cells', pp. 66–90.

108 G. Bertoni, *La Biblioteca estense e la cultura ferrarese ai tempi del duca Ercole I*, Turin 1905, pp. 229–33. See Werner L. Gundersheimer, 'Women, Learning and Power: Eleonora of Aragon and the Court of Ferrara', *Beyond their Sex*, ed. Labalme, p. 56. On Margaret of Austria, see Dagmar Eichberger and Lisa Beaven, 'Family Members and Political Allies: The Portrait Collection of Margaret of Austria', *Art Bulletin*, LXVII, 1995, pp. 225–48, p. 239 for description by De Beatis, and p. 239, n. 1. Margaret's library was wide-ranging and scholarly, attracting Erasmus and Dürer as students. I am grateful to Dagmar Eichberger for this reference; also to her suggestion (personal communication) that a number of noblewomen apart from Isabella d'Este had studies of their own, as she will suggest in forthcoming articles.

109 On the kind of texts read by women, and a manuscript owned by two women containing a typical assemblage, see Grendler, *Schooling in Renaissance Italy*, p. 95, n. 37. A volume of Petrarch seems however to have been an accessory for gentlewomen and courtesans alike: Lynne Lawner, *Lives of the Courtesans*, New York 1987, p. 52.

110 See a number of examples in Peter Thornton, *The Italian Renaissance Interior, 1400–1600*, London 1991, figs 40, 58–9, 161, 291 and 503.

111 Baxandall, *Painting and Experience*, pp. 46 and 48 for this passage and its interpretation.

112 Hilary Wayment, *King's College Chapel, Cambridge: The Side-Chapel Glass*, Cambridge 1991, pp. 31–4 for the cycle to which the panel belongs, p. 32 no. 4 for the panel. I am grateful to Hilary Wayment for a photograph of this panel, and to Jean-Michel Massing for showing me the panel itself.

113 Northern Europeans may have thought the same way: the first Earl of Cork records in his diary for January 1622 that he gave his brother's widow in marriage to Sir William Hull, 'and married together in the study at Youghal by Mr. Goodwin'. Dorothea Townshend, *Life and Letters of the Great Earl of Cork*, London 1904, p. 67.

114 Stanley Chojnacki, 'The Power of Love: Wives and Husbands in Late Medieval Venice', *Women and Power in the Middle Ages*, ed. Mary Erler and Maryanne Kowaleski, Athens and London 1988, pp. 127–48; for summary of this argument, p. 128, n. 11. Lisa Jardine, *Reading Shakespeare Historically*, Cambridge 1996, p. 114.

115 N. Krivatsky and L. Yeandle, 'Books of Sir Edmund Dering of Kent, 1598–1644', *Private Libraries in Renaissance England*, ed. E. Leedham-Green and R. J. Fehrenbach, vol. 1, New York 1992, p. 145.

116 On the Protestant sense of conscience, Patricia Crawford, 'Public Duty, Conscience and Women in Early Modern England', *Public Duty and Private Conscience in Seventeenth-century England*, ed. John Morrill, Paul Slack and Daniel Woolf, Oxford 1993, pp. 57–76, pp. 68–9.

117 See the mini-encyclopaedia for housewives on preserves and herbal remedies, *A Closet for Ladies and Gentle Women*, London 1608; Sir Hugh Platt's *Delights for Ladies, to Adorn their Persons, Tables, Closets, and Distillatories*, London 1609, for examples.

118 *Hamlet*, Act II, scene I. Jardine, *Reading Shakespeare Historically*, pp. 148–57, shows how a meeting between a man and a woman in a closet could carry a 'suggestion of the illicit, the indiscreet, certainly the secretive' (p. 151) to the extent that she sees the closet as 'crucial to the plot' of the play, since it is in the closet that the most sexually charged and emotionally pivotal encounters occur (Hamlet and Ophelia, Hamlet and his mother, Gertrude: pp. 149–56).

119 Stewart, 'Eary Modern Closet', pp. 82–3.

120 Jardine, *Reading Shakespeare Historically*, pp. 150–51, citing Stewart, 'Early Modern Closet', p. 81.

121 John Evelyn, *Diary*, ed. E. S. De Beer, 6 vols, London 1955, vol. 4, p. 423, entry for 14 March 1685.

122 Evelyn, *Diary*, vol. 4, p. 431, entry for 16 March 1685.

123 Henry Phillip Dodd, *The Epigrammatists*, London 1875, p. 184. On closets, see Peter Thornton, *Seventeenty-century Interior Decoration in England, France and Holland*, New Haven and London 1978, pp. 296–9; John Schofield, *Medieval London Houses*, New Haven and London 1994, p. 81; and Simon Thurley, *The Royal Palaces of Tudor England*, New Haven and London 1993, p. 141.

Chapter 5

1 Irene Favaretto, *Arte antica e cultura antiquaria nelle collezioni venete al tempo della Serenissima*, Rome 1990, p. 113.

2 Marilyn Perry, 'A Renaissance Showplace of Art: The Palazzo Grimani at Santa Maria Formosa', *Apollo*, CXIII, 1981, pp. 215–21, p. 220, n. 23.

3 Perry, 'Palazzo Grimani', p. 220 for a description of the room, a Tribuna-style design, perhaps that which can still be seen at the palace. Perry's identification of this room as the *studio* created by Grimani is however unproven; further details of its status cannot be ascertained until restoration of the palace is completed. I am grateful to Mario Piana, architect in charge of the project, for showing me round the palace, and to Sally Spector for current information about the restoration work.

4 Perry, 'Palazzo Grimani', p. 215.

5 Perry, 'Palazzo Grimani', p. 220 and fig. 7 for photograph of the *portone* admitting visitors to the rooms culminating in what she identifies as the *studio*.

6 Renate von Busch, *Studien zu deutschen Antikensammlungen des 16. Jahrhunderts*, Tübingen 1973, pp. 111–12 for Strada's account of 1575, and pp. 146–50. Strada's role in the display is discussed in Francis Haskell, *History and its Images: Art and the Interpretation of the Past*, New Haven and London 1993, pp. 36–9 and pls 21–2. H. Frosien-Leinz, 'La creazione dell'Antiquarium nella Residenza di Monaco e lo sviluppo della collezione di antichità da Alberto V a Massimiliano I', *Piranesi e la cultura antiquaria* (Atti del Convegno 14–17 novembre 1979), Rome 1987, p. 357; the sketches also in Clifford M. Brown and Anna Maria Lorenzoni, 'Our Accustomed Discourse on the Antique': Cesare Gonzaga and Gerolamo

Garimberto, Two Renaissance Collectors of Greco-Roman Art, New York and London 1993, pl. 21.

7 D. Coffin, 'Pirro Ligorio and Decoration of the Late Sixteenth Century at Ferrara', *Art Bulletin*, XXXVII, 1955, pp. 178–80. Illustrated in Brown and Lorenzoni, *Gonzaga and Garimberto*, pl. 20.

8 Claudio Franzoni, 'Le collezioni rinascimentali di antichità', *Memorie dell'antico nell'arte italiana*, ed. Salvatore Settis, vol. I, Turin 1984, pls 109–10 and pp. 315–16.

9 Franzoni, 'Collezione rinascimentali', pl. 110.

10 Favaretto, *Arte antica et cultura antiquaria*, pp. 144–5, and pl. 20. Favaretto is preparing an edition of this manuscript, Bodleian Library, MS d'Orville 539.

11 Hugh Tait, *Catalogue of the Waddesdon Bequest: The Curiosities*, London 1991, pp. 311–12, figs 342–3.

12 Ian Jenkins and Kim Sloane, *Vases and Volcanoes: Sir William Hamilton and his Collection*, exhibition catalogue, British Museum, London 1996, cat. 143.

13 Compare, for the *lattimo* body, a small enamelled vase in the British Museum: Hugh Tait, *The Golden Age of Venetian Glass*, exhibition catalogue, British Museum, London 1979, cat. 204, and for the form, an imitation chalcedony glass jug with handles, also in the British Museum's collections, cat. 167.

14 Michael Baxandall, 'A Dialogue from the Court of Leonello d'Este', *Journal of the Warburg and Courtauld Institutes*, XVI, 1963, pp. 304–26, p. 324.

15 Translation from *The Satyrs of Decimus Junius Juvenalis*, London 1726, p. 13.

16 Juvenal, *The Satires*, trans. G. G. Ramsay, London 1918, p. 49.

17 Isabella Palumbo Fossati, 'L'interno della casa dell'artista e dell'artigiano nella Venezia del cinquecento', *Studi veneziani*, VII, 1984, pp. 109–53, p. 147, n. 66.

18 G. Alberici, *Catalogo [. . .] de gli illustri scrittori veneziani*, Bologna 1605, p. 75.

19 John Pope-Hennessy, *Cellini*, London 1985, p. 177.

20 Benvenuto Cellini, *The Autobiography* (1538–62), trans. J. Symonds, ed. Charles Hope and Alessandro Nova, Oxford 1983, p. 191.

21 Pope-Hennessy, *Cellini*, p. 177.

22 Cellini, *Autobiography*, ed. Hope and Nova, p. 187.

23 Cellini, *Autobiography*, ed. Hope and Nova, p. 187. Charles Avery, 'The Bust and Medal of Bindo Altoviti', *Studies in European Sculpture*, London 1981, p. 4 and pls 13–14. D. Gnoli, 'Le demolizioni in Roma: Il Palazzo Altoviti', *Archivio storico dell'arte*, I, 1888, pp. 202–11.

24 Vincenzo Scamozzi, *Dell'idea dell'architettura universale*, Venice 1615, part III, p. 304. Quoted in Cristina De Benedictis, *Per la storia del collezionismo italiano: Fonti e documenti*, Florence 1991, p. 169.

25 On the use of *mischio di Seravezza* and other ornamental stone to complement bronze sculpture, see Nicholas Penny, *The Materials of Sculpture*, New Haven and London 1993, pp. 94–5, figs 86–7.

26 *Vasari on Technique* (Giorgio Vasari, Introduction to the Lives of the Most Excellent Painters, Sculptors and Architects), trans. Louisa Maclehose, ed. G. Baldwin Brown, New York 1907, pp. 37–9, 125–6; pp. 37–8 for Cosimo's commission.

27 'Due palle di mischio ed suoi piedi [. . .] una pila antica di pietra/Duoi vasetti di pietra antichi/Duoi lucerne una di bronzo e l'altra di terra antica [. . .] Una testa di leone di bronzo antico'; 'Sopra la scantia una testa di marmo col suo piede et una palle mischio di vetro': Caro 1578.

28 John Kent Lydecker, *The Domestic Setting of the Arts in Renaissance Florence*, PhD thesis, Johns Hopkins University, Baltimore 1987, Ann Arbor Microfilms 1987, p. 327.

29 'Dodese teste di stucco, co'sei balle di nero': Cornaro 1597.

30 '3 balle di marmora sopra la Nappa del Camin/Una testa di marmo del clarissimo signor Usper con il suo piede sotto indorado': Usper 1601.

31 Rafaello Borghini, *Il riposo*, Florence 1584, pp. 635–6.

32 Torquato Tasso, 'Il Malpiglio secondo', *Dialoghi*, ed. E. Mazzali, Turin 1976, p. 126.

33 A painting of St Paul by Antonio da Crevelcore (d. before 1525) includes carefully represented study objects, such as an inkwell, sander and candlestick, and also a black stone (possibly marble) sphere which rests on a window ledge at back left. This sphere may be an early representation of a marble sphere as a decorative study accessory. See *From Borso to Cesare d'Este: The School of Ferrara, 1450–1628*, exhibition catalogue, Matthiesen Fine Art Ltd, London 1984, cat. 15. I am grateful to Jeremy Warren for this reference.

34 L. Mauro, *Le antichità della città di Roma*, Rome 1556, pp. 202–12. Franzoni, 'Le collezioni rinascimentali', pp. 312–13. On Carpi, see Brown and Lorenzoni, *Gonzaga and Garimberto*, p. 194; for Aldrovandi, pp. 153–5.

35 Borghini, *Il riposo*, pp. 635–6. Wolfgang Liebenwein, *Lo Studiolo: Die Entstehung eines Raumtyps und seine Entwicklung bis um 1600*, Berlin 1977, pp. 73–4. De Benedictis, *Collezionismo italiano*, p. 210. F. Point-Wacquet, 'Les Botti: Fortunes et culture d'une famille florentine', *Mélange de l'Ecole Français de Rome*, XC, 1978, pp. 689–713.

36 Borghini, *Il riposo*, pp. 635–6.

37 Giorgio Vasari, 'Ragionamento Quarto' (c.1557), *I Ragionamenti e le lettere edite e inedite di Giorgio Vasari*, ed. G. Milanesi, Florence 1882, pp. 58–9.

38 Clare Robertson, *'Il Gran Cardinale': Alessandro Farnese, Patron of the Arts*, New Haven and London 1992, p. 50.

39 Robertson, *'Il Gran Cardinale'*, doc. 49, p. 299 and p. 50.

40 Robertson, *'Il Gran Cardinale'*, doc. 139, p. 315.

41 C. M. Brown, '"Lo insaciabile desiderio nostro de cose antique": New Documents for Isabella d'Este's Collection of Antiquities', *Cultural Aspects of the Italian Renaissance: Essays in Honour of Paul Oskar Kristeller*, ed. Cecil Clough, Manchester 1976, pp. 324–53.

42 C. M. Brown and Anna Maria Lorenzoni, *Isabella d'Este and Lorenzo da Pavia*, Geneva 1982, p. 220.

43 Brown and Lorenzoni, *Gonzaga and Garimberto*, doc. 113, p. 119.

44 Sabba di Castiglione, *I ricordi*, Venice 1560, p. 58. On Sabba, see *Dizionario Biografico degli Italiani*, vol. 19, Rome 1976, pp. 100–05.

45 Title as translated by Joseph Alsop in *The Rare Art Traditions: The History of Art Collecting and its linked phenomena wherever these have appeared*, Princeton 1982, pp. 420–21.

46 A. Luzio, 'Lettere inedite di Fra Sabba di Castiglione', *Archivio storico lombardo*, III, 1886, pp. 91–112.

47 Sabba, *Ricordi*, p. 58–9. For a recent critique of Sabba's bust of St John the Baptist, which its owner considered to be the work of Donatello, see Giordano Viroli, 'Il "San Giovannino" della Pinacoteca di Faenza', *Il Monumento a Barbara Manfredi e la scultura del Rinascimento in Romagna*, eds. Anna Colombi Feretti and Luciana Prati, Bologna 1989, pp. 153–56.

48 Sabba, *Ricordi*, no. 118, opening. Quoted in Edmond Bonnaffé, 'Sabba di Castiglione, notes sur la curiosité italienne de la Renaissance', *Gazette des Beaux-Arts*, XXX, 1884, pp. 19–154, p. 152.

49 On Mantegna's prints and their contemporary standing, see David Landau and Peter Parshall, *The Renaissance Print, 1470–1550*, New Haven and London 1994, pp. 100–02.

50 Giulia Bartrum, *German Renaissance Prints, 1490–1550*, exhibition catalogue, British Museum, London 1995, cat. 34.

51 On Junius and his patron, Thomas Arundel, see David Howarth, *Lord Arundel and his Circle*, New Haven and London 1985, p.84, n.17. I am grateful to Jeremy Warren for this reference.

52 J. Contareno will 1596. See also Favaretto, *Arte antica et cultura antiquaria*, p.94.

53 Bembo will 1544.

54 Paolo Manuzio, *Lettere volgari*, Venice 1560, book II, p.74. M. Foscarini, *Della letteratura veneziana*, Venice 1854, p.410. C. De Benedictis, *Collezionismo italiano*, p.226. Isabella Palumbo Fossati, 'Il collezionista Sebastiano Erizzo e l'inventario dei suoi beni', *Ateneo veneto*, XXII, 1984, pp.201–18.

55 'Che possano accrescere ornamento al suo bellissimo studio, e per conseguente alla nostra città': Manuzio, *Lettere volgari*, book II, p.74.

56 *Ambrosii Traversarii, Latinae Epistolae*, ed. P. Cannetus, Florence 1759, letters 412 and 417.

57 Marin Sanudo, *Diarii*, vol.12, Venice 1886, col.293, 5 December 1511. F. Ambrosini, '"Descrittioni del Mondo" nelle case venete dei secoli XVI e XVII', *Archivio veneto*, CLII, 1981, pp.69–71, p.69, n.1.

58 *Notizia d'opere di disegno nella prima metà del secolo XVI*, ed. J. Morelli, Bassano 1800. On Michiel, see *Venice: A Documentary History, 1450–1630*, ed. David Chambers and Brian Pullan, Oxford 1992, pp.423–6.

59 Vincenzo Mancini, *Antiquari, virtuosi e artisti: Saggi sul collezionismo tra Padova e Venezia alla metà del cinquecento*, Padua 1995, pp.41–3.

60 Mancini, *Collezionismo tra Padova e Venezia*, p.42, and pp.61–2 for the importance of Gerolamo Quirini's collection to visitors.

61 Francesco Sansovino, *Venetia*, Venice 1581, pp.137–9; expanded in Stringa's edition (Venice 1604) and Martinioni's (Venice 1666).

62 M. Perry, 'Cardinal Domenico Grimani's Legacy of Ancient Art to Venice', *Journal of the Courtauld and Warburg Institutes*, XVI, 1987, pp.215–44. Irene Favaretto, '"Una tribuna ricca di marmi", appunti per una storia della collezioni dei Grimani di Santa Maria Formosa', *Aquileia nostra*, LV, 1984, pp.206–39, pp.206–7.

63 Perry, 'Grimani's Legacy', pp.226–44.

64 L. Puppi, 'Vincenzo Scamozzi trattista nell'ambito della problematica del manierismo', *Bollettino del Centro internazionale di studi di architettura Andrea Palladio*, IX, 1967, pp.310–29.

65 Scamozzi, *Idea dell'architettura*, part III, p.306. *The Genius of Venice*, exhibition catalogue, ed. Jane Martineau and Charles Hope, Royal Academy, London 1983, cat.70.

66 Letter of Girolamo Gualdo, 30 November 1552, quored in G. Zorzi, 'Come lo *studio* di Valerio Belli transmigrò a Trento', *L'arte*, XVIII, 1915, pp.256–7; De Benedictis, *Collezionismo italiano*, pp.30 and 160.

67 Mancini, *Collezionismo tra Padova e Venezia*, p.47.

68 V. Ranieri, *Descrittioni di tutta l'Italia*, Bologna 1550, pp.393–4. Quoted in G. Schizzerotto, *Teatro e cultura in romagna dal medioevo al rinascimento*, Ravenna 1969, p.90, n.24.

69 P. Casadio, 'Un affresco di Girolamo di Treviso il Giovane a Faenza', *Il Pordenone* (Atti del Convegno Internazionale di Studio, Pordenone 1984), published Pordenone 1985, pp.209–13, p.210.

70 Quotation from Patricia Rubin, *Giorgio Vasari: Art and History*, New Haven and London 1995, p.117, on what she calls 'the culture of correspondence' and Vasari's place within it.

71 Paula Findlen, in *Possessing Nature: Museums, Collecting and Scientific Culture in Early Modern Italy*, Berkeley, Los Angeles and London 1994, takes this theme into the early seventeenth century.

72 Brown and Lorenzoni, *Gonzaga and Garimberto*, p.155.

73 Palumbo Fossati, 'Il collezionista Sebastiano Erizzo', pp.201–18; De Benedictis, *Collezionismo italiano*, p.226.

74 A. Luzio, 'Il Museo Gioviano descritto da Anton Francesco Doni', *Archivio storico lombardo*, 3rd series, XXVIII, 1901, pp.143–50; D. F. Fossati, 'Ritratti del museo Giovio', *Rassegna nazionale*, XV, 1893, p.380. On the formation of the collection, see Haskell, *History and its Images*, pp.44–50.

75 Cesare Vecellio, *De gli habiti antichi e moderni*, Venice 1590, p.219.

76 Giovanni Filoteo Achillini, *Epistole di Giovanne Philoteo Achillino al Magnificentissimo Missere Antonio Rudolpho Germanico, ove si narra[no] tutte le sorti di preciose petre, le Sibille, la varieta de l'armi antiche e moderni, Musici instrumenti, colossi, le nove Muse, diverse arbori, Cavalcature, antichi et moderni habiti, Altri dotti et giocosi tratti, et piu miraculosi accidenti* [n.p., n.d.], first letter, AIIII. Text published in Claudio Franzoni, 'Le raccolte del Theatro di Ombrone e il viaggio in oriente del pittore: Le *Epistole* di Giovanni Filoteo Achillini', *Rivista di letteratura italiana*, VIII, 2, 1990, pp.287–335. See Sandro de Maria, 'Artisti, "antiquari" e collezionisti di antichità a Bologna fra XV e XVI secolo', in *Bologna e l'umanesimo, 1490–1510*, exhibition catalogue, ed. Marzia Faietti and Konrad Oberhuber, Pinacoteca Nazionale, Bologna 1988, pp.17–44, p.32, n.89. There are copies of this rare book in the Marciana Library, Venice, and the Biblioteca Nazionale in Florence: the latter copy is referred to here. I am grateful to Jeremy Warren for this reference, and to John Goldfinch for locating this copy.

77 Landau and Parshall, *The Renaissance Print*, pp.99–100 and fig.89. Achillini knew Leandro Alberti, who appears as an interlocutor in his dialogue *Annotationi della volgar lingua*, Bologna 1536, in which he justifies the dignity of the Italian vernacular. See also Franzoni, 'Le raccolte', pp.309–10.

78 Achillini, *Epistole*, first letter, AIIII.

79 Of those mentioned, the firstnamed appears to have been invented by Sabba. Medals of Piccinino exist in bronze and lead, whereas the famous Gattamelata, best known from the equestrian statue of him by Donatello, is not recorded to have been figured on a medal. I am grateful to Luke Syson for comments on these references to medals.

80 The collector quotes a line of the *Doctrinale* from memory, 'Rectis as es a [dat declinatio prima]' on the singular endings for all first-declension nouns. On Alexander de Villedieu and his grammar, see Paul Grendler, *Schooling in Renaissance Italy: Literacy and Learning, 1300–1600*, Baltimore and London 1989, p.112.

81 Sabba, *Ricordi*, pp.58–9.

82 Sabba, *Ricordi*, p.58.

83 Raffaele Puddu, 'Lettere ed armi: Il ritratto del guerriero tra quattro e cinquecento', *Federigo da Montefeltro: Lo stato, le arti, la cultura*, ed. Giorgio Cerboni Baiardi, Giorgio Chittolini and Piero Floriano, 3 vols, Rome 1986, *Lo stato*, pp.489–94; Richard Goldthwaite, *Wealth and the Demand for Art in Renaissance Italy, 1300–1600*, Baltimore and London 1993, p.173, n.41, p.202.

84 For an assessment of Isabella d'Este and the role of antiquities as investments, see Lisa Jardine, *Worldly Goods*, London 1996, pp.412–24. I am grateful to Ian Jenkins and Jeremy Warren for this reference.

85 *Dizionario biografico degli italiani*, vol.19, Rome 1976, pp.669–73. Brian Pullan, *Rich and Poor in Renaissance Venice*, Oxford 1971, pp.117–18, 130–31. *Venice: A Documentary History, 1450–1630*, ed. David Chambers and Brian Pullan, Oxford 1992, pp.113–16.

86 Alessandro Caravia, *IL Naspo Bizaro*, Venice 1565, fols 140v–141r. I am grateful to Patricia Allerston for this reference and

87   Caravia, *Naspo Bizaro*, fols 140*v*–141*r*.

88   On his medal collection, De Benedictis, *Collezionismo italiano*, p. 172; on his prints, see Landau and Parshall, *The Renaissance Print*, p. 293.

89   Anton Francesco Doni, *I marmi* (1552), ed. S. Bongi, Florence 1863, pp. 257–8. De Benedictis, *Collezionismo italiano*, p. 201, Franzoni, 'Collezioni rinscimentali', pp. 343–4.

90   Paul Grendler, *Critics of the Italian World, 1530–1560*, Madison 1969, pp. 21, 189. On Doni as a moralist, see Francesco Sansovino, *Sopplimento delle croniche universali*, Venice 1575, p. 596, and preface to French edition of Doni's *I mondi* as *Les visions italiennes*, Paris 1634, pp. 3–5. Bernardo Macchietta's preface to *I mondi*, Venice 1597, p. 3, and John Florio's comments as quoted by D. G. Rees in 'John Florio and Anton Francesco Doni', *Comparative Literature*, xv, 1963, pp. 33–8.

91   Doni, *I marmi*, [1552] pp. 40–41. Jaynie Anderson, 'A Further Inventory of Gabriel Vendramin's Collection', *Burlington Magazine*, cxxi, 1979, pp. 639–49, p. 639.

92   Anderson, 'Vendramin's Collection', p. 639. A. Ravà, 'Il camerino delle antigaglie di Gabriel Vendramin', *Nuovo archivio veneto*, xxxix, 1920, p. 163.

93   'De sculptura mox loqui occepimus'; Pomponius Gauricus, *De sculptura* (c.1504), ed. A. Chastel and R. Klein, Geneva 1969, p. 40.

94   Luc'Antonio Ridolfi, *Aretefila, dialogo*, Lyons 1560. I am grateful to Neil Kenny and to Marie-Madeleine Fontaine for this reference; see the latter's article, '"Un coeur mis en gage", Pontus de Tyrard, Marguerite du Bourg et le milieu Lyonnais des années 1550', *Revue du XVIe siècle*, ii, 1984, pp. 70–89.

95   Ridolfi mentions the inscriptions in his introduction to Benedetto Varchi's *Lezioni d'Amore*, Lyons 1560, p. 84. Fontaine, 'Coeur mis en gage', p. 81, n. 22. A. Blunt, *Philibert Delorme*, Paris 1963, pl. 1 and p. 31, for description of the house.

96   Ridolfi, *Aretefila*, pp. 7–8.

97   Letter of 8 April 1476, quoted by Armando Petrucci, *Writers and Readers in Medieval Italy: Studies in the History of Written Culture*, ed. and trans. Charles M. Radding, New Haven and London 1995, p. 233, n. 158 (I have altered the translation slightly). I am grateful to Jeremy Warren for this reference.

98   'Et propositum eius, ut opinor, hoc erat ut non in sylvis sed in curia urbana, prope cubiculum suum, statueretur tam nobile studiolum, quo facilius et commodius ab externis oratoribus et poetis viseretur': Latin and Italian translation quoted in *Le Muse e il Principe: Arte di corte nel Rinascimento padano*, exhibition catalogue, ed. Andrea di Lorenzo, Alessandra Mottola Molfino, Mauro Natale and Annalisa Zanni, Museo Poldi-Pezzoli, Milan 1991, p. 328.

99   Luciano Cheles, *The Studiolo of Urbino: An Iconographic Investigation*, Wiesbaden 1986, p. 23.

100 Cheles, *Studiolo of Urbino*, pp. 21–2.

101 Luigi Michelini Tocci, 'La formazione della Biblioteca di Federigo da Montefeltro: Codici contemporanei e libri a stampa', *Federigo da Montefeltro*, ed. Baiardi, Chittolini and Floriani, vol. 3, pp. 9–18. John Pearson Perry, 'Practical and Ceremonial Uses of Plants Materials as "Literary Refinements" in the Libraries of Leonello d'Este and his Courtly Literary Circle', *La Bibliofilia*, xci, 1989, pp. 121–71, pp. 157–8.

102 Compare much the same fragile arrangement in the Castello di Torrechiara, near Parma, which also has a wooden panel folding out from the wall serving as a desk, surrounded by fine wooden panelling. I am grateful to Peter Thornton for drawing this arrangement on site for me.

103 Cheles, *Studiolo of Urbino*, p. 21 and fig. 149.

104 Cheles, *Studiolo of Urbino*, p. 86.

105 Cheles, *Studiolo of Urbino*, pp. 23, 91.

106 This attribution was made during the restoration work on the Urbino study from 1968 to 1973, during which the technique of chromatic modelling in wooden inlay was compared with Giuliano da Maiano's work on the Sacristy in Santa Maria del Fiore in Florence. Olga Raggio, 'Lo studiolo del Palazzo Ducale di Gubbio', *Piero e Urbino*, ed. Paolo dal Poggetto, Venice 1992, pp. 259–360.

107 Alessandra Angelini, 'Senesi a Urbino', *Francesco di Giorgio e il Rinascimento a Siena, 1450–1500*, ed. Luciano Belosi, Milan 1993, p. 332.

108 Francesco di Giorgio's role in planning the Ducal Apartments in Urbino in the 1460s and 1470s has been much debated: see Peter Thornton, *The Italian Renaissance Interior, 1400–1600*, London 1991, p. 392 for a summary of the argument.

109 Cecil Clough, 'Art as Power in the Decoration of the Study of an Italian Renaissance Prince: The Case of Federigo da Montefeltro', *Artibus et historiae*, xxxi, 1995, pp. 19–50.

110 'Unum liutum a sonando'; 'duas planettas': Monticuli 1413.

111 'Una palla di ottone, di astrologia, con piedistallo': Guinigi 1430.

112 Michael Baxandall, 'Guarino, Pisanello and Chrysolorus', *Journal of the Warburg and Courtauld Institutes*, xxvii, 1965, p. 196.

113 Lewis Lockwood, *Music in Renaissance Ferrara, 1400–1505*, Oxford 1984, p. 46, n. 5. I am grateful to Jeremy Warren for this reference.

114 Lockwood, *Ferrara*, pp. 48–63, 65.

115 Cecil Clough, *Federigo da Montefeltro's Artistic Patronage*, Liverpool 1978, pp. 10–11. Graziano Manni, *Mobili in Emilia*, Modena 1986, pp. 27–31. Jaynie Anderson, 'Il risveglio dell'interesse per le Muse nella Ferrara del quattrocento', *Le Muse*, ed. Andrea di Lorenzo et al., pp. 165–87, pp. 167–75 for Guarino and his sources. Thomas Tuohy, 'The Prince and the Muses', review of this exhibition, *Apollo*, cxxxiv, 1991, pp. 425–6.

116 R. W. Lightbown, *Mantegna*, Oxford 1986, p. 198. Luciano Cheles, 'The Inlaid Decoration of Federigo da Montefeltro's Urbino *Studiolo*', *Mitteilungen des Kunsthistorisches Instituts in Florenz*, xxvi, [1982], pp. 1–46.

117 Cheles, *Studiolo of Urbino*, p. 83, n. 128.

118 Iain Fenlon, 'The Gonzaga and Music', *Splendours of the Gonzaga*, exhibition catalogue, ed. David Chambers and Jane Martineau, Victoria and Albert Museum, London 1982, pp. 87–94, p. 87.

119 Fenlon, 'The Gonzaga and Music', p. 87.

120 On Isabella and the *frottola*, see William F. Prizer, 'The North Italian Courts', *Man and Music: The Renaissance*, ed. Iain Fenlon, London 1989, pp. 133–55, pp. 145–6. I am grateful to Stanley Sadie for this reference.

121 Prizer, 'North Italian Courts', p. 146 on printed music, and p. 146 on Petrarch.

122 Sabba di Castiglione, quoted in P. Thornton, *Italian Renaissance Interior*, p. 272.

123 Clifford M. Brown and Anna Maria Lorenzoni, *Isabella d'Este and Lorenzo da Pavia*, Geneva 1982, doc. 7. See also William F. Prizer, 'Isabella d'Este and Lorenzo da Pavia, "Master Instrument-maker"', *Early Music History*, ii, 1982, pp. 87–128, pp. 109 and 111 for her order for a *viole spagnole* in ebony.

124 Quoted in Lightbown, *Mantegna*, p. 199.

125 James Haar, 'The Courtier as Musician, Castiglione's View of the Science and Art of Music', in *Castiglione: Ideal and Real in Renaissance Culture*, ed. Robert W. Hanning and David Rosand, New Haven and London 1983, pp. 165–89.

126 Letter from Gerolamo Garimberto to Alessandro Farnese, 9 August 1566. In Robertson, *'Il Gran Cardinale'*, pp. 50 and 299 (doc. 49).

127 Amanda Lillie, 'The Humanist Villa Revisited', *Language and*

Images of Renaissance Italy, ed. Alison Brown, Oxford 1995, pp. 214–15.

128 Galileo Galilei, *Considerazioni al Tasso* (c.1589), in *Scritti letterari*, ed. A. Chiari, Florence 1943, p. 96. See also De Benedictis, *Collezionismo italiano*, p. 178. I am grateful to Dr De Benedictis for discussing her work with me.

129 De Benedictis, *Collezionismo italiano*, p. 38.

Chapter 6

1 Richard Goldthwaite, *Wealth and the Demand for Art in Renaissance Italy, 1300–1600*, Baltimore and London 1993, p. 243.

2 Letter to Ercole d'Este from Buda, 22 October 1501. *Modenai és velencei követek jelentései Magyarorsazág földrajzi és culturai állapotáról a XV és XVI*, ed. C. Foucard and G. Mircse, Budapest 1881, pp. 9–14, pp. 12–14. Shayne Mitchell, *The Image of Hungary and of Hungarians in Italy, 1437–1526*, PhD thesis, Warburg Institute, University of London 1994, p. 352. I am grateful to Shayne Mitchell for this reference.

3 Gianbattista Palatino, *Libro [. . .] nel qual s'insegna a scriver*, Rome 1560. O. Ogg, *Three Classics of Italian Calligraphy*, New York 1953, p. 239.

4 Ogg, *Italian Calligraphy*, p. 239.

5 Clifford M. Brown and Anna Maria Lorenzoni, *Isabella d'Este and Lorenzo da Pavia*, Geneva 1982, p. 242, n. 1. A particularly fine pair of scissors is shown being used to open a letter by The Blessed Pierre de la Palud in Tomaso da Modena's fresco in Treviso: Robert Gibbs, *Tomaso da Modena*, Cambridge 1989, fig. 32. I am grateful to Robert Gibbs for discussing Tomaso and the reading and writing accessories in his work with me.

6 Gibbs, *Tomaso da Modena*, fig. 48a.

7 'Uno bossolo con più puntelli da sugelli'; 'una scatola di sugelli in pasta': Chiaro 1424.

8 Charles Oman, *British Rings, 800–1914*, London 1974, pp. 29–31. Diana Scarisbrick, *Rings*, London 1993, pp. 30–34. Anne Ward, John Cherry, Charlotte Gere and Barbara Cartledge, *The Ring from Antiquity to the Twentieth Century*, London 1981, pp. 69–80. O. M. Dalton, *Franks Bequest, Catalogue of the Finger Rings, Early Christian [. . .] Medieval and Later*, London 1912, cats. 228, 230, 231, 257. I am grateful to my colleague John Cherry for discussing this with me.

9 Castellani memoranda, p. 129. The omitted phrase refers to the inscription to be engraved on the ring, which combines Greek and Latin. I am grateful to my colleague Ian Jenkins for his comments on the inscription and its interpretation.

10 I am grateful to my colleague John Cherry for discussing this with me.

11 Nicole Dacos, 'La role des plaquettes dans la diffusion des gemmes antiques: Le cas de la collection Médicis', *Italian Plaquettes*, ed. Alison Luchs, Studies in the History of Art, 22, National Gallery of Art, Washington 1989, pp. 71–89, pp. 72–3, figs. 1–3.

12 Dacos, 'Role des plaquettes', p. 72, n. 15, fig. 3.

13 Dacos, 'Role des plaquettes', pp. 72–3, notes 14 and 17. Ghiberti did not identify the subject-matter of the gem and described it incorrectly: Dacos attributes the latter to the fact that Ghiberti may have been writing from a plaquette (which would give the composition in reverse, with slight variations according with Ghiberti's description) and that, since Lorenzo's mark of ownership was engraved on the reverse of the gem, this may have been how it was displayed in his collections.

14 Dacos, 'Role des plaquettes', p. 73. The gem does not survive, but was reinterpreted in plaquette form in the mid-fifteenth

century. For a fine example, see a plaquette in the British Museum, cited by Graham Pollard, 'The Plaquette Collections in the British Museum', *Italian Plaquettes*, ed. Luchs, pp. 227–46, no. 38.

15 Brown and Lorenzoni, *Isabella and Lorenzo*, doc. 181, p. 134.

16 Sabba di Castiglione, *Ricordi*, Venice 1554, p. 366.

17 Yvonne Szafran, 'Carpaccio's *Hunting on the Lagoon*: A New Perspective', *Burlington Magazine*, CXXXVII, 1995, pp. 148–60.

18 Szafran, 'Carpaccio's *Hunting*', p. 158.

19 John Florio, *Queen Anna's New World of Words*, London 1611.

20 Ronald Lightbown, *Sandro Botticelli: Life and Work*, London 1989, p. 224 and fig. 91.

21 *Bronzen der Renaissance und des Barock, Katalog der Sammlung*, ed. Ursel Berger and Volker Krahn, Herzog Anton Ulrich-Museum, Brunswick 1994, cat. 3. I am grateful to Jeremy Warren for this reference.

22 R. Gobiet, *Der Briefwechsel zwischen Philipp Hainhofer und Herzog August der Jüngere von Braunschweig Lüneberg*, Munich 1984, p. 842. I am grateful to Jeremy Warren for this reference.

23 Gobiet, *Briefwechsel*, pp. 848, 842, 720 and letter 1467 for reference to another German sculptor making such paperweights.

24 *Natur und Antike in der Renaissance*, exhibition catalogue, ed. Herbert Beck and Peter Bol, Liebighaus, Frankfurt am Main 1986, cats. 269–75.

25 *Die Beschwörung des Kosmos: Europäische Bronzen der Renaissance*, exhibition catalogue, ed. Christoph Brockhaus and Gottlieb Leinz, Wilhelm Lehmbruck Museum, Duisburg November 1994–January 1995, cat. 104.

26 Anne-Elizabeth Theuerkauff-Liederwald, *Venezianisches Glas der veste Coburg: Die Sammlung Herzog Alfreds von Sachsen-Coburg und Gotha (1844–1900)*, Lingen 1994, pp. 62–7. Questions the dating of the Amerbach *millefiori* sphere, previously thought to be one of the 'Venetian' examples mentioned in the Amerbach inventory of 1578, p. 67. I am grateful to my colleague Aileen Dawson for this reference, and to Anne-Elizabeth Theuerkauff for going through the British Museum's collection of Sloane and Payne Knight pieces of this type.

27 Hugh Tait, *Five Thousand Years of Glass*, London 1991, p. 163.

28 'Due palle di vetri mischiati con fiori e altre opere': Strozzi 1494.

29 Gobiet, *Briefwechsel*, p. 843. I am grateful to Jeremy Warren for this reference and for translating it for me.

30 Peter Thornton, *The Italian Renaissance Interior, 1400–1600*, London 1991, pl. 76 and p. 70 on taffetas.

31 John Pearson Perry, 'Practical and Ceremonial Uses of Plants Materials as "Literary Refinements" in the Libraries of Leonello d'Este and his Courtly Literary Circle', *La Bibliofilia*, XCI, 1989, pp. 121–73, p. 131.

32 Perry, 'Practical and Ceremonial Uses', p. 131.

33 Letter from Buda of 11 November 1479 written by Antonio Probi to his chaplain Mathias. See L. Sorricchio, 'Angelo ed Antonio Probi, ambasciatori di Ferdinando I d'Aragon', *Archivio storico per le provincie napoletane*, XXI, 1896, doc. XII, pp. 163–4. I am grateful to Shayne Mitchell for this reference.

34 Letter from Benedetto Mastino to Marchese Lodovico Gonzaga of 9 August 1477. See D. S. Chambers, 'Francesco Gonzaga and the Mantuan Clergy', *Journal of Ecclesiastical History*, XXXVI, 4, 1985, pp. 605–33, p. 605. I am grateful to David Chambers for this reference.

35 On varying customs in setting books on shelves in the sixteenth century, see Graham Pollard, 'Changes in the Style of Bookbinding, 1550–1830', *The Library*, 5th series, XI, 2, 1956, pp. 71–94, p. 73. I am grateful to Anthony Hobson for this reference.

36 Anthony Hobson, 'The Pillone Library', *Book Collector*, VII,

1958, pp.28–37; Pierre Berès, *La Bibliothèque Pillone*, Paris 1957; Andrea Tessier, *Di Cesare Vecellio e de'suoi dipinti e disegni in una collezione di libri dei secoli XV e XVI*, Venice 1875.

37 Anthony Hobson, *Apollo and Pegasus: An Enquiry into the Formation and Dispersal of a Renaissance Library*, Amsterdam 1975, pp.37–63 on Claudio Tolomei and his patron Giovanbattista Grimaldi.

38 'Si formerà una libbraria finita, la qual v'ornarà prima lo studio, e di poi l'animo maggiormente': Hobson, *Apollo and Pegasus*, pp.41 and 202.

39 Hobson, *Apollo and Pegasus*, pp.10–11 on this feature, and pp.41, 202.

40 Hobson, *Apollo and Pegasus*, pp.95–6.

41 Hobson, *Apollo and Pegasus*, p.11.

42 John Hale, *The Civilisation of Europe in the Renaissance*, London 1993, p.588.

43 Hobson, *Apollo and Pegasus*, p.13, cat.67.

44 *On the Eve of the Reformation: 'Letters of Obscure Men'* (Ulrich von Hutten *et al.*), trans. F. G. Stokes, New York and London 1964, p.210. Hale, *Civilisation*, p.197.

45 John Earle, *Microcosmographie*, [1628] facsimile of Bodleian Library, Oxford, MS Eng.misc.f89, London 1966, fol.82.

46 Sabba, *Ricordi*, p.75.

47 Guido Fusinato, 'Un cantastorie Chioggiotto', *Giornale di filologia romanza*, 2nd series, IV, 1883, pp.170–83; Paul Grendler, *Schooling in Renaissance Italy: Literacy and Learning, 1300–1600*, Baltimore and London 1989, p.299, n.61.

48 Grendler, *Schooling in Renaissance Italy*, p.290, n.39.

49 Sabba, *Ricordi*, p.70.

50 Vincent Ilardi, 'Eye-glasses and Concave Lenses in Fifteenth-century Milan: New Documents', *Renaissance Quarterly*, XXIX, 1976, pp.341–60. Gibbs, *Tomaso da Modena*, pp.82–3. John Dreyfus, 'The Invention of Spectacles and the Advent of Printing', *The Library*, 6th series, X, 2, 1988, pp.93–106. I am grateful to Anthony Hobson for this reference.

51 Ilardi, 'Eye-glasses', p.350, n.21.

52 Grendler, *Schooling in Renaissance Italy*, p.78; different figure in Ilardi, 'Eye-glasses', p.357.

53 Michael Rhodes, 'A Pair of Fifteenth-century Spectacle Frames from the City of London', *Antiquaries Journal*, LXII, 1982, pp.57–73, pp.64 and 66. I am grateful to Geoff Egan at the Museum of London Archaeology Service for making it possible for me to examine a number of examples, including those described by Rhodes and more recent London finds.

54 Ilardi, 'Eye-glasses', p.345, n.13. David Chambers, *A Renaissance Cardinal and his Worldly Goods: The Will and Inventory of Francesco Gonzaga*, London 1992, p.69, n.155.

55 Ilardi, 'Eye-glasses', p.347.

56 Millard Meiss, *Patrons and Artists of Manuscripts: French Painting in the Time of Jean de Berry*, 2 vols., London and New York 1967, p.5. Ilardi, 'Eye-glasses', p.360, n.49.

57 Chambers, *Renaissance Cardinal*, p.69, n.156, p.53, n.28.

58 'Un cristallo da llegiere fornito dariento': Buonaguisi 1462.

59 Michael Cowell and Dora Thornton, 'The Armada Service: A Set of Late Tudor Dining Silver', *Antiquaries Journal*, LXXVI, 1996, pp.153–80, p.159, n.25.

60 Palatino, *Libro*; reprinted in Ogg, *Italian Calligraphy*, pp.121–247, pp.238, 236. On receipts for ink, see Christopher De Hamel, *Medieval Craftsmen, Scribes and Illuminators*, London 1992, pp.32–3.

61 Giovanantonio Tagliente, *Lo presente libro Insegna la vera arte dello excellente scrivere*, Venice 1524, followed by many later editions. See Ogg, *Italian Calligraphy*, pp.65–119. On the interrelationships between this and other writing books, see Stanley Morrison, *Early Italian Writing Books, Renaissance to*

Baroque, ed. Nicolas Barker, London and Verona 1990, esp. pp.65 and 76.

62 'Calamare di vetro mezzo azzurro e mezzo bianco': Luigi Zecchin, *Vetro e vetrai di Murano: Studi sulla storia del vetro*, Venice 1987, vol.1, p.62. These items were stolen along with paternosters and milk-white (*lattimo*) beakers.

63 'Uno calamaio di ariento in su quattro agnoletti i sul coperchio et co' paia di forbicine et due temperato di ferro': Trevisan 1465.

64 For the full story of this inkstand and Caradosso's activities as a goldsmith, see C. M. Brown and S. Hickson, 'Caradosso Foppa', *Arte lombarda*, CXIX, 1997 (forthcoming). I am grateful to Clifford Brown for this reference.

65 Sabba, *Ricordi*, p.51.

66 Emile Molinier, *Les bronzes de la Renaissance: Les plaquettes*, vol.1, Paris 1886, p.115. Eugene Müntz, 'L'atelier monetaire de Rome: Documents inédits sur les graveurs de monnaies et de sceaux', *Revue numismatique*, 3rd series, II, 1884, p.25. Luke Syson, 'Bramante and Caradosso: Questions of Attribution and Biography', public lecture. Brown and Hickson, 'Caradosso Foppa'.

67 *De Nola*, Venice 1514. On Ambrogio de Leone Nola see Roberto Weiss, *The Renaissance Discovery of Classical Antiquity*, Oxford 1969, pp.127–9.

68 For the reference to Leone as *philosophus huius tempestatis eximius* see Desiderius Erasmus, *Adagia*, I.ii 63; also II.iii 50 and III.vii 66. *The Contemporaries of Erasmus: A Biographical Register of the Renaissance and Reformation*, ed. Peter G. Bietenholz, vol.2, Toronto 1986, pp.322–3.

69 On *ekphrasis*, see Michael Baxandall, *Giotto and the Orators: Humanist Observers of Painting and the Discovery of Pictorial Composition, 1350–1450*, Oxford 1971, pp.85–7.

70 'Nam in unus illius latere nudi equis insidentes spectantur, qui auxilio cuidam ouero venerant, quem aquila eriperat in coelum; illi suspicientes alitem puereum deportantem, eum animum propositumque, ostenduntut evolare cum equis quoque velle videantur, ubi eiis figuris raptum Ganymedis ostendit. in altero pugna Centaurorum cum Lapithis est. tertio latere Hercules est, qua Cacum suppositum clavacque gutture illius presso genu altero cum violentia quadam stomachum calcante, alteraque ore stringente compulsat': Ambrogio de Leone Nola [Ambrosius Leo], *De nobilitate rerum natura*, Venice 1525, chap.CXLI (unpaginated). The translation has been kindly provided by Paul Gwynne, and differs slightly from that given in Brown and Hickson, 'Caradosso Foppa' (see above, n.64).

71 'Quarto vero Hercules leonem exossans specatatur, adeo pulcre exsculptus, ut hominem ira percitum, leonem dolore gementem prope sentiretis': Brown and Hickson, 'Caradosso Foppa' (see above, n.64).

72 Brown and Hickson, (see above, n.64) for the Leone reference to sulphur impressions of the relief panels of the inkstand.

73 John Pope-Hennessy, *Renaissance Bronzes from the Samuel H. Kress Collection: Reliefs, Plaquettes, Statuettes and Mortars*, London 1965, cats47–8. Brown and Hickson, 'Caradosso Foppa' (see above, n.64).

74 Pollard, 'Plaquette Collections', *Italian Plaquettes*, ed. Luchs, pp.227–45, cat.130. John Pope-Hennessy, 'The Study of Italian Plaquettes', *Italian Plaquettes*, ed. Luchs, pp.1–32, p.21. Syson, 'Bramante and Caradosso' (see above, n.64).

75 Pope-Hennessy, 'Study of Italian Plaquettes', p.21.

76 Brown and Lorenzoni, *Isabella and Lorenzo*, p.234; Brown and Hickson (see above, n.64) on whether this inkstand was that described by Leone or a later variant.

77 'Io ho grande desiderio veder un calamaro d'arzento lavorato da Caradosso, zoilero milanese, quale lui ha a Milano et perché

ne lo extraerlo gli occoreria datio, prego la signoria Vostra, a mia singulare gratificatione, sia contento concedere al prefato Caradosso una patente che lo exempti da ogni datio occurente nel portar et ritornar ditto calamaro per tutto quello dominio': Brown and Lorenzoni, *Isabella and Lorenzo*, p. 234; Brown and Hickson, 'Caradosso Foppa' (see above, n. 64).

78 'Uno calamaio di argento in forma di una cassettina alquanto grandetta cum le arme da Gonzaga et da Este in uno medesimo scuto in meggio dil coperto et cum quattro pedetti': Gonzaga 1549.

79 Brown and Lorenzoni, *Isabella and Lorenzo*, p. 236.

80 'Un calamaro con coperchio': Chigi 1497, p. 118.

81 Eric Maclagan, *Catalogue of Italian Plaquettes*, Victoria and Albert Museum, London 1924, p. 76. Pope-Hennessy, 'Study of Italian Plaquettes', pp. 19–35, p. 30.

82 Pope-Hennessy, 'Study of Italian Plaquettes', p. 30.

83 Maclagan, *Catalogue*, p. 75.

84 Pollard, 'Plaquette Collections', cat. 235–6.

85 Paul Grendler, 'What Zuanne Read at School: Vernacular Texts in Sixteenth-century Schools', *Sixteenth Century Journal*, XIII, I, 1982, pp. 41–54, p. 51.

86 'Un calamaro di ramo in forma de un busolo lavorato a la damschina': Gonzaga inventory 1483, p. 591.

87 Percival David, *Chinese Connoisseurship*, London 1971, p. 137.

88 'Un calamaro di ferro nel quale e posto dentro l'oro, lavorato alla ziminia'; 'con un sigillo legato a modo d'anello che imprime le pause, imprese di Madonna di bona memoria': Gonzaga 1549, p. 239.

89 Carmen Ravanelli Guidotti, 'Un singolare ritrovamento: Un piatto di servizio di Isabella d'Este Gonzaga', *Italian Renaissance Pottery*, ed. Timothy Wilson, London 1991, pp. 13–25, p. 15. Jörg Rasmussen, *The Robert Lehman Collection, X, Italian Maiolica*, New York 1989, cat. 66, pp. 246–51. Iain Fenlon, 'The Gonzaga and Music', *Splendours of the Gonzaga*, exhibition catalogue, ed. David Chambers and Jane Martineau, Victoria and Albert Museum, London 1982, p. 88. On Isabella's gown (*camora*) embroidered with *tempi e pause*, see Ronald Lightbown, *Mantegna*, Oxford 1986, p. 199.

90 Anthony Radcliffe, *The Robert H. Smith Collection: Bronzes, 1500–1650*, London 1994, cat. 4. Francis Haskell and Nicholas Penny, *Taste and the Antique*, New Haven and London 1981, pp. 308–10. Phyllis Pray Bober and Ruth Rubinstein, *Renaissance Artists and Antique Sculpture*, London 1986, cat. 203.

91 Ashmolean Museum, Oxford, 1888. CDEF.B1078, to be included in a forthcoming catalogue of the Fortnum Collection by Jeremy Warren.

92 Radcliffe, *Bronzes*, p. 34. I owe this reference to Jeremy Warren.

93 Elizabeth Pilliod, '"In tempore poenitentiae": Pierfrancesco Foschi's portrait of Cardinal Antonio Pucci', *Burlington Magazine*, CXXX, 1988, pp. 679–86, pp. 684–5, figs 8 and 15.

94 Radcliffe, *Bronzes*, p. 32, n. 4. Charles Avery, 'Giuseppe de Levis of Verona, Bronze Founder and Sculptor of the Late Sixteenth Century', *Studies in European Sculpture*, London 1981, pp. 53–70. Laura Camins, *Renaissance and Baroque Bronzes: Catalogue of the Abbott Guggenheim Collection in the San Francisco Museum*, San Francisco 1988, nos 2, 13 and 20.

95 Avery, 'Giuseppe de Levis'.

96 Camins, *Guggenheim Collection*, nos 13 and 20. Avery, 'Giuseppe de Levis', p. 66. Pope-Hennessy, 'Study of Italian Plaquettes', p. 31.

97 Pope-Hennessy, 'Study of Italian Plaquettes', p. 31.

98 Jennifer Montagu, *Roman Baroque Sculpture: The Industry of Art*, New Haven and London 1989, pp. 48–75 on the role of founders.

99 'Uno Calamaio quadro di rame con certi visi et centauri in su

100 'Una brancha di corallo con una cordellino d'ariento et parecchi spranghe': Pandolfini 1497. See Lightbown, *Mantegna*, p. 180, notes 30–31, and fig. XIV: *The Madonna della Vittoria*. On the coral trade, Geneviève Bresc-Bautier, *Artistes, patriciens et confreries, production et consommation de l'oeuvre d'art à Palerme et en Sicile occidentale, 1348–1460*, Ecole Française de Rome, 40, Rome 1979, pp. 116–17.

101 Nicholas Penny, *Catalogue of European Sculpture in the Ashmolean*, 3 vols, vol. I, Oxford 1992, cat. 230.

102 *Beschwörung des Kosmos*, ed. Brockhaus and Leinz, cats 86–8, 145–8.

103 Donald M. Bailey, *A Catalogue of the Lamps in the British Museum*, vol. 4, London 1994, Q3586 and pl. 16. I am very grateful to Don Bailey for discussing this lamp and others of its type with me.

104 Bologna, Museo Civico Medioevale, inv. 1473. I am grateful to Massimo Medica for kindly providing me with a photograph and for the information that this bronze probably derives from the Cospi collection.

105 The inkstand is described as 'Una lucerna cavata in un piede umano' in the Cospi inventory: I owe this reference to Massimo Medica. On the Cospi collection, see Laura Laurencich-Minelli, 'Museography and Ethnographical Collections in Bologna', *The Origins of Museums: The Cabinet of Curiosities in Sixteenth- and Seventeenth-century Europe*, ed. Oliver Impey and Arthur Macgregor, Oxford 1985, pp. 17–25, p. 22.

106 Fortunius Licetus, *De Lucernis antiquorum reconditis libbri sex*, Udine 1652, pl. VI cap. XIV, 667. Anthony Radcliffe, 'Bronze Lamps by Riccio', *Victoria and Albert Museum Yearbook*, III, 1972, pp. 29–58, p. 41.

107 Cecil Gould, *The Sixteenth-century Italian Schools: The National Gallery*, London 1975, cat. 299. Alessandro Bonvicino, Il Moretto, exhibition catalogue, Brescia 1988, cat. 72. P. Thornton, *Italian Renaissance Interior*, fig. 76.

108 Hugh Brigstocke, *Italian and Spanish Paintings in the National Gallery of Scotland*, Edinburgh 1993, cat. 2347. Mina Gregori, *I pittori bergamaschi: Giovanni Battista Moroni, tutte le opere*, Bergamo 1979, pp. 256–8.

109 *Natur und Antike*, ed. Beck and Bol, cat. 208.

110 Rosario Coppel Aréizaga, 'El collecionismo de pequenos bronces en Espana: Origen de la colleciòn del Museo arqueològico', *Archivio espanol de arte*, no. 264, 1993, pp. 373–92, p. 381. I am grateful to Jeremy Warren for this reference.

111 Malcolm Baker, 'Giambologna, Donatello and the Sale of the Gaddi, Marucelli and Stosch Bronzes', *Städel-Jahrbuch*, XII, 1989, pp. 179–94, pp. 185, 188, 190. Jeremy Warren kindly provided this reference.

112 Medieval and Later Antiquities, 1893, 6–14, 3; bought by Augustus Wollaston Franks from the collection of Fréderic Spitzer (*Catalogue des objets d'art et de haute curiosité antiques, du moyen-age, & de la Renaissance, composant l'importante et précieuse collection Spitzer*, sale of 17 April–16 June 1893, Paris, lot 661) and donated to the British Museum. The object will be fully catalogued by Timothy Wilson in his forthcoming *Catalogue of Post-classical Italian Pottery in the British Museum*.

113 The inscription incised on the sole has not been interpreted satisfactorily; it reads (in two lines of text) 'G F F 1569' and 'P I GIULIE. A SFORZA'. The first part is presumably a maker's inscription and the date of manufacture.

114 I am grateful to my colleague John Cherry for discussing this curious object with me.

115 Jeanne Giacomotti, *Catalogue des majoliques des musées nationaux*, Paris 1974, cats 1294–7.

116 Bailey, *Catalogue of Lamps*, vol. 2, London 1980, Q1136–8 for terracottas.

117 Letter from Girolamo Garimberto to Alessandro Farnese (details to come).

118 'Una testudine con una figura di sopra che serve per calamaro/Una figura con un calamaio sotto li piedi et con un bastone in mano': Gonzaga 1542.

119 'Uno sattiro de bronzo con venere legato a un albero/Una figura a cavallo de bronzo con un calamaio/Una figura de getto di bronzo': Usper 1601.

120 Usper 1601. See Bruce Boucher, *The Sculpture of Jacopo Sansovino*, New Haven and London 1991, p. 326.

121 'Un calamaio d'avorio/Uno di marmo/Uno di cristallo/Uno d'arcipresso': Minerbetti memoranda.

122 'Un calamaro di terracotta ed un uomo nudo sopra'; 'Un calamaro di mischio fatto a modo di sepoltura'; 'Un altro [calamaro] con un cavallo sopra': Caro 1578.

123 Sabba, *Ricordi*, p. 78.

124 'Uno calamaio a uso di chassetta quadro intarsiata all Napoletana usato di 1/2 braccia': Martelli n.d.

125 'Un calamaio a modo di libro': Buondelmonti 1563 and Correggaio 1560.

126 Giovanni Battista Giudicini, *Cose notabili della città di Bologna*, Bologna 1868, p. 462. I am grateful to Jeremy Warren for this reference.

127 Michael Baxandall, *Giotto and the Orators*, pp. 91 and 157–8. I am grateful to Michael Baxandall for this reference.

128 Baxandall, *Giotto and the Orators*, pp. 157–8.

129 Wendy M. Watson, *Italian Renaissance Maiolica from the William A. Clark Collection*, London 1986, p. 38 and pl. 3. Also Julia Poole, *Italian Maiolica and Incised Slipware in the Fitzwilliam Museum, Cambridge*, Cambridge 1996, cat. 325, p. 244 for the latest summary of research on Acole and his ceramic sculpture.

130 Timothy Wilson, *Ceramic Art of the Italian Renaissance*, exhibition catalogue, British Museum, London 1987, cat. 83.

131 Watson, *Italian Renaissance Maiolica*, p. 38.

132 'Uno callamaro grande cum uno Sancto Giorzo'; 'un callamaro cum una fontana cum diverse figure et uno altro quadro tutti di terra vedrati cum colluri': Frate Francheschino da Cesena 1489.

133 Pomponius Gauricus, *De sculptura* (c. 1504), ed. A. Chastel and R. Klein, Geneva 1969, p. 60.

134 Gould, *Sixteenth-century Italian Schools*, cat. 699. Francesca Cortesi Bosco, 'Il ritratto di Niccolò della Torre disegnato da Lorenzo Lotto', *Lorenzo Lotto* (Atti del Convegno Internazionale di Studi per il Centenario della Nascità), ed. Pietro Zampetti and Vittorio Sgarbi, Asolo 1980, pp. 313–24. I am grateful to Jeremy Warren for this reference.

135 'Uno calamaio di terra d'Urbino fatto a cassetta, in 7 pezzi'. See Marco Spallanzani, 'Maioliche di Urbino nelle collezioni di Cosimo I, del Cardinale Ferdinando e di Francesco I de'Medici', *Faenza*, LXV, 1979, pp. 111–26, pp. 122 and 119. Julia E. Poole, *Italian Maiolica*, cat. 435 and n. 1.

136 *L'istoriato, libri a stampa e maioliche italiane del cinquecento*, exhibition catalogue, Biblioteca Apostolica Vaticana, Rome 1993, cat. 51. I am grateful to Carmen Ravanelli Guidotti, and to Giorgio Assirelli, for information and the gift of photographs of this object.

137 *L'istoriato*, cat. 51.

138 Carmen Ravanelli Guidotti, *Ceramiche occidentali del Museo Civico Medievale di Bologna*, Bologna 1985, cat. 171.

139 *Lettere di un notaio ad un mercante*, ed. C. Guasti, Florence 1880, 2 vols, vol. I, p. 169. P. Thornton, *Italian Renaissance Interior*, p. 236.

140 Letter of 20 August 1391, *Lettere*, ed. Guasti, vol. I, p. 14. Iris Origo, *The Merchant of Prato*, London 1984, p. 233.

141 Gibbs, *Tomaso da Modena*, p. 85, n. 180.

142 Gibbs, *Tomaso da Modena*, p. 352 and pl. 38.

143 G. F. Hill, *A Corpus of Italian Medals of the Renaissance before Cellini*, 2 vols, London 1930, vol. I, no. 608. *Beschwörung des Kosmos*, ed. Brockhaus and Leinz, cat. 192.

144 I am grateful to Andrew Burnett and Luke Syson for their comments and translation of this Latin inscription.

145 Palatino, *Libro*, HIIII.

146 P. Thornton, *Italian Renaissance Interior*, p. 234 on inventory references, and p. 241 on mirrors in general.

147 P. Thornton, *Italian Renaissance Interior*, p. 237.

148 *Venice: A Documentary History*, ed. D. Chambers and B. Pullan, Oxford 1992, pp. 281–5, pp. 284–5, doc. 9. For the correct interpretation of this document, see Ingeborg Krueger, 'Glasspiegel im Mittelalter, Fakten, Funde und Fragen', *Bonner Jahrbucher des Rheinisches Landesmuseums in Bonn*, CXC, 1990, pp. 232–319, p. 259.

149 P. Thornton, *Italian Renaissance Interior*, p. 235.

150 Pietro della Valle (1586–1652) travelled between 1614 and 1626: his letters recording his experiences were published in sections, some during his lifetime, others by his four sons after his death. See W. Blunt, *Pietro's Pilgrimage*, London 1953, pp. 135–6.

151 *Canti carnivaleschi del Rinascimento*, ed. Charles Singleton, Bari 1936, p. 407.

152 Brown and Lorenzoni, *Isabella and Lorenzo*, doc. 49, p. 240.

153 'Il maestro che ha lustrato lo specchio dice non haverlo potuto fare ben netto per essere d'una mixtura molto trista': Brown and Lorenzoni, *Isabella and Lorenzo*, p. 241, n. 8.

154 Leonardo Fioravanti, *Dello specchio di scientia universale libri tre*, Venice 1564, p. 56.

155 Brown and Lorenzoni, *Isabella and Lorenzo*, pp. 240–42 for commentary and references to relevant documents.

156 R. Predelli, 'Le memorie e le carte di Alessandro Vittoria', *Archivio trentino*, XXIII, 1908, p. 130. *Kunsthistorisches Museum: Katalog der Gemäldegalerie*, vol. I, Vienna 1965, cat. 609.

157 Zecchin, *Vetro e vetrai*, vol. I, p. 46.

158 P. Thornton, *Italian Renaissance Interrior*, p. 236 and pl. 148.

159 Laura Gelfand, 'Girolamo Savoldo in the Cleveland Museum of Art: A Question of Mistaken Identities', *Apollo*, CXLI, 1995, pp. 14–19, pp. 16–17, n. 14 and fig. 4.

160 C. Gilbert, *The Works of Girolamo Savoldo: The 1955 Dissertation, with a Review of Research, 1955–85*, New York 1986, pp. 545–6 for identification of the sitter as Savoldo, upheld by Gelfand, 'Savoldo', but challenged in *Siècle de Titien*, exhibition catalogue, ed. Laclotte and Giovanni Nepi Scirè, Paris 1993, cat. 74, p. 452.

161 *Giovanni Gerolamo Savoldo, tra Foppa, Giorgione e Caravaggio*, exhibition catalogue, eds. Bruno Passamani and Creighton Gilbert, Milan 1990, cat. 1 26.

162 Sabba, *Ricordi*, p. 75.

163 Chambers, *Renaissance Cardinal*, p. 78, n. 221.

164 'Uno specchio quadro de azale ligato in ariento dorato cum otto camei, e col reverso de ariento cum l'arma aniellata': Gonzaga will 1483, p. 567.

165 Chambers, *Renaissance Cardinal*, p. 119, n. 123.

166 Brown and Lorenzoni, *Isabella and Lorenzo*, p. 240 and docs. 102, 114–22.

167 Brown and Lorenzoni, *Isabella and Lorenzo*, p. 240, doc. 102.

168 Brown and Lorenzoni, *Isabella and Lorenzo*, doc. 114.

169 Brown and Lorenzoni, *Isabella and Lorenzo*, doc. 116.

170 Brown and Lorenzoni, *Isabella and Lorenzo*, doc. 121 and p. 240.

171 P. Thornton, *Italian Renaissance Interior*, p. 236. John Kent

Lydecker, *The Domestic Setting of the Arts in Renaissance Florence*, PhD thesis: Johns Hopkins University, Baltimore 1987, Ann Arbor Microfilms 1987, pp. 119–21.

172 Will of Camilla Malipiero, 14 December 1538. E. A. Cicogna, *Delle inscrizione venetiane*, vol. 3, Venice 1830, p. 419.

173 'Un ritratto piccolo di donna di mano di Titiano in forma di specchio': Vittoria memoranda.

174 'A foggia di specchio': Michiel 1595 and Michiel 1601.

175 P. Thornton, *Italian Renaissance Interior*, p. 241, and pp. 239–41 on *restelli*.

176 For the mirror as an emblem of conscience, see *Renaissance Painting in Manuscripts: Treasures from the British Library*, ed. Thomas Kren, New York 1983, cat. 7, fig. 7b and p. 61. James Marrow, '"In diesen Spiegell": A New Form of Memento Mori in Fifteenth-century Netherlandish Art', *Essays in Northern European Art Presented to Egbert Haverkamp-Begemann on his Sixtieth Birthday*, ed. Anne-Marie Logan, Doornspijk 1983, pp. 154–63, p. 158.

177 Susan Haskins, *Mary Magdalen: Myth and Metaphor*, London 1993, pp. 257–8 and fig. 53.

178 Sabba, *Ricordi*, p. 60.

179 Florio, *New World of Words*.

180 Sabba, *Ricordi*, pp. 90–91.

181 Fioravanti, *Dello specchio*, p. 55.

182 Sabba, *Ricordi*, p. 60.

183 Quoted in Hale, *Civilisation*, p. 435.

184 Quoted in Peter Burke, *The Italian Renaissance: Culture and Society in Italy*, Cambridge 1986, p. 196.

185 *Canti carnivaleschi*, ed. Singleton, p. 407.

Conclusion

1 Richard Goldthwaite, *Wealth and the Demand for Art in Italy, 1300–1600*, Baltimore and London 1993, p. 238.

2 Peter Thornton, *The Italian Renaissance Interior, 1400–1600*, London 1991, p. 13, caption to fig. 4.

3 Goldthwaite, *Wealth and the Demand for Art*, p. 232.

4 On *ritratti in piedi* in merchants' *portegi*, see Isabella Palumbo Fossati, 'L'interno della casa dell'artista e dell'artigiano nella Venezia del cinquecento', *Studi veneziani*, VII, 1984, p. 145, n. 65 for references to three inventories. Vasari noted in his life of Titian that the works of Bassano are dispersed throughout Venice, and are valued highly, especially those of 'cose piccole, ed animali di tutte le sorti' (*Le opere di Giorgio Vasari*, ed. Gaetano Milanesi, 10 vols, 1878–85, reprinted Florence 1981, vol. VII, p. 455). Scenes of this kind are frequently listed *in tinello* or *in portego* in Venetian inventories.

5 On *restelli*, see P. Thornton, *Italian Renaissance Interior*, p. 269.

6 Goldthwaite, *Wealth and the Demand for Art*, p. 242.

7 'Isabella d'Este, Patron and Collector', *Splendours of the Gonzaga*, exhibition catalogue, ed. David Chambers and Jane Martineau, Victoria and Albert Museum, London 1982, pp. 51–64, p. 61; P. Thornton, *Italian Renaissance Interior*, pp. 16–17.

8 On the way in which Vasari's additions to the second edition of the *Vite* (1568) were informed by his own experience as architect to the Medici in the 1560s, see Patricia Rubin, *Giorgio Vasari: Art and History*, New Haven and London 1995, pp. 211–12. John Hale, *The Civilisation of Europe in the Renaissance*, London 1993, p. 587, citing P. Thornton, *Italian Renaissance Interior*, p. 392, col. 2, n. 15.

9 P. Thornton, *Italian Renaissance Interior*, p. 13.

10 *The Essays of Montaigne*, trans. Michael Screech, London 1991, p. 270.

11 I am grateful to Nicholas Cooper of the Royal Commission on the Historical Monuments of England for sending me draft chapters of his forthcoming book on English gentry houses, in which he shows how studies were increasingly common from the mid-sixteenth century onwards, a development which he associates with 'the enjoyment of privacy as a good'.

12 Simon Jervis, '*Les Blasons domestiques* by Gilles Corrozet', *Furniture History*, XXV, 1989, pp. 5–35, pp. 5–6.

Concordance of Inventories and Memoranda

The following list is arranged in alphabetical order of the short form of the inventories, account books and memoranda cited in this book. Where the profession, title or status of a given individual is provided in the inventory's preamble, or elsewhere, this is recorded. When a room is named as a study in an inventory, the word used to denote it is given here. References to secondary sources are included where appropriate. Such references are to published works only, and have been selected to guide the reader of Italian Renaissance inventories.

Abbreviations

The archival abbreviations have been used in the Concordance and the Notes; those for secondary sources apply to the Concordance only.

ARCHIVAL

A.S.: Archivio di Stato (State Archive, usually followed by the name of the relevant town; see also A.S.F. and A.S.V.)

A.S.F.: Archivio di Stato di Firenze (Florence)

A.S.V.: Archivio di Stato di Venezia (Venice)

B.: Busta (volume)

cod.: codice

M.D.P.: Magistrato de' Pupilli (Office of Wards)

P.A.P.: Pupilli avanti il Principato (before 1531)

P.D.P.: Pupilli del Principato (after 1531)

reg.: registro (register of notarial acts)

SECONDARY SOURCES

BM: Burlington Magazine

De Benedictis 1995: Cristina De Benedictis, *Per la storia del collezionismo italiano*, Florence 1995

Favaretto 1990: Irene Favaretto, *Arte antica e cultura antiquaria nelle collezioni venete al tempo della Serenissima*, Rome 1990

DBI: Dizionario biografico degli italiani, 45 vols (to 1995), Rome 1960–

JWCI: Journal of the Warburg and Courtauld Institutes

Levi 1900: Cesare Augusto Levi, *Le collezioni veneziane d'arte e d'antichità dal secolo XIV ai nostri giorni*, Venice 1900

Liebenwein 1977: Wolfgang Liebenwein, *Lo Studiolo: Die Entstehung eines Raumtyps und seine Entwicklung bis um 1600*, Berlin 1977

Lydecker thesis: John Kent Lydecker, *The Domestic Setting of the Arts in Renaissance Florence*, PhD thesis, Johns Hopkins University, Baltimore 1987, Ann Arbor Microfilms, 1987

Lydecker 1987: John Kent Lydecker, 'Il patriziato fiorentino e la committenza artistica per la casa', *I ceti dirigenti nella Toscana del quattrocento*, Impruneta 1987, pp. 209–21

Palumbo Fossati 1984: Isabella Palumbo Fossati, 'L'interno della casa dell'artista e dell'artigiano nella Venezia del cinquecento', *Studi veneziani*, VII, 1984, pp. 109–53

Palumbo Fossati 1985: Isabella Palumbo Fossati, 'Livres et lecteurs dans la Venise du XVIe siècle', *Revue française d'histoire du livre*, XLVI, 1985, pp. 481–513

Spallanzani 1978: Marco Spallanzani, *Ceramiche orientali a Firenze nel Rinascimento*, Florence 1978

Thornton 1991: Peter Thornton, *The Italian Renaissance Interior, 1400–1600*, London 1991

Weiss 1969: Roberto Weiss, *The Renaissance Discovery of Classical Antiquity*, Oxford 1969

Adiaceto 1573
Inventory of the estate of Tomaso di Adiaceto, 19 February 1573. A.S.F., M.D.P., P.D.P., B.2710. Consists of an unbroken list, without naming rooms: includes a fascinating shelf-ful of objects including Della Robbia products, for which see Jeremy Warren, 'Fortnum and the Della Robbia', *Apollo*, CXLV, 1997, pp. 55–7, p. 57.

Alatino 1620
Inventory of Vital Alatino, 16 April 1620, Venice. Guidici di Petizion, B.347/2. Ferrarese Jewish doctor of medicine. Inventory of his house in the Ghetto Nuovo in Venice includes a *studietto* with medical texts and surgical instruments.

Amulio 1590
Inventory of the estate of Hortensis Amulio, 11 March 1590. A.S.V., Cancelleria Inferiore, B.43. His name is apparently a form of Da Mula, that of a Venetian patrician family.

Balbiano 1584
Inventory of the estate of *magistri domini* Joannis Balbiano, 28 January 1584. A.S.V., Cancelleria Inferiore, notary Luca Gabrieli, B.43. Lists contents of writing-desk/cabinet (*scrigno*) in a bedchamber.

Bambelli 1573

Inventory of the estate of Antonio di Bartolomeo Bambelli, *cittadino fiorentino*, 18 September 1573. A.S.F., M.D.P., P.D.P., B.2710. Richly furnished house with many paintings.

Barbaro will 1570

Will of Daniele Matteo Alvise Barbaro, 9 April 1570. A.S.V., Atti Testamenti Vettor Maffei, B.657, n. 270. Barbaro (1514–70), a Venetian patrician, art patron and man of letters, was Patriarch elect of Aquileia, but is best known as a scholar and for his commentary on Vitruvius (published in 1567) and his treatise on perspective (1569). His will includes references to astronomical instruments 'both bought and made at home' (*comprati et fatti in casa*) and a bequest to his architect, Andrea Palladio. For text of the will and commentary, see Bruce Boucher, 'The Last Will of Daniele Barbaro', *JWCI*, XLII, 1979, pp. 277–82. See also *DBI*, vol. 6, Rome 1964, pp. 89–95.

Barzizza 1444

Inventory of the estate of Cristoforo Barzizza, 17 September 1444. A. S. Padua, Archivio Notarile, Liber Extens. Andree de Buvolento, *c*.834. Barzizza (*c*.1400–44), a native of Bergamo, became doctor of medicine and citizen of Padua in 1421 and taught there as professor from 1431 to 1444. He wrote orations and books on the practice of medicine. For his inventory, see R. Cessi, 'Cristoforo Barzizza, medico del secolo XV', *Bollettino della Civica biblioteca di Bergamo*, III, 1909, pp. 3–13, which lists the contents of his *studio*. For comments on his library, see P. Sambin, 'Cristoforo Barzizza ed i suoi libri', *Bollettino del Museo civico di Padova*, XLIV, 1955, pp. 145–64, and Thornton 1991, p. 164. See also *DBI*, vol. 7, Rome 1965, pp. 32–4.

Battaghini 1572

Inventory of the estate of Maestro Baptista di Rafaello Battaghini di Firenze, 1 September 1572. A.S.F., M.D.P., P.D.P., B.2709.

Bembo will 1544

Will of Cardinal Pietro Bembo, 1544, Biblioteca Correr, Venice, Codice Cicogna 3115/XL, *Testamenti due di Pietro Bembo, copiati [. . .] dall'ab. Jacopo Morelli*. Cardinal Bembo (1470–1547) was a famous poet, theorist on language and literature. For his will see Favaretto 1990, p. 103, n. 213. See also *DBI*, vol. 8, Rome 1966, pp. 133–51.

Benavides 1695

Inventory compiled by Andrea Mantova Benavides, a descendant of Marco Mantova Benavides (1489–1582), Biblioteca Communale di Padova, MS BP 5018. Lists household antiquities in the Casa Benavides, Padua. See A. Favaretto, *Andrea Mantova Benavides: Inventario delle antichità di Casa Benavides*, Padua 1978, and Favaretto 1990, pp. 108–15.

Berti 1594

Inventory of the estate of Domenico Berti, 18 July 1594. A.S.F., M.D.P., P.D.P., B.2714. Opens *Nello scrittoio da basso* and continues to list the contents of his richly furnished house.

Bianchini 1510

Inventory of the estate of Bartolomeo Bianchini, 20 March 1510. A. S. Bologna, Archivio Notarile, Rogito di Battista de Buoi, 2 May 1510. Bianchini [Blanchinus] was a Bolognese nobleman and humanist. The Bolognese Baptismal Registers for 1470–82 (ed. B. Caratti, Bologna, Biblioteca Communale, MS B.850 fol. 17), record his date of birth as 12 August 1471: I am grateful to Dottoressa Stagni for this reference, which she discovered in the course of preparing a forthcoming catalogue raisonné on Francesca Francia. He was renowned by contemporaries for his learning, looks, discernment in artistic and antiquarian matters, and for his friendship with artists: his *studio* testifies to his friendship with Francia. See L. Sighinolfi, 'Note biografici intorno a Francesco Francia', *Atti e memorie della Reale deputazione di storia patria per le Romagne*, 4th series, VI, 1916, pp. 1–21, and *DBI*, vol. 10, Rome 1968, pp. 182–3. See also Claudio Franzoni, 'Le raccolte del Theatro di Ombruno e il viaggio in oriente del pittore: Le *Epistole* di Giovanni Filoteo Achillini', *Rivista di letteratura italiana*, VIII, 2, 1990, pp. 287–335, pp. 299–300.

Borghetti 1594

Inventory of the estate of Alessandro Borghetti, 27 June 1594. A.S.V., atti G. A. Catti, reg. 3365.

Brazzo 1587

Inventory of the estate of Andrea da Brazzo, 1 June 1587. A.S.V., Giudici di Petizion, notary A. Nodaro, B.339/4. Includes entry for the *studio over contor in mezzo la scala*. See Levi 1900, p. LXV.

Buizzi 1594

Inventory of the estate of Giovan Francesco Buizzi, 3 June 1594. A.S.F., M.D.P., P.D.P., B.2714. A *scrittoio a mezza scala* is included in the inventory of the contents of his principal, richly furnished house, and a second study in his house in the *populo* of San Michele.

Buonaguisi 1462

Inventory of the estate of Piero di Cristoforo Buonaguisi. A.S.F., P.A.P., n. 80. See Spallanzani 1978, doc. 21.

Buondelmonti 1563

Inventory of the estate of Giovanbattista di Hypolito di Manese Buondelmonti, 8 February 1563. A.S.F., M.D.P., P.D.P., B.2708. Includes entry for the *scrittoio in camera grande*; his villa in the Valdarno also had one.

Calderini 1597

Inventory of the estate of Zuanfrancesco (Gianfrancesco) Calderini, 10 December 1597. A.S.V., atti G. Bianchini, reg. 492. Entry for furnishings *Nella camera che soleva habitar*, which includes *un scrittor dorado*, while a second cabinet is listed in another chamber. The inventory lists the contents of the richly furnished house of a wealthy Venetian merchant. See Palumbo Fossati 1984, pp. 109–53, p. 145, n. 65, p. 127, n. 38, p. 110, n. 4; and Palumbo Fossati 1985, pp. 481–513, p. 501, n. 28.

Calomelli 1556
Inventory of the workshop contents of Virgiliotto Calomelli, 17 December 1556. A. S. Faenza, Atti di Matteo Tomba, volume for 1556, II, fol. 15r–20v. Calomelli was a master potter of Faenza: the inventory includes many categories of ware, such as maiolica inkstands from the crude to the sculptural. See C. Grigioni, 'Documenti serie faentina: I Calomelli, maiolicari di Faenza', *Faenza*, XXII, 1934, pp. 143–153, and Timothy Wilson, *Ceramic Art of the Italian Renaissance*, exhibition catalogue, British Museum, London 1987, p. 149.

Calpurnio 1503
Inventory of the estate of Giovanni Calpurnio [Calfurnio; Calpurnius], 17 January 1503. A. S. Padua, Archivio Notarile, Abbrev. di Ambrogio da Ruina, LVIII, c.431. He was reader in rhetoric in the University of Padua from 1486 to his death. His inventory lists books and furnishings in chests in his academic bedsit. He left books to San Giovanni di Verdara, Padua: 229 volumes came to them in 1503, Greek and Latin manuscripts and incunabula, on which see Paolo Sambin, 'La formazione quattrocentesca della biblioteca di San Giovanni di Verdara in Padova', *Atti del Istituto veneto di scienze, lettere ed arti, 1955–56*, CXIV, 1959, pp. 262–80. On his tomb monument, see Volker Krahn, *Bartolomeo Bellano: Studien zur Paduaner Plastik des Quattrocento*, Munich 1986, fig. 97 and p. 201. See Vittorio Cian, 'Un umanista bergamasco, Giovanni Calfurnio', *Archivio storico lombardo*, XIV, 1910, pp. 236–48.

Caro 1578
Inventory of the estate of Annibale Caro, 8 November 1578, Biblioteca Apostolica Vaticana, Fondo Ferraiuoli 752. Caro (1507–66) was a poet, translator, courtier and critic. The inventory was compiled in the interests of his nephew, Fabio Caro. It is transcribed in Aulo Greco, *Annibale Caro*, Rome 1950, pp. 122–35: for the study in the family house in Civitanova Marche, see pp. 123–34 (with inaccuracies, misreadings and omissions; does not include the inventory of ancient coins, which was compiled a day before the rest). For Caro and his inventory, see Clare Robertson, *'Il Gran Cardinale', Alessandro Farnese: Patron of the Arts*, New Haven and London 1992, pp. 215–19, and Thornton 1991, p. 233. See also *DBI*, vol. 21, Rome 1977, pp. 497–508.

Castellani memoranda
Memoranda of Francesco di Matteo Castellani, A.S.F., Corporazioni religiose soppresse dal governo francese 90, convento di Santa Verdiana, 84. These are edited by Giovanni Chiapelli as *Ricordanze: Il Quaternuccio e giornale B (1459–1485)*, Florence 1995. For Castellani's biography, including the relations between his family and the Medici, see pp. 8–32.

Cecchi 1596
Inventory of the estate of Giovanni di Benedetto Cecchi da Pescia, 20 March 1596. A.S.F., M.D.P., P.D.P., B.2714. Starts in the *sala*, proceeds to *anticamera* containing books, arms, medals and coins.

Cellini 1570
Inventory of the estate of Benvenuto Cellini, 16 February 1570. A.S.F., M.D.P., P.D.P., B.2710. For the inventory see the following studies of Cellini as goldsmith, sculptor and autobiographer: C. Avery and S. Barbaglia, *L'opera completa del Cellini*, Milan 1981, p. 86; and John Pope-Hennessy, *Cellini*, London 1985, pp. 283–4, n. 36.

Chellini memoranda
Memoranda of Giovanni Chellini di San Miniato, Libro G, Archivio Saminiati, Istituto de Storia Economica dell'Università L. Bocconi, Milan. Chellini (1372/3–1461) was a doctor of medicine, prominent Florentine figure and art patron. He is perhaps best known for having received a bronze relief roundel (now in the Victoria and Albert Museum, London) from one of his patients, the sculptor Donatello, in payment for treatment. His memoranda are published complete, edited by Maria Teresa Sillano as *Le ricordanze di Giovanni Chellini da San Miniato*, Milan 1984; on the roundel, see p. 218, and Ronald Lightbown, 'Giovanni Chellini, Donatello and Antonio Rosellino', *BM*, CIV, 1962, pp. 102–4, p. 103. See also *DBI*, vol. 24, Rome 1980, pp. 417–18.

Chiaro 1424
Inventory of the estate of Giovanni del Chiaro, *orefice* (goldsmith), 1424. A.S.F., P.A.P., n. 41 c200v. The section of the inventory listing the contents of his study (*studio*) is published by Spallanzani 1978, doc. 13.

Chigi 1497
Inventory of silver in the possession of Agostino Chigi, 8 November 1497. Chigi (1465/6–1520) was a Sienese noble and papal banker, famous for his patronage of Raphael and for his Roman villa (later purchased by the Farnese and hence known as the Villa Farnesina). For the inventory, see G. Cugnoni, *Agostino Chigi*, Rome 1878, p. 118. See also *DBI*, vol. 24, Rome 1986, pp. 735–43.

Ciampoli 1564
Inventory of the estate of Chimeti di Francesco Ciampoli, 3 October 1564. A.S.F., M.D.P., P.D.P., B.2708. Lists contents of his *scrittoio*.

Colombe 1561
Inventory of the estate of Giovannini di Corso dalle Colombe, 23 April 1561. A.S.F., M.D.P., P.D.P., B.2708. Includes entry *Nello scriptoio della camera principale*, with jewellery, silver cutlery, maiolica and glass, books and *scritture*.

J. Contareno 1596
Will of Jacopo Contareno, 1 July 1596. Contareno was a Venetian patrician and collector: his will mentions the contents of his collection (*studio*). See G. Valentinelli, *Marmi scolpiti del Museo archeologico della Marciana di Venezia*, Prato 1866, pp. XVII–XVIII; M. Perry, 'The Statuario Pubblico of the Venetian Republic', *Saggi e memorie di storia dell'arte*, XIII, 1972, pp. 77–253, p. 96; Favaretto 1990, p. 167, n. 167; and De Benedictis 1995, pp. 228–9.

B. Contareno 1606

Inventory of the estate of Baldassare Contareno, 19 August 1606. A.S.V., Giudici di Petizion, B.343/8. Two of his paintings were glazed, as recorded in two rare references to a practice which may more commonly have escaped the notice of assessors: *Un quadretto con ritratto del sopra detto Illustrissimo Signore Baldissera coperto di vetro* and *Un ritratto della Madonna in un quadretto d'ebbano coperto di vetro*.

Cornaro 1597

Inventory of the estate of *clarissimo signore* Francesco Cornaro, 13 July 1597. A.S.V., Giudici di Petizion, B.344/9. Includes entry *in studio*. Cornaro is a variant spelling of Corner, a Venetian patrician family.

Correggaio 1560

Inventory of the estate of Francesco di Giorgio Correggaio, 3 February 1560. A.S.F., M.D.P., P.D.P., B.2708.

Donà 1587

Inventory of the estate of *clarissimo maestro* Zuansymon Donà, 3 February 1587. A.S.V., Cancelleria Inferiore, B.43. The Donà [Donado/Donati] are a Venetian patrician family: the collection of patrician portraits in this inventory demonstrate this individual's social standing.

Duodo 1586

Inventory of the estate of Francesco Duodo, 2 April 1586. Notary J. Figolini. A.S.V., Cancelleria Inferiore, B.43. His *studio* was in a corner of his bedchamber.

Fabbri 1616

Inventory of the estate of Ottavio Fabbri, 2 May 1616. A.S.V., Giudici di Petizion, B.345/10. Fabbri was a mathematician and a man of practical interests beyond his concerns as a Turkey merchant: he is named as an interlocutor in a dialogue written by Marcantonio Cornaro on the necessity of preserving the Venetian Lagoon for shipping; see E.A. Cicogna, *Delle inscrizioni veneziane*, vol. 6, Venice 1853, p. 569. For a description of Fabbri's *studio*, which was particularly rich in scientific instruments, see Levi 1900, pp. LXVI–LXVII; this quotes Francesco Sansovino (ed. Giovanni Stringa), *Venetia*, Venice 1604.

Fancielli 1592

Inventory of the estate of Antonio Fancielli, 28 August 1592. A.S.F., M.D.P., P.D.P., B.2713. One unbroken list, including medals, working drawings, models and sculptors' tools such as a set square, compasses and chisels.

Fece 1450

Inventory of the estate of Giovanni di Pietro di Fece, 28 February 1450. A.S. Siena, Archivio Notarile, K=DCCCIII. Includes a *studio*. For contents of the *studio* next to the principal bedchamber, which indicate the offices which he had held in his native city of Siena, see Curzio Mazzi, 'Una casa senese nel 1450', *Bollettino senese di storia patria*, XVIII, 1911, pp. 151–72, pp. 164–6. See also Thornton 1991, pp. 106, 303.

Fiesso 1484

Inventory of the estate of Francisco de Fiesso, 1 April 1484. A. Franceschini, *Inventari inediti di biblioteche ferraresi private del secolo XV*, Ferrara 1982, p. 130, lists contents of his *studio*.

Fiorentino 1585

Inventory of the estate of Lorenzo Domino Fiorentino, 29 October 1585. A.S.V., Giudici di Petizion, B.339/4 no. 22. Lists the goods in this jeweller's *bottega*.

Fontana 1583

Inventory of the estate of Antoniomaria Fontana, *zoieliero*, 7 March 1583. A.S.V., atti A. Brinis, reg. 460, fol. 53r. Inventory lists contents of his house and also of his workshop at Rialto. See Palumbo Fossati 1984, pp. 109–53, p. 127, n. 38, p. 129, n. 42.

Formenti 1611

Inventory of the estate of Clarissimo Signor Michiel Formenti, [illegible] August 1611. A.S.V., Giudici di Petizion, B.345/10.

Foscho 1582

Inventory of the estate of Andrea di Foscho, *intagliatore* (woodcarver), 24 April 1582. A.S.V., Cancelleria Inferiore, B.42. Notary F. Alcaini. For his career and inventory, see Palumbo Fossati 1984, pp. 109–53, pp. 118–37, and Palumbo Fossati 1985, pp. 481–513, p. 483, n. 5; on his architectural books, see Palumbo Fossati 1985, p. 493, n. 18.

Franceschi 1580

Inventory of the estate of Niccolo de' Franceschi, merchant, 26 June 1580. A.S.V., Cancelleria Inferiore, B.42. He owned a large collection of portraits of contemporary rulers, including two Holy Roman Emperors. See Palumbo Fossati 1984, pp. 109–53, p. 145, n. 65.

Frate Franceschino da Cesena 1489

Inventory of the contents of his *studio* and bedchamber, Cesena, 20 August 1489. A.S. Cesena, Archivio Notarile Mandamentale, Atti di novello Borelli, register for 1489. Frate Franceschino was the second librarian of the Malatestiana Library: on his appointment as custodian of the library, see A. Domeniconi, 'I custodi della Biblioteca Malatestiana in Cesena', *Studi romagnoli*, XIV, 1963, pp. 385–95, pp. 389–91. The inventory was published by Domeniconi, 'Un inventario relativo ad un custode della Biblioteca Malatestiana, Frate Franceschino da Cesena', *Studi romagnoli*, XVI, 1965, pp. 171–89 (some misreadings and errors in order of items listed). There is a typescript in the Warburg Library, London, of the inventory as prepared for publication by Domeniconi, sent to Roberto Weiss for his comments. For a few comments on ancient coins in the inventory, see Weiss 1969, p. 171, n. 1. See also Claudio Franzoni, 'Le collezioni rinascimentali di antichità', *Memorie dell'antico nell'arte italiana*, ed. Salvatore Settis, vol. 1, Turin 1984, pp. 297–360, pp. 310–11 and n. 310; Franzoni, 'Le raccolte del Theatro di Ombruno e il viaggio in oriente del pittore: Le *Epistole* di Giovanni Filoteo Achillini', *Rivista di letteratura italiana*, VIII, 2, 1990, pp. 287–335, p. 295. Thornton 1991, pp. 237, 273–9.

Fregoso 1426
Inventory of books belonging to Tomaso di Campo Fregoso, bound in with Latin manuscript, Bibliothèque Nationale, Paris, MS latin 5690, fol. 367, entitled 'inventarium eorum librorum qui inventi sunt in pulcherrimo studiolo'. Liebenwein 1977, p. 57.

Gianfigliazzi 1597
Inventory of the estate of Maestro Giovanbattista Gianfigliazzi, 5 August 1597. A.S.F., M.D.P., P.D.P., B.2715. Includes items *Nello scrittoio*.

Giocondi memoranda
Memoranda book (*Libro di debitori e creditori*) of Zanobi di Giovangualberto de'Giocondi. Archivio dell'Ospedale degli Innocenti, Florence, serie CLIV, 409, fol. 69. The memoranda include a section of expenses on his bedchamber and study (*Spese di chamera e schrittoio di Zanobi Giochondi*). See Lydecker 1987, pp. 209–21, pp. 218–19, notes 51–6. I am grateful to Kent Lydecker for drawing my attention to this manuscript, and to Dottoressa Maria Bortolotto for making it available to me with great courtesy and speed.

Giustinian 1587
Inventory of the estate of Leonardo Giustinian, 22 May 1587. A.S.V., Giudici di Petizion, B.339/4. He was a member of a famous Venetian patrician family.

Gondi 1578
Inventory of the estate of Alfonso di Simone Gondi, 26 September 1578. A.S.F., M.D.P., P.D.P., B.2712. Lists contents of his *scrittoio* in the Palazzo Gondi, which was heated by a portable brazier (*una cassettina da tenere fuoco*).

Gonzaga will 1483
The will of Cardinal Francesco Gonzaga, dated 20 October 1483. Published and edited by David Chambers in *A Renaissance Cardinal and his Worldly Goods: The Will and Inventory of Francesco Gonzaga, 1444–1483*, London 1992, pp. 132–41.

Gonzaga inventory 1483
Inventory of movables belonging to Cardinal Francesco Gonzaga (see above), 27 October 1483. Published and edited by Chambers, *Renaissance Cardinal*, pp. 141–88, followed by related correspondence, and prefaced by four introductory chapters on Gonzaga, his biography, career and the fate of his possessions after his death.

Gonzaga 1542
Inventory of Isabella's Grotta and Studiolo, compiled by the notary Odoardo Stivini three years after Isabella's death. Isabella d'Este (1474–1539) was one of the most gifted aristocratic women of her time. On her marriage to Francesco Gonzaga, Marquis of Mantua, in 1490, she dedicated her energies to building up a remarkable art and antiquities collection, which was carefully displayed in her apartments in the Castello di San Giorgio and the Corte Vecchia in Mantua. C. M. Brown published the entries in the inventory for the Grotta and Studiolo in *La Grotta*

di Isabella d'Este, Mantua 1985. A German translation of this section of the inventory has also been published by S. Ferino Pagden, 'La Prima Donna del Mondo', *Isabella d'Este Fürstin und Mäzenatin der Renaissance*, Vienna 1994, pp. 266–88. On the various copies of the inventory, see *Splendours of the Gonzaga*, exhibition catalogue, ed. David Chambers and Jane Martineau, Victoria and Albert Museum, London 1982, p. 168, cat. 118. For the inventory of jewellery which precedes that of the Grotta, see Daniela Ferrari, 'L'inventario delle Gioie', *Isabella d'Este: I luoghi del collezionismo*, Mantua 1995, pp. 11–15. Ferrari publishes the complete inventory as regards the Corte Vecchia in *Quaderni di Palazzo Tè*, n.s., 1, 1994, pp. 101–15. For the reference to Isabella's iron inkstand, see C. M. Brown, *Isabella d'Este and Lorenzo da Pavia: Documents for the History of Art and Culture in Renaissance Mantua*, Geneva 1982, p. 236, n. 5. See also A. Luzio, 'Isabella d'Este e il Sacco di Roma', *Archivio storico lombardo*, x, 1908, pp. 413–25.

Griffio 1594
Inventory of the estate of Giovanfrancesco de Griffio, 17 May 1594. A.S.F., M.D.P., P.D.P., B.2713. Includes a *studiolo*.

Guarinioni 1605
Inventory of the estate of Sebastian Guarinioni, 16 December 1605. A.S.V., atti G. A. Catti, reg. 3380. Includes a *studiol* with gems, plate, jewellery.

Guicciardini memoranda
Memoranda book of Jacopo di Piero Guicciardini, A.S.F., Archivio Guicciardini, Libri di Administrazione, ledger 12 (1503–1511), fol. 43, headed 'expenses in setting up my study' (*spese fatto in acconciare il mio scriptoio*). Guicciardini was a brother of the historian Francesco Guicciardini. See Lydecker thesis, pp. 137–40.

Guinigi 1430
Inventory of the confiscated estate of Paolo Guinigi, 29 August 1430. For the inventory (for which no precise archival reference is given), see S. Bongi, *Di Paolo Guinigi e delle sue richezze*, Lucca 1871, pp. 74–87 for section on the contents of his *studio* (see also Thornton 1991, pp. 49, 73, 218, 219, 370, 374). Guinigi (1376–1432) appointed himself Lord of Lucca and ruled from 1400 until he was deposed in 1430, when this inventory was compiled (Bongi, pp. 41–3). He was a renowned *condottiere* with considerable cultural pretensions, as documented by his library (listed in the inventory), his study made from wooden inlay by Arduino da Baese, and by his commissioning Jacopo della Quercia to make a funerary monument to his second wife, Ilaria del Carretto, for which he is now best remembered. The role of Lucchese silk merchants and bankers in Paris and Bruges explains Guinigi's interest in Burgundian plate and tapestries, Flemish paintings and Parisian goldsmiths' work; these interests are documented in *Carteggio di Paolo Guinigi, 1400–1430*, ed. L. Fumi and E. Lazzareschi, Lucca 1925. On Guinigi, see James Beck, *Jacopo della Quercia*, New York 1991, 2 vols, vol. 1, pp. 142–8; on the monument to his wife see also vol. 2, figs 3–13 and *Ilaria del Carretto e il suo monumento, la donna nell'arte, la cultura e la società del 400* (Atti del Convegno Internazionale di Studi, 15–

17 September 1994, Lucca), ed. Stéphane Toussaint, Lucca 1995, esp. pp. 119–63 on Guinigi's court. On Lucchese merchants and Guinigi, see Leon Mirot and Eugenio Lazzareschi, 'Lettere di mercanti lucchesi da Bruges e da Parigi 1407–1421', *Bollettino storico lucchese*, I, 1929, pp. 165–73. On jewellery in his possession, see R. W. Lightbown, *Medieval European Jewellery*, London 1992, pp. 37–8, and for two heraldic collars, Jenny Stratford, *The Bedford Inventories: The Worldly Goods of John, Duke of Bedford, Regent of France (1389–1435)*, London 1993, p. 102, n. 18. On the fate of the inlaid panelling from his study, which was removed to Ferrara for re-use by Leonello d'Este and was to have a long life there, see Graziano Manni, *Mobili in Emilia*, Modena 1986, p. 77; Adriano Franceschini, *Artisti a Ferrara in età umanistica e rinascimentale*, part I, 1341–1471, Ferrara 1993, doc. 389; and Thomas Tuohy, *Herculean Ferrara, Ercole d'Este 1471–1505, and the Invention of a Ducal Capital*, Cambridge 1996, pp. 81–2, doc. 59.

Helman 1606
Inventory of the estate of Carlo Helman, 2 January 1606. A.S.V., atti G. A. Catti, reg. 2281. Text of inventory in G. Devos and W. Brulez, *Les marchands flamands à Venise*, vol. 2, Rome 1986, pp. 799–811. On Carlo and his brother as Flemish Turkey merchants who resided in Venice and attained Venetian citizenship, see Umberto Tucci, 'La psicologia del mercante veneziano nel cinquecento', *Mercanti, navi, monete nel cinquecento veneziano*, Bologna 1981, pp. 43–94, trans. in *Renaissance Venice*, ed. John Hale, London 1974, pp. 336–78, pp. 357–70. For Carlo's will of 6 June 1605, see W. Brulez, *Les marchands flamands*, vol. 1, Brussels 1965, pp. 656–61.

Landucci memoranda
The memoranda compiled by the apothecary Luca Landucci of Florence between 1450 and 1516, continued by an anonymous author to 1542. Published by Iodoco del Badia, *Diario fiorentino dal 1450 al 1516 di Luca Landucci, continuato da un anonimo fino al 1542*, Florence 1883. Landucci's original section translated into English by Alice de Rosen Jervis, *A Diary from 1450–1516*, London 1927.

Laudo 1584
Inventory of the estate of Simon Laudo, *eques*, 2 January 1584. A.S.V., Cancelleria Inferiore, B.43. Lists goods *in terrazza* and *In un studio*.

Leniaco 1427
Inventory of the estate of Maestro Cristoforo de Leniaco, 18 August 1427. A. S. Padua, Archivio Notarile, Tabulario, XIII, 167r–168r. The son of a tailor, he was a notary and grammar teacher, owning Latin texts used for teaching by such ancient authors as Seneca, Virgil, Ovid and Cicero as well as Gasparino Barzizza's *epistolario*. The inventory was published in heavily edited form by A. Segarizzi, 'Inventario dei libri e dei beni di un maestro di scuola del secolo XV', *Bollettino del Museo Civico di Padova*, VIII, 1906, pp. 32–4.

Liena 1419
Inventory of the estate of Maestro Niccolao (Nicolas) di Ranuccio Liena, 16 January 1419. A. S. Lucca, Archivio

Notarile, notary ser Domenico Lupardi, n. 290, reg. I c. 35. He was one of the doctors who tended Ilaria del Carretto in her last illness. This inventory includes a *studio* with his medical books and travelling bookchest. See Eugenio Lazzareschi, 'Le richezze di due medici lucchesi della rinascenza', *Rivista di storia delle scienze e naturali*, VII, 1925, pp. 112–39, pp. 136–9.

Lippi 1504
Inventory of the estate of Filippino Lippi *di fra Filippo pittore*, 24 April 1504. A.S.F., notarile antecosmiano, serie 563, notary ser Giovanni di ser Piero del Serra (active 1497–1504), insert 4, cc. 330–333v. For the inventory, see Doris Carl, 'Das Inventar des Werkstatts von Filippino Lippi aus dem Jahre 1504', *Mitteilungen des kunsthistorichen Instituts in Florenz*, XXXI, 1987, pp. 373–91, pp. 384–91. Includes his *scrittoio*. See also Alfred Scharf, *Filippino Lippi*, Vienna 1950.

Lombardo 1569
Inventory of the estate of Julia Lombardo, Venetian courtesan, 30 April 1569. Istituzioni di Ricovero e di Educazione, Venice (IRE), Derelitti, Commissaria A. Leoncini, B.1 no. 50. Julia Lombardo apparently died intestate; her sister Angelica, who had lived with her, registered herself as sole heir to her sister's property, so that the inventory was not compiled until twenty-seven years after Julia's death. Includes two bedchambers with studies adjacent; one, referred to as a *studieto*, containing clothes in chests and toilet articles, and a more dignified and selfconscious *studiolo*; described as *Nel studiolo in ditta camera verso Sta. [Santa] Catta[Caterina]*. This was surely the courtesan's study, containing a bronze statuette, jewellery, a gold flask and needlecase, maiolica and porcelain and a small group of pictures (including a portrait of Dante) and unspecified books. For the inventory text and detailed commentary, see Cathy Santore, 'Julia Lombardo, *somtuosa meretrize*: A Portrait by Property', *Renaissance Quarterly*, XLI, 1988, pp. 44–83.

Loredan 1610
Inventory of the estate of Alvise Loredan, 24 November 1610. A.S.V., Giudici di Petizion, B.344/9. Member of a Venetian patrician family. Inventory includes furnishings *Nel studietto della camera in cavo il portego a man manca*.

Maiano 1498
Inventory of Benedetto da Maiano, 25 April 1498. A.S.F., Attoria, 1497, c. 141. Compiled at his death, it lists the contents of his and his brother's house and workshop, which includes two *scrittoi*. See L. Cendali, *Giuliano e Benedetto da Maiano*, Val di Pesa 1926, pp. 182–6; for excerpted text and commentary, see Maria Grazia Ciardi Dupré da Poggetto, *La bottega di Giuliano e Benedetto da Maiano nel Rinascimento fiorentino*, Florence 1994, pp. 41–3.

Martelli n.d.
Undated inventory of the estate of Baccio Martelli. A.S.F., M.D.P., P.D.P., B.2708. Includes a *scrittoio*.

Medici 1482
Inventory of the contents of the Villa Medici in Fiesole, 15 December 1482. A.S.F., M.A.P., CIV.4. Includes a *scrittoio* with

a panel painting of Saint Jerome. See Amanda Lillie, 'The Humanist Villa Revisited', *Language and Images of Renaissance Italy*, ed. A. Brown, Oxford 1995, pp. 193–215, pp. 204–5, notes 35–6.

Medici 1492
Copy (dated 1512) of the inventory of the estate of Lorenzo de' Medici (d.1492). A.S.F., Filza CLXV, Mediceo Avanti Principato. The definitive edition is that prepared by Marco Spallanzani and Giovanna Gaeta Bertelà, *Libro d'inventario dei beni di Lorenzo Il Magnifico*, Florence 1992, with introductory note on previous editions of the text and uses to which it has been put by scholars from the late nineteenth century. For the contents of the study (*scrittoio*), see Liebenwein 1977, pp. 71–9, 83, 121, 154. See also Thornton 1991, pp. 120, 157, 216.

Medici 1498
Inventory of the *substantie e beni* of Lorenzo de Pierfrancesco de' Medici (d.1503) and the heirs of his brother Giovanni, nominal date of September 1498. A.S.F., Mediceo avanti il Principato, CXXIX, fols 480–528. Lorenzo di Piero was the son of Cosimo Il Vecchio's brother, Lorenzo. Inventory references include a fitted desk in a *scrittoro* in a Medici villa at Fiesole; all entries with valuations. See J. Shearman, 'The Collections of the Younger Branch of the Medici', *BM*, CXVII, 1975, pp. 12–27, p. 26, section 41. See also Thornton 1991, p. 171, p. 380, p. 382.

Michiel memoranda
Unpublished diaries and records of Marcantonio Michiel (d.1552). Museo Correr, Venice, MS Cod. Cicogna 1022. E. A. Cicogna's fair copy of the original is also in the Correr (MS PD 684 C, pp. 586–7). See Jennifer Fletcher, 'Marcantonio Michiel's Collection', *JWCI*, XXXVI, 1973, p. 383, n. 11 for reference to a theft from Michiel's *studiolo* in the family palace.

Michiel c.1552
Inventory of the Michiel family collection in their palace at Santa Marina, Venice. Museo Correr, Venice, MS PD C 1267 (8). It was compiled in the interest of Marcantonio Michiel, grandson of the collector and critic of the same name (d.1552). The inventory was published (with a few domestic items omitted) by Jennifer Fletcher, 'Marcantonio Michiel's Collection', *JWCI*, XXXVI, 1973, pp. 382–5. Fletcher compares item descriptions with those in a Michiel inventory of 1595, Correr, Venice, MS PD C 1428 (7). On Michiel's career and collection, see Fletcher, 'Marcantonio Michiel: His Friends and Collection', *BM*, CXXIII, 1981, pp. 453–70, 601–9.

Michiel 1601
As for Michiel *c.*1522, but dated 1601. Museo Correr, Venice, MS PD C 1428 (1). See Fletcher, *JWCI* XXXVI, 1973, p. 384, n. 24.

Migliore 1579
Inventory of the estate of Messer Antonio di Fillipo Migliore, 23 May 1579. A.S.F., M.D.P., P.D.P., B.2712. Lists contents of a *studio*.

Minerbetti memoranda
Memoranda book (*Ricordanze*) of Andrea Minerbetti, Florence, Biblioteca Laurenziana, MS Acquisti e Doni 229, vol. 2. The memoranda include inventories of the contents of his palace at Santa Trìnita of 1493 (7r–8r), 1499, 1502 and 1546 (168r–171v). Attilio Schiaparelli, *La casa fiorentina ed i suoi arredi nei secoli XIV e XV*, Florence 1908 (reprinted 1979), pp. 184–187. See Joseph Alsop, *The Rare Art Traditions: The History of Art Collecting and its linked phenomena wherever these have appeared*, Princeton 1982, pp. 377–8 and notes 20–27 for the most accessible account.

Monticuli 1413
Inventory of the estate of Andrea de Monticuli, 17 October 1413. A. S. Udine, Archivio Capitolare, sezione XVI. Andrea came from a noble family originally from Verona, but well established in Udine. A lawyer, he was a leading figure in the *commune* in Udine, and served as Vicar-General to the Patriarch of Aquileia. His study (*studio*) is specifically described as being his: it appears to have been located close to his bedchamber. The inventory was published by Pio Paschini, 'La casa ed i libri di un giusperito udinese del secolo XV', *Memorie storiche foroglulesi*, XXXIII, 1936, pp. 121–49, with biographical account, pp. 121–38. See also Thornton 1991, pp. 106, 382.

Nero 1576
Inventory of the estate of Agostino di Piero del Nero, 25 May 1576. A.S.F., M.D.P., P.D.P., B.2711. His richly furnished house included an impressive group of marble busts; the *scrittoio* contained a large library, an armillary sphere and a globe.

Niccolini 1562
Inventory of the estate of Messer Otto di Messer Carlo Niccolini, 23 July 1562. A.S.F., M.D.P, P.D.P., B.2708. Lists contents of a *studio*.

Nigarelli 1419
Inventory of the estate of Maestro Davino Nigarelli, 8 April 1419. A. S. Lucca, Archivio Notarile, ser Domenico Lupardi, n. 290, reg. 2, c.24v. Includes his *studio*. On this doctor of medicine's inventory, books and career in Lucca, see Eugenio Lazzareschi, 'Le richezze di due medici lucchesi della rinascenza', *Rivista di storia delle scienze e naturali*, VII, 1925, pp. 112–13, 115–36.

Nuzio 1408
Inventory of the estate of Ugolino di Nuzio, 5 December 1408. This doctor of medicine's library included a travelling bookchest. See T. Gottlieb, *Ueber mittelalterliche Bibliotheken*, Leipzig 1890, cat. 658.

Odoni 1555
Inventory of the estate of Andrea Odoni, 23 June 1555. Lists contents of his *studio di sopra dell'antigaie (antigaglie)*. Odoni was a Milanese silk merchant and collector, resident in Venice, who was famously portrayed by Lorenzo Lotto and whose collection was described by Marcantonio Michiel in his manuscript notes on collectors in the Veneto and elsewhere in Northern Italy: for

an English translation of these, see *Venice: A Documentary History*, ed. David Chambers and Brian Pullan, Oxford 1992, pp. 424–7, introduced and translated by Jennifer Fletcher. The Lotto portrait, which is now in the Royal Collection and is displayed at Hampton Court Palace, is mentioned in the Michiel memoranda, p. 425. See Gustav Ludwig, 'Inventar des Nachlasses des Alvise Odoni, aus dem Nachlass Gustav Ludwigs', *Italienische Forschungen*, IV–V, Berlin 1911, pp. 56–74. See also Favaretto 1990, pp. 75–8; Thornton 1991, pp. 26, 48, 51, 110, 235–6, 237, 372, 378; and Liebenwein 1977, pp. 142, 233.

Pandolfini 1497

Inventory of the estate of Pierfilippo Pandolfini, 27 November 1497. Pierfilippo (1437–97) came from a wealthy and distinguished Florentine family of silk merchants and bankers. Taught by Marsilio Ficino, he was literate in Greek and Latin, and served as Florentine ambassador to Milan in 1480, Rome in 1489, and Livorno in 1496. He was also a client of Vespasiano da Bisticci, whose shop in Via del Proconsulo was near Palazzo Pandolfini. He died intestate, leaving children by his second marriage who were minors, among whom his estate was to be divided. Pierfilippo's son listed the books in the library. See A. Verde, 'Inventario e divisione dei beni di Pierfilippo Pandolfini', *Rinascimento*, IX, 1969, pp. 307–24, p. 314 for his *studio*. Annaclara Cataldi Palau, 'La Biblioteca Pandolfini: Storia della sua formazione e successiva dispersione, identificazione di alcuni manoscritti', *Italia medievale e umanistica*, XXXI, 1988, pp. 259–395, pp. 262–5 on his biography. Teresa de Robertis, 'Breve storia del Fondo Pandolfini della Colombaria e della dispersione di una libreria privata fiorentina, (con due appendici)', *Le raccolte della Colombaria: I incunaboli*, ed. E. Spagnesi, Florence 1993, pp. 7–285.

Panuzio 1493

Inventory of the estate of Francesco di Niccolò Panuzio, 20 May 1493. A.S.F., M.D.P., P.A.P., B.179. Spallanzani 1978, doc. 27 for the contents of his study (*scrittoio*) and p. 54 for mention of a piece of imported Spanish lustred pottery in his study.

Pasqualigo 1579

Inventory of the estate of Andrea Pasqualigo, 9 March 1579, notary Cesar Ziliol. Poet and patrician; his inventory includes the contents of his *studiol*. See Palumbo Fossati 1984, pp. 109–53, p. 147, n. 66 and Palumbo Fossati 1985, pp. 481–513, p. 499, n. 22. K. Pomian, 'Collezione', *Enciclopedia Einaudi*, vol. 3, Turin 1978, pp. 330–62.

Portigiani 1571

Inventory of the estate of Rinaldo di Michele Portigiani, 27 February 1571. A.S.F., M.D.P., P.D.P., B.2709. Includes a *studio* in his bedchamber, with which it was decorated *en suite*, all woodwork painted yellow and green.

Rinieri memoranda

Memoranda book of Bernardo di Stoldo Rinieri, banker (*Libro di creditori e debitori e ricordanze*), A.S.F., Conventi Soppressi 95, 212, libro rosso A. Mentions his *scrittoio*. See Lydecker thesis,

pp. 264–70, and Lydecker 1987, pp. 209–21, pp. 213–14 and notes 17–22. I am grateful to Kent Lydecker for this reference.

Rinuccini 1499

Inventory of the estate of Alamanno Rinuccini, 3 June 1499. Study with built-in desk, (*scriptoio*) in bedchamber on ground floor (*camera terrena*). See V. R. Giustiniani, *Alamanno Rinuccini 1426–1499*, Graz 1965, p. 42, and Thornton 1991, p. 113.

Rucellai memoranda

Memoranda of Giovanni Rucellai, Florentine patrician, banker and art patron. See *Giovanni Rucellai ed il suo Zibaldone*, ed. A. Perosa, 2 vols.: vol. 1, texts, London 1960; vol. 2, *A Florentine Patrician and his Palace: Studies by F. W. Kent, A. Perosa, Brenda Preyer, Piero Sanpaolesi and Roberto Salvini*, London 1981.

Scudieri 1560

Inventory of the library of Francesco Scudieri, 25 November 1560. A.S.V., Sant'Uffizio, B.15, Processo 49. He was a music teacher and reputedly a Lutheran, or in close contact with foreign pupils who were Lutheran, hence the inventory was drawn up at the demand of the Inquisition. Includes a specialised eight-sided music table and eight music stands: 'Uno tavolone da otto canton, con l'armario sotto con la chiave, et otto scabelletti da por i libri per sonar'. Ongaro (p. 363) suggests that the table would have been used by instrumentalists for household performances: all the printed music in the inventory could have been performed in this manner. See Giulio Ongaro, 'The Library of a Sixteenth-century Music Teacher', *Journal of Musicology*, XII, 1994, pp. 357–75; Iain Fenlon, *Music, Print and Culture in Early Sixteenth-century Italy*, Panizzi Lectures, 1994, London 1995, pp. 88–9, n. 117.

Seghieri 1592

Inventory of the estate of Messer Marco Seghieri, 16 September 1592. A.S.F., M.D.P., P.D.P., B.2713. Includes items *nella camera dello studio* and *Nello studio*, along with a large library.

Segizzi 1576

Inventory of the estate of Gasparo Segizzi, *miniatore*, 15 March 1576. A.S.V., Cancelleria Inferiore, B.42. See Palumbo Fossati 1984, pp. 109–53, pp. 138–46.

Serragli 1576

Inventory of the estate of Bernardo Serragli, 5 April 1576. A.S.F., M.D.P., P.D.P., B.2712.

Sodoma 1529

Statement of property removed from Sodoma's study by his pupil Girolamo Francesco Magagni, 20 July 1529. A. S. Siena, Archivio Notarile, Processi del 1529. See Lionel Cust, *Giovanni Antonio Bazzi*, London 1906, pp. 304–6. G. F. Hill, 'Sodoma's Collection of Antiquities', *Journal of Hellenic Studies*, XXVI, 1906, pp. 288–9. Weiss 1969, p. 182, n. 4.

Sodoma 1548

Inventory of the estate of Giovanni Antonio Bazzi, known as Sodoma, 14 February 1548. A. S. Siena, Archivio Notarile 1386, notary Ser Luca di Mariano Salvini d'Asciano, B.941. See Lionel Cust, *Giovanni Antonio Bazzi*, London 1906, pp. 337–8. Claudio Franzoni, 'Le collezioni rinascimentali di antichità, *Memorie dell' antico nell' arte italiana*, ed. Salvatore Settis, vol. I, Turin 1984, pp. 297–360, pp. 340–41.

Strozzi 1494
Inventory recording the division of 'glass and other things' from the estate of Filippo Strozzi between his heirs. A.S.F., Strozziana, 5th series, n. 54, *Libro verde, segnalato A, di Lorenzo e Giovan Battista Strozzi, eredi di Filippo Strozzi, tenuto da Selvaggia Gianfigliazzi, tutrice, c 9*. See Spallanzani 1978, doc. 25.

Terzo 1604
Inventory of the estate of Andrea Terzo, 13 January 1604. A.S.V., atti G. A. Catti, reg. 3378. Lawyer (*giurista*), whose inventory includes a *studio*. Palumbo Fossati 1984, pp. 109–53, p. 147, n. 66.

Tolosani 1584
Inventory of the estate of Luigi di Messer Giovanni Tolosani, 19 January 1584, A.S.F., M.D.P., P.D.P., B.2713. Lists contents of a *scrittoio*.

Trevisan 1465
Inventory of the collection of Cardinal Ludovico Trevisan, Florence, 20–21 April 1465. A.S.F., Notarile antecosmiano, 4823 (notary Piero Cecchi), fols 97–9, 106, 110, 115. He was one of the great collectors of his time, and many of his pieces were to be acquired by Lorenzo de' Medici. For the inventory, supporting documents and biographical note, see Rolf Bagemihl, 'The Trevisan Collection', *BM*, cxxv, 1993, pp. 559–3, pp. 561–3, doc. 2.

Tura 1483
Inventory of the estate of Maestro Bartolo di Tura, Siena. Biblioteca Medicea-Laurenziana, Florence, Codice Ashburnhamiano 1768. Bartolo was a doctor of medicine, at one point treating Pope Pius II, whose funeral oration was given by Agostino Dati and later printed in his *Opera*, Siena 1503, book v, *Augustini Dathi Oratio VI, De vita et obitu praecelentissimi et Philosophi et Medici Bartholi Turci Senensis, in toto Latio celeberrimi*. The inventory is written on vellum and entitled *Inventario de' Beni de figli di Bandino di Bartolo di Tura di Siena, fatto l'anno 1483 per parte di Donna onesta, vedova del Cavaliere Guido d'antonio di Biagio Piccolomini loro Nonna materna, Tutrice e Curatrice*. Donna Onesta was apppointed by the Office of Wards in Siena (*Magistrato de' Pupilli*) as guardian to Bartolo's grandchildren on the death of their father, Bandino. Two of the children were adult (Elisabetta and Eufrasia) and three were minors (Alessandro, Niccolo and Silvestro). The contents of the study (*studio*, as on fol. 9v–10r in the manuscript), are listed in Curzio Mazzi: 'Lo studio di un medico Senese', *Rivista delle biblioteche e degli archivi*, VI, 1896, pp. 27–48; the rest of the inventory is published in Mazzi, *La casa di Maestro Bartolo di Tura*, Siena 1900, with annotations and introduction. See also Thornton 1991, pp. 49, 65, 121, 164, 192, 248, 375, 385, 386, 389, 393.

Usper 1601
Inventory of the estate of Ludovico Usper, 25 February 1601. A.S.V., Guidici di Petizion, B.342/10. His profession as lawyer is evident from his papers, kept in one of two mezzanine offices. For reference to 'Una Nostra Donna de Bronzo opera di Sansovin' in Usper's inventory, see Bruce Boucher, *The Sculpture of Jacopo Sansovino*, New Haven and London 1991, 2 vols, vol. 2, cat. 17 and n. 2. Boucher suggests that this Madonna may have been the signed bronze in the Museum of Art at Cleveland 'or one of the later versions'. His globes are discussed by F. Ambrosini, '"Descrittioni del Mondo" nelle case venete dei secoli XVI e XVII', *Archivio veneto*, CLII, 1981, p. 69. See also Levi 1900, p. LXV.

Uzzano 1424
Inventory of the estate of Angelo da Uzzano, 2–4 May 1424. Inventory of the contents of the Uzzano family palace in the Via de' Bardi in Florence, which includes an entry for Angelo's study (*nello scrittoio d'Agnolo*) and two entries for studies belonging to Niccolò da Uzzano. For the text of the inventory and commentary, see Walter Bombe, 'Nachlass-Inventare des Angelo da Uzzano und des Ludovico di Gino Capponi', *Beiträge zur Kunstgeschichte des Mittelalters und der Renaissance herausgegeben von Walter Goetz*, vol. 36, Leipzig and Berlin 1928, pp. 1–29, nos 39, 80–96, 212–29 for the study entries. See also Liebenwein 1977, pp. 59–60 and notes 32–40, pp. 67 and 95. Thornton 1991, pp. 113, 114, 153, 164, 165, 173–4, 244, 277, 370, 382, 383, 389, 391.

Vendramin 1612
Inventory of the estate of Francesco Vendramin, 4 September 1612. A.S.V., Giudici di Petizion B.345/10. Lists art objects *In un studiol*.

Vittoria memoranda
Memoranda of the sculptor Alessandro Vittoria, Venice. These are published in Riccardo Predelli, 'Le memorie e le carte di Alessandro Vittoria', *Archivio trentino*, XIII, 1908, pp. 1–265, Part III, pp. 141–64; for mentions of the fitting out of his *studietto*, see pp. 158, 159, 163, 231. There is a photocopy of this rare publication in the National Art Library, Victoria and Albert Museum, 186.B.36. On Vittoria, see Bruce Boucher, *The Sculpture of Jacopo Sansovino*, New Haven and London 1991, 2 vols, vol. 1, pp. 169–71.

Vittoria will 1608
Will of Alessandro Vittoria, Venice, 27 May 1608. Lists contents of a small study (*studietto*) and the adjoining bedchamber (*la camera appresso il studietto verso l'horto*). See B. Giovanelli, *Vita di Alessandro Vittoria scultore trentino*, Trent 1858, pp. 132–3. De Benedictis 1995, p. 162.

Zarlino 1590
Inventory of the estate of the Reverend Gioseffe Zarlino, 20 February 1590. A.S.V., Cancelleria Inferiore, B.43. Notary Niccolo Doglioni. See Isabella Palumbo Fossati, 'La casa veneziana di Gioseffe Zarlino nel testamento e nell'inventario

dei beni', *Nuova rivista musicale italiana*, IV, 1986, pp. 633–41. I am grateful to her for this reference. See also F. Caffi, *La vita e le opere di Gioseffe Zarlino*, Venice 1836, and *The New Grove Dictionary of Music and Musicians*, ed. Stanley Sadie, vol. 20, London 1980, pp. 647–9.

Zuanelli 1587
Inventory of the estate of Antonio Zuanelli, *marangon*, 1 June 1587. A.S.V., Cancelleria Inferiore, miscellanea notai diversi, inventari, B.43, notary A. Brinis. See Palumbo Fossati 1984, pp. 109–53, p. 127, n. 39, p. 137, n. 52.

Index

Pages with illustrations are *italicised*